All of Us

Births and a better life: Population, development and
environment in a globalized world.
Selections from the pages of The Earth Times

D1208394

Books by Jack Freeman
All of Us: Births and a Better Life (Co-Editor)

Books by Pranay Gupte
All of Us: Births and a Better Life (Co-Editor)
Mother India: A Political Biography of Indira Gandhi
India: The Challenge of Change
The Silent Crisis
Vengeance: India After the Assassination of Indira Gandhi
The Crowded Earth: People and the Politics of Population

Books by Louis Silverstein
Design of the Times
American Taste

All of Us

Births and a better life: Population, development and
environment in a globalized world.
Selections from the pages of The Earth Times

Edited by Jack Freeman and Pranay Gupte
Design and Illustrations by Louis Silverstein

EARTH TIMES BOOKS
205 East 42nd Street
New York, NY 10017

ABOUT EARTH TIMES BOOKS

Earth Times Books is a venture of the Earth Times Foundation, a not-for-profit, nonpartisan organization that publishes The Earth Times in print and on the Internet. The Foundation also sponsors activities that enhance public understanding of global and local issues such as the environment, economic growth, population, trade, human rights, empowerment of women, children's rights, education, health, media, and science and technology.

Library of Congress Cataloging-in-Publication Data
Freeman, Jack; Gupte, Pranay; Silverstein, Louis
All of Us: Births and a Better Life: Population,
Development and Environment in a Globalized World.
Selections from the Pages of The Earth Times
p. cm.
Includes index

First published in the United States of America in 1999
by The Earth Times Foundation.
www.earthtimes.org

ISBN 0-9672909-0-2
1. Population—International. 2. Development—
International. 3. Environment—International.
4. United Nations. 5. Sustainable Development. I. Title

Manufactured in Canada
First Edition, September 1999

This book is dedicated by The Earth Times to:
A. M. Rosenthal
Seymour Topping
Arthur Gelb
Friends from the start

CONTENTS

FOREWORD

NAFIS SADIK, M.D.

The Earth Times came into being in 1991, a critical time in the history of the international community, the United Nations and the United Nations Population Fund (UNFPA)—the period just preceding the United Nations Conference on Environment and Development (UNCED). Although it certainly didn't seem propitious at the time, UNCED proved to be the springboard for the evolution of The Earth Times and for how the international community eventually came to view sustainable development and all its components, especially population and women's issues. The Earth Times, initially born to give coverage to the Earth Summit in Rio de Janeiro, found itself playing a key role in the effort to focus global attention on population issues and their relationship to development and the environment. In so doing, The Earth Times expanded its mandate and took the first steps to becoming the "development publication" of distinguished international standing it is today.

Rio was the first occasion in which The Earth Times played a significant role before the international community and international media. There were around 4,000 journalists attending the Earth Summit (as UNCED was also called). For many, it was their first exposure to an international meeting. Trying to make sense of the countless events that went on, not only at the UNCED but also at the sprawling meeting of nongovernmental organizations in downtown Rio, was daunting even to veteran reporters who covered the UN on a regular basis.

The coverage that The Earth Times provided at Rio proved to be the standard. Its lively tabloid pages not only provided in-depth information on the substantive issues, but also offered a balanced program of thoughtful comments as well as engaging human interest stories.

For us at the United Nations Population Fund, The Earth Times played a key role in the coverage it gave to population and family planning issues as they related to the UNCED process.

The Earth Times also gave coverage and—perhaps more importantly—recognition to the growing strength of the international women's movement which had coalesced around the population issue. The widening realization that the population issue was of great concern to women gave common ground to activist groups from both developed and developing countries and forged one of the most powerful political movements for change in the world today. The Earth Times was perceptive enough to see this happening and to cover it, not only with stories about parliamentary maneuvering aimed at putting population concerns in the UNCED Plan of Action, but also offering detailed, behind-the-scenes reportage of meetings of the women's caucus and carrying the viewpoints of women leaders in its opinion pages.

Because it proved to be reliable and accurate, other reporters were soon taking their cue from the upstart publication. Every morning, it was eagerly awaited by the delegates of the world's press.

As such, population became one of the burning issues at Rio, so much so that at times the media coverage gave the impression that the meeting at Rio was a conference on population and the environment.

Although the language in Agenda 21—the "blueprint" for environmental protection and economic growth fashioned at the Earth Summit—is not as strong as it should have been on population, it created a strategy for a battle that was to be fought over the next two years until it reached its triumphant conclusion in Cairo in 1994.

What Rio did was forge a determination in the international women's movement to assure that the lapses in focusing on population issues at Rio would not recur at the International Conference on Population and Development (ICPD) in Cairo, nor at any of the other international conferences of the 1990s.

And The Earth Times, which initially was to be an UNCED conference newspaper only, saw the linkages and value of the population story and decided to continue its work on an expanded basis.

In the years leading up to ICPD, The Earth Times gave exhaustive coverage to the preparations.

It provided daily coverage during various preparatory meetings at which complex—and delicate—diplomatic negotiations took place. While there were a number of other conference newspapers at Cairo, The Earth Times quickly became the unofficial paper of record of the ICPD because it gave such in-depth coverage and provided discussion of the key issues on a sustained and fair basis: the recognition of a broad reproductive health approach; the need to empower women by allowing them to exercise their rights; the open discussions of abortion and female genital mutilation as health problems rather than only moral or cultural issues; the Program of Action and the financial goals adopted at ICPD.

In the charged atmosphere that preceded and continued during the Cairo Conference, The Earth Times provided sophisticated coverage of the debate. At the conference, it offered a forum for opinions of leaders of non-governmental organizations and other prominent personalities. Women, men, religious leaders and ordinary people all had their say in the editorial pages of The Earth Times. In addition, it covered stories that commercial news organizations didn't or couldn't cover, and by doing so it brought an extraordinary range of information to delegates and the media covering ICPD.

The Earth Times was often quoted by global news organizations such as CNN, and American and European television networks as well as by numerous newspapers. While ICPD holds the record for attendance by journalists—more than 5,000—in the end it was The Earth Times that dominated and set the tone for the international coverage of Cairo.

In the media hoopla about the political issues at the 1995 Fourth World Conference on Women in Beijing, The Earth Times's coverage was a voice of reason, highlighting the close ties between the population issues discussed at ICPD and their relevance to the women's issues under discussion. In the end—and the media played a large part in this—issues from ICPD were actually strengthened at Beijing.

Because of the powerful media focus on them at the time, these two key conferences of the late 20th Century are now permanently linked as milestones in the struggle for women's equality and reproductive rights.

The Earth Times has kept population and its relevance to other development issues alive and before the delegates and media at the World Conference on Human Rights in Vienna, the World Summit for Social Development at Copenhagen, the International Conference on Human Settlements (Habitat II) at Istanbul, the World Food Summit at Rome, and other global conferences. Daily editions produced at annual meetings of the World Bank and the International Monetary Fund, and at other global conferences, have highlighted the connections between the environment and economic growth--—and the significance of population and reproductive-health issues.

International delegates now eagerly look for The Earth Times and have come to expect its brand of lively and informative coverage.

With major news organizations throughout the world decreasing rather than increasing their coverage of international events—especially of sustainable development issues—The Earth Times has, against all odds, not only survived but triumphed. Why? Because of its thoughtful writing and its variety of points of view, and because it always tries to be accurate and fair. The newspaper does not wield an ideological ax. It makes a special effort to highlight the work of men and women, and institutions, who are agents for positive change in their societies.

For those of us in the development field, The Earth Times is our newspaper. It keeps us connected. It keeps us challenged and moving forward. May it gather even more strength and support.

I am delighted that the editors of The Earth Times have launched a new enterprise, Earth Times Books. "All of Us: Births and A Better Life—Population, Development and Environment in A Globalized World," is the imprint's first title.

The selection of articles by Jack Freeman and Pranay Gupte covers a wide range of issues that affect not only policymaking but also the daily drama of development in different parts of the world. Louis Silverstein's remarkable illustrations tell a story by themselves. The editors have tried to be as inclusive as possible concerning the vast universe of sustainable development. These selections made for fascinating reading when they first appeared in the pages of The Earth Times, and they have held up very well indeed as a solid body of work that explains the human condition in our global commons.

INTRODUCTION

JACK FREEMAN

When I went to Rio de Janeiro in 1992 to cover the Earth Summit—the first of many international meetings that I've followed for The Earth Times over the last decade—I was made aware that nations were entering a new phase with the end of the cold war, which brought a whole new definition of human security. Instead of a world polarized between East and West, the critical distinction was now increasingly between the developing countries of the South and the industrialized countries of the North.

I also saw that, in an accelerated manner, many member states of United Nations were setting aside cold war suspicions and hostilities and were coming to grips with common global concerns such as rapid population growth, environmental degradation, lack of access to clean water and sanitation, poor education and inadequate health care facilities, and the low status of women in many parts of the world.

It was hardly a coincidence that the birth of The Earth Times—in 1991—occurred at the same time as the death of the cold war "old order." The Earth Times was created to direct renewed attention to the possibilities for change in the world and to seek out those who were engendering such change. This was the particular "universe" that the newspaper set out to cover, reporting on news-making developments affecting these common concerns, not only at the global level but at the grassroots as well.

At the heart of what The Earth Times does is a concern for human development—a perspective that sees population as more than just arithmetic, and development as more than just economics. The newspaper's reporters regularly travel to scores of countries around the world to provide first-hand reports on a wide range of issues—not only dealing with environment and sustainable development but also health, education, nutrition, human rights, gender concerns, children's rights, trade and, of course, population. The newspaper has evolved into a recognized forum in the world—in Washington as well as the chancelleries of various rich and poor countries alike, and among everyday audiences—for discussion of development and population issues. At the United Nations, it has become required reading.

Along the way the staff—which brings together veteran newshounds with idealistic young people drawn from many countries—has created what might be seen as a richer and more focused coverage of our "beat" than would ordinarily be found in almost any other publication.

The paper's coverage demonstrates the interconnectedness of global issues and priorities; it follows international meetings, speeches and processes through which high policy is fashioned on population, development and environment issues; it is sensitive to the cultural values of local communities in some of the planet's most isolated places—places that are often being exposed through "globalization" to Western lifestyles from which they have been completely insulated over long years. The Earth Times is completely independent and nonpartisan and it places no subject off-limits; and, though hopeful about progress, it is still unafraid to ask the hard questions and demand real answers from people in positions of power.

The Earth Times covers the details of what goes on in the field—the gritty work of implementing policy, often in places so extremely remote that one seldom reads about them in the so-called mainstream media. The content "mix" of the paper is constantly changing and expanding, with the result that off-beat and often surprising items find their way into our pages.

In the pages that follow you will see dozens of examples of such Earth Times reportage, under datelines from all over the globe, about people, governments, international bodies and nongovernmental organizations coming to grips with problems and issues related to population, sustainable development, environment, gender issues, human rights, health, children's rights, education and technology.

From the editorial and comment columns you will see essays and opinion pieces written by prominent political figures—Bill Clinton among them—and by leading thinkers and authorities in the population field, such as Dr. Nafis Sadik of the United Nations Population Fund, Jyoti Shankar Singh of India, and Steven W. Sinding of the Rockefeller Foundation.

You will also see thoughtful essays by noted developmentalists such as Sir Shridath S. Ramphal and Jim MacNeill. There are articles by diplomats such as Morris B. Abram of the United States and Nicolaas H. Biegman of The Netherlands. You will find extraordinary pieces written specially for our paper by well-known writers and editors such as A. M. Rosenthal, Seymour Topping, James W. Michaels, Flora Lewis, John Corry, Soon-Young Yoon, Tom Wicker and Audrey Ronning Topping; and you will savor reportage by young men and women just making their entry into the exciting world of international journalism such as Reshma Prakash, Erin Trowbridge, Kyu-Young Lee, Yasna Uberoi and Rabya Nizam. There is superb journalism by

Stella Danker of Singapore, and the late Richard F. Shepard. You will find reportage from the grassroots about individuals and institutions that are implementing change in their societies.

Everything selected for this anthology appeared first in the pages of The Earth Times or on its Web site (www.earthtimes.org). The selections reproduced here represent only a small percentage of all the items dealing with population, development and related concerns that the newspaper has published over the past eight years. They were chosen because they deal with important ongoing issues, they offer insights of lasting value, and they demonstrate how these issues of the human environment are intertwined and indivisible. The original publication date is given for each selection, and where possible we've tried to update the material without altering the meaning and context of the articles.

More than 50 years ago, as a high school student in New York, I stood in line for an entire night to attend the first meeting of the UN Security Council. I feel I am still on the front-line of the fight for human security—the actions being taken, largely by and through the United Nations, to deal with the interlinked problems of population, development, human rights and gender inequities—and I am happy to be there.

The Earth Times has been privileged to be a witness to this extraordinary period of human history, a decade in which, largely through the many global conferences sponsored by the United Nations, the people of the world have begun the task of claiming collective responsibility for the current and future well-being of this planet. Through the great UN conferences of the 1990s—notably the International Conference on Population and Development, held in Cairo in 1994, and the 1995 Women's Conference in Beijing—the international community has begun the arduous work of shaping the strategies needed to achieve the critical goal of global environmental security, economic growth and social justice.

The Earth Times—through its print and Web editions, its television programs and its new imprint, Earth Times Books—is there to cover this extraordinary story. And those of us who have been privileged to play a role in that coverage—and in the preparation of this anthology—feel a great sense of pride. This is a book about the linkages that increasingly shape our interdependent world in an age of globalization. We hope you will savor what our writers have to offer. And for more on the human environment, stay tuned.

We have come a long way from the days when people assumed that environmentalists believed that "Wildlife is good, people bad." Now everybody understands that the growth of human population and the concurrent rush of "globalized" development are in uneasy, indefinite and complex relationship with our needs to sustain the Earth's physical resources and aspects of soul-satisfying beauty. While we still hear stories about huge dam projects derailed because of a single species of tiny fish, the focus has moved to the much larger canvas of regional ecosystems. Solutions to environmental problems are no longer seen as "either-or" but as complicated balancing acts in which the needs of growing populations are recognized as part of vast systems where, indeed, a butterfly's fluttering wings in Japan can create a windstorm in North America.

Environmental protection and economic growth—two of the main elements of sustainable development—are now almost always factors in policy-making at all levels. From monumental World Bank projects to cleaning up the shoreline at Coney Island, hardly a project moves ahead without principles of sustainable development being addressed. Bill Clinton's essay written for The Earth Times, "A Blueprint for the Planet," tells the broad story, along with other pieces in this section. We also report on cases where environmental concerns were not sufficiently addressed. The "environment" is about more than ecology; it's a matter of people, as both Sir Shridath S. Ramphal of Guyana and Ingar Brueggemann of Germany put it.

SECTION 1

PEOPLE AND THE ENVIRONMENT

A BLUEPRINT
FOR THE PLANET

WILLIAM JEFFERSON CLINTON
November 1992

The Earth Summit was truly a turning point in history. Never before had so many world leaders come together—drawn by a common sense of concern about and a dedication to take action on problems that have now reached global proportions.

Whether it is rapid deforestation and desertification, or depleted and poisoned ground water resources, or soils that will no longer bear crops, the problem is the same: We are failing to meet pressing human needs and at the same time we are destroying the very resources upon which our ability to meet those needs depends. The Earth Summit was about nations joining together in common resolve to do a better job in the future and to offer our children the hope for a brighter tomorrow. The centerpiece of this international effort was an extraordinary blueprint for our planet, Agenda 21, which world leaders adopted by acclamation.

In dedicating themselves to this effort, many industrialized countries came to realize that taking action to solve environmental problems is also good for the economy. Reducing emissions of greenhouse gases, for example, can most readily and effectively be achieved by improving the efficiency of every sector of the economy. And improved efficiency enhances productivity and competitiveness. Moreover, the commitment to improved efficiency acts as a strong incentive for the development of new environmentally sound technologies. These technologies are in demand and a $200 billion market awaits those who will be aggressive in developing them.

We cannot ignore both the peril and the promise of our environment and development challenges. And we must work even more vigorously toward creating a healthier and more prosperous planet. Though the United States is responsible for more greenhouse gas emissions than any other nation on Earth, we were the lone holdout among the industrial countries in agreeing to reduce those emissions to 1990 levels by the end of this century.

Though we know that species are being driven to extinction at a faster rate than at any time since the age of the dinosaurs, we gave little attention to the negotiations on the biodiversity convention and in the end failed to join the 154 signatory nations. To truly achieve sustainable development, every nation will have to use natural resources more wisely.

Al Gore and I know that our children's health and well-being depends on having clean air to breathe and pure water to drink. We know that the health and safety of our laborers depends on safe working conditions. And we know that the very best within each of us is touched and inspired by the majesty of nature. Care for the environment is a concern that unites us.

We have heard the argument that excessive environmental regulations are a leading cause of our economic problems, and that Americans will have to choose—either we can have a healthy environment or a strong economy but we cannot have both.

It's a false choice. If this argument were right, Germany and Japan—which enforce regulations that are as stringent as or more stringent than US environmental protections—would be in dire economic straits. If this argument were right, then the Eastern European nations—which made that choice—would be economic powerhouses. If this argument were right, then the one sector of our economy that has shown impressive growth over the last four years—the environmental products and services industries—would have been dead in the water like most other important sectors of the US economy.

The fact of the matter is that economic strength will increasingly depend on sound environmental performance. Our competitors understand that achieving a healthy economy and a healthy environment are complementary, not contradictory, objectives. One of the reasons German workers make 25 percent more than the average American worker is that their industries use half the energy to produce the same amount of goods as US firms. Japanese companies enjoy a 5 percent competitive price advantage in the global marketplace because of higher energy efficiency.

Developing countries are also an increasingly strong presence in the global marketplace. In 1991, while the economies of many of the industrialized countries were stagnant, the economies of many of the developing countries grew at some 6 percent. In 1991 these countries also purchased more than a third of all US exports. What types of products and processes are these countries demanding? Now suffering the effects of economic growth policies that did not consider environmental impact, these countries are demanding technologies and services that will fuel economic growth without destroying the environment. Mexico, for example, is closing down factories not because their economic performance is poor but because Mexican citizens are literally choking to death on the thick pollution. Mexico needs to get those factories up and running again; Mexico needs to purchase equipment that will enable those factories to run cleanly.

Will US firms meet that need?

Other developing and newly industrialized countries are making similar policy choices. Taiwan, for example, has experienced record industrial growth over the last two decades, but has failed to date to deal with the toxic by-products of that growth. Millions of tons of hazardous wastes are simply dumped in unlined landfills, in rivers and streams every year and a very small fraction of industrial waste water is treated or purified. The air too has been poisoned as millions of cars spew sulfur dioxide and other particulates virtually without control. To tackle these problems, the Taiwanese government and industry leaders have committed to spending more than $20 billion over the next eight years to clean up past problems and to build the infrastructure necessary to limit future problems.

Will US firms meet this demand?

Over the next 15 years, experts estimate that developing nations will need to install a trillion dollars' worth of energy technology to meet growing energy needs. These countries want clean and efficient sources of energy.

Will US firms meet this demand?

Not if the United States sits on the sidelines of the environmental revolution that is under way. Not if our businesses are told that concern for the environment is a fad that will pass and that the old, polluting ways of the past will be acceptable in the future. The evidence is unmistakable. We have seen important markets slip away from us. In 1980, the United States had three quarters of the world sales in solar technology. In 1990, German and Japanese competition had cut our share to 30 percent. We also used to supply the world with air pollution control technologies. Today, we import more than 70 percent of those technologies. And the list goes on.

'Al Gore and I know that our children's health and well-being depend on having clean air to breathe.'

Al Gore and I believe that the time for posing false choices has passed. For our children's sake, for the sake of improving worker health and safety, for the sake of enhancing the living standard of every American, and for the sake of preserving our planet's precious natural resources, we cannot afford the practices of the past.

The Clinton Administration will work for a better future for the American people. It will be a future built on a genuine commitment to leave our children a better nation whose air, water and land are unspoiled; whose natural beauty is undimmed; and whose leadership for sustainable global growth is unsurpassed. This approach will challenge Americans and demand responsibility at every level from individuals, families, communities, corporations and government agencies to do more to preserve the quality of our environment and our world.

Our country's leaders must be willing to exert international leadership on issues threatening the health of the planet. The cold war is over and we have entered a new era in which threats to our security are less evident, but no less dangerous, than before. If we do not find the vision and leadership to defeat the unprecedented new threats of global climate change, ozone depletion, habitat destruction and desertification, then those threats may well defeat us.

But the message of Rio was powerful. Nations are ready to meet this challenge. They are eager to move ahead. They looked to the United States for leadership—or at least for us to join them in the cause. We must not disappoint the world community, and we must not fail to represent the real concerns and aspirations of the American public on these issues.

Al Gore and I are determined to make progress to protect the land we cherish, the values we share, and the only Earth we have.

TUNISIA: DEVELOPMENT, YES POLLUTION, NO

ELIZABETH BRYANT
October 1994

BIZERTE, Tunisia—To the thousands of European tourists who flock here yearly, Bizerte, with its winding streets and peeling Andalusian houses, is close to paradise. But trouble lies just out of sight of the town's wealth of dazzling beaches and azure waters, an hour's drive north of Tunis.

Nearby industries still dump largely untreated waste into the Mediterranean, already one of the world's most polluted oceans. At night, the town's oil refinery casts an orange glow on the beaches and serves as a reminder of potential oil spills from rigs just offshore.

For a country in which tourism is the third largest business, such environmental blights are worrisome indeed. Not only this, but a myriad of environmental problems have come to the fore. Piles of household waste, declining water tables, soil degradation—all are side effects of an economy that is expanding faster than the environment's ability to cope.

The work of Tunisia's three-year-old Ministry of Environment and the emergence of stricter legislation highlight the country's desire not to walk the same development path as the West.

Passed in 1988, the law requires, among other things, that industries develop environmental impact assessments before launching new projects.

"Before, there was no environmental politics in Tunisia," said ministry spokesperson Fethi Debbabi. "This has changed with education and with the environmental law. Now there's lots of awareness, especially with large industries, on ways to recycle. They win and the environment wins."

While it may be early for such sanguine assessments, the country's latest four-year development plan, passed in 1992, earmarked roughly $1.4 billion for environmental projects, including $598 million in direct investments. The money will be spent through a series of ambitious programs recently launched by the ministry, programs dealing with everything from coastline to desert.

To reduce soil erosion and desertification that cause annual losses of almost 50,000 acres of arable land, the government has launched a massive reforestation project. Money is also going toward conserving biodiversity and promoting ecotourism as an alternative to sun and sand. The programs are implemented by Tunisia's environmental agency in partnership with related ministries such as agriculture and health.

Cleaning up Tunisia's overpopulated coastline may be the greatest concern. The coast is home not only to tourists but to the majority of the country's industries and people. To reduce the heavy quantities of toxic and other wastes, the government is establishing pollution reduction measures such as building wastewater treatment plants and levying fines on polluters. Other projects include efforts to control coastal erosion and petroleum spills. In November 1994 Tunisia is scheduled to host a Med21 conference in which participating countries will draft a Mediterranean-specific Agenda 21.

To date, the country's efforts have largely won praise from outside experts. "Generally, I think Tunisia has done an excellent job," said George J. Lombardo, program manager for the New York-based World Environment Center, which conducts environmental audits in Tunisia.

Lombardo ranks Tunisia's environmental program as one of the most effective in the Middle East. "There seems to be a consciousness among Tunisian industries and people toward the environment. Beyond just consciousness, you're seeing moves by the government for industries to clean up their acts," he said. Earning such praise has not been easy. Private industries complain of being squeezed in one direction to make heavy investments in pollution prevention and cleanup technologies and in another to compete under the country's recent privatization initiatives.

'If you tell us to invest in the environment, we don't have the means.'

"We have a dilemma. For us the priority is employment and economic growth," said Tarak Cherif, the Tunisian chairman of Philips Whirlpool and head of an environmental association of chemists. "If you tell us to invest in the environment, we don't have the means."

Others say the government is investing too heavily in cleanup technologies, rather than reducing the amount of pollution emitted to begin with. "In Tunisia there are legal incentives for new projects to reduce pollution," said Rachid Nafti, director of the Environmental Pollution Prevention Project (EP3), an environmental auditing firm. "But what about existing projects?"

Some of these criticisms were raised in a recent Work Bank study, which found Tunisia slow to implement its environmental programs and enforce its "polluter pays" principles, said World Bank program officer Ramzi Fares. "They could do more," Fares said, but he still praised Tunisia's efforts overall. "The question is, can they do more without inciting a large amount of displeasure among the industries? If you add another financial burden on them, you might have industries falter and more people on the streets—and unemployment is already 15 percent. It's a very explosive situation."

Public environmental awareness is also lacking. Despite what some describe as excellent educational material provided by the government, Tunisia recycles little but bottles. People dump household and industrial waste in fields where sheep graze. Other fields are heavily irrigated, depleting the country's scarce water supplies and, at times, causing salt to build up in the soil.

Still, many experts believe Tunisia has time on its side. With an economy based mainly on agriculture, textiles and tourism, Tunisia is spared the massive cleanups needed in countries like Russia that have a lot of heavy industry. To help finance its programs, the government has recently negotiated a few debt-for-nature swaps with European governments, Debbabi said. Other governments have also assisted with generous grants.

"In the end, you can't separate environment from development," Debbabi said. "But you also can't be fundamentalist about the environment."

ENVIRONMENT IS A HUMAN ISSUE

INGAR BRUEGGEMANN
July 1997

L ONDON—Family planning has a key role to play in achieving the right balance between population and resources, and therefore in sustainable development. But without the provision of adequate women's education and radical improvements in the status of women, family planning cannot fully succeed.

Before Rio, environment tended to be an issue seen in isolation. But the evidence is that people need to be at the heart of the discussion on environmental issues. Investments in people, particularly in their health and education, go a long way in helping to achieve wider environmental objectives. As Rio's program of action, Agenda 21, explained, sustainable development is the way to reverse both poverty and environmental destruction.

This is why the International Planned Parenthood Federation(IPPF) thoroughly endorses the conclusion of the latest Human Development Report of the United Nations Development Programme that greater sex equality should be a goal in order to win the fight against poverty. Women and children are more likely to suffer poverty than adult males. The connection between the status of women and the pace of development has become increasingly clear: economic growth and improvement in quality of life have been fastest in those areas where women have higher status and slowest where women face the greatest barriers to equality.

Twenty-five years ago the Club of Rome forecast an environmental cataclysm due to uncontrolled population growth that would outstrip the Earth's carrying capacity. At that time the world population growth rate was 2.1 percent per annum, corresponding to a population doubling time of 33 years. Despite the heralded success to date of national and international development cooperation efforts to make information and services available—which has been effective in slowing the rate of growth to 1.48 percent—the numbers are still increasing by some 81 million persons annually.

According to United Nations projections, annual increments are likely to remain around 80 million until the year 2015, and it seems clear that the world population will pass the six billion mark by 1999. By the year 2050, the United Nations' low projection shows a world population of 7.7 billion people and the high projection a population of 11.1 billion people.

As Elizabeth Dowdeswell, Executive Director of the UN Environment Programme, pointed out at the International Conference on Population and Development (ICPD) in Cairo: "Population growth has caused the 'resource pie' to shrink, leaving people without food and literally forcing them into acts of environmental degradation."

Two groups in particular are responsible for a disproportionate share in the consumption of resources involved in environmental degradation: the world's billion richest and billion poorest people. The richest countries consume the largest slice of the Earth's resources and generate enormous quantities of waste and pollution. As one delegate at Cairo pointed out, the 24 million people added to the population of the United States in the last decade will consume more of the Earth's resources than the 750 million people living in Africa. According to the latest census prediction, the US's population alone will grow by more than 120 million by 2050.

Women need to be at the center of any progress for environmental protection.

The poorest countries have the highest fertility rates. Poverty is the cause of many choices that lead to environmental degradation because of the need for immediate survival. Poverty and environmental degradation have come to reinforce one another in many developing countries, along with illiteracy (especially among women), inadequate family planning availability and other factors which are incompatible with sustainable development.

The interdependence and mutual reinforcement of economic development, social development and environmental protection for sustainable development was emphasized in the Platform for Action at the Fourth World Conference on Women in Beijing in September 1995. Throughout the developing world, mainly women manage the land; they grow and process food; and they collect water and firewood as well as maintain homes.

Therefore, it is women who are directly interacting with the natural environment and need to be at the center of any environmental protection progress. Yet the environment for women in the least developed countries is mostly one of poverty, illiteracy, frequent pregnancies, malnutrition, anemia and too-heavy workloads. Family planning has a crucial role to play here, as part of an integrated approach to sustainable development.

The World Fertility Survey found women would have an average of 1.41 fewer children if they were able to choose the size of their families. In about 30 years' time this could make a difference of approximately 1.3 billion people in the world's population. But access to family planning is still a problem; 300 million couples know about family planning methods but have no access. Between 120 and 150 million more women would use family planning now if they had access to sexual and reproductive health information and services.

Nafis Sadik, Executive Director of the United Nations Population Fund, recently pointed out that if this need for family planning is satisfied, the world's population in 2050 would be significantly closer to the UN's low projection. She indicated at the launch of the 1997 State of the World Population Report that an ultimate world population of under 9 billion is "do-able."

The need for, and right to, sexual and reproductive health care was fully recognized at the Fourth World Conference on Women in 1995 and at ICPD in Cairo in 1994. It is time to honor the commitments made at these conferences. We have had much discussion and too little action. Promises won't result in an improved environment and reduced population pressure, but effective investment in participatory sustainable development programs will.

After many years of providing successful family planning services, organizations like IPPF and the Family Planning Associations are well qualified to take on an outward-looking advocacy and service delivery role in working with governments, intergovernmental organizations and national and international voluntary organizations to address the crucial importance of family planning for a sustainable environment and sustainable development—and to help reduce crippling poverty. IPPF is committed to working alongside agencies and national groups that put an integrated approach to development, including health and environmental concerns, at the top of their list of priorities.

In many countries IPPF piloted joint environmental and family planning integrated efforts.

For example, in Nepal, a family planning and agro-forestry project was set up by local women's groups in conjunction with the Family Planning Association. Guava trees, indigenous to the area, are grown, then sold in Kathmandu. The tree nurseries are run by women, which increases their income. Fodder trees are also grown, along agro-forestry principles, so that main food crops are safeguarded, while soil erosion is offset. Activities still include sexual and reproductive health and family planning, but also include immunization and the community's own microcredit bank.

In the Jamalpur District of Bangladesh, the Family Planning Association worked under an Oxfam-funded flood relief program in the late 1980s. The self sustaining program is now run with the local community and includes agro-forestry, fish farming, basic health care, a community store so that workers can sell the grain with which they are paid when prices are favorable, and tube-wells for safe drinking water. The benefits of such an integrated approach to poverty have become clearly visible. The association has begun using its successful experience in this project to conduct similar programs in other parts of Bangladesh.

World population will continue to grow well into the next millennium and, as consumption levels rise, the impact on the global environment will increase. The only way to ensure a balance between population and sustainable resources is through sound family planning as an essential feature of reproductive health available to all. Satisfying people's reproductive needs at the same time contributes to the macro-world of a sustainable environment in all its dimensions. People in most parts of the world want smaller families; failure to respond to that need not only condemns millions of women to suffer the misery of unintended pregnancy—and even death from abortion—but it may well prove the deciding factor in the long-term survival of the fragile ecosystem that is Planet Earth.

THE IMPACT OF POPULATION ON THE ENVIRONMENT

MOHAMED T. EL-ASHRY
September 1994

The 1994 Cairo Conference on Population and Development presented world leaders with a timely opportunity to adopt the necessary actions to stabilize global population levels and contribute to the betterment of people's livelihoods. By the year 2030, the world will have almost three billion more people—two billion of them in countries where the average person earns less than the equivalent of $2 a day.

The world is becoming too inured to the suffering and damage created by overpopulation:

• Witness the soaring numbers of environmental refugees escaping environmental disaster regions;

• Witness the mushrooming slums worldwide;

• Witness the thousands of families forced to live on flood-prone sand banks, deltas and low-lying areas in a number of South Asian countries;

• Witness the large-scale land degradation accompanied by famines and human suffering in parts of sub-Saharan Africa.

The impact of human population on the environment can be divided into two components. The first is the impact imposed by the basic needs of people for food, fuel, clothing, shelter and transport. Everyone needs a minimum of 1,000-2,000 calories a day, for example. This component of the impact is proportional to sheer numbers of people. The impact of producing the calories, fuel, shoes, and shelter will intensify with the 90 million people swelling the world's population each year.

This impact also must be multiplied by almost 6 billion, the number of people currently inhabiting the Earth. But this is inadequate. People are not on Earth to subsist at the lowest level compatible with life. Therefore, alleviation of today's poverty is imperative. The paramount goal of economic development is to raise consumption of the poor above this level. That is why acceleration of technology transfer is so important for developing countries.

The second component of the impact of humans on the environment is consumption. Developed country consumption creates 70-75 percent of global environmental impacts. Wasteful use of energy has led to risky accumulation of carbon dioxide and other pollutants in the atmosphere. (For example, the United States releases almost 30 times as much carbon dioxide per capita as India.) There is major scope to produce the same amount more efficiently, with less waste and less impact. Second, there is an opportunity to reduce consumption in general; less consumption would improve health and welfare. Possibly the biggest contribution the Organization for Economic Cooperation and Development (OECD) could make to approach global environmental sustainability is to accelerate the transition to renewable sources of energy. This would be a significant contribution in terms of carbon dioxide and other forms of pollution, and in terms of land lost to agriculture by unprecedented urbanization.

In the transition toward environmentally sustainable development, population stabilization must become a high-priority goal. If we cannot provide for the poorest 20 percent of the human population at today's relatively low population, how will we be capable of improving living standards when the world population approaches 10 billion? These staggering numbers have serious implications for any country's development ambitions. Huge development and environmental rehabilitation efforts will be required just to maintain the status quo. Indeed, whether any "development" is achievable in some places is open to question.

EXPLOITING NATURE

STELLA DANKER
May 1999

M ountains and beaches are some of the most attractive places to which
people flock to escape the stresses of their lives. But as more people are
drawn to the beauty of nature, these places are literally being overwhelmed by
the attention.

The mountains of Nepal, for example, drew only 20 nature lovers in
1964. By 1996, though, the mountains were besieged by some 17,000
trekkers—so many that, at the height of the tourist season, there were five visitors to every Sherpa, according to Mountain Agenda, an informal group
interested in promoting mountain tourism. This group researched 17 mountain attractions from Baguio in the Philippines to Canada's Whistler
Mountain and found that, in many places, while visitors hiked away their individual stress, their sheer numbers brought significant environmental stress to
the area.

In the case of Nepal, the onslaught of people has turned the world's
highest mountain, Mt. Everest, into the world's highest junkyard. Trekkers
have turned the hike to the Everest base camp into a garbage trail. Empty
beer bottles waiting to be airlifted greet visitors arriving at Lukla and
Syangboche airports. There is an estimated 17 metric tons of trash for every
kilometer of trail, which is deteriorating because of the numbers hiking it.
Trees outside the protected national park are disappearing fast as they are cut
for firewood and timber.

A careful balance has to be found to protect nature and benefit local
people while allowing visitors to bask in the beauty of a place without loving it
to death. Take the Hawaiian island of Maui, for example. It manages to amuse
some two million sun-lovers yearly while conservation groups, major landown-
ers, corporations, and federal and state governments fiercely protect 100,000
wilderness acres. Maui largely looks after itself. Only a quarter of the island's
729 square miles is inhabited because much of the terrain is rugged and hard
to reach. On that, 100,000 people live. As for the tourists, they congregate on
the island's windward side, soaking up the sun in plush resorts. Maui has one
of Hawaii's largest tracts of native forest and its waters are a marine sanctuary

where baby whales frolic. The second largest of Hawaii's eight volcanic islands, it had been the winter retreat of Arctic humpback whales long before Polynesian seafarers chanced upon it 1,500 years ago.

These 80,000-pound giant whales swim the 3,500 miles to Maui to have their babies. Others mate. The endangered humpbacks love Maui's shallow (300-foot-deep) Alalakeiki Channel, which is sheltered by the nearby islands of Molokai, Lanai and Kahoolawe. For this reason, almost two-thirds of the 3,000 humpbacks living in the North Pacific make the pilgrimage there. The whales, which can grow up to 45 feet long, are easily seen from land because they hug the shoreline, particularly the nursing mothers. When they are in Maui's waters from December to May, they are protected by federal and state laws, encouraging them to breed and return. All thrill craft like jet skis and parasailers are banned. Water vessels have to stay more than 100 yards from the whales. Aircraft may not fly lower than 1,000 feet overhead.

The coastline is fringed with 33 miles of beach with sand of white, gold, black, green and crushed garnet, while the now-dormant volcano rules the interior. The many hues of the sand are a result of the metallic content of the lava and cinder flow, exposed by erosion—rust from iron and yellow from sulphur.

The waters hide a maze of coral reefs and lava formations, a haven for the colorful fish, manta rays and green sea turtles. Every winter the whales return, making the highest and lowest pitch sounds that can be heard by people. Humpbacks are the only whales to hold a tune as we know it, singing together in phrases and themes. They all sing the same tune, refining it gradually over the season. When they return the next winter they pick up the final version of the previous season's song.

From the sound of their music on the southern coastline, one of the world's fastest-climbing roads goes up in just 40 miles from sea level to the 10,023-foot summit of the volcano named Haleakala, Hawaiian for "House of the Sun." Its last eruption in 1790 and streams from centuries of rainfall have cut deep channels into the slopes. A dozen or so cinder cones emerged in renewed volcanic activity—smaller volcanoes within a volcano, some almost 600 feet high. Clouds whoosh down the valleys formed by the cones within the crater. Up in the sky with the clouds and stillness, ancient Hawaiians felt close to the gods.

On the far rim of the crater, they marked out with stones their *heiau*, or holy ground. Here, the early Marquesan settlers of 1,500 years ago worshiped and sometimes made human sacrifices to appease their gods. These sacred slopes also hide and protect the mana of the ancient *alii* or chiefs. Hawaiians believed that a person's inner spirit, holding all one's wisdom and power, could be stolen on death. To stop this happening to the *alii*, their dead bodies were stripped of flesh, the bones wrapped in wicker and hidden in the tiny caves formed by the lava tubes. The entrances were camouflaged by rocks.

Today hikers, mule-riders and campers go down the 4,000-foot-deep crater, which at 21 miles across is as big as Manhattan. There are no New Yorkers living here, only some 50,000 Ahinahina. This silvery rosette, about three feet across, lives from five to more than 30 years, flowering once before it dies. A central upright stalk erupts to six feet. From this sprout 500 purple-red flower heads, each with several hundred blossoms. In the same family as the sunflower, it is highly adaptable, surviving with little moisture in the extreme of a Haleakala summer day to the frigid cold of its wintry night. Its spongy finger-shaped leaves curl inward, protecting the stalk and creating a bowl that collects and stores rainwater. So far, the crater is quite pristine. But the number of hikers should be controlled so that magnificent plants like the Ahinahina will continue to thrive.

CHINA'S THREE GORGES DAM

AUDREY RONNING TOPPING
March 1998

The forced relocation of almost two million Yangtze River refugees is causing such serious trouble in China that opponents of the Three Gorges Dam believe it may force the government to scale down or even terminate the world's largest and perhaps the most hazardous hydroelectric project. This new view of the mega-project that most people thought was beyond the point of no return has surfaced because of a recent report by a prominent Chinese social scientist who toured five areas of the river valley scheduled to be flooded by the 1.3-mile-long, 610-foot-high dam which will create a 385 mile long reservoir which the Chinese refer to as a "lake within the gorges".

The author, who has concealed his identity to protect his career, reports that the resettlement program—that has already evacuated 100,000 people from their ancestral homes—has been plagued by official corruption, false reports of progress by local officials to national leaders, inadequate compensation, lack of farmland and a severe shortage of jobs. This is all fomenting dangerous anger and frustration among the evacuees. The report was distributed recently by International Rivers Network and Human Rights in China.

The account was no surprise to opponents of the dam. Dai Qing, a woman journalist and the chief voice for the opposition in China, has long been warning about the folly of the project to this reporter for publication in The Earth Times. She was jailed for ten months for writing a critical book "Yangtze! Yangtze!" Undaunted, she has just completed another book of essays by China's top scientists and archeologists, "The River Dragon Has Come." (M. E. Sharpe, New York and London, 1998.) The book details the dangers of the project. The scientists

> *The world's largest and perhaps most hazardous hydroelectric project.*

were not allowed to present their views to the People's Congress while the decision to build was being discussed. In 1997, while Prime Minister Li Peng was exclaiming, "The damming of the Yangtze River is successful!" and Chinese leaders cheered the completion of the first phase of construction of The Three Gorges Dam, opponents accused him of jumping the gun and vowed to continue the fight to either stop or force a scaling down of the dimensions to lessen the dangers of what they believe to be the most hazardous hydroelectric project ever attempted. Even as China's leaders attempted to exploit the completion of the 350-feet-wide and almost a mile long diversionary channel into a major political event, the critics claimed it as a prime example of putting politics before responsible engineering.

Is China putting politics ahead of responsible engineering?

President Jiang Zemin declared it to be a symbol of China's emergence as a world power. "It vividly proves once again," he claimed "that socialism is superior in organizing people to do big jobs."

Owen Lammers, executive director of International Rivers Network, saw it as "merely the most recent evidence that science and engineering are taking a back seat to political agendas in order to erect this monument to China's hard-line regime."

Opponents of the dam are basing their hopes on the ascension of China's economic czar Zhu Rongji who has replaced Li Peng as Prime Minister. Dai Qing points out that Zhu is the only Chinese leader who has never expressed enthusiasm for the project.

By 2009, the Government says that 1.2 million people will have to be resettled. Unofficial accounts estimate 1.8 million. Many of them are resisting but this is being hidden by false reports. The account said that when Prime Minister Li met with residents of a doomed town, the people who expressed anger at the lack of compensation and jobs were barred from the meeting and replaced by others not even slated for relocation. They were bribed to serve as the audience for Li's speech.

"Foot-dragging opposition to resettlement is widespread, presaging a major crisis if the dam project continues as planned," wrote the Chinese researcher, "...raising the specter of unrest."

A coalition of 45 international groups which have opposed the project for environmental dangers and violating basic human rights, is calling on international banking institutions to stop financing the project. They claim the only way now to keep the Yangtze flowing is to halt the flow of foreign financing. Peter Passell, reporting on China's economic scene in the New York Times on March 12, 1998, stated that "Chinese leaders have said they will increase spending, with $750 billion to $1 trillion devoted to new construction over three years." Passell claims this is "virtually impossible short of a total mobilization of the economy in the manner of Chairman Mao's Great Leap Forward." Passell was comparing the Three Gorges enterprise to Mao's plan to rapidly industrialize China which resulted in a terrible economic and human disaster.

The estimated cost of the dam has risen from $17 billion to $75 billion and many investment firms are having second thoughts. Public pressure in Japan has led at least one investment company to stop offering bonds for the State Development Bank of China. The US Export-Import Bank has refused to finance loans for the project and the World Bank, after a thorough investigation, declined financial aid. Ignoring the American example and the tragic history of catastrophic dam failures in China, Canada's publicly funded Export Development Corporation is backing Canadian firms that want to supply 26 giant turbines for the dam.

'We are fighting to expose the issues the government is trying to suppress because we want basic rights, more power and a better government.'

All public debate on the project has been banned in China since 1989. Dai Qing claims that the megadam represents much more than a political and ecological debate. She sees it as a metaphor of China's changing society, a microcosm of what is happening in the whole of China. She claims the fight in China is for a better, freer society without resorting to revolution. "We are fighting to expose the issues the government is trying to suppress because we want basic rights, more power and a better government in China. On the surface, the struggle is about the dam and the resettlement of over a million people. But it is really the story of how the Chinese people suffer and how we are working for a better future."

"The Three Gorges Dam is a special case," she continued. "China is undergoing rapid change. The politicians who seek power by supporting the dam have all the characteristics of the old society—authoritarianism, one-party system, no regard for the individual—and allow no democratic discussion. Opponents of the dam, that is, the majority of China's intellectuals, are concerned about the environment, human rights, the welfare of others as well as our ancient roots which will be washed away forever by the reservoir. These people have all the characteristics of the new society. We want the freedom to be heard. What is the government afraid of?"

The leaders, however, seem so blinded by their own pride that they refuse to take the advice of their own hired consultants.

Author's Note: On May 24, 1999, Chinese Prime Minister Zhu Rongji admitted that severe problems bedevil the giant Three Gorges Dam Project. In a widely published speech, he announced a major change in the strategy for resettlement of the reservoir evacuees. Instead of moving the people to close sites above the lake, they now plan to send them to distant parts of the country. But critics claim this solution may be just as unworkable.

WHAT IS SUSTAINABLE DEVELOPMENT?

THEODORE W. KHEEL
September 1992

The term "sustainable development" dominates and informs the texts of the decisions that emerged from the 1992 Earth Summit in Rio. It is the guiding principle of the Rio Declaration on Environment and Development, the predicate of the action-oriented programs of Agenda 21, and the foundation on which the principles of forestry management are based. The convention on climate change recognizes that the signatory parties "have a right to and should promote sustainable development" and cooperate on policies and measures that lead to "sustainable economic growth and development." The convention on biological diversity employs a substitute—sustainable use—for the obvious reason that it addresses the conservation of species, not their development.

That convention said that sustainable means "use of components of biological diversity in a way and at a rate that does not lead to the long-term decline of biological diversity, thereby maintaining its potential to meet the needs and aspirations of present and future generations." In the context of development, that could be the definition of sustainable development. As the climax to its emphasis on sustainable development and related activities, the Earth Summit recommended that there be established a Commission on Sustainable Development to ensure effective follow-up to the conference.

The key word in all of this is, of course, the adjective "sustainable." In addition to sustainable use, it is the designated modifier of most other activities set forth in the texts. There is a reference to "sustainable management" in the convention on climate change. In the first 100 pages of Agenda 21 alone, there are references to sustainable livelihoods and environmental protection, sustainable agriculture, sustainable consumption, sustainable economic growth and prosperity, sustainable lifestyles, environmentally sound and sustainable use of renewable resources, sustainable human settlements, sustainable community involvement in environmental health activities, sustainable land-use planning and management, and sustainable energy and transportation systems. Nowhere in the texts is the term sustainable development defined. Its meaning, however, emerges from the context in which it is used.

Sustainable development is obviously the link integrating the twin concerns of the conference: environment and development. It is used both as a goal and a process to encourage development without damaging the environment. Obviously, it contemplates far more than the dictionary meaning of the words that make up the term. Taken literally, it would mean development that continues indefinitely. One pundit suggested that it might be viewed as an intellectual oxymoron.

It appears that sustainable development first came into prominence in 1980 when the International Union for the Conservation of Nature and Natural Resources presented the World Conservation Strategy with "the overall aim of achieving sustainable development through the conservation of living resources." In 1987, it was adopted by the World Commission on Environment and Development (the Brundtland Commission) and defined in the Commission's report—"Our Common Future"—as "development that meets the needs of the present without compromising the ability of future generations to meet their own needs." That report defines as the "major objective" of development "the satisfaction of human needs and aspirations." It then says that meeting essential needs depends in part on achieving full growth potential and that "sustainable development clearly requires economic growth in places where such needs are not being met." The report describes in detail the operational objectives necessary to protect the environment through sustainable development. In summing up, the report states that "sustainable development is a process of change in which the exploitation of resources, the direction of investments, the orientation of technological development, and institutional change are all in harmony and enhance both current and future potential to meet human needs and aspirations."

In 1991, a writer for a learned publication concluded that the description of sustainable development in the report of the Brundtland Commission represented the mainstream of sustainable development thinking but was internally inconsistent. He maintained that clarification and more precise articulation was necessary if sustainable development "is to avoid either being dismissed as another development fad or being coopted by forces opposed to changes in the status quo."

But the use of the term sustainable development goes marching on, gaining meaning from the extensive ways in which it was used by the Earth

Summit and the preparations leading up to the Summit. Sustainable development, for example, was the main theme of a book, "Changing Course," published by the prestigious World Business Council on Sustainable Development. It was also the centerpiece of a statement by 30 commercial banks, with assets of over $1.5 trillion, committing themselves to environmental assessment as part of their lending policies. It is being widely used for such purposes by international development agencies, including the World Bank.

In Rio, sustainable development was freely and frequently included in the discussion of the delegates. It was known to and thoroughly understood by the 35,000 persons who attended the conference. Sustainable development is a consensus builder. It may not provide room in the same text for environmental purists and developers bent on business as usual. But it does seek development that meets human needs and aspirations. It asks in return that the development not compromise the ability of present and future generations to meet their needs.

The conflict between environmental protection and economic growth is severe. President Bush used his allotted seven minutes of speaking time in Rio to defend his refusal to sign the convention on biodiversity on the grounds that it would result in loss of jobs in the middle of an economic recession. The leaders of all other countries disagreed. Many believe that sustainable development can create jobs and generate profits not only for its practitioners but for the developers and purveyors of new technologies as well. It offers a neat solution that can accommodate economic growth with environmental protection.

Sustainable development suffers from one major weakness at the present time. It is not known to the vast majority of this planet's inhabitants. Yet, it is understood by the relatively small group intensely involved with the Earth Summit's concerns. But it is far from being part of our common parlance. Nor is it ever likely to achieve widespread notoriety. It is not a simple concept that can readily be appreciated. It was given a major forward thrust by the Earth Summit. It is now critical that the general public, including journalists as well as political leaders and opinion makers, become fully aware of this unifying concept.

RICH AND POOR: THE TIME BOMB IS TICKING

SIR SHRIDATH S. RAMPHAL
April 1994

A scientist at Cambridge University suggested to a recent conference that Britain's population should be reduced to about 30 million—about half its present level—so that the British people could enjoy the optimum quality of life while preserving the environment and conserving natural resources. The scientist was not advocating anything drastic or draconian by way of immediate action; he thought that if public policies continued to encourage small families and fertility was maintained at its current rate of 1.8 children born to each woman, the population would slim down to 30 million in 150 years.

I start with this reference to make the point that while the problem of rapid population growth is one faced essentially in developing nations, the problem of environmental impact and of pressure on resources has to be confronted in both developing and developed countries—and, in some crucial aspects, especially in developed countries.

The principal cause of human pressure on the environment is human consumption. Population acts as a multiplier. The total impact can therefore be reduced by moderating human consumption or human numbers or, optimally, by doing both.

None of the industrialized countries are, as far as I am aware, contemplating any significant program to cut per capita consumption or make their population smaller; but ecological compulsions, leaving aside considerations of global equity, may well require them to do so in the not too distant future. Instead of waiting for the leisurely, pain-free "Cambridge" process of a slow decline in numbers to produce results, they may need to opt for more resolute action to reduce consumption. But I will return to this later.

World population is now increasing by 1.7 percent a year. That does not seem an alarming figure by itself. It is when the percentage figure is translated into absolute numbers, into the incremental increase in numbers that occurs each year, that the enormous dimensions of present-day demographic change become clear.

When the Rev. Thomas Malthus was writing his "Essay on the Principle of Population" 200 years ago, world population was edging toward its first billion. It took just over 100 more years to reach the second billion. The third we added in 30 years and the fourth in 15, the fifth in 12. From 1960 to 1987, world population increased by 2 billion—the figure it had taken all the millennia from the emergence of Homo sapiens until 1930 to reach. From 1930—in my own lifetime—world population has trebled. We are now adding almost a billion every 10 years—an India each decade, a Mexico each year.

We cannot speak with much certainty about future population growth except for the next 20 or 30 years. Beyond that, demographers can only offer projections, extrapolating from current trends and making assumptions about variable factors like the pace of economic growth and the spread of family planning. They can only speculate about future technological advances or ecological constraints. Estimates of what the numbers are likely to be in the longer term are therefore imprecise. So demographers offer us high, medium and low variants and we use their medium projection as a working basis.

As you know, the latest medium projection by UN demographers has world population, now 5.5 billion, touching 10 billion by the middle of the next century, and continuing to grow for another 100 years or so before leveling off at about 11.6 billion. If human behavior were to correspond closer to the high projection, the numbers would swell by another two or three billion before peaking, but there are even higher projections that take us to 19 billion by 2100.

Whatever the increase, as much as 95 percent of future growth in human numbers will be in the developing countries, whose population is growing at the average rate of 2.1 percent against an average of 0.5 percent for the developed countries. There is no room to doubt that the pressure exerted by populations expanding at this pace will have serious environmental impact.

Scientific advances have so far helped to frustrate Malthusian predictions of doom. Some technological optimists, who feel that our scientific ingenuity will continue to defeat ecological challenges, may still be around. But the consensus of scientific opinion does not share such blithe confidence.

In an unprecedented joint statement in 1993, the Royal Society in Britain and the National Academy of Sciences in the United States issued a warning: "If current predictions of population growth prove accurate and patterns of human activity on the planet remain unchanged, science and technology may not be able to prevent either irreversible degradation of the environment or continued poverty for much of the world."

These fears do not reflect a sudden loss of confidence among leading scientists but are influenced by the present scale of population increase and the extent of pressure already exerted on the environment. The impact of people on their habitat is, of course, a complex one and is affected by several factors. Geography and climate, the distribution of wealth, the availability, ownership and fertility of land, the level of income, economic policies, technology, and agricultural practices all have a bearing.

In poor countries, as numbers rise there is generally more pressure on the land. Farming becomes more intensive: fallow periods between crops are abandoned, and more pesticides and fertilizers are applied. The result is early exhaustion and degradation of the land. Farming is also extended to more fragile areas—leading to soil erosion or desertification—or to forest land, resulting in the loss of trees and of species. Poor people needing land to grow food for themselves cause more deforestation than loggers seeking timber.

Increase of yields per acre or hectare may be possible in some countries, but Green Revolution technologies have faced not just social costs but other problems as well. Soil erosion, salination and other forms of land degradation and ecological impacts erase about half the gains from technology-based improvements in grain production, holding output gains below the rate of population growth.

Population increase exacerbates other environmental problems as well: Water scarcity, inadequate sanitation and lack of fuelwood are all part of the daily environmental experience of millions in the South. Rapid population increase also spurs migration from rural areas, adding to congestion in urban areas and the environmental strains that go with it. Migration is no new phenomenon: it has long been a survival strategy among the poor; but it is now assuming worrying proportions. The term "environmental refugee" has joined "political refugee" in the humanitarian lexicon.

Sign of our times: Environmental refugees are growing.

Environmental refugees have so far largely been the products of desertification and famine in Africa, and the host countries that have had to accommodate and support them are also in that region. Future movements, however, will not be confined to these causes or this continent.

Trans-border movements apart, the likely future pressures on the cities of the third world are sufficient cause for concern. In 1960, of the 10 largest cities in the world, seven were in developed countries and only three in developing countries. Now the proportion has been reversed: Seven are in developing countries. By the end of the decade there will be 20 cities with more than 11 million people each; 17 of the 20 will be in developing countries. Mexico City, the largest, will have as many people as the Netherlands and Belgium put together.

The trend to megacities, what The Economist has termed "monsteropolises," is continuing unabated. Today 45 percent of the world's people live in urban areas; this is expected to rise to 65 percent by 2025. As Calcutta and Saõ Paulo testify, developing countries are already hard put to maintain even the barest environmental standards in congested urban agglomerations.

Neither rural nor urban areas of the third world will therefore escape environmental degradation if population growth continues unchecked. The people of the developing world will be the principal victims. Whether it is the lack of land or its diminished fertility, the shortage of fuelwood, bad sanitation or poor housing, whether it is hunger or malnutrition or water-borne disease, it is the poorest who will suffer. It is therefore in the interests of these countries and their people that the problem of rapid population growth be tackled.

And it has been tackled resolutely and with considerable success. The overall number of children per woman (the fertility rate) declined in developing countries from 6.1 per woman in 1960-1964 to 3.9 per woman in 1985-90. The result has been 70 million fewer births per year in the developing world throughout the latter years of the 1980s—a momentous demographic change given all the difficulties that developing countries have experienced. They achieved that decline in less than 30 years. The time it took to go from an average family size of 6.5 to 3.5 for the United States was 58 years. For Indonesia (by no means the prime example of fertility decrease) it was 28 years.

In three decades, the prevalence of contraceptive use has risen from 10 percent to more than 50 percent in developing countries. The challenge ahead for developed and developing countries alike is to assist the acceleration of these overall trends. It has been estimated that 100 million more women would use contraceptive services if they were available or of high quality. If these needs were met, contraceptive prevalence could be raised to about 60 percent, but this is not the only need. Let us remember that the demographic transition in Europe was achieved without the benefit of modern contraceptives.

Economic development and rising prosperity were the primary means of achieving fertility decline. If the world is serious about bringing down population growth rates, our global community must help to create conditions in which couples in the developing world consciously and voluntarily seek a lesser number of children—of surviving children. Reducing poverty, improving the standard of health and education, raising the status of women and increasing their opportunities: these are the conditions that can increase the impact of available contraceptive services. If we are to influence reproductive behavior in poor countries in favor of small families, development—especially social development—is a necessary complement to family planning services. But this is precisely the time when development assistance is stagnating and development cooperation weakening.

At a recent meeting of the North-South Roundtable held in Bretton Woods, New Hampshire, where the postwar economic order was established in July 1944, a call was made for a new framework for development cooperation. It came with the recognition that one of the principal motivations for development assistance in the last few decades was to seek allies in the cold war, and that while the cold war has ended, current allocations of assistance still carry its scars, with only slender links to the objectives of poverty alleviation and human development. The point was illustrated with examples pertinent to a discussion of the centrality of development, and development assistance, in securing global sustainability:

•Egypt receives $370 of development assistance per poor person, compared to $4 for India.

•El Salvador received more US assistance last year than Bangladesh, even though Bangladesh has 24 times the population of El Salvador and is five times poorer.

•Only a quarter of official development assistance (ODA) goes to the 10 countries containing three-quarters of the world's poor.

•Twice as much ODA per capita goes to high military spenders as to more moderate military spenders.

•About 95 percent of the $15 billion in technical assistance every year is spent on foreign experts and equipment from industrial countries rather than on national capacity building in developing countries.

•Only 6.5 percent of bilateral (country-to-country) assistance is earmarked for human-priority concerns of primary health care, basic education, safe drinking water, nutrition programs and provision of family planning services.

Of even more direct significance in the context of the need to moderate population pressure is the fact that only 1 percent of all development assistance flows is devoted to population programs.

The weakening of development cooperation beyond aid is, in my view, even more inexcusable. The European Community's economic relations with Africa, the Caribbean and the Pacific are covered by the Lome Convention. It is a Convention for preferential market access, yet the substantial experience is that of continued trade barriers, especially in products covered by Europe's Common Agricultural Policy such as sugar, beef and vegetables—all still subject to quotas and market restrictions. Protectionism over a wider area is a fact of economic life for developing countries. Despite all the talk about free trade and the insistence that developing countries open up their markets, the United States and the European Community in particular have adopted a kind of apartheid doublespeak in a range of right-sounding trade wrongs: "orderly marketing arrangements," "voluntary export restrictions." There is now a second generation of these perverse labels: "managed trade," "results-oriented negotiations," "European preference," "social dumping," "strategic industries." So how does the third world export, how does it sell, how does it develop in ways which encourage the demographic transition?

Egypt's Boutros Boutros-Ghali, former Secretary General of the United Nations, has given a stark description of Africa's debt crisis: "External debt," he said, "is a millstone around the neck of Africa... Easing the Continent's debt burden must be a priority for the international community." Latin America is often thought of as the center of the debt crisis. It is, if you are a Western bank and a creditor. Africa, in fact, is considerably more "debt distressed" than Latin America, where external debt is 37 percent of GNP, while for Africa it is more than 100 percent.

For many developing countries, economic protectionism is a way of life.

As the excellent Oxfam report "Africa Make or Break" recently depicted it: "Every Zambian man, woman or child has the dubious privilege of owing the country's creditors around $766—more than twice the average annual income level. Mozambique is embarking on a process of postwar reconstruction shackled by a foreign debt equal to four times its national income. How does Africa make the transition to small families that economic transformation encourages?

This matter of financial resources for development has acquired a particular focus in relation to implementation of Agenda 21, the set of recommendations that came out of the 1992 Rio Earth Summit. At the Earth Summit, there was no definitive conclusion, no firm commitment of "new and additional resources." The question of resources from rich countries for implementation of Agenda 21—the 20 percent of the resources required to catalyze the much greater contribution from the poor themselves—was deferred: at best, for consideration by the rich among themselves; at worst, ad infinitum. Agenda 21 was agreed to, but in effect made subject to the provision of resources.

The logo of the Rio Earth Summit depicted the Earth "In Our Hands." It represented that sustainable development required a shared effort by all the world's people, a partnership for survival in which each country has a role that is related to, sometimes integrated into, the roles of others. The partnership, of course, is not between equals. Developed and developing countries are unequal in responsibility for getting it wrong and in capacity for setting it right. Aristotle, in his "Ethics," instructed us a long time ago that equity between unequals requires not "reciprocity" but "proportionality." His dictum holds in this ultimate domain of environmental restoration. Proportionality must be the ethical touchstone of the role of developed and developing countries in their partnership for survival through sustainable development.

Cannot the European Community do better itself and give an enlightened lead to the world—first of all in the area of financial resources, particularly European cash, where European concern clearly is? And cannot the European Community—the world's premier regional community—help in practical ways to fill out the vision of world community, showing how loyalty to our human neighborhood is not a substitute for, but a necessary complement to, our loyalties to country and region? It is particularly necessary that Europe (which on the whole knows better) should not allow the Community's enlightened position on some of these matters to be canceled out by the negative policies of allies, however strong—as they were prior to the Earth Summit at Rio. Europe has, I would suggest, a wider solidarity than that with military, economic or cultural allies alone. An awareness of human solidarity will lead it to look more critically not only at what it might do to help others to sustainable development through easing the pressure of populations on the planet, but also to what its people can do themselves to that same end. One is as necessary as the other.

Why are we concerned about a population explosion? Why do we think of it not as a flowering of the species but in the negative sense of an overgrown garden? If we are, as we believe, the best thing that has happened to the planet, why shouldn't more of us be welcome? There is good reason why we worry, although we seldom fully present the case. The real reason, the ultimate reason, for our concern is sustainability—the sustainability of life on the planet. In scientific terms, it is described as Earth's "carrying capacity"; less formally, it is our impact on the biosphere measured by what we use and what we waste. When we ask whether planet Earth can sustain double its present human population, the answer has to do with consumption. If we continue to draw from nature at the rate we do today—if, overall, we consume at today's level—such a doubling may not be sustainable: The population explosion could threaten survival. Remember the words of the British and American scientists: If current predictions of population growth prove accurate and patterns of human activity on the planet remain unchanged, science and technology may not be able to prevent either irreversible degradation of the environment or continued poverty for much of the world. "If... patterns of human activity in the planet remain unchanged": They were talking about consumption.

In 1986—while the Brundtland Commission was still working—an American scientist, Peter Vitousek (and others) published in "BioScience" a study entitled "Human Appropriation of Products of Photosynthesis." Photosynthesis is nature's solar-powered food-making process. Its product is the material that sustains all life. Only 70 years ago human requirements took about 10 percent of the life-sustaining product of photosynthesis on land—10 percent of annual growth. Hence the prevailing belief, then and long afterwards, that nature was limitless and inexhaustible. Vitousek and his colleagues calculated that by the mid-1980s the five billion people on Earth had raised that appropriation to 40 percent. As our numbers double to more than 10 billion, they concluded, it may be impossible for human appropriation to double to 80 percent. In other words, it may not be possible—let alone desirable—for us to continue on our present consumption path.

To succeed in doing so, we would have to preempt other animal life in a desperate human scramble to enlarge land cultivation and garner all its product for ourselves. Science and technology may increase the solar-powered productivity of nature's plants, but we are also cutting back production as desertification, urban growth, soil erosion and pollution all steadily decrease the extent of Earth's green cover.

In any event, after taking 80 percent of Earth's life-sustaining material around 2050, humankind would not be far from the absolute limit of 100 percent. Like a plague of locusts we would have eaten ourselves out of house and home. Like locusts we would move on, but the only thing left for us would be aquatic plant life. Our processing technologies would turn them to human use, but most likely they would provide nothing but fractional relief. Of course, well before our continental food stores ran out, men, women and children would have been embroiled in a primitive internecine struggle for survival—a struggle over consumption.

The problem, however, is not only the level of human consumption but also its skewed pattern. At present, about one quarter of the world's population (mostly in industrial countries) accounts for about three-quarters of the world's net annual consumption of resources of all kinds. The industrial world consumes 75 percent of the world's commercial energy, 90 percent of its traded hardwood, 81 percent of its paper, 80 percent of its iron and steel, 70 percent of its milk and meat, 60 percent of its fertilizers. The other three-quarters of the world's people must get by altogether on the remaining one-quarter of the resource pie.

Estimates vary as to the overall consumption of the rich and poor in the world. In the UN Development Programme's 1993 Paul Hoffman Lecture, the President of the Population Council, Margaret Catley-Carlson, used the estimate that "every child born in the North consumes over a lifetime from 20 to 30 times the resources and accounts for 20 to 30 times the waste—year in and year out—of their counterparts in developing countries." The British ecologist Norman Myers has made a similar point: "The average British family," he wrote, "comprises two children, but when we factor in resource consumption and pollution impacts, and then compare the British lifestyle with the global average, the 'real-world' size of a British family is more like 15 to 25 children." On this basis, the 1.2 billion people of the North could be taken as the equivalent, in relation to consumption, of 24 billion people in the developing world—using conservative estimates. They already impose on the planet the burden of a century of the unborn of the South.

As we have seen, the world's population now increases at around 1 billion persons per decade, and will continue to do so over several decades. Of those increases, only 5 percent will be in the developed world. But from a consumption standpoint, the 5 percent that will be added in the North will impose on the planet a greater burden than the 95 percent born in the South.

So where is the timebomb ticking? The truth is that there are many explosions in the making. The 95 percent of world population growth that will take place in the South is one of them—in sheer numbers alone, and with dire implications for people in the South. But the 5 percent of world population growth attributable to the North is as large or larger an explosion—not in relation to numbers but to what the numbers imply for the planet. Perhaps the whole analogy of timebombs ticking away is misleading: for the bombs have been detonated already; the explosions have occurred. What is needed is containment of them: rolling back consumption levels in the North, reducing population growth in the South.

There is a further point about consumption. It is palpable—or should be—that we cannot realistically project population growth in the South into the 21st Century at the same levels of consumption that prevail there today. The South will not remain abysmally poor. Already East Asia is showing the way to other developing countries, and not just in marginal development. By the first decade of the 21st Century, the world's economic center of gravity may have shifted away from North America and Europe to East Asia, perhaps to an East Asian Economic Community in which Japan will occupy a prominent place. Latin America will be next and then South Asia and, last of all, Africa—Africa assuredly not for many a decade to come. Moreover, it is going to be in the world's interest—very specifically in the interest of reducing population growth rates—that development should be a reality throughout the South.

But what development? Development which, through "CNN" and "Sky" and "Star" and all the other communication wonders that lie in store for us, mimics the consumption culture of the West, requiring the governments of the South to deliver a development that more and more approximates the lifestyles of the West? If so, we can think of the burden on the planet, in what the economists call "real terms," not as a doubling but as something nearer a tenfold increase in the world's population—in short, of an Armageddon long past the horrors of the Vitousek projection.

Our intelligence should tell us that we have to lower the levels of consumption in the North, that we have to lower the levels of population growth in the South, and that they are not an either/or proposition. It is not enough to be concerned about population and development; almost nothing we do about population and development is really going to suffice unless we do something earnestly and quickly about consumption as well.

In the final analysis, the answer to the population problem lies in development: more real and sustainable development in the South and a better quality of development, a better quality of life, at lower levels of consumption, in the North.

PATAGONIA: DEVELOPMENT WOES IN A PRISTINE ECOSYSTEM

ERIN TROWBRIDGE
August 1998

PUERTO MADRYN, Argentina—Along the coast of Southern Argentina, the dry, dusty pampas give way to one of the richest natural habitats in the world. The seemingly endless horizon of the plains finally breaks into a splendid coastline with whales lolling about just yards from the beach, sea lions playing on the rocks in the bay and penguins waddling around on the sand.

The coastline, 1,800 miles long, is the breeding ground and habitat for a diverse array of marine creatures from elephant seals to endangered species of whales. However, the coast of Patagonia is also rich in oil deposits and has, according to the United Nations Development Programme (UNDP), the world's fastest growing commercial fishing industry.

Environmentalists say that unless strict laws and restrictions are put in place and methodically observed, the Patagonian haven could be destroyed. On the other hand, if all goes well, the nongovernmental organizations working along the coast say that within 30 years the Franca Aural Whale can be taken off the list of endangered species. After centuries of depletion, the whale population is now increasing at an annual rate of 8 percent, which many credit to the work of a small group of environmental specialists focused on preserving the natural habitats and wildlife of this region.

In 1989, a team of scientists, researchers and resource managers from all over Patagonia formed the Fundacion Patagonia Natural, a nonprofit organization for the protection of the wildlife and habitat of the coastal region. Now armed with $2.8 million in funding from UNDP and the Global Environment Facility (GEF), the foundation for the Patagonian coast has developed a management program for the entire bio-region. Fisheries, oil tankers and careless tourists are all being told to either clean up or get out.

"In general, people are very concerned about Patagonia and very supportive of our efforts," said Guillermo Harris, Director of the Fundacion

Patagonia Natural. "This area is famous the world over for its wildlife, and saving it doesn't require coercion for government officials and people living in the area. In that respect we're very lucky. In the private sector, working with the fishermen, it took no time for them to agree to our programs and ideas. Protecting the habitat of Patagonia is in their long-term best interests. By implication, we're protecting their livelihoods."

In 1992, the foundation began the first phase of its work, consisting mainly of collecting data, conducting research, educating the people living off the profits reaped from the coastal zone and, finally, getting legislation passed that laid down the law of what fisheries and oil tankers could and could not do. Researchers combed the coast, documenting the types of mammals, seabirds and animals living there and, for the first time, created a comprehensive study of the natural balance between these species and their habitats.

The foundation has received, in general, great cooperation from the government and most industries, said Dr. Enrique Alberto Crespo, a biologist and vice director of the foundation. "We're lucky because there aren't too many people living here and it still has the feeling of a small town," he said in his office at the science laboratories outside of Puerto Madryn. "It's hard for the government to ignore us when I pass the ministers and governors on the street in town. They're not so hard to get to and they tend to have more open minds when they see people as people, not numbers."

The difficulties, though, said representatives of the foundation, arise from the fact that the economy of Patagonia is almost wholly dependent upon the three industries that most threaten the environment: tourism, fisheries and oil. According to Harris, fisheries alone bring $500 million a year to what is otherwise a quiet, middle-class economy. The oil industry in southern Argentina accounts for more than one billion dollars in annual revenues. The other side of the coin, said Harris, is that over-fishing and water pollution are destroying the fragile balance between flora and fauna. The oil tankers, traveling the long coastal stretch from Tierra del Fuego to the Buenos Aires port, often spill small amounts of oil as they dump excess water stored in old oil drums.

"While its rare to see an actual tanker spill, what we do see is no less disconcerting," said Harris. "The penguin population has dropped by as much as 20 percent due to oil spills. We've seen thousands of 'oil penguins' and, even if you wash the oil off of them, it has already destroyed their ability to protect themselves from the cold and the water. They slowly suffocate or starve."

Tourism, seemingly the most benign of the three industries, poses no less a threat. According to Harris, tourism in Puerto Madryn, situated just miles from the Valdes Peninsula where the whales come each year to find mates, grew from 4,000 people a year in 1990 to 150,000 in 1997.

"We don't have to promote tourism," said Harris. "The reputation of the beauty of this natural area is already spreading like wildfire. Our task is to ensure that tourism is done properly and conducted responsibly. If we can increase the revenue brought in by tourism, if we increase entrance fees to the national parks, for instance, we can cut down on the number of people allowed in without hurting the people who depend on the tourist dollar."

Puerto Madryn's summer tourist season runs from November to March, when thousands of travelers come from Buenos Aires and other northern cities to vacation at the beach. From May to September, even more come to "whale watch" on large charter boats that leave the port town every half hour, full of life-jacketed tourists. Representatives of the foundation said they have not yet been able to determine just how much the presence of the boats disturbs the whales' mating practices. A boat captain at the harbor, though, said he can tell when the whales get angry and that in September, when tourism is especially heavy, the whales sometimes bump the boats and nudge them away.

"Speaking as a biologist," said Crespo, "there is absolutely no good that comes of tourism other than the money it brings in to local families. What we have done is encourage tour directors, hotel managers and others who can profit off the industry to promote better practices," such as water conservation and recycling. "The task at hand is through education to control the problem before it even becomes one."

CLINTON'S ENVIRONMENTAL POLICY

TOM WICKER
August 1996

When Bill Clinton telephoned on January 30 to congratulate Oregon's newly elected Senator—Ron Wyden, the first Democrat the state has sent to the Senate in 34 years—the President proclaimed himself "the second happiest man in the land." No wonder. Analysts agree that Wyden—a 46-year-old liberal who had trailed in the polls, was expected to lose and who was undoubtedly "the most happy fella" that night—won primarily because of his stand in favor of environmental protection. President Clinton, himself facing an election this year, lately has been plugging hard on the same issue and appears to be depending heavily on it to bring him a second term.

It was not always so. Clinton's environmental actions often have earned him severe criticism, not least in states like Oregon, where clean water, pure air, healthy forests and other natural resources have been highly valued. In 1995, for instance, the President ultimately signed a measure he originally had vetoed because it threatened renewed logging in the Northwest's old-growth forests. Some changes had been made in the measure after the veto, and when Clinton signed it he said the new provisions provided adequate protection against logging.

He was wrong. Lawyers for the timber industry persuaded a federal judge to agree that the new legislation still permitted logging in previously protected areas. By late 1995, environmentally damaging clear-cutting had been resumed in old-growth areas, also threatening rivers, streams and fish as well as a federal program to restore overcut national forests—and angering Oregon's numerous environmentally conscious citizens.

Ultimately, deploring legislation he himself had signed, Clinton conceded that he failed to perceive that even the amended bill retained the potential to cause "grave environmental damage." He failed, too—though he did not say so—to grasp that the fatal logging provisions actually had been sponsored by timber interests eager to get at those old-growth forests.

Clinton's inconsistency—or perhaps his "stupidity or cave-in," as charged by Tim Hermach of Oregon's Native Forest Council—is a major reason why many environmentalists take with a grain of salt the President's recent posture as a stand-up fighter for their interests. Almost none believes that Bill Clinton has undergone a conversion from near indifference, in the first half of his term, to real enthusiasm in the second. Most think, instead, that as the approach of November has forced the President to focus on this year's election, he has belatedly understood that protecting the environment is good politics, favored by a public grown wary of the intentions of the Republicans who control Congress. A White House "political strategist" said as much to Doyle McManus of the Los Angeles Times: "The environment is one of the issues we can use to appeal to swing voters and suburbanites."

"They've finally figured that out," drily observed Gene Karpinski, the Washington representative of the US Public Interest Research Group. It's not just "swing voters and suburbanites" who look with hostility on threats to the environment. A recent survey by Lake Research of Washington—which often polls for Democrats—found that 71 percent of respondents believed the environment should be the "top" of a "very important" priority for the President to be elected in November. Sixty-five percent said they would either "definitely" or "probably" vote against a presidential candidate who wanted to relax clean water protection; 53 percent were equally hostile to one who threatened clean air regulations.

This measure of opinion seems to have been borne out in the Oregon Senate race. An after-election poll for the Sierra Club and the League of Conservation Voters found that the candidates' stands on the environment were an "important factor" to three out of four voters. Sixty-six percent of those voters supported Ron Wyden. And, though environmental support groups poured more than $200,000 into advertisements backing him, Wyden actually had been outspent by $2 million by his conservative Republican opponent, Gordon Smith, much of it from Smith's own funds. [Gordon Smith later won the seat of retiring Senator Mark Hatfield.]

Ironically, the Oregon election only tends to confirm the view of many environmentalists that Bill Clinton's has been a political, not a heartfelt, conversion. Few can forget the disappointments of his first two years in office, when an administration of which they perhaps expected too much either avoided or blundered away numerous chances for significant environmental advances—notably reform of the antiquated Mining Act of 1872, which blatantly favors mining interests, and raising the low fees for stock grazing on public lands. Now, with a conservative Republican Congress mostly setting the legislative agenda, Clinton's new environmental position has to be essentially defensive—protecting regulations and requirements long in place—with no real hope for new initiatives.

Still, after two years of disappointment, even skeptics among environmental activists have been encouraged by these developments—even if they were motivated by re-election politics.

What Karpinski calls "the three E's"—education, environment and the elderly (Medicare and Medicaid)—have become part of Clinton's "short mantra" of defiance against proposed Republican budget cutbacks. In January, the President declared that a balanced budget should not "prevent America from giving Medicare to senior citizens ... or educational opportunity to young people or environmental protection to us all," and in his State of the Union message he cited a clean environment as one of the seven great challenges facing the nation.

•In September, Clinton specifically pledged to veto any bill that would permit drilling for oil in the Arctic National Wildlife Refuge, as the Republicans had proposed—a promise since reiterated by the President, Vice President Al Gore and other administration officials.

'The most anti-environment Congress in the history of this country.'

•In November, owing largely to new administration pressures, the House of Representatives voted 227 to 194 to instruct its conferees on an EPA appropriations bill to drop 17 riders that would have drastically curbed the agency's powers to enforce its regulations.

•In December, Clinton vetoed an appropriations bill for the Interior Department that would have favored developers in the use of public lands and curtailed protection of endangered species, and another for the EPA, on which Congress still sought to impose severe budget cuts.

•Interior Secretary Bruce Babbitt has accused the Republican Congress of "the worst onslaught on public lands and the environment in this century," only to be topped by Gore, who called it "the most anti-environment Congress in the history of this country." Though they are the most prominent "greens" in the administration, neither is likely to have spoken in such partisan terms without White House approval.

•Loud Democratic criticism, led by Babbitt, persuaded enough voters that a Republican proposal for a commission to study the national park system was part of a plan to sell national parks to private interests. The pressure from an alarmed public became so severe that the Republicans dropped the idea.

• The number of House Republicans opposing their own party's proposal to restrict environmental regulation mounted steadily last year—pushed by public opinion but also, Washington observers think, by the administration's more combative rhetoric, in particular the President's veto threats.

Republicans in the House of Representatives, acting against their leadership's wishes, cast 48 votes against the Interior Department appropriations bill that Clinton later vetoed, and 63 Republicans were among the 227 House members who instructed their conferees to drop the 17 riders that would have restricted EPA enforcement powers. The latter vote was a gain of 13 Republicans from an earlier test on much the same issue.

This rising Republican opposition to their leaders' drastic environmental proposals probably reflects—as does Clinton's more combative opposition—new public fears. Representative Sherwood L. Boehlert, Republican of New York, the leader of his party's environmental moderates, explains that they're "catching hell back home" because of voters' perception that the Republican Congress is trying to weaken or repeal important environmental protections.

Numerous polls, as well as the Oregon election, tend to sustain Boehlert. The Harris organization, for instance, reported in December that 86 percent of its poll respondents "think the Environmental Protection Agency is needed as much as or more than it was when it was founded in 1970"—a reminder, incidentally, that the EPA is not a product of Democratic "big spenders" but was established by Richard Nixon in the wake of the first Earth Day. In the Harris poll, 76 percent of Republican respondents agreed that the agency was still needed.

Indeed, since the days of Theodore Roosevelt, conservation—if not contemporary environmentalism—has usually been a Republican standard. Today, in the opinion of Tim Mahoney of the League of Conservation Voters, "The vast majority of Americans consider themselves environmentalists." In ordinary circumstances that's not necessarily "the driving motive behind their votes," but Mahoney thinks that "now the public has received the message that the environment is under assault" in Congress, and is reacting against the attempt.

The fabled "Contract with America" that formed the Republican platform for the party's 1994 Congressional triumph did not even mention the environment. So the public, including Republicans, was not alerted to planned environmental "reforms" until they began to arrive on the House floor. As a result, that same Harris poll found that only 7 percent of respondents have much confidence that the "GOP-controlled Congress" will protect the environment; 36 percent had "hardly any" such confidence.

President Clinton did not score much better—16 percent reported "a great deal" of confidence in him as an environmental protector but 19 percent had "hardly any." The President's personal poll standing, nevertheless, has increased substantially. A New York Times/CBS poll found in the last month of 1995 that, for the first time in two years, more than 50 percent of respondents approved of Clinton's White House performance—as against only 26 percent who approved of the way the Republican Congress had done its job, and 29 percent who supported Speaker Newt Gingrich's performance (down from 34 percent in October).

Opinion on environmental issues was not specifically sampled, but the Times/CBS poll found that 49 percent of respondents believed Republican efforts to cut or slow the growth of "social programs" were too drastic, even in the drive to reach a balanced budget. That finding probably has encouraged President Clinton in his rising opposition to Republican cutbacks, including those affecting the environment.

Republican leaders seem to fear that environmental protection can be a profitable issue for the Democrats and the President in November. Speaker Gingrich, the Republican intellectual and political leader, has acknowledged that he and his party "mishandled" the matter by trying to cut too deeply into environmental regulations. Linda DiVall, who polls for Republican candidates, has warned that on environmental issues "our party is out of sync with mainstream American opinion." Representative Tom DeLay of Texas, the House Republican Whip, has been even more candid: "I'll be real straight with you," DeLay confessed to The Wall Street Journal in December. "We have lost the debate on the environment."

It's not just the Oregon election that suggests DeLay may have been correct. Bill Roberts of the Environmental Defense Fund notes that B.A.S.S. Inc., an organization of professional bass fishermen in the South—hardly a liberal group—is expressing dismay over the Republicans' clean water proposals. Similarly, hunters in the West, fearing loss of access to public lands, have organized effective opposition to a Republican-sponsored bill that gives states the opportunity to take over 270 million acres of federal land.

Wary environmentalists, however, are not yet ready to accept Tom DeLay's judgment, owing partially to their doubts that the President's newly stiffened spine will remain sufficiently rigid under the pressures of a hard-fought reelection campaign, a conservative Congress, business interests that often have pushed him around in the past, and the hard choices inevitably posed by most environmental questions.

Chuck Clusem of the Natural Resources Council is among the cautious. "As threats to the environment have increased and become more dangerous," he concedes, Clinton's "involvement has increased and he's been more positive." But, he asks, "Can we count on him?" The same legislation, after all, that permitted renewed old-growth logging—which the President now says he made a "mistake" in signing—also reduced wildlife protection, restricted listing of new hazardous waste sites and offered states relief from some provisions of the Clean Water Act.

Though the President has vowed to prevent any threat to safe drinking water or adequate waste water treatment, when the crunch comes will he compromise or cave in—or make another "mistake"? Vetoing an inadequate EPA appropriation, for instance, will not in itself produce enough money for the agency's needs. And the Endangered Species Act is still a prime Republican target. Moreover, Democrats have developed considerable respect for Gingrich's leadership and the ferocious determination of freshman Republicans to reduce the role of government—certainly including the protection of the environment.

Clinton may nevertheless have turned a political corner on environmental protection in late 1995, and if that issue is crucial, as the Oregon election suggests, he will have put himself in a greatly improved position for 1996. Moreover, the criticisms heard in 1993 and 1994 may never have been entirely fair. Mahoney believes, for instance, that most really were "criticism of the ideal"—which should seldom be expected from a political figure.

Clinton was elected by only 43 percent of the vote in 1992; his supporters in the 103rd Congress, with relatively small majorities, were reluctant to take many risks—delaying action on such issues as clean water and endangered species, in hopes of being able to do better in the next Congress. Needless to say, the 104th Congress dashed that expectation, which was probably unrealistic to begin with.

Besides, a "political conversion" may be more effective than an ideological conviction in a President facing an election. Richard Nixon was by no means an environmentalist when he responded to public pressures by establishing EPA and signing the first modern environmental legislation. If Bill Clinton is now feeling the hot breath of voters, that may move him more profoundly than any number of pleas from the environmentally convinced.

COVERING THE HUMAN ENVIRONMENT

SEYMOUR TOPPING
January 1993

The oil gushes into the sea off the Shetland Islands from the grounded tanker Braer. Once again we see television images of anguished coastal folk and oil-drenched corpses of sea creatures. And, once again, a disaster befouling Mother Earth captures the attention of the world press.

Yet experience tells us that this media wakening of the public to the immediate danger of lasting damage to the environment will soon subside. We know that not long after worldwide alarms have been sounded about such threats as pollution of the seas, global warming, thinning of the ozone and loss of bio-diversity, there ensues a return to a "snore"—as The Economist once characterized typical news coverage of the global environment.

This is the problem that is the despair of journalists who write about the environment and, of course, all those who would mobilize public opinion behind efforts to nurture the Earth. There is unending debate among environmentalists as to whether the blame lies principally with a fickle public or editors who shy from the technical and prefer to concentrate coverage on "human interest" or sexier topics, if you will, that will attract larger audiences. Editors acknowledge that they might do a better job of stimulating public interest, but they also remind us that media owners concerned about the bottom line do not want the customers bored excessively.

In the months before the United Nations Conference on the Environment and Development in Rio, when more than 150 heads of government were to assemble to sign a new Earth Charter, there was little coverage of the preparatory meetings which drafted the treaty texts. These texts were to form the basis for Agenda 21, the program that was to activate measures to safeguard the planet between 1993 and the year 2000 and beyond. But the process was flawed by a lack of press and public attention that might have generated more commitment. Governments failed to come forward with sufficient funding. The lack of attention in Washington was an eventual factor in the refusal of the Bush administration to sign the biodiversity treaty. The Earth Summit itself in June evoked a frenzy of news coverage, with 8,000 journalists participating in what was part negotiation and part spectacle. After the heads of government shoulder-to-shoulder provided a final photo opportunity (George Bush and Fidel Castro, no less, posing for the same take), the lens and front pages switched focus to other subjects.

By contrast to the Rio press extravaganza, in the last weeks of 1992 very little media coverage was given, at least in the United States, to the critical negotiations at the United Nations which led to the creation of a 53-member Sustainable Development Commission to implement the agreements reached at Rio. Also largely unreported was the creation of the Earth Council, an international nongovernmental body sited in Costa Rica, to monitor compliance with the agreements. The Council is being chaired by Maurice Strong, who served as Secretary General of the Earth Summit. These will be the organizations assigned the tasks of bringing Agenda 21 to reality so that the Earth Summit will not slip into history as principally another photo opportunity.

The news media in Europe, Japan and the developing countries have been more preoccupied than the press in the United States with environmental issues, largely because their concerns are more immediate. Europeans have been contending with the environmental devastation in Eastern Europe uncovered after the fall of Communism. Japan has been highly sensitive to its own environmental vulnerabilities and eager to exploit a growing market in pollution control technology. The developing countries, which blame the industrial North for most of the ecological damage besetting the planet, are seeking financial assistance and access to technology needed to relieve poverty and to put their economies on an environmentally sound footing.

The advent of the Clinton administration, with a Vice President who has been America's leading advocate of global reform, has renewed interest in the environmental agenda, given the prospect of stronger leadership in Washington. As a measure of that interest, Al Gore's book, "Earth in the Balance," was a bestseller for months.

The Vice President, once an investigative reporter himself for the Nashville Tennessean, has been an occasional critic of press coverage of the environment. While still a Senator, writing in reply to questions posed by the Freedom Forum Media Studies Center, Gore said: "When the smoke clears after a harsh [environmental] battle, when the earth settles, the story recedes from public view and, therefore, from public consciousness, though the issues behind the struggle remain critical." A central problem cited by the Senator was what he described as striking a "dangerous imbalance."

"When more than 700 members of the National Academy of Sciences wrote President Bush urging action on global climate change," Gore recalled, "six or seven members took the other side of the argument, but they were given equal billing with the 700. Our most eminent scientists are telling us we face a problem of unforeseen proportions. Yet the media, compelled to search high and low for 'the other side,' find those who say there is no problem and amplify those voices so that soon the protests of a few are as powerful as the concerns of the many."

Gore's remarks were relevant to the ongoing debate among journalists as to what approach should be taken to environment reporting, with some insisting on advocacy forms, given the urgency of the problems. Others are adamant such advocacy in reporting would compromise the integrity and independence of the press. However, Gore insisted in his comments that he was arguing not for "one-sided reporting, but rather for reporting that recognizes the subtleties involved in this issue and that accurately weighs opinions and research. As importantly, it is an argument for reporting that educates the public."

Few will dispute that media coverage of environmental matters has improved dramatically in the two decades since the Stockholm Conference and that the Earth Summit further heightened awareness of the issues in every country.

Whitman Bassow, contributing editor for Environmental Protection magazine, says: "I think the coverage of environmental issues has improved enormously in the 20 years that I have been observing environmental matters. The issue has been attracting talented and hardworking journalists. The stories are getting increased exposure in print and broadcast media. However, there are still roadblocks in comprehensive coverage. These roadblocks are: insensitivity of editors to the issues, and the complexity of environmental issues themselves that require more scientific and economic knowledge than most reporters possess."

There is in progress among journalists considerable self-examination as to the adequacy of environmental coverage. Speaking to a recent national conference of the Society of Environmental Journalists, Robert Giles, editor and publisher of the Detroit News, made these points: Too many journalists do not have enough knowledge about the subject they cover, too many editors don't know enough about the content of the stories they assign, edit or decide where to put in the paper. The greatest worry is found in a report that the number of newspapers with environmental "beats" has decreased by 60 percent in recent years. Reporters without a fundamental grounding in the sciences and economics simply are no match for their sources, who know more and have more media savvy.

Jack Cox, president of the Foundation for American Communications (FACS), put it more strongly. "Sending a general assignment reporter out on intricate stories without background in the topic is wrong and even unethical."

There is a growing perception in the media industries that specialized education is essential for responsible reporting of an increasingly complex world. Larger newspapers have been adding specialists to their staffs. Gene Patterson, editor and president emeritus of the St. Petersburg Times and Poytner Institute, has called for a closer marriage between the media and the university. FACS, the American Press Institute (API), Poytner and other professional organizations offer seminars on environmental reporting. The Scientists' Institute for Public Information has more than 25,000 scientists on file who are willing to answer questions from the media.

While press coverage of global environmental issues tends to be inconsistent, reporting on local issues ranging from irresponsible use of pesticides, pollution of waterways, depletion of forests and wetlands to protection of sea turtles in the Gulf of Mexico, is very much in evidence. Pulitzer Prizes and other journalistic recognition are awarded frequently for such environmental reporting. Reporters and owners, particularly of smaller media, often risk the hostility of subscribers, advertisers and officials in investigating and reporting on local environmental abuses. Correction of abuses sometimes results in the shutdown of businesses with the loss of jobs, or the adverse publicity may be enough to discourage tourism and investors.

There are a few newspapers, however, like the New York Times, which has been the leader in environmental reporting and commentary, that have urged their readers to think seriously about the need to accept the high costs of a gasoline or carbon tax to cut down on carbon dioxide emissions from fossil fuel use. The United States accounts for 23 percent of such emissions, which are suspected of causing about half of the global warming effect.

Peter Passell, of The Times, may have summed up the central obligation of the press in environmental coverage when he quoted scientists as saying: "To make sensible choices between greater safety and the alternatives, Americans need more and better information, presented in ways that stimulate a sense of perspective."

Dedicated grassroots work by social-minded activists in health, population, education, sanitation and every other aspect of human and social life existed, of course, long before the term "non-governmental organizations" was coined and conveniently shortened to "NGOs." The term, awkward as it is, nevertheless gave these grassroots workers an organizational identity and a platform from which they could voice their views and be heard by the officials and bureaucrats who make policy.

The NGOs have made an enormous jump: From mere well-meaning "do-gooders" on the edge of national and UN deliberations, they have jumped to become invited—even sought-after—participants. At the 1992 Earth Summit in Rio, for example, the NGOs made their mark with a parallel but separate meeting called the NGO Forum. With each successive UN conference—on human rights, population, urbanization and the others—the presence of the NGOs has become stronger. At the 1996 Habitat II conference in Istanbul, for example, not only were civil organizations invited onto the official agenda, but also individuals from the local level—from mayors and businessmen to architects and labor union activists.

As the flow of international aid money steadily decreases—grants from the donor countries in 1999 are expected to be barely $45 billion, a decline of 10 percent from 1998—the policy makers are turning to the grassroots to take up the slack. Here, after all, is where the specific daily and often grinding work is being done. Here also is where the almost disenfranchised poor can be organized, taught and helped to develop voices loud enough to be heard.

SECTION 2

GROWTH AND CHANGE AT THE GRASSROOTS

CIVIL SOCIETY IN ACTION

JYOTI SHANKAR SINGH
November 1996

I was recently asked to speak at an international conference of legislators on the role of "civil society." What does the term "civil society" imply? It obviously encompasses nongovernmental organizations (NGOs), which in turn include advocacy groups concerned with such issues as population, the environment, women's empowerment, trade, aid and development, and protection of ethnic and religious diversity.

But the list cannot be confined to NGOs alone. Ahmed Kamal, the current Ambassador of Pakistan to the United Nations in New York, identifies a host of other actors in civil society—trade unions, cooperatives, local community groups, the media, religious organizations, youth organizations, and research and academic institutions. He goes on to say, "We might have to include lawmakers and legislative bodies as components of a broader civil society." I would not go so far as to include legislative bodies or parliaments in such a list. But it should include, in my view, parliamentarian groups which have been formed in recent years to undertake advocacy activities on such topics as food, population and the environment.

> *Nongovernmental organizations are only part of the picture.*

Another attempt at defining civil society identifies it as the third component of a trio, the other two being the state and the private sector. This would imply that various actors in civil society seek to influence through their actions the other two actors on policy and program issues that affect the society as a whole. While the interaction with various branches of the state (executive, legislature and judiciary) focuses on a whole range of political, economic and social issues as well as issues of democratic governance, transparency and accountability, that with the private sector focuses on the economic and social implications and consequences of the market economy, the role of business companies and the role of transnationals.

Twenty-five years ago, when I joined the United Nations Population Fund (UNFPA) as the NGO Liaison Officer in the Secretariat for the 1974 World Population Year, the term "civil society" was not in vogue. But Rafael M. Salas of the Philippines, the executive director of UNFPA, who had been given overall responsibility for World Population Year, was cognizant of the need for UNFPA to work with all the major groups and entities that seek to form and influence public policy. In the early 1970s population was relatively a new topic, and Salas felt that, in order to promote better knowledge and understanding of population and related development issues, we had to work not only with governments and the UN agencies but also with nongovernmental organizations and the media. He told me to pay special attention to youth, religious and women's groups and asked the secretariat as a whole to promote close contacts with the media, academics and parliamentarians in all the regions of the world. Our task thus was to identify and work with a wide variety of actors in the sector now being called "the civil society."

The role of civil society may differ from country to country. But civil society groups have developed many common concerns that cut across national borders. The preparatory processes for the major UN conferences that began with the Rio Earth Summit and the Rome Food Summit, accelerated the development of international coalitions of NGOs to focus on such issues of common concern as the environment (Rio), human rights (Vienna), population (Cairo), social development (Copenhagen), women (Beijing) and food (Rome). The experience gained over the past six years by these coalitions, along with NGOs and other civil society groups, tells us a lot about the evolving role of such groups vis-a-vis national governments and the international community.

First, these groups have been increasingly successful in connecting people with specific major issues on the international agenda and mobilizing national support through their affiliates and associates for targeted action on such issues. On reproductive health and women's empowerment issues, there was no clear agreement or consensus when the preparatory process for the International Conference on Population and Development (ICPD) began. By strongly advocating well articulated positions, groups were able to influence the stands taken by national delegations at a various preparatory conference and meetings. As Executive Coordinator of ICPD, I had the opportunity to work closely with NGOs as we sought to enlarge and strengthen their involvement and participation in the ICPD process. I was extremely

Twenty-five years ago, the term 'civil society' was not in vogue.

impressed by the role played by NGOs in influencing the outcome of the Cairo Conference. The consensus recorded in the ICPD Program of Action on reproductive health and the role and status of women owes much to strong advocacy by NGOs.

Second, civil society groups have gained valuable experience in bridging wide differences among themselves and between the groups and national governments. In their effort to get others to accept their points of view they have learned how to negotiate and compromise. Susan Davis, then Executive Director of the Women's Environment and Development Organization (WEDO), says of women's groups, "We found ICPD extremely challenging in bridging wide differences among NGOs to create a strong Women's Caucus during that process. By creating a strong women's caucus, which met daily during preparatory committee meetings, and by networking among their members, women's groups were able to exercise a decisive influence on the Cairo process and to those relating to Copenhagen and Beijing as well."

Third, civil society groups have been able to persuade many governments to accept the concept of partnership in decision-making. Many parliamentarians and NGO representatives were invited to serve as members of national delegations to preparatory committee meetings for Cairo and Beijing and finally to the conferences as such. In the period following these conferences,

Women's groups have been able to exercise a decisive influence.

efforts have been undertaken both by governments and by civil society groups to cooperate and collaborate with each other on the implementation of the Programs of Action adopted at these conferences; and it is partly as a result of the pressure exercised by the civil society groups that the UN agencies and organizations have accepted the need for a "common framework" to follow up on these conferences.

There is also a general willingness on the part of the UN system to keep civil society groups fully involved in the followup. The process is far from perfect. Many governments do not fully trust NGOs, and many NGOs are wary of closer involvement in government-sponsored programs for fear of compromising their independence. But on the whole the process, I believe, is moving in the right direction.

The three key concepts of advocacy, dialogue and partnership are crucial in strengthening the role of civil society groups in decision-making and in promoting popular involvement and participation in all future efforts aimed at seeking solutions to urgent issues of global and national concern. The Geneva meeting of parliamentarians discussed several issues of concern to parliamentary groups—population growth and food production, food security and environment, and community development.

It will be important to ensure that government, civil society groups and the international community, having agreed on what needs to be done, work together in concert to implement their agreements. This process may indeed seek to involve the private sector as well, insofar as private sector companies and organizations are expected to play an increasingly important role in promoting food security and development.

IRAN: PRESERVING UNDERGROUND GARDENS

RESHMA PRAKASH
April 1999

TEHERAN—Hajj Abdullah Bardal has inherited a priceless treasure that has passed down through five generations of his family—not rubies or diamonds but, in the desert land he lives in, something even more precious: a garden.

No rivers run here, and rain-fed irrigation is impossible because it hardly ever rains. Temperature can reach 120 degrees Fahrenheit (50 degrees Centigrade), scorching the earth into a hard and brittle mantle hostile to life.

Once a thousand vineyards bloomed here in the desert. Now there are only eight remaining, and nobody can say how long they might survive.

Yet, here in the hot and arid province of Bushehr in southern Iran, in a village called Sabzabad, lies a little oasis of green.

Bardal is the owner-guardian of an ancient vineyard using water technology that researchers say dates back 4,000 years to the Elamite period in Persia's history. Instead of growing grapes on vines planted in surface soil, this vineyard has plants growing out of underground cultivation chambers or cisterns that trap and preserve the water supplied by the occasional flash floods that tear through the region. Gnarled and knotted with age, these plants grow out of chambers big enough for a man to comfortably stand in, and they spread their vines over a water-starved land, producing a rich harvest year after year.

There used to be a time when a thousand such vineyards dotted the land, with Bardal himself owning seven, but now there are just eight of them left in all of Iran. Like so much flotsam on the tide of modernity, the other vineyards have either been abandoned by people who moved out to the cities or destroyed by the construction of a military base in the area.

"These vineyards are born of the desert and have a very clever way of harvesting the little water that the region gets," said Abbas Abdollah Garrousi, a specialist in rural affairs who says he "discovered" the vineyards 32 years ago when he was working with the Ministry of Agriculture. He was so intrigued by them that he came back years later to document the few remaining vineyards before they too faded from man's memory, their precious wisdom lost for eternity.

> *The vineyards are so ingenious that the plants survive even if it doesn't rain for three years.*

The technology is deceptively simple, said Garrousi, but reveals a deep understanding of the climate and geology of the land. Stone pathways and a stone wall more than 160 feet (50 meters) in diameter were built to surround each vineyard, directing the water from the flash floods into underground chambers that are about 20 feet (six meters) in depth and 10 feet (three meters) wide.

Expert well diggers, using the simplest equipment, constructed these chambers, digging into the earth until they reached a greasy layer of soil they called "shol." Upon reaching this layer, they waterproofed the walls of the chamber using local clay and filled the chamber with topsoil. The chamber was then ready to be cultivated, said Garrousi.

Each January, at the beginning of winter, farmers plant branches cut from older plants in some good soil to sprout. In March, the saplings are transferred to the chambers and are watered and nurtured through the first dry months of summer. "They need to be watered only during that period," said Garrousi. "After that they needed no more watering for the rest of their lives. Even if it doesn't rain for three years, these chambers remain wet all year through and sustain the plants," he added.

When the vines grow out, they are trained onto stone pillars called khaens. When harvest time comes around, the farmers crouch under the vines to pick the bunches of grapes, said Garrousi. A single vineyard produces up to two tons of grapes per year. As many as seven varieties of grapes are grown in the region, he said, and some of these vines are 400 to 500 years old.

According to Garrousi, the single biggest reason for the disappearance of most of these vineyards, and the ancient tradition of growing grapes, was the construction of the military base nearby. "The old and new authorities nationalized the land to build the base, bulldozed the land, ruined the soil and the underground chambers have collapsed," said Garrousi. "They interfered in what they didn't understand and they have upset the natural ecosystem of the place. Without their land, most people migrated to the city or started to work in the military plant. The few farmers who are left fear that even more land will be taken away, but they still cling to hope. They're stubborn, they don't want to give up on the old ways."

Garrousi now works as a researcher for one of Iran's oldest and most prominent nongovernmental organizations called Center for Sustainable Development or CENESTA. He said that CENESTA has asked the government of Iran to protect the remaining gardens by declaring them a cultural heritage site, and that the government is considering the request.

INDIA: CREATING A BETTER LIFE FOR RURAL WOMEN

ASHALI VARMA
May 1997

PITTIWAS, India—In this remote village, 40 miles from the city of Jodhpur in Rajasthan State, women who have no access to clinics or hospitals are buying "safe delivery sets" for when they give birth. The sets, which cost less than four rupees (the equivalent of 15 cents), consist of a clean razor blade, gauze, a strip of cord to tie the newborn's umbilical cord and a bar of soap for the midwife. For another four rupees they can buy a plastic sheet, which is an important item because mothers in this area often give birth on the sand and have a high rate of infection. Free tetanus shots are also given to pregnant women.

Pittawas is off the beaten track for tourists and even government agencies have neglected it. But for the women of Pittawas, change came in the form of one woman whose passion for India translated into action. Jacqueline de Chollet started the Veerni Project in India in 1992. Veerni means "strong women" in Hindi. Today, five years later and at a total cost of $90,000, 17 villages with 7,000 families now have access to reproductive health care, contraception, primary health care, immunizations, prenatal and postnatal care and treatment of infections.

In India, the maternal mortality rate is 500 per 100,000 live births per year, compared with 7.4 deaths per 100,000 births in the US. Village women rarely have their choice of contraceptives, and 85 percent of family planning consists of sterilization.

Jacqueline de Chollet, who lives in London, New York and Jodhpur, describes how she became determined to do something for the women and young girls eking out an existence on the very edge of survival.

"In 1991, I was traveling in Rajasthan and I found myself in a remote village near the Pakistan border. It was far from the main road, off a deeply rutted dirt track," de Chollet said. "In a one-room house with an earthen floor, I met a woman weaving with a baby in her arms. Her other children were outside. The girls were very thin. There was little food and almost no water—she had to walk hours each day to get it. She looked worn out. I told her I would buy the shawl she was weaving. But the moment I gave her the money, a man came in and took it. It stayed in my mind that the woman had managed to make something and sell it, but her gain had been taken away from her. I thought something must be done, something has to change, and it started from there."

She approached a local nongovernmental organization, Parivar Seva Sanstha (PSS), which had been working in the field of reproductive health care for many years, and the Veerni project was born. All of the money de Chollet raises for it goes toward providing health services to families in the villages. "PSS manages the project and has done a wonderful job under extremely difficult circumstances," de Chollet said.

"The women in these areas were very tradition-bound. They were not allowed to leave their villages," she said, and were kept secluded by the purdah system (veils covering the face). "At first we had to approach the men of the community and convince them of the benefits of the services we were going to provide, before they would let their women come to meetings to discuss their health and other problems," she said.

The project has an office in Jodhpur and, to reach the villages, bought a mobile clinic in 1992 at a cost of 200,000 rupees ($6,000), de Chollet said. The van goes to two or three villages every day, traveling as much as 80 miles over roads that vary from dusty and rutted in the winter to almost impassable during the rainy season. It is equipped with medical supplies and benches and can handle simple medical procedures wherever they are needed. Dr. Rashmi Mishra and two field educators, Jaspal and Shehjadi, provide the services, which include checkups not only for women but for children and the men as well.

Free immunization, contraception and screening for tuberculosis are included in the project's primary health care services, de Chollet said. Through videos, lectures and meetings, the field educators teach the women about cleanliness, hygiene, nutrition and the importance of taking care of themselves and spacing their pregnancies.

In addition, immunization camps and general health camps are also held to bring primary health care to the families.

"One of the biggest changes we have noticed in women's reproductive health is the introduction of sanitary napkins. Previously the women and their daughters had to use rags, and there was a high incidence of reproductive-tract infection," de Chollet said. The Veerni project makes and sells sanitary napkins for 10 rupee (30 cents) for a package of 10, well below market prices and even below the cost price. "Not only are women buying them for themselves but they also buy them for their daughters," she said.

The project also provides oral rehydration therapy (ORT) kits, which can be effective in saving the lives of children and babies suffering from diarrhea. "In fact the ORT kits are even used by women who suffer dehydration from working long hours in the field under the hot sun," de Chollet said.

To encourage women to take better care of their children, the Veerni project organizes well-baby celebrations and gives prizes for babies who are clean, healthy and have had their immunization shots. In the words of Jaspal, the Veerni field educator, in the last five years, "There have been so many changes. Women are removing their veils to speak. Their children are clean. If their children are sick, they know where to get the right tablet. Before, they believed that sickness was out of their hands."

"What we are trying to do here is to create a demand for services and make those services available," de Chollet said, "But how can women demand services when they don't know that they exist? We are trying to create awareness. In time the government will provide these services, but we will be here for as long as it is necessary. It's a long-term commitment on our part," said de Chollet.

The project's plans include buying another mobile clinic and adding another 15 villages to the service area this year. So far the money for Veerni has come from the Global Foundation for Humanity, which was set up by de Chollet and her husband, Robert Towbin, and is funded by individuals. "Foundation funding would be very valuable," de Chollet said, "but so far it has proved difficult."

DOCTOR OF HAPPINESS

ERIN TROWBRIDGE
December 1998

SOLO, Indonesia—Along the thin, bumpy roads winding through Central Java, miles away from the smog-laden capital of Jakarta, the scents of bitter clove trees, sweet supria flowers and earthy cashew trees fill the air. Industry out here means a tired, three-walled shack, charred black with great clouds of smoke swirling about as several men stoke a fire, burning bits of wood to sell later as charcoal. Most of the work in Central and East Java is rural, either farming or industry at its most basic, scaled-down level.

Old men, faces wrinkled and hollowed, ride decrepit bicycles loaded down with 30 to 40 pounds of cassava. They pass painstakingly up and down the steep hills, carrying the root vegetable to the markets to be sold. A bag of rice big enough to feed a family of four for a week costs less than 25 cents— and yet people here are still starving, unable to afford even this.

Ajahi, a grandmother waiting in line with her daughter and grandchildren to buy subsidized rice and noodles, admits that it has been three months since she has eaten two meals in one day. Talk about economic policy or financial monitors that may improve Indonesia's economic situation doesn't interest her or the others in the line. She says, simply, that she's afraid her newborn grandchild can't get the nourishment he needs. Feeding him is all that matters right now.

That's how it is for most people in rural Indonesia: For them, the global tremors caused by the economic crash in East Asia aren't the real issue. Poverty really comes down to getting less than 2,000 calories a day—and a staggering number of people are not getting anything close to that level of nutrition. In the last year, the number of people living below the official poverty line has doubled.

In response, the country's newly installed government has been adapting and reinforcing social policies to address the needs of the new poor scattered throughout the more than 13,000 islands making up the Indonesian archipelago. It is working to develop a social safety net to keep any more people from falling through the cracks.

Indonesia's recent economic devastation, currency devaluation, student riots, political ousters and allegations of gross human rights violations have dominated the news all over the world. The economic crisis that began in mid-1997 has caused East Asian currencies to depreciate by 15 to 75 percent, and stock prices have plunged as much as 65 percent. Indonesia is one of the nations that has been hit the hardest (at one point its currency and stock market index were both down by 90 percent). And financial analysts say the hitting has only just begun.

The Jakarta government estimates that by the end of 1998 almost half of the population will fall below the poverty line. That's roughly how bad the situation was 28 years ago, when 60 percent of the population was living in poverty and former President Soeharto instituted social welfare programs to provide relief. These programs had been heralded throughout the development world as paradigms of success—raising all but 11 percent of Indonesians above the poverty line by 1996—but they crumbled as soon as the rupiah's value began to collapse. "The enormous strides we made in the last two decades can be absolutely attributed to the comprehensiveness of the social programs established under Soeharto," said Djoko Suharno, Deputy Assistant of the Health Division in the Ministry for People's Welfare and Poverty Alleviation. "The systems themselves, the programs, are good. The question is running them properly. That was a failure under Soeharto—too much favor-granting. In some respects, the programs were so good—and had done what they set out to do—that they lost their priority status. Now, we have to rethink, debate and re-address the problems. We call this period now the 'Euphoria of Democracy.' Right now we have riots, protests and marches every day. But eventually the ideas and groups will crystallize and the programs will be reinvigorated, but with a degree of democracy that Habibie is bringing in that was truly lacking under Soeharto."

The man responsible for coordinating and bringing life back to the poverty alleviation programs for all of Indonesia is Dr. Haryono Suyono, Coordinating Minister on Social Welfare and Poverty Alleviation, a post created in Soeharto's last months in office but really invigorated under Habibie's new regime. Haryono's task, he says, is to make sure that the right hand knows what's going on with the left. The ministry oversees the activities of several different branches of government, from trade and agriculture to migration and women's affairs, with a specific focus on poverty alleviation, human resource development and preparations for natural disaster activities going on in each department. Right now, of course, Haryono is most concerned about the poverty alleviation activities, and his approach is nothing short of a revolution in Indonesian social policy.

Haryono explains that his preparation for this new position included 25 years' experience in running Indonesia's family planning and reproductive health programs. "The two are very connected and complementary," he said. "Our tactic here is to apply the outreach techniques we developed in family planning programs and apply them to poverty alleviation programs. Our approach within reproductive health was to provide family-centered, comprehensive programs that would benefit everyone from the father and mother to the livestock in the field behind the house. We look at it in terms of family, in terms of households, because that is the unifying factor. We develop programs that address the needs of families; they are the foundation of our culture."

He went on: "When you hear from the statistics department of the government that there are 79.4 million people living below the poverty line, it is only a number. Before this position was created, poverty programs just looked at that number. Now we've applied the principles of the family-centered approach and we can tell you where, exactly, those 79.4 million people are, how well they eat and what they need to pull themselves out."

The global tremors of the East Asian economic crash aren't the real issue. Poverty really comes down to getting less than 2,000 calories a day.

To ensure that the impoverished citizens of Indonesia know that the government's priority is to ease their burden, Haryono and ministers from other departments travel to small towns and villages throughout the archipelago each weekend. The gesture is symbolic, Haryono admits. Planting one banana plant in a single village, buying the products made by community support groups, distributing 10 kilograms (22 pounds) of rice—these aren't going to change the current of the crisis. But Haryono says he believes that it will give people a certainty that the government cares and a hope that the mechanisms are in place to change the present chaos back to a stable, growing environment.

"This is the new part of the program," said Haryono, driving into the outskirts of a small town in central Java where he was going to visit a reservoir project that will provide jobs and help prevent flooding. "Before, the goal wasn't poverty alleviation but programs for the poor. There wasn't a concerted effort to really target poor families. Now we target them so that, within the same family, the mother is connected with a community group for income generating projects, the father gets a loan to help him buy farming supplies, and the child gets a fellowship from the Ministry of Education so that the child can continue schooling without being pressured to just go to work. The integration, the holistic nature of these programs, will go much further not only in addressing the needs on a very large scale, but giving people the tools and the safety net to ensure that this won't happen again."

Haryono said that while the social unrest and the riots continue on the streets of Jakarta and in villages throughout Indonesia, the rage has never been directed at his department. Most people, he said, understand that the work done through the Ministry for Poverty Alleviation stands outside of the political ins and outs. The work needs to be done whether it's President Soeharto or President Habibie in office.

"Our goal is just to find a way out of poverty and give people control," said Haryono. "In that sense, my job is a mixture of government official, anthropologist and sociologist. As sociologist, I stand back and collect enormous amounts of data regarding every aspect of the situation of poverty. As anthropologist, I look at the cultural idiosyncrasies that will impact the development of different programs and examine the strengths that already exist and how they can be integrated into projects. And as minister, I develop and enact the policies born of this research. Each aspect depends upon and is invigorated by the other."

The poverty level in Central Java isn't so much about earnings or savings. According to the ministry's standards, poverty here means having only one set of clothes, no access to doctors, eating less than three times a day and living on dirt floors. The number of people surviving this way is staggeringly high. Haryono's goal in this area is not only to provide relief but also to help rebuild confidence that the situation can change. "In the past—and by that I mean a year ago—20,000 rupiah was like 10 dollars," said Haryono. "Now it's more like two dollars. But, you can still see that it means something. You can see the difference it makes. Even one dollar a day makes a difference. People want to work, want to have something, anything coming in."

The ministry's plan is to not only provide the immediate support and supply of food but to set up programs and projects that will help sustain the community.

"It's not our aim to just hand out food here," said R. Ricarda, chairman of Jabbaru Abaca Surya, a nongovernmental organization that helps to distribute food. "If a family is utterly, wholly poor, we give them rice and noodles for free. But if they can buy it, even at a very low cost, we charge them that subsidized price because it helps them feel that they are still able to put food on the table, still able to make ends meet, and ultimately feel that they have control of their own fate. It brings dignity and pride back to people who have already lost so much."

For people of the lowest classes, pride isn't just about pulling yourself up by the bootstraps. In Java, it also has to do with lower-middle-class people who may not enjoy luxuries but are still able to sleep in a bed, feed their children and go to work. The government, particularly Haryono's ministry, targets these people as much as the others. In community groups, people from this stable class work closely with those who are living far below the poverty line.

"Within these community groups, of which there are hundreds of thousands throughout Indonesia, we have maybe nine middle-class women and men working with four very poor men or women," said Haryono. "They use simple tools and items provided by the government to make crafts, food, jewelry, anything that can be sold for a small profit. In time, they can take out loans and make their business better and better. But we need those that are stable economically to really teach and help those who aren't. We need the ones who have suffered and have lived this way for a long time to learn how to manage a small business, how to apply for a loan, how to save profits. We can't just expect them to know this."

Integrating the classes goes beyond just placement in community groups. As the ministers travel throughout the island villages, their wives travel with them, buying the items for sale in the small markets dedicated to displaying and selling the goods that come from the local community groups. The wives, said Haryono, demonstrate to upper and middle-class women that not only are the products good, but purchasing them is socially responsible. "I can't lie, it is very difficult to work with the impoverished families," said one middle-class woman from a community group in a village outside of Solo. "It becomes frustrating having to teach everything from the ground up. But it is also not something I would back out of. It is good for the society and it is also a matter of social status. We are respected for this work."

These empowerment programs give small loans to the community groups to help them purchase supplies and learn needed skills. The groups, mostly made up of women, are focused on home industries. They buy wooden mallets and tin frying pans to break cassava root and fry it into chips. Others buy small electric stoves to bake cakes and breads which can be sold locally. Some weave baskets, others crack open cashews and bag them. The outcome is simple, but the profit is real. The groups divide the money equally, putting some of the profit toward paying back the loan, some into a group savings account with high interest, and the rest goes to the individual members. It may provide a supplementary income of only $10 a month, but in Central Java $10 goes a long way.

"It's different here because the poverty has been around for a long time," said Ricarda. "In other parts, like Jakarta, the economic crisis has devastated millions who had stable lives and incomes. Here, the devastation has never stopped. This is a mostly agricultural area so we're working with them to develop long-term economic and social safety nets for the future."

In Minggir, a farming community only 10 miles away from the village where former President Soeharto grew up, the 800 people living in the town feel more like centuries away from the political and social upheavals that have followed in his wake. In Minggir, even the doe-eyed children seem tired and hardened beyond their years as they help their parents carry produce and count out tiny portions of rupiahs to pay for supplies.

In a thatched hut tucked beside a bend in the dirt road leading out of town, 10 to 12 people come each morning at 8 to start working. The heavy scent of a wood-burning stove hangs over the workers as the morning sun starts to burn off the fog and mist of the night before. Suragi, in his early twenties, sits cross-legged on the dirt floor, using a knife to slowly peel thin strips of bamboo. Though his hands are fine-boned and delicate, his fingers are calloused and scarred from cuts. Working for 5,000 rupiah a day, just over 50 cents, he uses his fingers to nimbly pull at the nicked edge of the bamboo. Head down, he can peel long, thin threads to be woven into fine, intricate baskets, or thick, uneven pieces for more utilitarian containers that can be balanced on the back of a bicycle.

The KeraJinan community group works out of the hut six days a week. Mostly, the same eight people are there every day. Some weave, some peel, some ready the branches and some dye. Inside, in the workroom, it is silent. The work is carried on without a word except to pass a piece along or call for a thicker weave. The clack of the weaving loom and the rip of bamboo shreds are the only man-made sounds to be heard above the chirping of the birds outside.

Although the town is sparsely populated, there are more than a hundred such groups in Minggir alone. Most make baskets, some produce baked goods and others make jewelry. The KeraJinan group makes 50 to 100 baskets each week, depending on the design, and they are sold in sets of three for less than one dollar. Trays, picture frames and baskets of all shapes and sizes are stacked ceiling-high in the front room. Pariyo, the director of the cooperative, said that the baskets are exported to the Netherlands, Canada and Japan.

KeraJinan was founded in 1996, and in this year alone it has made almost enough to finish paying off the loan it received to start the group up.

In the villages surrounding Yogyakarta, like Minggir, the middle class—meaning those who are able to eat more than twice a day and who live in homes with four walls and floors—has shrunk from 57 percent to 31 percent of the population in the last year. Most of the people working in community groups like KeraJinan used to do it as a means of supplementing the earnings from their farms or livestock. These days, many of the people work in the community groups full-time. They've lost their farms or their outside work.

"It is affecting this community in smaller ways," said Dr. Koeslan, director of the Yogyakarta division of the Family Planning Ministry. "But the urban people who work within industry, they're the crestfallen ones, the ones who have had the carpet pulled out from under them. Here, perhaps, the parents are now eating tempeh where before they had chicken. The people here weren't used to a high life, and when you don't have very much anyway, you don't have so much to lose. In some ways, they're better off here. They already had support and community groups going to sustain those who weren't making ends meet. Now, the groups mean bread and butter for a lot more people, but no one had to fall all the way to the bottom before getting back up on their feet."

In Bali, poverty has a different face. It is hard to compare life, even hard living, on this lush, fertile land to that in the rocky, haggard mountains of Eastern Java. Somehow it seems that it would be easier to live here, even without the middle-class luxuries, than in the tough land on the island lying just miles away to the west. From the ministry in Jakarta, the poverty alleviation programs are developed for the whole of Indonesia. The different terrain, practices, cultures and traditions of each island must be considered as programs are developed to accommodate the specifics of each place. Between Java and Bali, only a hair's breadth apart on a map, those differences could not be more pronounced. Bali's faith is Hindu to Java's Islam. Tourism is the main industry in splendorous, green Bali while agriculture dominates in most parts of Java.

Bali, with its Hindu traditions, has a leg up when it comes to community group projects, said officials working on the poverty alleviation programs developed for this island. In addition, throngs of Australians and Japanese visit the island constantly, cutting out the need for middlemen to sell handicrafts to export markets.

In the small town of Sampian there are only three families living below the poverty line. The other two hundred households in town help support their work and products, creating a demand for their baked and fried foods and buying out the steady supply of baskets another family makes. Wayan Wati said it took two years for her family to save enough money to build a real house—just yards away from where their old house still stands. The new house, a two-room sheetrock and wood construction, cost almost $1,000. The old one, a roughly assembled collection of sticks and branches with dirt floors and three walls, serves as a storage space now. Wati says it also stands as a reminder of the way of life that she shared with her husband and children for 10 years.

"In Bali there are very powerful social, cultural groups called Banjars," said Dr. Gde Butu Abadi, Coordinator for Poverty Alleviation for Bali. "These Banjars are a fundamental part of Hinduism here and they've existed for hundreds of years. They're made up of two leaders and all of the townspeople. The groups are dedicated to the betterment of the community as a whole. We only had to enlist the Banjar leaders in our work to bring the benefits to the whole community. The structure, impact and respect were already in place. We only had to set up loan programs and projects for income-generating activities and the Banjars would carry them out. Our philosophy here, as Hindus, is that to prepare for the next life it is necessary to make living conditions better for everyone around you. Poverty alleviation programs go very well here. They work with the natural organization of the people."

> *'When you don't have much, you don't have so much to lose.'*

THE ORPHANS OF CHIANG MAI

SATYA SIVARAMAN
October 1998

CHIANG MAI, Thailand—As one travels through northern Thailand's picturesque Mae Rim District, the first sight that catches the eye is the area's lush green farmland, presenting a picture of abundant prosperity. In the villages around the fields, however, the reality is different—with family after family losing members to the HIV/AIDS epidemic, leaving behind orphaned children in the care of aging grandparents.

"I have lost three members of my family—my daughter, my son-in-law and a granddaughter—to AIDS, all in the past one year alone," said Supaporn, a local grandmother who is now beginning her life all over again at the ripe old age of 67. Apart from providing for her ailing husband, she now has the responsibility of bringing up two grandchildren. For the children it is an abrupt end to childhood and the start of an uphill struggle for survival.

Supaporn's story is typical of the way the HIV virus is destroying the middle generations of families throughout northern Thailand. Health workers say that the growing numbers of orphaned children will soon become one of the biggest social fallouts of the epidemic. According to an estimate made by the Thai Ministry of Public Health, there are already more than 48,000 orphaned children in Thailand. Worldwide there are over 8.2 million orphans as a result of the HIV epidemic.

Realizing that the problem is only going to get worse in the coming years, Thailand is making considerable efforts to mitigate the impact of this trend. While many orphaned children—some of whom are themselves HIV-positive—continue to be cared for by their immediate families, several hundreds are now being looked after in orphanages.

"Initially our staff was hesitant about working with HIV-positive children. But they now look after them with love and are an example to people in the community," said Dr. Mayuree Yoktree, Director of the Viengping Home, a state-run orphanage in Mae Rim district which has pioneered work among children affected by the HIV epidemic in Thailand. The orphanage has more than 200 children, of whom almost 100 are HIV-positive since birth and many others who were orphaned as a result of the epidemic.

Officials from the Viengping Home carry the knowledge and expertise gained in their orphanages to the village communities to help them cope with the growing problem. Orphanage officials are also seeking ways of giving children affected by the HIV epidemic a new life outside their own institutions by encouraging adoption.

Along with the growing number of orphans, an equally worrying phenomenon is the rise in the number of children who are born HIV-positive. "We have not been successful enough in getting men to change their behavior and be faithful to their wives," said a health worker in Chiang Mai. "What that means is that HIV is now entering the family, and more and more pregnant women are passing on the virus to their babies."

Though the first cases of HIV in Thailand were detected among intravenous drug users, heterosexual activity is now the biggest source of transmission, health workers say. Again, though sex workers initially had the highest rates of HIV incidence, in the past few years more and more housewives are becoming HIV-positive—contracting the virus from their husbands. Every year in Thailand more than 20,000 HIV-positive women give birth to children, many of whom get the virus from their mothers during delivery.

Many Thai women complain that men, whatever their social class, refuse to tell their spouses about their HIV status because of their big egos and fear of humiliation among other men. "It is this silence which is the primary cause for the rapid spread of HIV among housewives in Thailand," said Phimjai Inthamun, 34, coordinator of the Community Health Center at Mae Rim, 18 miles (30 kilometers) north of Chiang Mai. Still, health workers report that more and more Thai women are mustering the courage to question the behavior of their husbands and insist on their using

Many Thai women say that men fail to tell their spouses about AIDS.

condoms during marital sex, although the majority quietly accept whatever happens as "good luck" or "bad luck" in line with the Buddhist notion of karma.

One ray of hope that has emerged for preventing more newborn babies from contracting HIV is provided by recent studies showing the effectiveness of the anti-retroviral drug AZT in cutting down transmission of the virus to newborn babies. Hailed worldwide as a major breakthrough, clinical tests jointly conducted by the US-based Center for Disease Control and Prevention (CDC) and Thailand's Ministry of Public Health in February 1998 showed that a short course of AZT given late in pregnancy and during delivery reduced the rate of HIV transmission to infants of infected mothers by half. The Thailand study, which began enrollment in 1996, provides the first conclusive scientific data on the preventive effectiveness of a short-course regimen of AZT. The trials have not been without controversy, however, and have attracted much criticism from nongovernmental organizations in the US for their use of placebos as part of the study.

The rationale behind studying the efficacy of administering a short course of AZT to pregnant women arose from the prohibitive costs of the longer courses that are used regularly for preventing HIV transmission to newborn babies in developed countries. The short regimen is expected to cost just $80, compared with almost $1,000 for the longer course. The dramatic reduction in costs is hailed as beneficial to developing countries where almost 90 percent of HIV infections occur.

Even at these reduced costs, however, the drugs are still beyond the reach of many poor Thai women. While some international agencies are subsidizing the drug further, the efforts are still far short of what is required, given the scope of the problem.

REPORT FROM SOUTH AFRICA

PRANAY GUPTE
May 1995

One morning in South Africa, I was sitting inside a one-room shack in the black township of Khayelitsha, a sprawling collection of corrugated-iron structures in the shadow of Cape Town's fabled Table Mountain. On the walls were posters with messages such as "Making love is beautiful; making unwanted babies is stupid." In front of me was a red Formica table on which family-planning brochures were placed, and beyond the table was a neatly arranged row of white plastic chairs. The chairs were occupied by local women who had gathered to talk about health services and family-planning and primary schools and sanitation and street crime and the AIDS pandemic. It would ordinarily have been a routine weekly meeting for the women, but what made this session special was that it fell on the first anniversary of the April 1994 election—the country's first full democratic election after the apartheid era—an occasion that the government of President Nelson R. Mandela had designated as "Freedom Day."

Some 750,000 blacks are said to live here and Khayelitsha is growing at the rate of 5,000 new arrivals a day. The newcomers are from the old tribal "homelands" of Transkei and Ciskei, and they come to this township because, of course, they expect jobs in Cape Town, a gem of a city at the southernmost tip of continental Africa. But Cape Town, like other large South African cities, has few new jobs to offer, at least not for unskilled laborers. This cohort of young job-seekers has grown nationally to some 11.5 million people, or around 27 percent of the country's overall population of 42 million. Most of the women in that small room in Khayelitsha were jobless, as were many of their husbands and boyfriends.

I had been brought here by Anna van Esch, an energetic veteran of South Africa's family planning effort, to see for myself how the community's women lived and what their problems and aspirations were. The world's focus on South Africa, until recently, had been on the human-rights abuses perpetrated by apartheid. Now that the long political revolution was over and the black majority had come to power, I wanted to see how South Africans were faring in another revolution—this one against disease, illiteracy, crime, AIDS, economic deprivation and gender inequality. This revolution was open-ended, with no election at the end to render a verdict on its success. Neither would there be political prizes for the victors, no spoils of office. The only dividends would be a more secure life and a more sustainable society for all South Africans.

Khayelitsha seemed as good a place as any to start in this huge country, and Anna van Esch proved to be immensely obliging. A tall blonde woman who had worked in community development and adult education much of her adult life, Anna cautioned that in South Africa, as in much of sub-Saharan Africa, numbers were a problem. "We really have no clue as to how many people live in Khayelitsha," she said as we drove on a six-lane highway out of Cape Town toward the black township. In the old apartheid days, a draconian law aimed at "influx control" prevented blacks from migrating to anywhere near sparkling white-only cities such as Cape Town. Now that the law had been lifted and communities such as Khayelitsha had mushroomed, the challenge lay in providing proper health, education and sanitation services to community residents. "The government doesn't have adequate resources in providing public health," said Anna, who is the Cape Town branch director for the Planned Parenthood Association of South Africa. "So it is the nongovernmental organizations that must play a role in such things as family planning and women's health education. We've made a small start in Khayelitsha with our Masikhanyise project." In the Xhosa language, "Masikhanyise" means "bringers of light." For the Planned Parenthood Association, "Masikhanyise" is a project for women's "wellness and advocacy," according to Anna; it is a project for the advancement of women for whom the "New South Africa" is much like the old one. Anna told me that although hundreds of nongovernmental organizations (NGOs) had sprouted in the country, the Planned Parenthood Association was the only NGO working in reproductive health. No program concerning the well-being of women could be effective unless it dealt with reproductive health, Anna said.

Perhaps it was the anniversary, or perhaps it was the presence of a first-time foreign visitor to what everybody in politics and the media was calling the "New South Africa," or perhaps it was the frustration that had built up among the Khayelitsha women to a point where they simply had to fulminate vigorously. Whatever the reason, the conversation in the shack this morning was quite spirited. No holding back here, no disguising problems in euphemisms.

"Talk is very good these days among our politicians," said Dikeledi Xorile, a local trainer for the "Masikhanyise" project, who led the discussion, "and many promises are being made. But progress is slow for us women. Where are the jobs, the positions of leadership? Are we being abused less? Has rape decreased in our townships? So what's changed for women? Little has changed."

Implicit in her words was disappointment with the African National Congress, which won 62.7 percent of the votes in the April 1994 election and which, with 252 seats, enjoys a comfortable majority in the 400-member National Assembly. The ANC, which has had a rocky time making the transition from a liberation movement into a ruling party, pledged to institute gender equality: 30 percent of all elected officials at the national and regional levels will be women, the ANC has promised, but in reality only three women are cabinet members in President Mandela's Government of National Unity and few women sit in regional councils in South Africa's nine provinces. Nelson Mandela has urged his people to be "patient," and indeed they have been, for the most part. But it doesn't take much digging to discover that in post-apartheid South Africa, women are yet to be accorded significant roles on the national stage.

The women of Khayelitsha keep track of such things. Said Nomzi Abrahams: "We don't want South Africa to become like other countries where women do all the work and it is the men who decide everything."

Health is something else that women here follow closely.

"What about the men who sleep around with many girlfriends and bring AIDS home to their wives?" said Nomvuyo Ntyeko, tapping her feet on the fading linoleum carpet. "Our men refuse to accept the seriousness of the situation," Nomvuyo said. "They ask, 'Where is the disease? Is it like plague? Is it like cholera?' How do you explain that AIDS is a disease like no other?"

Nomvuyo and the other women were expressing in the most elemental terms what troubled them locally, but what they said echoed larger concerns that I was to encounter in subsequent days during my South African journey. In South Africa as a whole, there are an estimated 500 new HIV infections each day; at the current rate, almost 20 percent of the country's population would be infected in another 25 years. The Department of Health has estimated that almost a million South Africans are HIV-positive, and that more and more women are giving birth to infected babies. Women, already victims of a societal double-standard under which male philandering is often condoned, overwhelmingly feel that AIDS is being increasingly brought home by husbands who tend to wander.

Vivienne Gongota, a sprightly young community worker who collaborated with Anna van Esch and is the project coordinator of "Masikhanyise," spoke up. "We know that women here are so oppressed by law and culture," she said. "But let's not forget what we have been able to start in our community here. Women are starting to find their own identities. Our message is that people should take responsibility for their own lives." She mentioned a local project called "Delta," which is the acronym for "Development Education Leadership Team in Action." The Delta program aims to develop self-confidence and skills in a variety of areas for local women, Vivienne told me. The idea is to foster a network of mutual support which will encourage women to accept leadership roles.

Vivienne, like Dikeledi Xorile, helps other women improve their own lives and that of their neighborhoods. This is accomplished at one level by teaching women how to express themselves more clearly and how to organize small cells to attend to civic matters such as cleaning up their neighborhoods; at another level, these women are taught to sew or become family-planning educators so that they can find jobs locally, maybe even start small-scale businesses.

At still another level, the women are taught to work with their menfolk—perhaps the hardest of the tasks before the educators because the women of the "Masikhanyise" project constantly run into male resistance. In many local homes, domestic tensions between husbands and wives increased after the women started participating in "Masikhanyise" sessions. Vivienne later told me that the two most frequent rejoinders she got from Khayelitsha's men were: "Hope you aren't going to put the spirit of defiance into our women," and, "Are you training our women to become preachers?" The answer, of course, is neither. Vivienne—whom local women call a "bringer of light"—said that her trainees often focus on relatively simple things such as persuading their husbands to start wearing condoms or accompany them to local health clinics for regular check-ups—especially if sexually transmitted diseases are suspected.

I asked a young mother named Nophelelo Tshaka how she felt about all this. Speaking in Xhosa—which was translated into English by Vivienne—Nophelelo said that she was pleased by the easy availability of contraceptives in the community. Already the mother of two, she did not wish to have more children, she said, and something as relatively simple as being able to walk to a community health center to obtain contraceptives was, for her, a major thing. Did her husband go along? No, Nophelelo admitted, but she was confident that she would get him to start wearing condoms one of these days.

"Change here is incremental," Vivienne said to me later. "What we tell our women is that all social change must start with self-development. Little things matter a lot."

As she spoke, it occurred to me that this 30-year-old woman had the wisdom to recognize a fundamental truth that applied to all nations, rich or developing—but especially to South Africa—that while political events can race ahead with bewildering speed, social change by definition moves at a much slower pace. Governmental systems—even evil ones such as those based on racism—are transformed far more readily than long-ingrained cultural attitudes. And no attitude is more difficult to change than the way men think they should treat women.

Several days later, when I visited the national headquarters of the Planned Parenthood Association in Johannesburg, I was discussing my Khayelitsha visit with Audrey Elster, the organization's national development manager, or fund-raiser. How grim, really, was the picture for South Africa's poor black women, I asked, and how different was their situation from women in any other developing society? Audrey, a bespectacled young woman who speaks with more than a trace of a Scottish accent, said: "I don't know where to start. I would say that black women in South Africa have been doubly oppressed in this country—by their color, and oppressed by their own people. Black women in this country are still at the bottom of the pile. And no respect is given to them. The African culture looks on women as bearers of their children. It's the common attitude, even amongst young people. There is the idea that you're not a man until you've fathered a child. And, often, that you're not a woman until you've given birth. And that gives rise to teenage pregnancies. And there is the attitude, amongst young men, that it's quite all right to father children with many women—because then you're a real man, then you're a real stud. It's a very macho, paternalistic culture. And that basically has African women completely disadvantaged. I mean, they have no purpose whatever in this kind of society. Black women have been completely disempowered. The temptation is obviously to try and assist them in some way, to try and give them some skills to help them. But the structure of their society is such that they can't get out of it until you do something about the wider issues that affect their lives. That is why the Khayelitsha project emphasizes self-help and developing self-esteem. "

"It's farcical to talk about women's empowerment in today's South Africa because that empowerment is not going to come from men," Audrey continued. "I think there's not the will, really, to put women in positions of power, to really do something about improving their opportunities and giving them a chance to get out of the situation and the positions that they're in. On paper, and even when they stand up and make big speeches, our male leaders have talked about helping women, or doing things for women. But when it comes to the real crunch, when it comes to issues such as abortion, when it comes to issues such as putting women in positions of power, it's not being done. I think prior to the election last year, there was quite a euphoria about, you know, how the situation for women was going to change radically. But it's not changed so radically. You see far more black women in offices now than you might have seen before—but they tend to be secretaries and clerks. You see far more black people, in general, living in the more affluent suburbs. But it's the black men who are driving the BMWs and the Mercedes. So I think we've got a long way to go before women's lives will really qualitatively change in this country."

Anna van Esch drove me to the nearby community of New Crossroads. In the distance were the crenelated ramparts of a hilly range, with the wide expanse of the Atlantic Ocean rolling out from the edge. In front of me was a lawn, violently green from recent rain. Children were playing. The sky was now blue and cloudless and a gentle wind carried the faint bouquet of tropical flowers. Jacaranda trees were in full bloom.

I was quickly reminded that this was less than a picture-postcard tableau. For beyond the lawn where the children played stretched miles and miles of shacks, home to almost a half-million dispossessed blacks. The children wore shabby clothes. The roads that meandered through this township were rough and pocked with potholes, metaphors for the violence that punches through the fabric of daily life here. In South Africa, according to the Ministry of Safety and Security, a serious crime is committed every 17 seconds: a murder every 30 minutes; a rape every 18 minutes; a house break-in every two minutes; a car is stolen and a robbery committed every five minutes; and someone is assaulted every three minutes. During just one weekend that I was in the country, 23 people were killed and 36 women raped in Johannesburg. (Reuters reported that a senior World Bank official was accused of raping a cleaning woman but that no formal charges were filed.) The police said it had been a "normal weekend" for South Africa's commercial capital. "The statistics are actually not too high for a normal weekend," Warrant-Officer Andy Pieke told Reuters in Johannesburg, a city dubbed the most violent in the world outside a war zone. Pieke said the weekend's crime

Governmental systems are transformed far more readily than ingrained cultural attitudes.

tally also included 557 break-ins, the hijacking of 11 trucks and 28 cars at knife or gunpoint, robberies at 25 businesses and the theft of 256 cars. (Belgium has pledged the equivalent of US$5.5 million to help South Africa combat crime and transform its 13 police agencies into a single community service, Reuters reported, although few South Africans expect the crime picture to improve in the near future.)

A visitor can get depressed by such information. But South Africa is also other things besides a country of rising crime: It is the most significant military and economic power in Africa, as the author and journalist Allister Sparks has put it, "a regional superpower in the world's most marginalized continent, the one country that could perhaps provide the engine to pull Africa out of its mire of poverty and desperation." South Africa's gross domestic product is $104 billion, or 60 percent of all the other 45 sub-Saharan countries combined—and nearly four times the $28 billion of Nigeria, Africa's next most-developed country. South Africa's per-capita income is $2,600—more than 10 times that of Nigeria. Princeton University political scientist Jeffrey Herbst says that post-apartheid South Africa is important because "it is a vivid example of the worldwide democratic movement, it is a potentially significant emerging market, and it is one of the very few bright economic spots in Africa." To quote Allister Sparks again: "A successful new South Africa, embodying as it does all the elements of the global divide and striving now to overcome them, could develop into a model for the gradual solution of the North-South divide. With a leader of Nelson Mandela's international stature, it has the chance to be the interlocutor between the developed and underdeveloped worlds."

'A model for the gradual solution of the North-South divide.'

These two worlds are plainly in view. They exist separately but side-by-side in contemporary South Africa, as they have for 350 years since Jan van Riebeeck and the first Dutch settlers sailed into Table Bay. Cape Town, with its beautiful Dutch-style and English colonial homes, its wide boulevards lined with stately old oak trees and its sparkling shopping malls, is one world. New Crossroads, with its dusty roads and ramshackle buildings, is another. Even today, a year after Mandela and his black-dominated government took over this country's leadership—ending three centuries of white domination and almost 50 years of rule by the white-oriented National Party—it is possible to roam the streets of Cape Town neighborhoods such as Newlands and not encounter a single black. And in the black townships, it is equally rare to spot a white face. The Western Cape—of which Cape Town is the capital—is in fact one of only two provinces that do not have a black majority: its population of 3.6 million is 55 percent "colored," 25 percent white, 19 percent black and 1 percent Indian. This province has the highest literacy rate and the lowest infant-mortality rate in the country—but, of course, the statistics are less encouraging in the black townships. As we drove into New Crossroads, a young black man, who was clearly inebriated, lurched across the road in front of us, almost running into our car. He stopped, looked at Anna van Esch, and shouted in Xhosa, "Hey, mlungu!"— "Hey, whitey!" But he did so with a smile, and Anna assured me that he meant no insult.

I had expected Anna to take me to yet another shack in New Crossroads, and I became morose at the prospect. But she wheeled her little Japanese-made car into a side street. There, parked in splendid isolation, was a sturdy brick building. It had its own courtyard, and Anna pulled into a driveway and we got out. We had come to the New Crossroads Youth Center, a truly remarkable enterprise.

It is remarkable because, in the first place, the center exists at all. New Crossroads can be called, without risking hyperbole, a tough place. During the inflammatory years of South Africa's freedom struggle, there was much political agitation here, mainly violent clashes between the United Democratic Front—which included Mandela's African National Congress—and groups of government collaborators and agitators. Along with such violence there was crime—muggings, rapes, murders. Hundreds of youths—some no more than 10 years old—came to possess deadly knives and guns. Now that the freedom struggle is over and black-majority rule is here, the political confrontations have abated somewhat in New Crossroads. These days, some of the mostly jobless youths employ their weaponry in the pursuit of crime—a fact of life that worries many national leaders. Nelson Mandela, in a speech back in 1992, expressed concern that unless the ANC satisfied the economic needs of its black constituents, the country faced "dangerous prospects." Mandela warned about a potential conflict between South Africa's haves and have-nots, not just between whites and blacks. "The youths in the townships have had over the decades a visible enemy, the government," he said. "Now that enemy is no longer visible, because of the transformation that is taking place. Their enemy now is you and me, people who drive a car and have a house. It's order, anything that relates to order, and it is a very grave situation."

The Mandela Administration is addressing this situation by promoting, among other things, what is called the Reconstruction and Development

Program, an ambitious $10 billion effort to create 2.5 million jobs and build a million new homes by 1999, when the next national election will be held. The RDP, according to Anton Harber and Barbara Ludman of the Weekly Mail & Guardian, was designed to right the economic wrongs that apartheid inflicted, and six chapters constitute the main economic program of Mandela's Government of National Unity. The RDP, say Harber and Ludman, is also "the article of faith of all who believe in the new South Africa."

The RDP, of course, is many things to different people. For some businessmen, it is about more investment in telecommunications; for South Africa's powerful unions, it is about gaining advantage in management/labor relations; for diehard socialists, it is about redistributing land still heavily owned by white farmers. Most of all, the RDP means massive government spending on housing, health and jobs. Like the Program of Action that was adopted last year at the International Conference on Population and Development in Cairo, the RDP acknowledges that investing in people, in their health and education, is the key to sustained economic growth and sustainable development. For the youths of communities such as New Crossroads, the RDP has created rising expectations about jobs. With almost 40 percent of the country's population under the age of 15, you can imagine the potential for social explosion if these rising expectations aren't met adequately.

"It's important to offer these kids a channel for their energy," Anna van Esch said to me as we approached the youth center. "Their expectations about better education and decent jobs may not be immediately fulfilled. But what we can do is to give them facilities for recreation and help instill a sense of purpose. It's important to take these kids off the streets."

The center, run by an enthusiastic white man named Allister Butler, has a nice library, a computer training facility, rooms where seminars on sex education and youth leadership are conducted and recreation rooms where local boys play furiously at basketball, carom and miniature pool. Crayon drawings by local kids were tacked up on the library walls; there were posters that said: "Don't bend the corners of the page," and, "Be on your best behavior," and, "Books are not hats for use when it rains." Allister, who has worked in youth programs in the United States and Britain, told me that one of his biggest problems was dealing with resentment from older youths—those above 20 years of age, for the most part—who weren't eligible to participate in the center's activities, which cater to those between 10 and 19 years of age. Some of these older youth also resented the fact that the five-month-old center wasn't around when they were eligible to join.

"New Crossroads kids, like kids anywhere else, respond well to mentors," sais Allister, a chunky man in his mid-30s. Clearly, he seemed the sort of person whom the local youths would regard as a mentor and, indeed, in the time that I spent at the center I saw how easily he and they got along. Butler joked with the kids and engaged in occasional playful mock boxing. He would inquire about their folks. He would compliment them on their dunking skills. More than 400 kids show up here every day, and Butler is convinced that the number will soon double. He frequently meets with local parents to discuss the young people's personal problems so that he can better understand his wards.

The new Crossroads Youth Center represents an unusual cooperative effort among some 20 nongovernmental organizations—including Anna van Esch's Planned Parenthood Association—to address social problems in impoverished communities by pooling resources. The center was fashioned after careful research, according to Elizabeth Seabe, who conducted the early studies that provided local demographic and related data under the supervision of Dr. Mamphela Ramphele, deputy vice chancellor of the University of Cape Town, whose brainchild the New Crossroads Youth Center was. The Carnegie Corporation of New York funded some of Elizabeth's research. The Independent Development Trust—a semi-official organization—along with the Rockefeller Foundation, a number of businesses and nongovernmental organizations came up with the equivalent of $300,000 that it took to build the center.

Elizabeth was a pleasant young woman who took me around the center and spoke animatedly as we wove our way between sweaty youths who chased one another in the raucous manner of teenagers everywhere, and younger kids armed with books who were headed for the center's library. One kid, whom everybody called Skollie, kept doing cartwheels and flips and at one point drew my attention to a bulletin board with photographs of the center's youths. At the age of 7, Skollie was obviously highly popular—or highly assertive—because he could be seen in virtually every picture. When Skollie wasn't at school he was at the center—which obviously pleases Allister Butler and Elizabeth Seabe. They say they are confident that Skollie is turning out well-adjusted.

"Young people in our urban ghettoes have been marginalized," Elizabeth said, "and you won't find too many programs around the country aimed at preventing further marginalization. Most of these youths say to us, 'I don't have enough space.' When there are constraints on physical space within households, kids are forced out into the street, where they are vulnerable to peer pressure. So experimentation with smoking, drinking, drugs and sex forms part of their life experiences from an early age. This has serious consequences for themselves as individuals—and for society as a whole."

The center had become quite full by now. I tried to start a conversation with one of the youths, but his mind was on a carom game. When I started taking pictures, however, the kids abandoned their activities and posed excitedly for me. Some of them had seemed quite graceful on the basketball court, and when I mentioned this to the Planned Parenthood Association's educator, Noxolo Ntenetya, she told me that perhaps that grace flowed from the fact that quite a few of them took dance lessons at the center. Noxolo comes to New Crossroads three days a week to give workshops on sexuality education and reproductive health. She also offers a contraception service. Noxolo's work is sponsored by the Planned Parenthood Association at the center's request. About 22 kids attended the workshop, she told me, adding that one of her objectives was to educate them about sexually transmitted diseases. "We discuss family relationships in our workshop as well," said Noxolo, a slim 23-year-old with a sculptured face and a closely cropped hairstyle. "I think it is essential that these kids also learn the difference between love and infatuation. This is not the kind of education they get in our schools."

The center's activities are not designed to replace schoolwork but to complement formal education. It doesn't take much insight to understand that the center's responsibility toward its youth is heightened by the fact that the school system is unsatisfactory in townships such as New Crossroads. School buildings are dilapidated, teaching equipment is old or nonexistent and school books are in short supply. To cope with overcrowding, some schools have adopted double or triple teaching sessions.

The government, Elizabeth said, still spends four times as much on a child in traditionally white areas as on a child in a black area. In 1994, only 48.5 percent of all black final-year school pupils passed, compared with a white pass rate of 97.3 percent. Until last year, the national educational system was governed by 18 education departments—for white, black, "colored" (non-tribal black) and Asian pupils. A single education department has now been announced, although each of the country's nine provinces has also been given clearance to establish its own education department. The Mandela government, under the RDP, has allocated $28.4 million to rehabilitate and upgrade schools in black areas, but these funds have yet to reach New Crossroads. No one seems to think that the money is going to arrive any time soon.

South Africa is a breathtakingly lovely country, with stark deserts, craggy mountains, huge stretches of game parks, long, flat plains and thousands of miles of coastline dotted with beaches and scooped by natural bays. The climate, for the most part, is salubrious. It is not difficult to imagine how the early visitors to Africa's southern tip must have felt when exposed to this

Population control is not the same as controlling fertility.

place. South Africa's great physical beauty was first recorded by the seafarers of the Vereenigde Oostindische Compagnie—the United East India Company—who came to the Cape around 1652. They were the forebears of the Afrikaners who established farming settlements in the lush interior. The British came later, annexing the Dutch Cape Colony in 1795, and went on to create modern South Africa, discovering diamonds and gold and launching the only industrial revolution in Africa. Certainly, their wars against the Xhosa and Zulu tribes constitute the stuff of this nation's mythology and history.

From South Africa's western coast I flew to its eastern coast, to KwaZulu-Natal, home to many of the country's 8.5 million Zulus. Audrey Elster of the Planned Parenthood Association had suggested that I meet Tim Phiri, who worked on reproductive health issues with fellow Zulus in a community called Gingindlovu, about a hundred miles north of Durban, a teeming commercial city on the Indian Ocean. I could not pass up this opportunity to visit Zululand. The romance of history beckoned.

To get to Gingindlovu in time for a full day's visit, I had to catch a bus at 7 o'clock one morning at a location near Durban's City Hall. I had wanted to walk from my sea-front hotel on tony Snell Parade, a corniche distinguished by tall hotels and apartment buildings, and a beach with an amusement park featuring a miniaturized model of Durban. The bus stop was some 20 minutes away by foot, but the receptionist advised me to take a taxi.

"Lots of muggings these days," the receptionist, who was of Indian origin, said.

The taxi-driver, who was black, expressed some surprise that I had chosen not to walk. I told him about the receptionist's warning.

"Ah, some people panic when there is no need to panic," he said. The tenuous relationship between South Africa's blacks and Indians has a way of drawing attention to itself in a thousand little ways. It is a relationship exacerbated by the perception of many blacks that the Indians had preferred the National Party to the ANC; in the 1994 election, the National Party won overwhelmingly in the traditionally Indian section of Chatsworth in Durban. Obviously there is also the great economic divide between Indians, who are mostly businessmen and professionals, and blacks, who are mostly poor.

Still, the receptionist's observation about muggings could not be entirely dismissed: Durban, like most South African cities, was experiencing rising crime rates.

The bus stop was on Pine Street, a short block away from Church Square and City Hall, an ornate Victorian structure. A small sign nailed near the ceiling of the bus shed said "To Zululand." I had read up on the Zulus' proud but bloody history, about their great 19th Century King Shaka and his martial exploits. I had also followed closely the newspaper accounts of contemporary turmoil in KwaZulu-Natal. The Zulus' Chief, Mangosuthu Buthelezi, was much in the news, having had public rows with President Mandela over the decision by Buthelezi's Inkatha Freedom Party to boycott the process of writing a final constitution for post-apartheid South Africa. The Reuters news agency reported that Buthelezi, who was seeking a large measure of autonomy for the Zulus, said the ruling African National Congress had reneged on an agreement to accept international mediation in disputes in drafting the charter. The agreement was made during talks in April 1994 that brought Inkatha into South Africa's first democratic elections, which Buthelezi had threatened to boycott. The flamboyant Zulu chief was now home-affairs minister in Mandela's Government of National Unity, but a continuing irritant nonetheless.

The disagreements between the ANC and the IFP would ordinarily be considered as political disputes like those that characterize most any democratic system. But the level of violence that the disputes have spawned is scary. More than 300 political murders were reported in KwaZulu-Natal in the run-up to the April 27-29 elections last year. The ANC and the IFP, of course, blame each other for the deteriorating situation. (The IFP won control of the province after the elections.) Regardless of who is to be blamed, the terrible fact is that, in the past decade, more than 20,000 people have died because of the political rivalry, according to the Human Rights Committee, a national watchdog organization. It said that 78 people were killed for political reasons in KwaZulu-Natal in April 1995, an increase of 37 percent from March. "This province is the only area where old-style political violence continues," the HRC said in its April report. Many killings were in rural areas and villages among lush green hills in KwaZulu-Natal, according to the group.

Now here I was, in a comfortable bus, headed toward those very hills. I had paid the bus driver the equivalent of $12 for the privilege of seeing first-hand what the fuss, and the killings, were all about. Although I was a relative newcomer to the issues here, it did not take much convincing that if the violence in KwaZulu-Natal escalated, it would surely spread to other areas of the country. And that would hurt South Africa's prospects for economic growth, political and social stability—and much-needed foreign investment.

The road to Gingindlovu moves out of Durban in a leisurely, winding manner, past expensive weekend homes and signs that point to discreet little resorts with names like Zinkwazi Beach and New Guelderland. I was struck by how well maintained the roads were in the province—in fact, roads most everywhere in South Africa seem in excellent shape, except, of course, in the black townships. The bus turned inland about an hour out of Durban, then began to climb into short, rolling hills that were carpeted with sugar-cane fields. At one point, the bus driver obligingly stopped so that I could take pictures. He told me that although the landscape looked dramatically green because of a good rainfall, the rainy season had been delayed for months. The area, the driver said, was still feeling the effect of a severe drought in 1992. "Food prices are going up all the time as a result," he said.

I later learned through a news dispatch by the Inter Press Service that, because of the inadequate rainfall, South Africa would be forced to import one million tons of corn this year from Argentina and the United States. These imports are likely to cost $133 million. Commercial farmers this year could plant only 2.95 million hectares (7.4 million acres) of corn, compared with the 3.4 million hectares (8.5 million acres) they normally farm, the IPS report said, quoting the National Maize Producers Organization. IPS said that South Africa consumed 3.6 million tons of corn a year as its staple food. Farmers expect to reap about 2 million tons this season. That, plus a 700,000 ton carry-over from last season, is expected to produce a shortfall of almost one million tons, IPS said, adding that consumer prices were likely to rise by another 40 percent.

Gingindlovu was a small town with one main street. The bus let me off at the post office, a small colonial building that was perched on a grassy knoll. In front of the building was a parking lot where Tim Phiri was waiting for me in a Toyota van. Tim turned out to be a large man with a soft voice, and a tendency to alternate deeply worried expressions on his face with broad smiles. He invited me for tea and toast at a fast-food place on Main Street; I was sorely tempted to buy guavas and apples instead from a street vendor nearby, but Tim had already walked into the eatery.

The tea was strong and flavorful and the toast was thickly buttered. Tim told me that, as an "educator" for the Planned Parenthood Association, he spent 10 hours a day visiting Zulu families and distributing contraceptives. He also conducted workshops on reproductive health at factories that are strewn around this mostly rural area. As he talked, I noticed a small sticker on the wall that said: "AIDS warning: Practice safe sex."

Tim shook his head. "Most of the men around here are anti-condom," he said. "They don't believe that they can contract AIDS. And the young people, who understand the problem better, often have to hide contraceptives because their parents say that condom use will make these kids promiscuous. But I say, better safe sex than being dead."

The waitress came by to serve more tea. She said something to Tim in Zulu, and he explained to me that the young woman had attended one of his high-school workshops on sexual education. Her name was Doris Mhlongo, and she had had to leave school in order to support her family. I asked her what she had learned in Tim's workshop.

"I learned about family-planning methods, and about hygiene," Doris said, shyly. "I think most students learned a lot from the open way in which he spoke."

Tim told me that Zulu culture was, by and large, fairly conservative, and that things such as sex education weren't easily relayed. Being a teacher from the area worked in his favor, but "it still takes an awful lot of convincing on my part." This means that Tim must make repeat visits to homes; at factories, he works with management officials who then direct him to workers. It is important that in both home and workplace, he observe hierarchical etiquette. That is part of the culture here.

The culture, however, isn't kindly disposed toward notions of family planning and population control. This is not surprising, given the controversial status of "population" during the apartheid era.

A couple of days before I arrived in the country, Nafis Sadik, Executive Director of the United Nations Population Fund (UNFPA), had delivered a major address at a government-sponsored meeting in Pretoria in which she noted that one unfortunate legacy of the apartheid era that needed to be overcome was the widespread tendency in South Africa to interpret the term "population control" as referring to "fertility control," particularly of the country's black majority, while approving population growth for the white minority. "The family-planning program of the 'old' South Africa has been criticized both at home and abroad for not being completely voluntary or oriented to the needs of the clients," Dr. Sadik said. "Many say that the program was excessively driven by numbers and motivated by factors other than people's welfare."

Since 1948, successive white governments explicitly or implicitly had a "population control" policy. White people were offered tax incentives to have children. Blacks were offered not reproductive-health education and a choice of contraceptives, but only one contraceptive—the controversial Depo-Provera, which is injectible. In Johannesburg, the Planned Parenthood Association's Audrey Elster told me that if you looked at the contraceptive use rate in this country you will find that it's quite high—about 50 percent. But something like 80 percent of black women use Depo-Provera. "I think the government definitely had a very racist population control policy during the apartheid years, and people are still quite sensitive to that," Audrey said. Like many others I met during my South African journey, Audrey felt that the historical background and social sensitivities to population issues virtually ensured that the Mandela administration would move slowly in developing a national population policy.

As the authoritative Weekly Mail & Guardian reported, there is ambivalence over the role of Abe Williams, Nelson Mandela's Minister of Welfare and Population Development. According to the newspaper, Williams was nominated to the cabinet by his National Party as a token of appreciation to the affluent Western Cape's colored voters for their support in the 1994 election. Colored support was a major factor in the National Party's winning power in the provincial council—the only province in which the white-dominated party holds power.

In a belated move that was widely welcomed by NGOs and social activists, Williams' ministry published in late April a "Green Paper" aimed at opening up a national debate about how population issues relate to development issues in South Africa. The idea behind the document was to invite public feedback so that an overarching development policy that integrated population concerns could be framed. Jay Parsons, the UN Population Fund's representative in Pretoria, told me that the document was concerned with two key questions: What were the inadequacies of the Reconstruction and Development Programme and how should the RDP take into account the impact of population trends on development activities? And what institutional structures were needed to properly take into account South Africa's population and development trends?

Parsons, a tall, friendly American whom I had first met more than a decade ago when he was UNFPA's representative in Indonesia, cautioned me, however, that the "Green Paper" did not set out to question existing policies and programs of various ministries, including that of Abe Williams. Rather, the intent was to see how these policies and programs could be streamlined in the light of the burgeoning population and development challenges facing the New South Africa.

Khayelitsha and New Crossroads seemed like another world as I drove in Tim Phiri's van through Zululand. There wasn't much traffic. From time to time we came across small groupings of kraals, round huts with thatched roofs that are a housing staple in these parts. It was difficult to accept that such beautiful territory could contain an explosive political situation and harbor tensions that were fostered, at least partially, by a deteriorating health, education and economic situation. Tim was taking me to Sundumblu to meet Theodora Thoko Kubheka, principal of the Imbewenhle Junior Primary School.

Bucolic though the scene was, I soon got a glimpse of the encroaching future—a small chemical manufacturing factory whose chimneys were belching soot that was the only intruder in the clear blue sky. Outside the grilled gates, I spotted a group of women sitting in the dirt. Tim told me that they were waiting to see if the factory would hire them for the day, a familiar sight in these parts: There weren't enough jobs in agriculture, and the few factories were inundated with applicants for temporary employment. Sometimes these women—and men, too—waited for hours, only to be informed that there would be no jobs, at least on that day. Tim said he frequently waded into these job lines and spoke to people about health and family planning issues while they waited. "My captive audiences," he said, chuckling.

We got to Theodora Kubheka's school just as pupils were assembling in the courtyard for a homily prior to dismissal for the day. They were all wearing blue and white uniforms—all school children in South Africa are required to wear uniforms—and as the principal spoke to them it was apparent that, in the manner of children everywhere, the students could scarcely wait to go home. When they were dismissed, a collective squeal was let loose and then there was the thunder of a thousand pair of feet racing away. The students were between 6 and 11 years of age, and Theodora told me later that enrollment in the school—for which parents pay a token sum—was increasing at the rate of 10 percent annually.

This increase reflected two things, said Theodora—a short woman who wore a black beret that made her look stern: one, an enhanced campaign by national and local officials to get parents to send their children to school; and two, population growth in recent years that had resulted in more and more children becoming school age.

"But we need more classrooms to accommodate this demand," Theodora said. "We need photo-copying machines, we need typewriters, we need overhead projectors."

And computers?

She smiled, then said: "Soon."

What was really on her mind, Theodora said, was the question of sexual abuse of children. I was startled to hear this. Was it any more of a problem here than elsewhere in the country?

"Yes," Theodora said. "Our children are very much abused. That is because housing conditions are so crowded around here. It is especially common to see fathers raping daughters. We have started a parental education program, but you can imagine how sensitive all of this is."

It is so sensitive a subject that even a seasoned educator like Tim Phiri must tread gingerly when discussing it with parents suspected of child abuse. Theodora told me that some months ago, four children—between the ages of 9 and 12—were raped and strangled in the area, and in each case a father was involved. Murders, of course, are rare, but the prevalence of sexual abuse of children, especially of girls, suggests to Theodora that there is a need to get more social workers to deal with the problem. Where possible, of course, people like Tim Phiri get involved; but Tim has many other constituencies he must deal with, and what Theodora needs in her area are full-time social workers who deal exclusively with the question of parents violating their children.

These days, Tim Phiri involves teachers at Theodora's school in his reproductive health programs. He said that sexuality education courses—with a special emphasis on AIDS—are given by the school's teachers from the first grade onward because "kids start experimenting early around here." Teenage pregnancies are sharply on the rise in KwaZulu-Natal, according to official statistics, and between 30 percent and 40 percent of babies born to blacks in the province are HIV-infected. It may seem a perfectly reasonable thing to get teachers to include AIDS awareness in their curriculum, but such courses were traditionally resisted by bureaucrats during the apartheid era. Even today, with bureaucracies still largely staffed by holdovers from that era, there is some opposition. Why? "Because textbooks now have to be rewritten, and that means spending money on education," Theodora said.

What about reaching kids who aren't at school? Theodora acknowledged that their numbers were growing in the region. Small towns like Gingindlovu were experiencing an alarming increase in street children—youths who either were homeless or who hadn't been enrolled at school and had no jobs either. They frequently turned to crime in order to earn a livelihood. Most any evening you can see some of these kids on Gingindlovu's Main Street, cadging cigarettes or trying to pick fruit from vendors without paying, or occasionally roughing up a passer-by.

From Theodora's school we went to meet a group of local activists with whom Tim has developed a program of workshops on reproductive health. Tim had invited them to his office, a small room on the second floor of a commercial complex. The office had a plethora of family planning brochures, boxes of condoms and other contraceptives and plenty of posters on AIDS. "This is my replenishment center," Tim said, adding that he came to the office only when he needed more supplies for his workshops. Having an office at all is a luxury for Tim; his earlier assignment as an educator had been in an isolated area near the Mozambique border, where his van served as both a vehicle and an office—and sometimes as a home as well on long overnight trips when no hotels could be found.

Of the four women whom Tim had invited, two were nurses who ran family planning clinics run by the government and two were social workers. In South Africa, all major family planning services are government-operated; during my time in Zululand, and in other rural areas, I also saw mobile clinics—large vans staffed by nurses—that the government sponsors. One of the nurses, Bongiwe Cynthia Khanyige of the Mangete Clinic, said that almost 100 women visit her facility each day. In addition to her clinic work, Sister Khanyige also spends part of each day visiting medical cells at factories. She told me that people brought not only their medical problems to her but also their domestic and economic ones.

"The main problem around here is poverty," she said. Echoing the findings of a recent study by the World Health Organization, Sister Khanyige said that virtually everyone she met identified better housing, jobs and water supply as their critical requirements. Because childbearing outside marriage was relatively common in the region, she said, many mothers ask for child care facilities. Sister Khanyige is convinced that because of the high birthrate here—the average woman gives birth to six children during her lifetime—family planning services badly need to be expanded. "We can't talk of development as a means of controlling population growth without providing proper family planning services," she said.

Surrounded by the vast open spaces of KwaZulu-Natal, by its sugar-cane fields and guava and mango orchards, it is difficult for a visitor to fully grasp the implications of rapid population growth. South Africa's population of 42 million is expected to double in 30 years, and this will put severe pressure on both urban and rural authorities to provide better municipal services, more jobs and schools, and improved health care. The population growth rate of 2.3 percent a year has outstripped economic growth for the last five years: The annual economic-growth rate for South Africa between 1988 and 1993 was barely 1.8 percent—the low growth rate was substantially the result of apartheid, which drew international sanctions against South Africa so that the country's exports suffered. Contributing to the sluggish economy was the decline in the manufacturing sector, while South Africa's reliance on mining and base metals rose: Gold accounts for up to 40 percent of annual export revenues; and if you factor in revenues from metal exports, then minerals and metals account for up to 80 percent of export revenues. The jobless rate pushed up beyond 33 percent in 1993, and it has yet to fall. The economy is now said to be improving—in 1994, the economy grew at 2.3 percent, and in 1995 the growth rate may rise beyond 3 percent—but few people expect that the gains will be such that everyday South Africans will reap benefits any time soon.

The Mandela government's new "Green Paper" notes that South Africa's previous apartheid government had set up a "Population Development Program" in 1984 aimed at lowering the population growth rate; the program's proponents argued that population growth needed to be equal to or lower than economic growth in order for people to obtain the best of economic gains. But beyond pushing for the lowering of black numbers, the white minority government failed to fashion any meaningful national development strategy.

This failure has had lasting consequences for urban and rural areas alike, according to the women of KwaZulu-Natal. One consequence certainly has been the slow economic growth here and the widening of poverty and crime. But another consequence, according to these women, has been far less publicized—the fact that South Africa's politicians tend to acknowledge urban problems but rarely the country's rural ones. "Black or white, the government isn't interested in this area," one of the women said to me. "The people in government should come here more often and look at the way we live. If they understood what places here looked like, then maybe there would be change."

The country's politicians tend to acknowledge urban problems but rarely rural problems.

She did not want her name used for fear of repercussions from the local authorities. I told her that this was the "new" South Africa, a democracy, where speaking with journalists wasn't necessarily a crime. Besides, I did not think that she had said anything especially incendiary. But the woman insisted that her name be withheld.

The episode preyed on my mind. Wasn't this "free" South Africa? Could a rural nurse really get into trouble with the authorities for just speaking with a visiting journalist? Some days later, I got a much different perspective. I was having lunch in a Johannesburg suburb with Achmat Dangor, one of South Africa's leading novelists. Dangor told me about how much the society had been freed up from draconian measures since Mandela took office. Dangor recalled the time, a few months earlier, when he was returning to his country from a visit to Germany. As his plane descended toward Johannesburg's Jan Smuts Airport, he instinctively searched his briefcase for any anti-apartheid literature that might incriminate him and possibly fetch him a prison term. "Then I realized that there was no need for my caution," Dangor said. "I realized that I lived in a free society now, where apartheid was no longer the policy and where I could carry any literature I wished. But old habits die hard."

• • •

They call him "Mfundisi We Cisi"—"the priest with an earring"—a sobriquet that Dennis Bailey has earned because of the small gold cross he wears on his left earlobe. He is an Anglican clergyman of British origin and he works with disadvantaged youths—which is to say, he spends his time with black kids in urban Pietermaritzburg and the hilly district of Mzumbe, some 150 miles from Durban. During the 1980s, when the apartheid regime's security forces were committing all sorts of excesses against those protesting human rights abuses, Dennis was especially active in standing up for young men and women. He was therefore always being harassed by the police and under 24-hour surveillance. He has now expanded his focus to promoting AIDS awareness among youth.

'Then I realized that I lived in a free society now.'

I was taken to see him by Mbusi Hadebe, who works in family planning in Durban, and we drove one morning to a community called Nhlangwini in the "highflats" area south of Durban. The last 40 miles were beyond the blacktop highway, and the gravel road, although quite smooth and wide, slowed us down somewhat.

We passed vast plantations of gum trees that sat on the sides of hills, and rich green fields of corn and sugar-cane. Mbusi commutes this distance every morning; his wife is a real estate agent in Durban, where their small children also go to school, and even though his work requires him to spend 12 hours every day in the hills of Mzumbe, Mbusi has opted to continue living in Durban. Along the way, we stopped near a little village because Mbusi spotted Engeline Sibiya, a "abasizi" or community helper. Engeline was making her round of local homes.

This morning Engeline was talking to residents about the importance of family planning. I asked her what her central message to them was. "It is not how many children people should have," she said. "I ask them, 'How many kids can you afford to have?'" Engeline typically puts in eight or nine miles on foot every day because homes in Nhlangwini are quite far apart. The "abasizi" are selected by the local community and paid by the local authorities. NGOs such as the Planned Parenthood Association assist them by supplying contraceptives and family planning literature, and, in fact, one of Mbusi Hadebe's tasks is to ensure that these community helpers do not run out of supplies. Indeed, several miles farther down the road we encountered another community helper, Constance Hadebe—no relation to Mbusi—who asked Mbusi for a box of contraceptives. Mbusi opened the trunk of his car and gave her a box.

Dennis Bailey's office was, quite literally, on the top of the farthest hill that I could see in this magnificent landscape. Mbusi suggested that we stop at some homes along the way. I met with two women who lived in kraals on two contiguous hills. Each of the kraals had a vegetable patch and a courtyard, and each family had two huts—one that served as a kitchen and another as family quarters. The first woman, Maggie Masango, the mother of 12 boys and girls, ruefully told me that she wished she had listened to the family planning messages of people like Mbusi. "Twelve children—too many for one mother to properly take care of," she said in Zulu, which Mbusi translated. Her neighbor, Sylvia Nglolo, said she would probably have had more than her five children but that she was able to space her children after learning about modern contraception from a family planning worker. "Life is difficult enough as it is," Sylvia said. "We have water problems here, and our husbands work in factories in Pietermaritzburg—so we are forced to look after our families by ourselves. Five children is all I can properly handle."

Life is indeed hard for these women on the hills. Electrification is not universal, sanitation is elementary, and it can get very cold in winter. On the way we passed a hill on whose top sat a palatial estate; several Mercedes-Benz cars were parked in the driveway. The property looked incongruous. Mbusi said it belonged to the local Zulu chief. Beyond the chief's estate was a little valley in which workers were tending to a large vegetable garden. Mbusi proudly told me that he was responsible for starting the enterprise, which supplements the ordinarily poor diet of Nhalangwini residents. The vegetables are sold cheaply, Mbusi said, and sometimes even distributed free to the very poor.

A few miles before we were to make another turn toward Dennis Bailey's office, Mbusi asked me if I would like to visit a "creche," a pre-school facility. It turned out to be at the home of a woman named Nokuthula Sosibo, who had converted a small kraal in her compound into a school. As we approached the creche I could hear the voices of children singing. The facility accommodated 22 children, Nokuthula told me, including three of her own. Why did she start the creche? "Because I had the space and because these children needed something like this," was her reply.

Nokuthula persuaded a friend, Khanyisile Sosibo, to become the teacher. Local mothers bring their children to the creche at 8:30 in the morning and the children are picked up at 1:30 PM, after a lunch of eggs, rice and a sweet dish. School instruction is in English and the kids are taught elementary hygiene as well, Khanyisile said.

"My problem often is getting the food for the children," Nokuthula said. "Sometimes I have to use my own money." The provisions are supposed to come from municipal authorities, but their attention to education-related matters is not always high around here.

Dennis, a tall, hirsute man dressed in casual clothes, turned out to be a virtual volcano of opinions. I could barely keep up in my note-taking. It was clear that he cared passionately about South Africa's youth. In Nhlangwini, he said, some 60 percent of the population of almost 80,000 people was under the age of 25. And a recent study showed that 85 percent of this under-25 population was infected with some form of sexually transmitted disease. One reason for this high incidence of STDs was that much of the male population was migrant, often traveling to Durban or Pietermaritzburg for employment. The men frequently brought STDs back home with them. Health care was inadequate because the nearest hospital was 40 miles from here and the local population had access to only two thinly-staffed government health clinics.

> *'Education is the key here, and there isn't enough of that.'*

The dropout rate in schools was equally alarming, Dennis said, as much as 35 percent. The dropouts generally tend to be girls who get pregnant. "You have a massive population of randy young men who are largely unsupervised because their fathers are away in the big cities," Dennis said. "So there's a lot of sexual experimentation. Yet these kids are also ignorant about their own sexuality. Result? High disease rates, high teenage pregnancy rates."

The pressing need was for more funding so that Nhalangwini and other economically underprivileged localities could get more teachers and better educational facilities, Dennis said. And the prospects for this? Very slight.

"But we've got to lobby the people in power," he said. "We've got to convince them that unless they get their act together, the social bomb that they're sitting on will go off. Once apartheid killed us. Now it is disease, AIDS, backwardness. And the effect is the same. It drives people to militancy."

Although Dennis was too modest to tell me himself, I found out that he was also a published novelist. One novel, "Khetho," is about the sexual abuse of children; another, "Thatha," is about the political abuse of children. The fiction is based on his life experience, particularly the hard years of apartheid when he rescued youths who'd been remanded into custody, often for something as innocuous as shouting anti-racist slogans. His novels are primarily intended for teenage audiences, but they are popular among adults as well. His forthcoming literary works will deal, among other things, with the AIDS pandemic. He says he writes as much for his three teenage sons as he does for the countless teenagers in South African schools who desperately needed better education about sex.

I asked Dennis why the people of Nhalangwini were being victimized by the pandemic. "Education is the key here, and there isn't enough of that," Dennis said. "There is even resistance to something as simple as wearing condoms. The resistance stems from the fact that you are, in effect, attacking gender issues, attacking male status. But people have got to understand why they're dying. It's not apartheid now, or being black. It's being negligent in sexual practices."

"In the end, there isn't any South African who isn't grim about the future," Dennis said. "It's going to be uphill all the way, especially for the women. As a relative new citizen of this country, I've thrown in my lot with South Africa. I'm engaged by it. I'm an activist—I've grown tired of the verbosity of people. I know I'm giving myself a hard time, but the only alternative is going back to the amnesia of the West. I've come here to live and contribute, but I've no illusions about what it's going to take."

What Dennis Bailey said about "lobbying" those in power was something that lodged in my mind. One afternoon in Johannesburg, Audrey Elster of the Planned Parenthood Association was discussing the need for more resources for her organization. "We need the resources to have someone in advocacy on our behalf, on a big public media level," Audrey said. "Someone who talks about women, about the need for a pro-choice government policy. We have no experience in lobbying, other than resistance lobbying. And I don't know if you call that lobbying. But resistance politics in this country has been a way of life. And now we need to be engaged in a constructive dialogue with the government. We don't have the resources to do that. And we don't have the skills to do that. The people who have those kinds of skills are probably white academic women. And in this country, in order to give your argument weight, it has to be coming from a black woman. And so every time we're invited on TV, we make sure that the person who goes on TV is a black woman. But there is just a tiny group of black women who are able, who have the skills and the experience to articulate these things—apartheid has seen to that."

• • •

As much as anything articulated by the people I met during my all-too-brief time in this extraordinary country, something that the novelist Achmat Dangor said seemed to capture the ethos of Nelson Mandela's brave new world—the South Africa where the color of one's skin isn't supposed to matter at long, long last.

"Well, we're still together as people, tentatively as a nation," Dangor said. "The country's not in flames and the 'chicken-run' [the trickling out of panicky whites and their capital] has slowed; some say it has even reversed. Above all, we have achieved the moral miracle that the world needed at a time when idealism was floundering as a guiding force and we were resigned to leaving human fate entirely in the hands of the 'market' and market forces. Of course, we've only built about a thousand houses and the crime rate is up. Few new jobs. So what's new? Ask Bill Clinton or John Major, let alone Boris Yeltsin. Everybody presides over failed expectations these days."

INDONESIA: FAITH AND FAMILY PLANNING

ASHALI VARMA
August 1994

MERANGGI, Indonesia—Mothers with small children and some fathers gather together, once a month, at a Posyandu, an assembly held in the village center, where health and family planning services are provided. Five portable tables are set up, some outdoors, some partly shaded, where the infants are weighed and immunized and parents are provided with family planning counseling and nutritional and hygienic advice.

Staffed entirely by volunteers from a family welfare movement called PKK, the Posyandu has been cited as a major factor in the success of rural family planning programs, along with the overall improvement in maternal health and child care. More than one million trained volunteers are scattered throughout 66,744 villages on Indonesia's 6,000 inhabited islands.

Today 95 percent of all Indonesian women know about modern contraceptive methods and more than half of the eligible couples are using family planning. Since the early 1970s, Indonesia's fertility rate has declined by 46 percent.

Wardani, a 23-year-old woman who is a PKK volunteer in Meranggi, told The Earth Times, "I took on this responsibility because I would like to participate in the development of my community and motivate other families to improve their lives. Here mothers learn how to take care of their babies and are taught about nutrition, health and immunization. They are also given information on family planning."

Wardani has a three-year-old child and says she is waiting to send him to school before planning her second child. She works with her husband making bricks.

Unpaid volunteers such as Wardani come from all walks of life and are the backbone of the family planning movement started by President Soeharto more than two decades ago. Even then it was felt that without the participation of people, especially at the grassroots level, family planning programs would not succeed. An all-out campaign was developed to engage the cooperation of the media, religious leaders, heads of communities and the people.

"The most challenging task," said Dr. Haryono, Minister of State for Population and the architect of Indonesia's family planning movement, "was to change the people's mentality that family planning was not a medical problem. We overcame this step by step, by showing the community that the local leaders, village heads, religious persons could speak with authority on family planning. And this became the accepted norm, which helped to spread information and awareness and educated the villagers."

Another important goal of the movement was to promote the role of women. "In communities we made them leaders," Dr. Haryono said. "We focused on mothers, who are often the weakest links and the most vulnerable since they bear the greatest burdens. Apart from establishing a health infrastructure, we also started income generating schemes for them."

In the city of Yogyakarta, in Central Java, leaders from the local communities, successful entrepreneurs and officials from the Family Planning Program (BKKBN) gathered to celebrate the third anniversary of the region's effort to promote income-generating activities. Festive stalls were set up by women's clubs selling cooked food, fresh vegetables, sauces, handicrafts and leather goods. Each group had been given low-interest loans to encourage young wives to start small businesses, so villagers could have successful employment and income-generating activities in their own areas and not have to migrate to already overcrowded cities to work. One woman persuaded the Minister to buy some food and then hitched up her sleeve to proudly display a Norplant implant, saying, "I have one child and am now busy earning an income." Later Dr. Haryono told The Earth Times that 20 years ago women in Indonesia would not even look directly at a man and today they had no reservations about discussing their choice of contraception with the Minister.

At this event, individuals and corporations made donations in cash and kind. A decree by President Soeharto makes it mandatory for all public sector companies to lend between 1 and 5 percent of their profits to community development. Some institutions will donate 1,000 sheep and 300 cows to low-income families. To make them financially independent, farmers are allowed to keep two-thirds of the profits, with the remaining one-third given back to a social foundation to help others in need.

Equally important to the success of Indonesia's family planning program is the access and free availability of counseling and contraceptives to families both in rural and urban centers. The Radensaleh Clinic in Jakarta specializes in reproductive health services and is affiliated with the General Hospital. Dr. Suryono, who works in the clinic, told The Earth Times, "We cater to about 60,000 clients a year and offer IUDs, pills, injectibles, Norplant and even sterilizations. People with problems who cannot be served by rural clinics are referred to us. We also train doctors, midwives and paramedics and medical personnel from foreign countries."

The clinic has a collaboration with the Johns Hopkins Institute and the World Health Organization. More then 5,000 midwives from rural areas have been trained in counseling and family planning care. Treatment is free for those who cannot afford to pay.

At the Jakarta Islamic Hospital, Dr. Lathifahsati, a woman doctor specializing in general medicine, spoke about the change in attitudes toward family planning. "Now women feel that family planning is a basic need," she said. "They want to plan their families and have time to pursue careers and give their children the best of education. The fact that couples come on their own and want to pay for contraception shows that they really want these services."

The most challenging task is to change people's view that family planning is just a medical problem.

According to Indonesian government rules, all hospitals must offer basic family planning facilities. At the St. Carolus Catholic Hospital in Jakarta, which is the largest of 53 Catholic hospitals in Indonesia, Sister Christophora said the hospital offered family planning consultations, counseling and contraceptives. "We tell mothers to return here 40 days after delivery and at that time we inform them of the family planning options that we offer," she said.

The Mother and Child Clinic at the hospital provides pills, implants, injectibles and condoms as well as information on the so-called natural method. "The natural method is not easy for uneducated women," she said. "And all women indicate a preference for more reliable forms of contraception."

Dr. Endang, who works in the Mother and Child Clinic, said that more than 200 women who have never used contraceptives before request the hospital's services every month. "We give these women general information on our program and counsel them on how to have smaller and healthier families," he said. He added that this hospital "is one of the motivating hospitals where we train midwives to care for women in rural areas, especially in the areas of family planning, health and education."

In an interview with The Earth Times, Ginanjar Kartasasmita,

Indonesia's Minister for Planning and Development, said: "Population is a very important element of our development plan. In fact, all development plans should be based on population projections—and the most important objective of the plan is to create jobs. It is also important to decentralize the government and try to develop plans away from urban areas and to empower regional governmental institutions."

According to Sister Christophora, some women seek religious counseling to help them in making family planning decisions. "Sometimes the midwife will call the religious leaders for a panel discussion," she said, "so the women can ask whether a specific family planning method adheres to the tenets of their beliefs." She noted that priests in the Catholic Church offered motivational and educational assistance in addition to pre-marriage counseling, in which they explain the benefits of regulating families and give advice on how to raise a happy family and manage a household.

Although some experts in the population debate contend that population growth rates cannot be reduced until the general economic condition of the people is raised, the Indonesian family planning movement proves that a constructive, cohesive and committed approach to family planning can be very successful, provided that people at the grassroots level are actively involved in the programs and there is a political commitment to improve their lives.

At the Human Rights Conference in Vienna in 1993, the cry that was heard the loudest was, "Women's rights are human rights." The following year, at the International Conference on Population and Development in Cairo, "reproductive rights"—the rights of women to avenues of health, education and physical well-being for themselves and their families—became the central focus.

"Reproductive rights" thus became the battle cry, taking over from controversial phrases such as "population time bomb," which concentrated on numbers of children born and clearly was failing as a rallying cry for many parts of the world.

Today, as The Earth Times's reporters and columnists consistently point out, economic and political "empowerment" of women is increasingly seen as an important part of the picture whenever a nation's general well-being is measured. Progress on gender issues—women's rights, health, family and well-being, job status and political place in society, among others—is seen increasingly as a necessary attribute of any positive development program. And yet few governments have fully lived up to their pledges to dedicate more resources for the education and employment of women, especially in the least developed countries.

SECTION 3

GENDER ISSUES AND HUMAN RIGHTS

POPULATION AND HUMAN RIGHTS

NAFIS SADIK, M.D.
October 1993

Reproductive freedom through family planning as a basic human right has been recognized by the international community for more than 25 years. In 1968 the International Conference on Human Rights stated that "parents" have a "basic human right to determine freely and responsibly the number and spacing of their children." This language was modified in 1974 at the World Population Conference in Bucharest to read "individuals and couples."

Reproductive freedom has been affirmed in a number of subsequent international documents. Among them are the 1979 Convention on the Elimination of All Forms of Discrimination Against Women, the 1984 International Conference on Population and the 1985 World Conference to Review and Appraise the Achievements of the United Nations Decade for Women. The United Nations Population Fund (UNFPA) is dedicated to making the right to family planning a reality for individuals worldwide. This includes providing support for the provision of family planning information and quality services. It also involves promoting social change in order to empower women and to enhance and secure their status in society, independent of the roles they play as mothers.

In addition to responding to women's concerns in its programming, UNFPA takes an active advocacy role, calling attention to the disparity of opportunities between women and men at all stages of their lives and the need to redress this imbalance. If women are to realize their full potential in their productive and community roles, they must be guaranteed reproductive rights and must be able to manage their reproductive role. This means that they must have access to reliable information, to quality family planning services, and to the health care services necessary for the prevention and treatment of debilitating infections.

The ability to decide freely and in an informed manner the number and spacing of one's children is the first step in enabling women to exercise other choices. When a woman realizes that she can make decisions regarding reproductive functions, this autonomy empowers other aspects of her life. It enables her to pursue diverse opportunities and make pivotal decisions.

However, experience and research alike have shown the heavy toll that discrimination takes on women and girls. A widespread denial of education limits women's access to employment, social services and decision-making positions. For each woman, this constricts her ability to exercise her human rights and makes her dependent on others for her basic human needs. For society, it means leaving undeveloped 50 percent of its human resources.

Education for women is essential. It is one of the strongest factors influencing the use of family planning. In all societies, the more highly educated the woman, the smaller her family. Education makes women stronger and more confident in dealing with the world. An educated woman can make her own decisions, among them whether she wishes to become pregnant or not. An educated woman asks questions, among them where she can find reproductive health and family planning services. It has been found that, even among countries with similar per capita income and similar investments in the social sector, those that have closed the gender gap between men and women in education have better indicators of social welfare, including more use of modern family planning, better birth spacing and smaller families.

Reproductive choice is a human right of critical importance to women, because the ability to carry out their multiple roles in the family, the workplace and the community hinges on good health care, nutrition and reproductive well-being. The denial of reproductive self-determination and neglect of reproductive health are an affront to human dignity and individual as well as communal well-being.

Each year 500,000 women die from complications related to pregnancy and childbirth. Ninety-nine percent of these women live in developing countries, where the lifetime risk of maternal death is 50 to 100 times greater than in developed countries. Many of the women who survive suffer serious and often permanent impairment as the result of complications incurred during pregnancy and childbirth. Access to contraceptive education and services, combined with wider access to education and quality health care, enables women to exercise both their right to reproductive choice and their right to health.

I believe there must be an increase in political support for effective measures to secure women's reproductive rights and reproductive freedom. Central to all other elements is the ability of women to have full control over their fertility, which requires that family planning information and services are provided with utmost respect for voluntarism and attention to high quality care. Reproductive choice enables women to pursue a wider range of opportunities and to increase their participation in public life. Family planning is therefore an essential means of enhancing women's autonomy. It also has a bearing on the prevention of sexually transmitted diseases, the consequences of unwanted pregnancy, infertility, sexual health, child survival and safe motherhood. Population policies must seek to guarantee for women the human rights to equality, health and reproductive choice.

The pressing need is to improve the situation of women through education, training, skill development and economic activities. The fund is also a sponsor of the Safe Motherhood Initiative, which focuses on the needs of women, particularly girls and adolescents, and on the provision of quality maternal and child health care and family planning services. In order to increase the knowledge base on women, our agency recognizes the importance of working closely with the United Nations Statistical Office in disseminating data on women and development.

The experience of UNFPA during the past three decades has convincingly demonstrated the importance of addressing the moral and ethical dimension of population and development issues. It has illustrated the need to focus on reproductive rights as a basic human right and on the need to implement development policies and programs that are equitable and appropriate and that acknowledge the centrality of women to the development process. Population policies and programs need to be continually responsive to national and local circumstances—so that the basic human right to development is promoted and extended to all.

CHINA: A NEW PHOENIX ARISES

SOON-YOUNG YOON
September 1998

BEIJING—In the inner courts of the Forbidden City, a carving of the mythical phoenix decorates the outer wall of the empress's palace like a talisman warding off evil spirits. The phoenix was the court's favorite symbol of the empresses' power. According to legend, the phoenix was destroyed in a fiery death but arose again out of the ashes of its own destruction. No wonder empresses held the phoenix dear. They probably thought that heavenly portents had guaranteed them immortal powers. That was the traditional Chinese symbolism. But I think a modern variation is equally telling.

Like the mythical bird, Chinese women have had their historical moments, wielding power and then vanishing from sight. Yet in each era their political spirit was reborn, usually with a different identity. Today, Chinese women are transforming themselves again—striving to gain political power that is based on democracy, not imperial rule. That makes all the difference.

This decade is a propitious time for a new Chinese phoenix to rise. Ideological "certainties" are being reexamined and serious cracks have developed in the plan for socialism's paradise on Earth. In China, as in many other one-time Communist strongholds, things didn't turn out quite as expected. Today, isolationism, big government and central planning are unpopular artifacts, vying with internationalism, private enterprise and free markets.

In that atmosphere of transition, Chinese women needed only an opportunity to become the center of national attention. The Fourth World Conference on Women in 1995 provided that chance. As the political folklore goes, the country's bid for the Olympics crumbled just when political liberals were seeking to showcase the "new" modern China on an international stage. Whether or not women's rights were foremost in the minds of political leaders was not the point. They probably weren't. The United Nations women's conference was the only major event on an otherwise empty international calendar. Thus the tides were turned. The country's leaders shifted their attention from Ping Pong and wrestling to women's rights.

The positive impact of the Beijing women's conference on Chinese women is indisputable. According to scholars at Beijing University, the most immediate result of the conference was a 1990s great leap forward in women's political participation. As one women's studies doctoral dissertation attests, more Chinese women than ever are running in local elections—and winning.

Wu Qing, a distinguished professor of American studies at the International University and a recently elected representative to the People's Congress, is a leading evangelist for the cause. Touting a grassroots political philosophy, she travels around the country, speaking to community and women's groups.

Her main message is that women must take advantage of their constitutional rights. She urges her listeners to exercise their rights by voting and holding their local representatives accountable. Wu believes that the future of women's political power lies in mobilizing their political consciousness and encouraging more independent-minded women to run for office. That kind of conviction is hard to beat.

Wu Qing speaks from her own experience as a successful independent candidate for the prestigious People's Congress. In her spare time she opened her university office to her constituency to stay in touch with their concerns. "They tell me about everything—family problems, illnesses—and I listen," she explained. Her views may stray from the party line, but she says that everything she espouses is legal. Some people who know her well ask, "What statute are you quoting these days?" Her favorite saying is that the representatives to the People's Congress must be at the service of the people. Leadership, in her philosophy is about power sharing, not power grabbing.

The women's conference also marked a turning point for the largest women's nongovernmental organization in the world—the All China Women's Federation. Strictly speaking it is not a political institution, but that depends on your definition of "political." I have always been intrigued by its enigmatic role in a society where public criticism of government policies was, until recently, near taboo. While officially upholding the existing order, its function is to provide a social critique on behalf of women. Founded in 1949, it is a mass organization whose purpose is to "represent and uphold women's rights and interests and promote equality between men and women." As a resource for mass mobilization, it is as powerful as they get. An umbrella, quasi-governmental organization, it is affiliated with virtually every officially recognized women's group in the country, including university groups, trade unions and professional associations. Since most Chinese women belong to some form of association, the majority of Chinese adult women are affiliated with the federation. In all, its membership covers almost one million grass-roots committees.

The conference provided a big boost in status to the federation and gave new life to its long administrative arm. Paralleling official administrative units with councils from the village up to the provincial and national levels, the federation's reach is remarkable. As such, it works either as a mechanism of social control or as an extraordinary organization for political reform. I suspect it is capable of doing both at the same time.

Access to stable financial resources has strengthened its political clout. The ACWF has considerable government and international donor backing to provide services that Chinese women need. The federation has launched popular anti-poverty and literacy campaigns that plan to reach millions of women. Its departments include human resources development, publicity and education, children's work and international liaison. A publishing house, several magazines and the China Women's Daily are also affiliated. These social services, combined with strong media outreach, guarantee that the federation is a major player in the country's struggle for social and economic reform.

While the progress since the women's conference has been significant, the new environment has produced new challenges as well. As Liu Yazhi, the Vice Minister of Labor and Social Security, explained, the most urgent problem is massive layoffs, particularly in female-intensive industries like textiles. Government enterprises that formerly thrived are currently being dismantled as part of the privatization and restructuring of the economy. Just as in the West, many Chinese women workers have been released into the labor market and replaced by temporary and part-time workers who do not have full social benefits.

International experts say that the resolution of the economic problems of Chinese women will depend largely on external factors—Asian financial stability, expanded world trade and economic growth. No doubt this is true, but the experts are perhaps underestimating the importance of the quiet social revolution taking place within China. If Chinese women follow their current course of action, they can seize the moment and translate their growing political clout into new economic strength. Compared with the rest of the world's women, they have a good head start. Few countries can measure up to the civil and economic rights Chinese women have had on the books since the 1960s. Public policies defend women's basic economic rights as human rights, and principles such as equal pay for equal work are well supported. Even with the demise of large state enterprises, many social support systems such as low-cost health care and day care centers remain intact. The organization is waging a national campaign to lighten women's work at home by promoting the equal sharing of household duties by men and women. All this could give Chinese women a competitive edge in the international business and labor market, but they have to assert their rights with greater confidence.

The Beijing women's conference didn't turn China upside down by itself, but it clearly contributed to the country's political renaissance. Above all, it helped to encourage many Chinese women to see themselves as leaders in the forefront of China's modernization. Striving to be assertive and demanding "self-respect," young women in particular are making progress toward personal power. They are challenging traditional authoritarian models of centralized power and heavy-handed rule.

For the new leaders of the Chinese women's movement, the imperial manner of authoritarian leadership is part of the old order. The feminization of politics in China has taken on a new purpose of women's equal participation and leadership in a democratic society.

May the new phoenix grow fast and strong before it is too late.

MONGOLIA: 'WOMEN STILL HAVE A LONG WAY TO GO'

KYU-YOUNG LEE
November 1997

ARVAIKHEER, Mongolia—Sambaa was quickly but skillfully blow-drying the hair of one of her clients. With every pass of the dryer, sparkling dust swirled in the light which shone through a single window into the small room. Her client's face, reflected in the mirror, seemed eager, awaiting the end result. Behind her were seated young boys, middle-aged women and school-girls patiently waiting for their turn. "Sometimes," Sambaa said, "it's hard to keep up."

Sambaa is one of 80 women in this aimag (province) center who have received an interest-free loan from the local government under one of Mongolia's poverty alleviation programs. The modest loans, which range from about $30 to $200, are coordinated by the Women's Federation, a nongovern-mental organization (NGO) with branches in all of the aimag centers in Mongolia. The federation was instrumental in getting women's development programs like microcredit made part of the national poverty alleviation pro-grams. It also acts like a bank, issuing and collecting payments while monitor-ing the progress of the local women.

Sambaa was given 25,000 tugriks, or about $33, which she is expected to pay back in three months' time. After paying back her first loan Sambaa will be eligible to receive a second one of closer to $200.

On her table sat a hairspray can, oils, curlers, scissors, pins and a number of brushes and combs. "I bought all this with that money," she said, "many of my clients, they are satisfied with my work and they just keep on coming back." Sambaa speaks in soft tones but does her work confidently as her fin-gers move deftly over her client's head, despite the distractions of the ques-tions. She exudes the feeling of inclusion and participation in her community, perhaps the most important result of microcredit.

The federation helped set her business up on the first floor of the main government building, which holds the offices of all the local officials and administrators of the center—including a few of Sambaa's clients.

Outside the salon, in a room down the hall, is one of the offices of the federation. Inside, women were learning how to balance the books from the businesses they had started with the loans received.

E. Myagmarsuren, a recipient of a loan herself, sat at a desk drawing empty charts for the other borrowers to fill in. Working with her husband and six children, she designs and weaves carpets at home. "Before when we were making carpets," she said, "we made only enough money to feed ourselves. With the loan we bought more yarn and tools from Ulaanbaatar so that we could make more carpets and more money. Soon we were able to save."

Beside her stood her six children, who range in age from 16 to 26 and gleam with pride at their mother for what she has been able to do. "None of my children had a job," she continued, "but I taught them how to weave, and now we have our own family business." The average carpet that her family makes costs about 12,000 tugriks (about $16), a fairly large amount for the average household. "Often we accept other forms of payment," she said, "like perhaps some meat for one carpet, or even a whole sheep."

The main headquarters of the federation, located in Ulaanbaatar, was established in 1921. Back then, however, it was under the auspices of the Communist Party and was meant to unite the different women's organizations under party control. It was only in 1990 that the organization became an NGO, said Gerelsuren, director of the federation. She added that the group had done a lot since then.

The federation comprises 45 different women's organizations, among them teacher and other professional, religious and local groups. Gerelsuren said that the group had a number of other roles including conducting skills training courses, teaching reproductive health and policy advocacy for women's rights in the parliament.

But, like most organizations in Mongolia, the federation has not been immune to the problems of the transition economy. Once fully subsidized by the government, it now has to explore new possibilities for generating income for itself as well as for women in Mongolia.

Among its other activities the federation holds classes teaching skills such as sewing and typing. The average class costs 10,000 tugriks ($13) for two months; at a private institution the same classes can cost almost double.

"Based on Mongolian tradition," said Gerelsuren, "men can live on their own power. But women can survive only if educated." In the countryside, she said, women are more likely than men to go to school because men usually end up working at home.

"The women in Mongolia are doing well status-wise," Gerelsuren said. And, indeed, the country has the statistics to prove it. The literacy rate for adult women in Mongolia is around 96 percent, close to that for men. In medical schools 95 percent of the students are women. They also constitute 70 percent of the lawyers, 80 percent of medical doctors and 64 percent of the workforce in education. "But when it comes to wages, politics and domestic issues, women still have a long way to go," said Gerelsuren. Out of a total of 76 seats in Mongolia's Parliament, women account for only seven. The rate of women's employment has fallen steadily over the past 10 years, mostly as a result of the transition. The federation has been seeking to reverse this trend.

Gerelsuren is practical when listing all the activities her group is involved in, reflecting on the amount of patience needed to see progress come about. She said that assistance provided by the federation is not always in the form of money. From 1993 to 1996, she said, the United Nations Population Fund (UNFPA) gave the federation $170,000 to help promote income-generating projects. That money was used mainly to supply women interested in running their own businesses with technical assistance and supplies, she said. Myagmatseren of UNFPA said that the assistance ranged from giving the women animals to teaching them how to bake bread.

Of the 2,500 women who took part in the project, all attended seminars on family planning and 1,500 of them eventually received credit. "It was a very good project," said Gerelsuren, "because it reached so many women on the sum [local community] level and enhanced reproductive health activities in those remote places." She also said that 90 percent of the primary loans had been paid back in monetary form and that second loans consisted of either money, machinery or more animals.

Domestic violence has also been a concern for the federation in recent years. Gerelsuren said there is no formal law dealing with spousal abuse. Previously, in fact, she said, "It wasn't even an issue. I feel that it should be treated just like any other crime in a court of law."

Resistance to such thinking, however, does not always come on the political front but rather is born from the minds of the people. She said this is where the most change is needed—change in tradition.

ONE DAY, ONE SIDE OF HONG KONG

HELEN ABBY BECKER
October 1995

Hovering on the edge of the vast Asian continent, like a bright peripheral star, Hong Kong's glass and steel towers cast a thousand shadows as they point upward into the hot noonday sun. Anyone who doubts that "the Asian Century" is coming hasn't been here yet. From the waters of Fragrant Harbor and Repulse Bay to the top of Victoria Peak, a first-time visitor sees narrow streets filled with people, shops, taxis and buses. Huge apartment houses vie with the commercial buildings for standing room to provide living space for six million residents in the 3,861 square miles (10,091 square kilometers) of Hong Kong, Kowloon and the New Territories. One senses the money, the power, the energy while still in the final approach of the descending airplane.

In early September 1995, when we were there on our way home from the Women's Conference in Beijing, the national holiday of the "Mid-Autumn Festival" was in full swing. The streets and restaurants and shops and squares were crowded with families enjoying thousands of lanterns and fire dragons and the music of clanging gongs. In the parks, everyone ate mooncake pastries filled with lotus seeds—pastries served only at this time of year. The festival, although now a family occasion, was primarily a women's celebration in ancient China, one of the concierges at the splendid Mandarin Hotel told me, reflecting the essential female character of the moon.

"But this is only one side of Hong Kong. Have you ever been here on Saturdays and seen the Filipino girls?"

Saturday night. No relief from the intense heat. Statue Square and a small area nearby, become a pedestrian mall on weekends for families and tourists, eliminating the ceaseless traffic and creating a safe area for strolling.

Filipino housemaids, many of them college graduates, brought in by employment agencies to meet the great demand for domestic workers in the prosperous city, flock to the square by the thousands on their one day off a week.

"Each girl earns about HK$4000 [about $520] month," the concierge told me. "No Hong Kong woman would work for that. But for the Filipinos it is much more than they can earn at home, even as nurses with graduate degrees. They work very hard, very long hours. They probably put up with a lot of abuse, they send much of their money home, and they return home after a few years. If they are really lucky they marry Hong Kong boys. Of course, with the new government, who knows what will happen to them?"

Some of the young women sat and talked in small groups, some danced in the well-lit little park near the square, others strolled arm-in-arm in the humid Hong Kong night air. The voices of thousands of Filipino women became a giant sound, brushing against the buildings like the wings of 10,000 birds fluttering against a huge glass cage.

COLOMBIA: SPEAKING UP, SPEAKING OUT

ERIN TROWBRIDGE
March 1998

BOGOTA, Colombia—From her hospital bed in the Materno-Infantil Clinic in the impoverished southern section of this city, Juanita rolled over slowly and closed her eyes for a second. After three abortions, four births and one miscarriage, this 42-year-old (who did not want her real name used) was recovering from the birth of her son four days prior. She had barely survived, said her doctor. High-blood pressure, a disease responsible for many complicated pregnancies in this clinic, had almost killed her and her baby. She had only just learned that another pregnancy would mean her death—no two ways about it, her doctor said.

She asked to remain anonymous because she was afraid of what her husband would say if he knew she shouldn't have more children. She would tell him, she said, but until she did she really couldn't discuss her medical options or talk on the record. Her husband hadn't been in to visit her yet, nor was she sure about when he was coming. "He's a construction worker," she said. "They're very busy."

The hallways of the three-story Materno-Infantil Clinic, housed in a hundred-year-old colonial-style building, are filled with women and girls in various stages of pregnancy. Adolescent mothers-to-be shuffle meekly through the long corridors wearing sheer nightgowns, seeming unaware of their sexuality despite their protruding bellies. Women addicted to drugs toss and turn, sleepless in their beds, waiting to hear how their newborns are doing.

An entire section of the hospital is dedicated to women like Juanita, who are suffering from high blood pressure and traumatic birth, lying very still in unlit, pale yellow rooms. The city's most renowned service provider for pregnancy difficulties, the clinic is noticeably devoid of men. "Of course they're allowed to come," said Dr. Pio Ivan Gomez Sanchez, director of the clinic. "Most just feel that pregnancy is exclusively a women's issue."

This is a Roman Catholic country where, although half-naked women adorn almost every advertisement, condoms are still considered a bit scandalous and abortions are illegal. Though promiscuity and adultery are discussed as facts of life, the influence of the Catholic Church still reigns supreme in matters of politics and morality. Organizations working on the status and health of women in Colombia face obstacles; graffiti and stone-throwing are common assaults on their buildings. Iron gates surround both large and small offices and hospitals like Materno-Infantil have strict security to check everyone coming or going. It is not a simple task to carry the message, but it is one carried out with staunch determination.

Groups that work for reproductive health rights and services in this country have a multifaceted function. Organizations like Profamilia, the United Nations Population Fund (UNFPA) and La Liga Colombiana de Lucha Contra el SIDA (the Colombian League for the Fight Against AIDS) are not only providers. They hold classes and have outreach programs to inform women of their legal rights, help them find counseling for abuse, and teach adolescents about pregnancy and sexually transmitted diseases, including AIDS. Abuse and violence, they say, are not just matters of hitting. Neglect and misinformation about sex education is a critical front on which these organizations battle.

"The major part of our work here is in lowering the maternal mortality rate," said Mercedes Borrero, Auxiliary Representative of UNFPA. "But what any kind of work in women's human rights leads to here is the confrontation of a social condition that utterly and wholly debilitates women."

It is difficult, say the directors and social workers of these organizations, to tabulate exactly how many women suffer abuse in Colombia. It is not clear what qualifies as "abuse" in a nation where violence is so common, but there is every reason to believe that abuse is under-reported. Women who see a doctor for a black eye will say it resulted from an "accident," not an "incident."

"The fact that there are abuses to women's human rights is really a matter of common sense," said Borrero. "Colombia is the most violent country in the world, and people here have unfortunately grown accustomed to fear. Women, in particular, are affected because not only is violence and abuse prevalent, it is also historically directed at them by default. When men feel they've been wronged in society, they take it out at home. For this reason we've widened the scope of family planning information to include women's rights reproductively, legally and socially."

Programs throughout this capital have become the pilot projects incorporating these ideas. Profamilia sends social workers and consultants out to social security buildings to teach classes on birth control both for prevention of pregnancy and protection against AIDS and sexually transmitted diseases (STDs). Claudia Hernandez, who has worked with the organization for 14 years, wears the signature Profamilia uniform, a beige and olive green skirt and jacket, and in front of a projector and chalkboard explained to a steadily growing classroom audience the realities of condoms and the benefits of Norplant, a contraceptive implant.

Hernandez explained that human rights don't exist unless they are accessible. She asked the 34 people in the room if they understand how to petition a lower court for their right to education and then asked if they understand that full access to family planning methods is part of their rights. When the topic of responsibility arose and one of the women in the classroom asserted that it is, indeed, a woman's responsibility to use protection, Hernandez retorted, "Does a woman get pregnant alone?" After the laughter died down she launched into the importance of including men in the dialogue of contraception.

She discussed the myths of contraception and ways in which sexually transmitted diseases (STDs), including AIDS, can be acquired. The men present shifted a bit uncomfortably as the women admitted that the main reason they don't use condoms is that men say it makes sex less pleasurable. Hernandez asked whether unwanted pregnancy or an STD is any more pleasurable.

"That class was 28 women and four men," she said, leaving the building. "I feel one of my biggest responsibilities now is to bring the men—most of whom just came with their wives, not of their own volition—into our conversations and encourage the women to carry on the dialogue with the men who aren't there and encourage them to come next time. Men need to realize that this is an issue that involves them too."

Colombia's Ministry of Health recently launched a media campaign directed at both men and women, adolescents and adults, to promote the use of condoms. Pilar Arrazola, director of the campaign, said that while many of the ads and posters were seen as controversial, she is convinced they will eventually change the lackadaisical attitude many people have toward contraceptives, specifically condoms.

"In our research for the campaign we found two startling realities," said Arrazola. "One reason girls between the age of 10 and 14 go to the hospital is for a problem relating to pregnancy, a botched abortion, complications, etc. The other thing was that if an adolescent boy gets an STD, he doesn't go to the doctor. He goes to the pharmacy and gets a temporary medicine that doesn't work. We found that people in general just aren't using condoms.

They think that condoms are only a means of preventing pregnancy. Our research also demonstrated that most people don't realize that AIDS is an STD; they think it is a disease you get like cancer or something. People also think that if they put the condom on at the last minute they'll be fine, and more than 30 percent of teenage girls think that the pill will protect them against STDs/AIDS. This is the reality we have to contend with."

The public-information advertisements aggressively target teenagers. Arrazola says that they are still forming their habits and can learn from these ads, while people in their twenties and thirties aren't going to change their patterns of behavior. Using bright colors, slang, young faces and sexy posters, the commercials address the isolation many teens face, the possibility of adolescent pregnancy and the pain of STDs/AIDS.

Many organizations working to promote condom use in Colombia have similar campaigns and have found similar results in their research. The lesson, they say, is a frightening one that demands immediate attention.

"Here in Colombia birth control and contraception are a means of establishing equality and protecting people from STDs/AIDS," said Borrero. "There is a lot of promiscuity here, and unfortunately about 97 percent of the women who are HIV-positive or have AIDS got it from their husbands, many of whom have already died and left their wives not only with the illness and the stigma, but to take care of the children and the household."

La Liga, a group that originated as advocates for AIDS patients and gay men's rights, has set up workshops in poor neighborhoods outside Bogota to educate people about the importance of condoms and to use the information they gather to further their research into common social practices.

In the small town of El Carmen, nearly 20 women turned up to meet with social workers from La Liga. Some of the women were young mothers and toted their children along to play while they talked. Others, in their fifties, sat quietly while the younger women dominated the conversations. The workshops normally incorporate play-acting as a way to open women up to discuss their problems at home or the fears they may not want to air publicly. One social worker, herself a young mother who is HIV positive, said she can see an enormous change in attitude since La Liga first came into the area. Women are realizing that HIV/AIDS is a disease that affects everyone, not just prostitutes and gay men. They realize, she said, that maybe their husbands say they don't have sexual relationships with other women, but the reality may very well be different.

"Before I attended these workshops," said Hilma Garzon, 48, a participant, "I really believed that the AIDS campaign was just a means of trying to prevent prostitution. I thought that was the only way you get it. This workshop has met only six times and already our horizons have expanded so much that we will continue to gather even after La Liga has finished its work. For us, it is a way to vent our feelings, and some of the younger women here have taken condoms back to their husbands and said, 'I trust you and I love you, but we are going to use these just in case.'"

The younger women are more open, more willing to discuss their sex lives and tell how they convinced their husbands to use condoms. The older women respond more to the discussions of violence, asserting that there need to be outlets for abused women and also for children who grow up seeing their mothers getting hit. One woman said that her sons learned to strike and her daughters to accept it from their husbands because she never stood up to her husband. As she spoke, her tone was grave and hushed, and the chatter, laughter and teasing that bounced around the room moments earlier was silenced.

Carolina Garcia, a consultant with La Liga, said that although the women in workshops vary in age and class, they share many of the same assumptions. Almost 70 percent, she said, are economically dependent on someone else and have a hard time understanding that they have certain unalienable rights. The workshops address the concept of machismo, the realities of promiscuity, violence and the importance of education about STDs/AIDS.

"The classes and discussions show that attitudes are changing and women are learning that they have rights that must be met," said Borrero. "The clinics and hospitals, though, still show that the situation is dire. Women are dying of toxemia and complicated pregnancies. Teenage girls are showing up at the point of giving birth, never having seen a doctor. I remember almost 20 years ago my maid went into premature labor. When she arrived at the maternity hospital the nurses called her a prostitute, they left dirty blankets and bloody sheets laying around. Now Materno-Infantil is one of the best reproductive health clinics in the world and there are doctors whose entire careers are centered on creating a better environment for Colombian women. There are signs that the changes are beginning to take hold and, frankly, we're a nation of strong, determined women. Once we get a sense of what is rightfully ours, nobody will ever be able to take it away again."

.

PAKISTAN: GIRLS AS A RESOURCE FOR DEVELOPMENT

ERIN TROWBRIDGE
May 1999

HOPER, Pakistan—Anywhere one drives in the northern region of Pakistan, more often than not women and girls duck inside or cast their eyes downward in the presence of strangers. On the streets it is considered deeply offensive for visitors to take pictures of anyone without permission, but especially of women. Even if permission is requested, more often than not the request is denied.

"It's a custom in this area, one that is made up of a predominantly conservative Islamic society, that it is considered inappropriate for a woman to be seen by men other than her immediate relatives," said Safiullah Baig, a program officer with the Aga Khan Development Program. "But reaching women has to be an integral part of development work," he said. "Improving their status, health services and education is critical if the aim is to truly improve the standards of living here."

Although in some towns in the northern area, primarily those along the highway, girls have had access to schooling and professional training for years, in many places the concept is entirely new.

Outside stone schoolhouses, young boys wearing burgundy sweaters and navy trousers sit in neat lines, their school books balanced on their thin legs. The girls, though, if they are in school at all, are in small, windowless rooms, packed in tightly. If a stranger approaches the boys they shout out greetings and proudly recite from their readers. Girls look down, avoiding eye contact, and busy themselves with the folds and pleats of their dresses. A question directed to their class elicits little more than a mumbled response.

Despite the girls' timidity, though, the teachers in their schools say that they want to be there. "There is still a bit of chaos in the thinking, but slowly people are realizing that in order to see progress, things have to change, especially with regard to women," said Mussarat, a teacher in the village of

Zhayan. "Fathers are starting to understand that their daughters should learn to read and write," she said, "and that if they do, they will be more of an asset to the family. My own father, 10 years ago, had to be persuaded to allow me to attend school, but now he's proud and talks to other fathers here to encourage them to do the same. So far, since the school started, only three girls have dropped out this year and that was because they could not afford the fee," which is less than three dollars a year.

But as more and more girls go to school, the faces of the villages are changing dramatically, and some wonder whether the traditional social structures can sustain the transition. In a region where 90 percent of the people are subsistence farmers, working the land for immediate consumption, women have played a fundamental role in planting and harvesting. Men can be seen hauling the goods from fields to the road or to their homes, but the field work is almost entirely done by women.

"I know there will be dropouts once the young girls grow up a bit and are able to work in the fields," said Sobider Bashir, a former army officer and now a member of the school committee in Hoper. "Right now the girls are young and they're missed in terms of watching the other children while they are in school. But in the coming years our community is going to have to adapt to their absence in the fields. Men are going to have to share in the labor and prepare for their daughters to maybe even leave home and attend college."

The degree to which communities support girls' going to school varies. In areas of Chitral, where there is a strong Taliban influence that has been carried down from Afghanistan, even broaching the idea has proved controversial for local educators. Other towns, like Hoper, which resisted the notion for years, have seen the economic and social development of towns nearby and are following their models. One of the first links to success, they say, is education, and in order to catch up, kids must go to school.

On a break from the school day, the children come outside to play and welcome the visitors to their town. Playful, they smile and then hide behind their parents' skirts. Their cheeks are rosy from windburn and their eyes rimmed with charcoal powder. Although all the children, boys and girls, are in school, the boys stand proud before their schoolhouse, talking with adults, while the girls squat on a nearby wall and run away when asked a question.

BANGLADESH: THE YOUNGEST WORKERS

PERNILLE TRANBERG
August 1998

DHAKA, Bangladesh—There she is. A young girl sewing clothes in the middle of a big group of hardworking women cramped together in a factory in downtown Dhaka. The two inspectors from the International Labor Organization (ILO) assume she is a child worker and take her to the manager's office to interview her.

The girl is called Aleya, but she doesn't know her age because most poor people in Bangladesh don't have birth certificates. Therefore, the two inspectors check out her hands and put her arm around her head to see if it reaches the other ear. They ask her if she remembers the terrible flood in 1988, if she has sisters and brothers in school and what classes they are in. Putting the answers together they decide that she is 13, too young to be working. The factory owner is told to keep the girl in the job until the inspectors return with papers giving her access to a school financed by the ILO and United Nations Children's Fund (Unicef).

Then the inspection team moves on to visit the next factory, the fourth visit out of seven it was to make that day. They quickly find the factory owner, get access to the factory floor and check out every corner, look under every table, behind every door and in all big boxes. Very few children have had time to disappear because the visits are unannounced.

The ILO program in Dhaka, called the International Program on the Elimination of Child Labor (IPEC), is the first of its kind in the world. All too often, the issue of child labor is a neglected area of the worldwide human rights campaign. Three times a week over a period of three years, a team of two ILO inspectors, a representative from the government's labor department and a representative from the employer's association, Bangladesh Garment Manufacturers and Export Association (BGMEA), have visited the 2,100 exporting garment factories in Bangladesh.

"Child labor has almost disappeared in this industry," said Rijk van Haarlem, chief of the program and an expert on work environment from

Holland. "We find child labor in less than five percent of the factories today. When we started in 1995 we found children in 43 percent of the factories."

Though there are still a lot of children working in the industry, and millions of them in other sectors, the IPEC program shows that it matters when consumers in rich countries demand better working conditions in the developing world. The program is such a success that it has already been established in Pakistan and will soon be copied in Brazil, Tanzania, the Philippines, India and Indonesia.

It all began in 1994 when the US Senate approved the so-called Harkin Law, which forbids the importation of goods made by children. At that time, however, the Americans did not think of the consequences of just forbidding something without giving the children an alternative. "Within a day, the garment factories in Bangladesh fired 50,000 child workers," said Haarlem. "It could have been 20,000 or 100,000—nobody knows. But a lot of children ended up in other working conditions, often more dangerous, such as in the machine or auto industry or as prostitutes. Their parents could not afford to send them to school," said Haarlem.

> *'Within a day, the garment factories in Bangladesh fired 50,000 child workers.'*

Some of the children contacted Unicef, the ILO and the American Embassy to inform them about the new situation. Later that year the government of Bangladesh, BGMEA and the ILO signed a historic agreement to send the children in the exporting garment sector to school.

Since 1995 more than 10,000 children have been sent to school. Today 4,300 children are in 252 Unicef schools. Every child gets a stipend of 300 taka ($8) a month, which is supposed to compensate a little for the wages they used to earn in the factories.

"This has happened only because of pressure from the buyers in Europe and America," said Haarlem. "Without that, nothing would have happened. Earlier the government totally denied there were child laborers. But the garment sector brings this country $3 billion a year, so they listen to the buyers."

One of the biggest hurdles faced by the IPEC program was the need to make the government and BGMEA realize that there was a problem. "Before, we thought it was better for the children to work for us than not to work, because the families need money," said Tipu Munshi, Vice President of BGMEA. "But now when they can go to school, of course, it is best. And by listening to the American consumers we hope we get more orders from the US."

Others believe it is ridiculous to remove the children from the factories because many of them just go to work elsewhere. That is the belief of the manager of the factory where the ILO inspectors found Aleya.

"We are going to lack workers in the future because when we give the children an education, they don't want to work for such a low wage as they get now, and then we can't sell our products," said Mamunul Huq, who exports shirts to the European market. "And it will be more difficult to train the workers because they are easier to train when they are very young."

Though the ILO finds only between 90 and 170 child workers each month in the export garment sector—out of a total labor force of 1.4 million in the sector—the child labor problem is far from solved.

IPEC has put only 10,000 children on the school bench. According to the ILO there are at least 6.3 million children working in Bangladesh, and that is a conservative estimate. Nine out of 10 work in the informal sector collecting garbage, crushing stones, selling stuff on the street, working as prostitutes or in agriculture. But although such work is far more dangerous than in the clothing factories, there is no pressure or money from the rich countries to get those children off the job and into school.

MONITORING HUMAN RIGHTS

MORRIS B. ABRAM
May 1999

GENEVA—When we speak about improving the lives of people everywhere, in rich and poor nations alike, it's not enough to just speak of increasing the level of employment, building hospitals or improving schools. In order for populations to enjoy any of the economic fruits of development, they must have access to political and civil rights as well.

Human rights are difficult enough without worrying about the main international body charged with their protection. But political gamesmanship, structural problems and misguided priorities continue to plague the United Nations Commission on Human Rights, which meets every year in Geneva.

The Commission's mandate to discuss "civil liberties, the status of women, freedom of information, the protection of minorities, the prevention of discrimination on the basis of race, sex, language or religion" has not been adequately upheld at recent Commission sessions.

In years past, the Commission contributed significantly to the recognition of human rights as a legal concept and as practical protection against horrible abuse. It produced the seminal Universal Declaration of Human Rights in 1948. It drafted the International Covenant on Civil and Political Rights and the International Covenant on Economic, Social and Cultural Rights in 1966. In the last two decades it has forged a Special Procedure System that, among other things, appoints experts to investigate and report on alleged human rights violations around the world.

This year the candor and passion of UN Secretary General Kofi Annan's remarks distinguished him from most other speakers. "No government has the right to hide behind national sovereignty in order to violate the human rights or fundamental freedoms of its peoples," Annan said in reference to the genocide in Kosovo. He was honest and direct even though he risked agitating some significant state powers.

These words of the Secretary General contrast with the political and rhetorical speeches that flourish at Commission meetings. Some addresses by

Commission members are ludicrous in light of their governments' actions and accomplish little more than to mock the Commission's noble aims:

A representative of the Chinese delegation asserted that the Chinese people enjoy "the freedoms of speech, publication, assembly and association" and that "people's courts…at all levels exercise their power independently, free from interference by any administrative organs."

The Sudan said it "is a multi-racial, multi-cultural, multi-religious and multi-ethnic society" that "has managed to 'coalesces' [sic] this diversity and to build a dynamic interacting community"; and that the "right to equality, freedom of movement, freedom of creed and worship are guaranteed." This from a country whose "government security forces were responsible for forced labor, slavery and forced conscription of children" in 1998, according to the US Department of State.

Ministers from nations around the world come with their press corps, take advantage of the photo opportunities and pay due obeisance to human rights principles. But they rarely take a stand against the human rights abuses of countries with which they have close relations. And they overlook some of the most horrible state practices and discriminations—female genital mutilations in some parts of Africa and Asia, or restrictions on women in some Arab countries, to name just a few.

The increase in the Commission to 53 members, up from the original 15 in 1946, has altered the Commission's dynamic and led to ever-greater politicization and confrontation. With more than a hundred observer government delegations, it has grown into a miniature General Assembly with all its attendant faults.

Moreover, qualification for membership depends almost solely on geography rather than on a demonstrated dedication to human rights. The result is a roster of members, each elected for three-year terms, with questionable human rights records.

Are present Commission members like China, the Sudan, Cuba, the Democratic Republic of Congo, Indonesia and Niger really interested in upholding human rights around the world when they suppress them within their own borders?

When I served as the US representative to the Commission in the 1960s, it was a 21-member body generally wedded to the primacy of civil and political rights, which are, in my opinion, the "rights of man."

Today the 53 member states represented on the Commission tend to link these rights with the popular but amorphous right to development. This coupling is a convenient way for some countries to obscure their records on fundamental rights like free speech, free press, freedom of assembly and the rights to life, liberty and property.

Moreover, proponents of the right to development have taken advantage of its vague interpretations to demand the cancellation of debts owed to international institutions and lenders. The poverty in some parts of the world tugs on the conscience. But, in countries without the rule of law and which lack transparency and accountability, debt relief has encouraged corruption and poor monetary policy.

Some further contend that civil and political rights can be realized only after development. The examples of North Korea and East Germany show that this is the wrong approach. These countries guaranteed their citizens material minimums at the price of the surrender of their civil and political liberties. Both languished, and today the people of North Korea are starving. Material progress as well as freedom has been forfeited.

Lack of development is not an excuse for restricting human rights. The Foreign Minister of Germany, Joshka Fischer, stated it best: "We believe that granting democratic rights, not suppressing them, is the only viable basis for sustainable development."

Minister Fischer's frank words and the Secretary General's speech show that the Commission could be the UN's preeminent human rights forum. But for that to happen, countries must cease their political posturing, strengthen conditions for state membership in the Commission and address the world's most pressing human rights concerns.

THE HORROR
OF LANDMINES

ASHALI VARMA
August 1997

World War II, 1941, North Africa. A young Lieutenant from the Corps of Indian Engineers is given the task of clearing a track through 55 miles of mine fields. Speed is of the essence for the troops to advance. For 96 hours non-stop the officer and his men carry out the perilous task. His carrier is blown up twice and his driver loses his life. With both eardrums damaged he moves on with his men clearing 15 mine fields of thousands of mines. His commanding officer calls it "the longest feat of sheer cold courage." He was later awarded Britian's Victoria Cross for his bravery, the first Indian to receive the honor.

The Olympic Games, Atlanta, 1996. Maria Mutola from Mozambique, winner of the Bronze medal for the women's 800 meter finals makes a moving appeal for the ban of landmines. In her country, which is trying to recover from a devastating 16-year civil war, the work of reconstruction and of families trying to get back to work is hampered by the silent, menacing presence of landmines which kill and maim women working in the fields, children going to school or playing in areas that were once mined. She says that in many African countries, athletes do not have the luxury of training cross country. Every time an athlete runs there is the real fear of stepping on a mine and being blown up.

Over 50 years have passed since World War II but the war machinery continues to churn out antipersonnel landmines. Mary Wareham, Coordinator of the US Campaign to Ban Landmines, said, "Landmines have killed more people than chemical, nuclear and biological weapons. Every 22 minutes somewhere in the world, a child, a man or a woman becomes the victim of an antipersonnel landmine. And the numbers are increasing. There are 250,000 landmine disabled living in the world today."

There are over 100 million hidden landmines in 68 countries. They cost as little as $3 to $30 to produce but cost from $300 to $1000 to remove. To remove even 50 million mines at the lowest rate of $300 would cost about $15 billion and take several years. Countless lives would be lost and many more would have to live with disabilities. The even more shocking reality is that for each mine cleared an estimated 20 new ones are laid.

Historically, the US has been one of the world's most influential exponents of landmine warfare doctrine as well as one of the world's major landmine producers and exporters. From 1969 through 1992, the US exported 4.4 million antipersonnel mines. Military records show landmines caused 33 percent of all US casualties in Vietnam and 28 percent of US deaths were attributed to landmines. Even more startling is the fact that military records from the Vietnam war report that 90 percent of all mine and booby trap components used by the National Liberation Front against US troops were of US origin.

> *Development isn't simply a matter of economics. Concerns for human security must figure in policy formulation.*

According to a report titled "Exposing the Source" released by Human Rights Watch in April 1997, there are 47 US companies that have been involved in the production of antipersonnel mines. The best known are General Electric (GE), Alliant Techsystems, Lockheed Martin and Raytheon. The one that is a household name in the US is GE which says "we bring good things to life."

When Human Rights Watch in a letter to Jack Welch, GE's Chief Executive Officer, requested that the company issue a statement regarding any past or present involvement in the manufacture of antipersonnel landmines or their component parts, GE responded, "Based on a review of GE's business, we know of no active GE contracts or any direct sales of GE products or materials in which we are involved with manufacturers of antipersonnel mines, mine components or mine delivery systems...The reported presence of our materials at a particular company cannot be construed as evidence of a current direct relationship with GE."

However, GE's involvement in the landmines business first came to Human Rights Watch's attention when GE showed up on a 1994 Pentagon list of suppliers of landmines and mine components. The Department of Defense confirmed GE's past production activities in a February 10, 1997 letter stating that GE was a supplier of "integrated circuit components for self-destructing landmines," and that GE is still considered by the Department of Defense (DoD) to be one of the several "potential sources of supply" for landmine components.

Further research by Human Rights Watch showed that GE had had business ties with the Italian ex-landmine producer Tecnovar Italiana. In a letter to Human Rights Watch, Technovar stated that GE's Dutch and US subsidiaries supplied Lexan plastic powder and synthetic rubber components to Technovar to manufacture 1.6 million antipersonnel mines and 1.2 million antitank mines from 1979 to 1993.

Managing Director, V. A. Fontana of Technovar also wrote to Human Rights Watch to say, "Regarding our raw material producers we can confirm that our main suppliers were General Electric Plastics (GEP) for plastic components using the Lexan polycarbonate produced in the GEP factory in the Netherlands; General Electric Plastics US. All suppliers were aware of our production."

When contacted by The Earth Times, Bruce Bunch, GE's spokesman said,"When Human Rights Watch first called us in 1994, we told them we had no involvement in land mine production then." "We have no involvement in landmine production today or plans for future involvement," he added. He also went on to say that the report cites Tecnovar as an ex-landmine producer but not GE as an ex-supplier.

'We believe that we have an obligation and a unique opportunity to proactively support the elimination of antipersonnel mines.'

Stephen Goose, Program Director of the Arms Project of Human Rights Watch, told The Earth Times, "What we have asked of GE is to openly acknowledge that they were a past supplier of landmine components and to definitively renounce future production of landmine components. As far as I am aware they have not committed to this."

Typical in the arms trade is that the eventual destination of arms is often not the first country that bought it. Egypt bought 1.4 million antipersonnel mines from Tecnovar from 1979 to 1993. Some of them, the exact numbers unknown, found their way elsewhere.

In 1996, some of the mines exported to Egypt were among weapons captured from rebel Hutu militia groups.

One of the most promising outcomes of the report by Human Rights Watch was that 17 US companies have said they will no longer be involved in antipersonnel mine production. Leading among the companies was Motorola. In July 1996, Motorola pledged to "do everything reasonably possible to make sure that Motorola does not knowingly sell any part that is intended for use in an antipersonnel mine...[W]e believe that we have an obligation and a unique opportunity to proactively support the elimination of antipersonnel mines."

According to the Human Rights Watch report, Alliant Techsystems Inc. "is the company that appears to have profited the most from landmine production contracts. Alliant was awarded DoD antipersonnel and antitank landmine production contracts worth $336 million in 1985-95; its Wisconsin subsidiary Accudyne Corp. was awarded similar contracts worth $150 million in 1985-95."

In response to Human Rights Watch's appeal to cease production, CEO Richard Schwartz replied in a letter dated August 22, 1996: "The International Campaign to Ban Landmines has served an invaluable role in shedding light on a terrible problem that must be addressed," but he insisted his company's landmines were not to blame. "It is irresponsible to imply that companies such as Alliant Techsystems have contributed to the world's landmine problems. To do so wrongly maligns responsible US citizens and diverts resources that could be applied toward stigmatizing the governments that violate international law."

'US companies should contribute to the solution not to the problem.'

The report states: "Thirty companies rejected Human Rights Watch's humanitarian appeal to forgo any further production of antipersonnel mine components—17 companies directly, in writing, and thirteen through silence."

"US companies should acknowledge the humanitarian crises created by antipersonnel mines and make the moral decision to get out of the business now," said Andrew Cooper, Human Rights Watch Arms project researcher and author of the report. "The international community is moving rapidly toward a complete ban on this weapon, and US companies should contribute to the solution, not to the problem."

NGOs feel that for a ban on land mines to be truly effective governments have to sign on to an International Treaty that will be negotiated in Ottawa in December 1997. The treaty calls for "an effective legally binding international agreement to ban the use, stockpiling, production and transfer of antipersonnel mines."

Nongovernmental organizations around the world, including the International Red Cross, have been instrumental in an advocacy campaign to convince governments to sign the Ottawa treaty.

The US Campaign to Ban Landmines (USCBL) is a coalition of 225 nongovernmental organizations across the country and is a part of the International Campaign to Ban Landmines (ICBL), an organization which was nominated for the 1997 Nobel Peace Prize.

Leading up to the Ottawa process was the Brussels Conference, in June 1997. It was attended by more than 150 governments, 138 NGOs from forty countries, including landmine survivors and mine clearance experts.

"We have been calling for a ban since 1992," Wareham said, "and we were called Utopian. Now ninety-seven countries have pledged to sign the Ban Treaty in Ottowa this December. The group includes all of Latin America, most of Africa, all of Europe with the exception of Finland, Greece and Turkey. Asian countries include Malaysia. Eastern European countries have agreed as well."

The US Administration, however, has not yet made a commitment to sign. According to US NGOs at the Brussels Conference, US delegates "tested the waters to see how many holes could be shot in the treaty in order to accommodate US policy."

"We are particularly concerned that US delegates, through bilateral consultations, are pressing for an explicit exception for new use of all mines in Korea and the continued use of smart mines indefinitely anywhere in the world," said Stephen Goose of Human Rights Watch and Chair of the Steering Committee of the US Campaign to Ban Landmines.

This action is at odds with a White House that has previously pledged its commitment otherwise. On May 16, 1996, President Bill Clinton said, "Today I am launching an international effort to ban antipersonnel land mines...The United States will lead a global effort to eliminate these terrible weapons and to stop the enormous loss of human life."

'Antipersonnel mines are not essential. Thus, banning them would not undermine military effectiveness.'

According to the USCBL, the Administration is bowing to pressure from the Pentagon. This, despite a strong and growing support for the ban from Senators and Congressman and retired generals. In an open letter to President Clinton in The New York Times, April 2, 1996, 15 retired generals including former US Korean commander Lieutenant General James F. Hollingsworth, General H. Norman Schwarzkopf, and General David Jones wrote, "Given the wide range of weaponry available to military forces today antipersonnel mines are not essential. Thus, banning them would not undermine the military effectiveness or safety of our forces, nor those of other nations."

In June 1997, some 57 senators led by Patrick Leahy, Democrat of Vermont, and Chuck Hagel, Republican of Nebraska, introduced a bill that would ban future American use of antipersonnel land mines. A bipartisan group of 160 House members has also urged the Administration to back the Ottawa process.

The Administration favors negotiating a ban through the United Nations Conference on Disarmament in Geneva but this decision was criticized by the US Campaign to Ban Landmines "as an effort to avoid rapid progress toward a ban, given the notoriously slow pace of the Conference on Disarmament."

Another concern of the Clinton Administration is that countries like China, India, Pakistan and Russia are not participating in the Ottawa process, but participants of the process say that if 97 countries can produce a good treaty in Canada this year, there would be additional pressure on the countries that are not a part of it.

On June 12, 1997 at a news conference on the Leahy-Hagel Landmine Bill, Senator Patrick Leahy said, "Landmines have some marginal military value. So, for that matter, do chemical weapons. But the damage done by these hidden killers long after the guns fall silent and the armies have gone home far outweigh whatever small benefits they add to our enormous and unsurpassed military arsenal."

The victims are not only innocent civilians. Many of them are American soldiers.

He pointed out that "The victims are not only innocent civilians. There were more than 64,000 American casualties from landmines in Vietnam. If that is not appalling enough, the overwhelming majority of those mines contained US components. They were made here, and they killed and maimed our soldiers half-way around the world."

Leahy made it clear that although the purpose of the legislation was to exert US leadership, it is no different and, in fact, does not go as far as what others have already done, including Great Britain, Canada, Germany and South Africa. These countries "have unilaterally renounced their production, use and export of these weapons, and are destroying their stockpiles," he said.

Meanwhile, the American NGOs continued to put the pressure on. On July 21, Human Rights Watch and the Vietnam Veterans of America Foundation released a joint report called, "In Its Own Words: The US Army and Antipersonnel Mines in the Korean and Vietnam Wars."

"The report is going to undercut the Pentagon argument in favor of using and making antipersonnel landmines. We are doing this by showing that US landmines used in the Korean and Vietnam conflicts had a blowback effect on US troops," said Cooper .

But the question, some countries might well ask, is: "What if the 100 million mines were hidden on American soil, one for every 2.5 citizens, would American companies or the US government even debate the issue?"

Author's Note: In December 1997, the International Campaign to Ban Landmines was awarded the Nobel Peace Prize. In the same month an international conference to ban the use of anti-personnel landmines was held in Ottawa. The Ottawa Convention urges countries to sign and ratify the prohibition of the use, stockpiling, production and transfer of anti-personnel landmines. As of April 1999, 135 countries had signed the Convention and 72 had ratified it. The US is not one of them.

The term "development" has many meanings, most often associated with physical, economic or commercial efforts that lift, in one way or another, a community's economic status. "Human development," on the other hand, deals with the individual person—the capacity to better fulfill the individual's potential for a better existence. The means for this are seen in down-to-earth concerns ranging from education and health services to access to electricity, proper toilets and freedom from official corruption. But what really constitutes a better existence? Here a consensus breaks down. For some it's MTV on television, Big Macs at the village bus stop and the hope for a Disneyworld tourist center down the road. For others a fulfilling life is simply the enjoyment of the best parts of the indigenous traditional ways, free from the wrenching influences of "globalization," "ecotourism" and the inequities of world trade, which have put whole populations out of sync with the hurtling speed of international development.

SECTION 4

PROMOTING HUMAN DEVELOPMENT

EGYPT: 'THE CORNERSTONE FOR OUR ECONOMIC REFORM'

JACK FREEMAN
September 1994

ALEXANDRIA, Egypt—Nobody ever had to write a job description for Hosni Mubarak. As President of Egypt, or as President of the recently concluded International Conference on Population and Development (ICPD) in Cairo, he is one man who knows precisely what is expected of him. And it can be summed up in one word: leadership.

In an exclusive one-on-one interview he granted to The Earth Times at the Ras el-Tin Presidential summer palace here, he focused on Egypt's leadership role in the global population effort and his own role in promoting family planning, within Egypt and elsewhere in the world. It was largely because of that role, and its extraordinary effectiveness, that he was honored last month as the United Nations Population Award laureate for 1994.

Leadership, says Mubarak, is Egypt's duty because it is at the center of the Islamic world and is the largest nation in Africa, the largest nation in the Arab world. That, he says, is why his country feels it must take the lead in South-South cooperation, in the Middle East peace process, and in population matters as well.

"I took action on population as soon as I became President," he told The Earth Times, "but I realized the need for family planning in Egypt long before that."

He said that efforts to develop Egypt, to make economic reforms, create jobs and increase food production had been failing because the progress they brought was overwhelmed by sheer numbers of people added to the population each year. Between 1950 and 1976, the country's population doubled.

"Before I took office," Mubarak said, "infrastructure here in Egypt was below zero. No water, sewage treatment had deteriorated, there was not enough energy, enough electricity." In the past 10 years, though, according to government figures, Egypt has invested roughly $35 billion dollars in improving its infrastructure.

If you drive between Cairo and Alexandria, the evidence of that effort can be seen all along the Desert Road: the irrigated orchards and croplands blooming where there was once only dry sand, the new cities and factories under construction everywhere one looks.

"We have built 13 new cities," said Mubarak, "and we have plans for another 10 or 15, in the desert, built from scratch. If you go to one of these new cities now you'll see 1,000 factories in operation, producing, and you'll feel how many thousands of workers are working there. This," he said, "is the cornerstone for our economic reform."

Such development has also impacted on Egypt's population problem, adding to the effectiveness of the country's family planning program. Now, after 13 years as President, Mubarak can tell how his national population program has made dramatic progress, dropping the annual population growth rate from 3.1 percent to 2.2 percent. The effect has been astonishing, since each 1/10th of 1 percent in the rate represents almost 200,000 babies.

"And now we are working to reduce the rate even more," Mubarak said, "by convincing the people, by getting them to understand that big families reduce their standard of living. You have to take an approach that the people feel in their daily lives."

It is an approach that he has used, successfully, ever since the program began, going on television to talk about family planning and using virtually every speech as a platform to stress its importance to the people of Egypt.

You have to make people understand that having big families reduces their standard of living.

"I explained to them in the most practical way," he said, "how it is going to affect our economy, the standard of living of our future generations, if we didn't work for family planning.

"I gave them one simple example: We have two families, one with four persons, the other with 10 persons; the income is the same, say $100. If you divide the $100 by four, each has $25—for housing, for food, for clothing, for education, for health care—$25. On the other hand, if that $100 is divided by 10, each will have only $10. The living standard of the four will, for sure, be far better than the living standard of the 10. When people analyzed this situation, it changed their minds."

Mubarak points out that Egypt's family program is entirely voluntary, "not forcing anything on the people but educating the people, advising the people, leaving the family planning to each wife and husband."

It was this same philosophy that animated the Egyptian President's words when he told the Conference on its opening day:

"The population problem facing our present world cannot be correctly solved on the basis of handling the demographic dimensions only, but should be dealt with within its close relation to the problems of social, economic and cultural development, which aims at raising the individual's capacities and participation in production and consumption."

He said also that the cornerstone of any successful population policy must include "working on improving women's conditions, especially in the developing countries."

Still, Mubarak told The Earth Times, in order to motivate people to act you must make them aware of the problem—and its global dimensions.

"In this our new era in the world," he said, "we are all part of the globe—Egypt, the United States, Israel, Saudi Arabia—the contact is so close, and the communication now is completely different than ever before. So I think the Cairo Conference has given information to people all over the world to let them understand the reality and the danger that we face without family planning."

Poor countries are barely managing to sustain good standards at current population levels.

"The rate of increase of world population," he went on, "is almost 100 million persons every year. By the year 2025 it will be another three billion. In the world there are now 500 million unemployed. If we add another three billion persons on Earth, how can we find jobs for these people? How can we feed them? It would be a disaster."

And what does Mubarak intend to do about this threat? "We will keep doing what we are doing," he said. "We are increasing the rate of convincing the people—and this conference showed them many points."

Statistics show that among Egyptian women awareness of family planning has risen to 99.6 percent. Since 1980, contraceptive use has more than doubled, from 24 percent to just over 50 percent.

But Mubarak made clear that contraceptive awareness campaigns are just one aspect of the effort that is needed. "We are looking after education now," he said, "giving great attention to education: building schools, improving the standards of our teachers and professors. Also health care. We have a lot of work to do for the people here."

He said he planned to meet personally with the 2,000 young Egyptians who served as conference aides. "We are going to use them to advise the people all over the country about family planning. They represent new leadership."

And he intends to pursue the new channels of South-South cooperation.

"The population in the North is very stable," he said. "No increase in Germany and Italy and these countries. That is why their standard of living is getting very good. But in the South—poor, and the rate of increase in population is very high. I don't know how we are going to live. If we are barely managing to keep good standards for our people now, what is going to happen after 15 or 20 years? I think we will not be able to afford that."

THE 200 MILLIONTH INDONESIAN

HELEN ABBY BECKER
September 1994

JAKARTA—There are eight crystal chandeliers in the reception area of the Indonesian Presidential palace. Two hundred or so gold chairs are arranged, row after row, in readiness for an event that two hundred or so Indonesian public health and family planning people are waiting to fill.

These people, village field workers, local public officials, the press and friends are gathered here to witness President Soeharto sign the first issue of a new stamp commemorating the birth of the 200 millionth Indonesian child. This is indeed something to celebrate. Indonesia has been waging a war on the poverty of its people for the last 20 years, and in that time family planning experts have estimated that if not for education and the huge campaign that the Ministry of Population has waged, an additional 80 million children would have been born. Had they been born, many of them would have died of neglect or starvation. So this 200 millionth child is a triumph to celebrate.

Dr. R. Hasan Mohammad Hoesni is a member of the National Family Planning Coordinating Board, and while we were waiting for the ceremony to begin in the great chandeliered room, he told me family planning tries to teach "that each family have two children, that girls are just as desirable as boys, that the government will help them in their old age, so they don't need so many sons to take care of them. This is further enhanced by a policy of no free education for the third child. It has worked, so the 200 millionth child, not the 300 millionth child, is born this year. All of these people here are Family Planning workers, and all of them have contributed to this program." Dr. Hoesni was educated at Johns Hopkins University in Baltimore and has been a pioneer in family planning. "I am very pleased to be here today," he said.

A whisper ran through the crowd, there was a flurry of activity, and we were all ushered into the large room to hear Haryono Suyono, the State Minister of Population, praise the hard work of all the people present. He is a small, serious man and I had been told that his dedication and creative approach to the cause of family planning had been an incentive to everyone.

Then President Soeharto, looking like a person in an Italian Renaissance portrait with his square Indonesian cap and full-length black coat, spoke briefly, commending everyone present for their hard work in educating the public in family planning, and then he signed the order approving the stamp as the television cameras followed his every word.

Everyone was given a copy of the stamp and a small breakfast was served. While I was balancing a glass of delicately fruited iced water and a plate of exotic cookies, the gentleman who is second in command of the family planning program under Haryono, Pudjo Rahardjo, proudly pointed out that other nations had been coming to Indonesia to learn about its family planning programs, "including the Chinese."

Pudjo also wanted me to know that many diseases had been successfully eliminated in Indonesia. "Smallpox, of course, but also tuberculosis and polio and, yes, malaria—we have no more malaria." Life in his country, he said, had changed drastically in the last 30 years of independence from Dutch rule.

"Indonesia consists of 300 islands which stretch from Malaysia in the west to Papua New Guinea in the east. When we won our freedom it was said of us that as a people we were indolent—not a pejorative, you know, because it was true. If it didn't get done today, there was always tomorrow or next week—that was our attitude. But now as you can see from being in Jakarta, we have changed our work ethic and, as you can see, are as time-conscious as any. And we try to be efficient."

Pudjo discussed the enormous building boom in Jakarta—new hotels and office buildings and apartment high-rises climbing out of the ashes of slums and vacant land. I mentioned seeing elegantly designed new apartment buildings near the airport.

"Oh," said Pudjo, "but they are very expensive. In US dollars, 1,500 a month for two bedrooms. I never could afford that on my salary as a public servant." But he made it clear that he would not trade his accomplishments in family planning for a richer life. "Wherever my family and I live, we are content."

NEPAL: NEW ENERGY IN AGE-OLD VILLAGES

ASHALI VARMA
October 1996

SYANGJA, Nepal—There is a quiet revolution taking place in the mountains of Nepal—changing the pace of life and age-old systems in remote little hamlets where for generations people have existed with the barest of necessities.

This is a country where mountains dictate distance and distance is not measured by miles but by the days it takes to trek to a village. And though to the casual observer the terraced mountains and little hamlets where women still walk miles to cut fodder for livestock might seem untouched by modern times, in the villages men and women are working together, saving money, making vital decisions in an effort to improve their lives.

In Syangja Bazaar, a small town about one and a half hour drive from Pokhara, more than a hundred women gathered in the local district development headquarters. Women who just four years ago would never have dreamt of leaving their villages, much less speak about their trials and triumphs, had come from several villages to be heard. They were all members of Amma Tolis (Mothers Groups).

Prem Kumari Regmi spoke about how she had started the Amma Tolis in villages and how the women had organized themselves and started savings schemes.

"We collected money through cultural programs and in two years we have built 250 resting places along the route that women travel, helped to build two primary school buildings, conducted literacy classes for women, broadened village trails for easy access to villages and helped to maintain springs and wells for water supply," she said.

The labor for all this activity was provided by the women themselves. Regmi said that at first the men were reluctant to cooperate with them but slowly they realized the benefits and have started helping out. The Amma

Tolis have been helped in some of their activities by UN Children's Fund (Unicef), UN Development Programme (UNDP), UN Population Fund (UNFPA) and the local government.

From the savings schemes, women get loans to start income generating activities. Chet Kumari Arya, a shy, pretty young woman of 27, spoke about how the group had helped her. She lives alone with her 7-year-old son. Her husband works in a factory in India. To supplement her income she keeps buffaloes and sells the milk. She got a loan of 1,200 rupees ($21) from the women's group and started ginger farming. She was able to make 3,000 rupees ($54) when she sold the ginger. In addition she was taught how to sew clothes. Although she went to school only until the fifth grade, she has been trained in bookkeeping and is the secretary and bookkeeper for her group.

> *With a stake in their own economic futures, women feel the need to improve their surroundings.*

There is no dearth of ideas for income generation activities, and the women have ventured into painting fabric, weaving, opening tea shops, poultry and farming. With a stake in their own economic futures, they also feel the need to improve their surroundings. Many women spoke about tree planting ventures and how the group meetings had helped raise their awareness of health and sanitation, child care and family planning.

One group is even involved in making smokeless stoves (a recent report states that the smoke from wood burning stoves used by the poor is as carcinogenic as smoking 100 cigarettes a day).

Subadra Arya, a 46-year-old widow with four children, said, "Before we got organized I did not know how to read and write and my only income came from a few livestock. I went to train in vegetable farming in Pokhara and today I am earning twice as much as I used to, growing ginger and vegetables."

None of the women had heard about the big UN Women's Conference in Beijing, but by organizing they had gained collective strength and they didn't think twice about stating their needs. Yam Kumari Arya stood up to say that she felt family planning was biased toward women. "Men should also be partners in this," she said.

The women also said they feel that more of the local government's resources should be channeled to their groups. They told the Chairman of the District Development Committee that they wanted at least half of the funds to be allocated to their projects. They also said they needed more training in accounting and management skills.

Jay Singh Sah, who has been involved with the South Asia Poverty Alleviation Program, comes from the Terai region of Nepal and is UNDP's man on the ground. "We encourage the villagers to get mobilized and to work for both community and individual benefits," he said.

There are three important elements in this drive toward village participation, he added: developing capacity at the grassroots level, providing and generating capital (UNDP gives a one-time seed grant for irrigation or water supply, depending on what the village organization needs), and skill enhancement.

Once organized, the villagers are encouraged to start a savings scheme and to lend money to families for income-generating activities.

Sah said the success of these ventures lay in creating linkages, "In all of our programs we try to have linkages between the local people, NGOs and the government authorities, so that it can be sustained. Our projects are much more people-focused now so we use local people."

Manoj Basnyat, UNDP Unit Chief, is Nepali and is enthusiastic about the new thrust toward the grassroots approach. "Early in 1994 we felt that we should focus on getting women organized. We worked with the Amma Tolis and today they have become such a force that they want to be mainstream as far as resources are concerned," he said.

He feels it's necessary for the Nepalese to be managers of the programs. "We know and understand the culture and traditions of the people we are working with. It is not just a question of money but mobilizing the people and resources from within." He said that the transfer of expertise from international experts to local managers has had an impact on other donors as well, and is yielding results.

JORDAN: WHAT THE CHILDREN NEED

ELIZABETH BRYANT
September 1996

A MMAN, Jordan—After slashing infant mortality rates, boosting literacy and launching specialized services for the handicapped, Jordan's children's activists have hit a snag: success.

The impasse comes as Jordan seeks assistance for a newly established national children's task force aimed at consolidating the agendas of disparate children's groups and eradicating remaining strongholds of poverty, malnutrition, abuse and illiteracy that continue to plague this country's youth.

"Jordan's image is good," said Dorrit Alopaeus-Ståhl, area representative for the United Nations Children's Fund (Unicef), summing up the country's overall development dilemma. Unicef pours about $1 million annually into Jordan's mother-and-child programs and is one of the national child task force's few initial investors. "But because Jordan's image is so good, donors think there's no need in Jordan."

Statistics say otherwise. If basic health care is widely available, it remains underutilized, Unicef reports. Literacy rates are among the best in the Arab world, but failure and dropout rates are also high, particularly among girls. Many Jordanians have six or more children, and only 35 percent of women use any form of birth control.

"We have done extremely well for developing countries—and, in some areas, even relative to the progress made in some of the developed countries," said Jordan's Queen Noor in a recent interview at her office in Al Ma'wa Palace, as she assessed her country's progress on women and children. "But there remains a great deal to be achieved in other areas."

Indeed, experts say, there are still too many cases like El Ham Masaud for comfort. After nine pregnancies, seven childbirths and two miscarriages, the 35-year-old Palestinian woman is pregnant again.

"I don't want any more but my husband wants more," Masaud told her family doctor, Sahar Ezzat, who visited her home recently in Amman's Prince Hassan refugee camp. Her 6-year-old son, who has a huge, untreated growth spreading from his temple, stood near her, staring at the visiting health care workers. "My husband keeps asking for more boys."

The couple's 14 children are crowded into a dirty three-room house, furnished only with a refrigerator, three small chairs and mats for sleeping. Seven of the children belong to Masaud; the other seven are children from her husband's previous three marriages. Masaud's husband is unemployed, his wife said. Food is purchased with money scraped up from odd jobs and neighborly kindness.

Masaud's uterus is split in two, making an intrauterine device ineffective, Dr. Ezzat said. It also means that each of her pregnancies has been with twins. Ezzat said he doubted Masaud's assurances that she used the pill.

"How can you love your wife if you get her pregnant all the time?" Ezzat asked Masaud's scowling husband, lounging by the door.

"She's still young," was the answer.

"It's *haram* to get pregnant all the time and not have anything to feed the kids," Ezzat said, citing Muslim religious laws against such a deed. "And your wife is sick."

Ezzat heads a recently established community health program at Prince Hassan, a Palestinian refugee camp established in 1965. Armed with funds from Unicef and the Adventist Development and Relief Agency, an international nongovernmental organization, the program aims to boost immunization rates, lower pregnancy rates and teach basic health and hygiene to some 1,000 women in the camp and surrounding areas.

Already the project has achieved some notable successes. More than 90 percent of the children at the camp have been immunized, thanks to a car-toting loudspeaker campaign, inviting kids out for shots. And women, the health workers say, are slowly beginning to listen to them.

But Ezzat wondered how much the project could accomplish during its three-year life span. "I feel this project has much effect on women. The women start talking about secrets and finding solutions," she said, as she climbed up a steep, rutted road to visit Palestinian squatters near the camp. "But three years is nothing. Nothing at all."

Still, Jordan has come a long way in a few short decades, children's experts say. Infant and maternal mortality rates are far lower than those of many other Arab countries, according to Unicef. Jordan's 85 percent literacy rate is one of the region's highest.

Founded last year by Jordan's Queen Noor, the National Task Force for Children aims to tackle a myriad of concerns, from drug abuse and homelessness to basic health care and family planning. The task force is also expected to coordinate the efforts of various children's agencies in Jordan.

Children's rights is one area the task force will address, even as it treads a delicate line between state and family authority.

"We can improve the legal coverage, if you will, of their rights as individuals in the society," Queen Noor said. "But the family is the unit of authority, and not the state. The challenge is to try to achieve a balance between the children's rights as individuals in the society and the family as the guarantor for the authority over its members."

Some legal strides have been made, the Queen said. A two-month-old labor law prohibits employment of children under 16 years and allows working mothers 10 weeks paid maternity leave and a year's unpaid leave. Some children's activists are trying to raise the legal working age to 18.

But, Queen Noor added, "children are very precious in our society and culture. They are basically very well protected by an enduring and cohesive family unit."

Although one arm of the task force—a research and database on children—has received financing, no money has been pledged for next year's operational costs, said Hayat Yashi, the task force's coordinator. But as a primarily volunteer-driven organization, the task force expects its costs to be minimal, officials say.

Despite the high-powered backing of Queen Noor and other royal family members, some experts fear that children's issues may remain a nongovernmental organization cause. Of Jordan's almost 600 preschools, for example, almost all are run by NGOs, according to Unicef.

"The concern is that you have these big NGOs and the distinction between them and the government is being blurred," said one children's expert. "And the children are falling more and more into their agenda." If the NGOs dissolve, he said, the framework supporting children's interests could be lost.

GUATEMALA: HAPPY THE WAR IS OVER

ERIN TROWBRIDGE
October 1997

GUATEMALA CITY—Avilio Isidro Porras Montufar, 31, grimaces and tugs on a layer of Reina Arias' hair, trying to measure it against the layers he has just trimmed. With a tight frown, he trims off another inch and then smiles, telling her she's finished and handing her a mirror to admire his work. He bends down and brushes the hair off his black leather army boots with a quick, almost reflexive gesture. Out of habit, he keeps them polished and shining even though he's been out of the army for months.

Montufar is the only man taking beautician classes at the Feminine Technical Institute, which was set up to provide training for the women who had worked as cooks and laundresses for the military. The institute was founded through donations from the United Nations Development Programme(UNDP) and Fonpaz, Guatemala's Foundation for Peace. Classes in sewing, baking and hairdressing are offered to recently demobilized members of Guatemala's army.

This program is one of many that have sprung up in the year since the Guatemalan government signed a peace agreement with the guerrilla. After 36 years of a civil war that left 150,000 civilians dead, thousands "disappeared," and dozens of mass graves filled with bones of the unknown, the country is making an effort to pull out of decades of living a temporary sort of existence where immediate survival was the primary concern for most of the population.

Montufar, an explosives expert formerly with an elite squadron of the army, decided to learn to cut hair because his own father used to give shaves and trims to earn extra money in his hometown of Marjas Jalapas. Even though his army buddies tease him about his choice, he's proud, he said, to follow in his father's footsteps.

Most of the soldiers he fought with have gone into private security work, he said. With an increasing number of kidnappings being reported this year, Guatemala's wealthiest feel threatened. There is no shortage of jobs in the field of protection, but Montufar says he's had enough of carrying a gun. Cutting hair sounded like a much better future to him.

A scholarship for 900 quetzales ($150) from UNDP is paying for Montufar's schooling. When he left the army, after 11 years of service, he was supposed to receive a payment of 5,000 quetzales ($833), but he never got it. The army was taken apart so quickly, he said, that in many cases soldiers didn't get the money that was coming to them.

Another money problem: Because his salary as a barber is less than half what he used to make as a soldier, he said he will also have to work on a farm outside of Marjas Jalapas to make ends meet.

"I was proud to serve in the army, but I'm happy the war is over," Montufar said in the back of a classroom filled with wigs, mannequins and the smell of nail polish remover.

"The change to civilian life has been hard, but I'm glad the risks are over. It was harder out there in the mountains," he said, pointing through the window to a mountain range just outside the city. "I'm a campesino too, from a small town. The war came from the city and they asked us to kill men who could have been our brothers. I looked more like the men I was fighting than those I was fighting for."

Montufar glanced up quickly, brushed some stray hairs off his white barber's jacket, and smiled. His next client had arrived and, fortunately, this one didn't have so many layers.

COSTA RICA: EVEN SUCCESS CAN HAVE PROBLEMS

JACK FREEMAN
November 1994

S AN JOSE, Costa Rica—By no stretch of the imagination could Costa Rica be described as overcrowded: According to recent figures, it has a population density of only 163 people per square mile (63 per square kilometer). Vast areas of the country are under cultivation, growing coffee, bananas, oranges and many other crops, and some 25 percent of its land has been set aside as wilderness conservation areas.

And yet, population remains a concern. The reason: Although Costa Rica's fertility rate has declined sharply from 7.3 births per women to its present level of 3.1 births, the country's population is still expected to double in less than 40 years. (The best estimates put the population growth rate at 2.4 percent.)

Another factor adding to population concerns is immigration, much of it illegal. Costa Rica's minister for natural resources, Rene Castro, told The Earth Times that hundreds of thousands of illegal immigrants have fled political and economic problems—worsened by a five-year drought that has destroyed subsistence crops—in neighboring Nicaragua and El Salvador. Those immigrants, he said, now constitute 10 percent of Costa Rica's population.

"And," he added, in a jibe at California's latest referendum barring services to illegal aliens, "we don't kick them out of the schools."

Education has long been one of this country's greatest strengths. But ironically it is precisely because of those strengths that some observers are concerned about the future. They worry that the fertility rate seems to have stopped declining, even though Costa Ricans do not fit the profile of a high-fertility country: They enjoy remarkably high standards of health care and education—the literacy rate among women is 93 percent—and are less troubled than their neighbors by widespread poverty.

Another ironic cause for concern is the high level of families using family planning: 75 percent. That's the highest rate in Central America, more than three times the contraception rate in neighboring Guatemala.

Add to that the fact that the government of Costa Rica has been actively addressing its population problems, with the help of the United Nations Population Fund (UNFPA), since 1970—and the country's relatively high fertility rate becomes even more difficult to understand.

Along with their concern about excessive population growth, government planners are also troubled by the trend toward urbanization. Costa Rican cities are expanding at an annual rate of 3.6 percent. And roughly two-thirds of the country's population is crowded into the Central Region (the area surrounding this capital city of San Jose), which occupies only 20 percent of the country's land.

To deal with the overcrowding of its cities, Costa Rica has begun promoting the development of small rural population centers and has decentralized some of its services. It is also encouraging people in rural areas to participate in local government, as a way of inducing them to stay where they are and not pull up stakes and head for the cities.

To promote family planning, the government has tried advertising on radio and television, with special emphasis on reducing the rate of teenage pregnancies.

Costa Rica's government is also trying to address regional differences in social conditions and access to family planning services. With UNFPA's assistance it has embarked on a program of trying to improve the condition of women in the Caribbean coastal province of Limon, bordering Panama, which is one of the country's least developed regions. Reports suggest that among the young women of Limon (age 15 to 24), the rate of contraceptive use is only 5 percent. Their fertility rate is among the highest in the country.

BIG MACS, MARLBOROS AND COLOR-CODED CONTRACEPTIVES

RESHMA PRAKASH
March 1998

HO CHI MINH CITY, Vietnam—This city used to be known as Saigon, the Paris of the East, evoking images of French colonialism, plantations and Catholic missionaries. It was then Saigon of the American occupation and a symbol of a country divided, torn by civil war and beset by a corrupt government. When it "fell" to the Communists at the end of a bloody and protracted war in which more than a million people were killed, it was expected to unleash a ripple wave of unrest as the nations of South East Asia fell like dominoes before the Communist juggernaut. Or so it was thought.

Reborn as Ho Chi Minh City after the war, the metropolis has prospered through more than two decades of Communist rule. Indeed, capitalism is alive and well here, and with the active encouragement of the government.

The signs of change are everywhere in Vietnam. The cities are teeming with small shops. A mere five minutes away from HCM City airport, gleaming new buildings house local branches of Kentucky Fried Chicken, McDonald's and UPS, announcing the arrival of a new American presence. Billboards displaying advertisements for Foster's beer, Marlboro cigarettes, Kodak film and other foreign products tower over the streets. It seems as if everyone on the streets is selling something, from the women sitting on the pavements with fruits spread out before them, to the men pushing carts filled with bottled water. Construction workers are busy building new houses, and the numerous stores were filled with people buying clothes, home appliances, vegetables and other consumer goods. There are motorbikes everywhere. The most popular means of transportation is a motorbike called the Honda Dream II, and prices for motorbikes are dropping as companies like Yamaha and Suzuki challenge Honda for bigger market shares.

Even though Vietnam ranks among the world's poorest countries, with per capita income of only $190 a year, it has made some progress on the social front. On the United Nations Development Programme's Human Development Index—which weighs health, education and social development—it ranks as number 116 out of 173 countries. Today, almost 90 percent of its people are literate.

One of the key areas in which Vietnam has demonstrated its progress toward "developed" status is the lowering of its birthrate. The country has experienced such a rapid decline in fertility that some people are calling it the "reproduction revolution."

The number of children born to the average woman has fallen from six in 1961 to 3.8 in 1989 and 3.1 in 1995. It is projected to decline to 2.5 by 2000. Life expectancy now stands at 65 years, a rise of 20 years since 1960. Infant mortality has fallen from a high of 219 per 1,000 live births in 1960 to 46 per 1,000 in 1994.

The initial emphasis of the government's population and health policy was on family planning. Although family planning activities began in North Vietnam as early as 1963, it wasn't until the country was united under one government in 1975, at the end of the war, that population programs were introduced to the whole country. At first the Ministry of Health, which was responsible for population programs, worked extensively with mass organizations such as the Women's Union, Youth Union and Trade Union, which were allied with and supported by the Communist Party. These organizations, with large memberships and branches all over the country, not only helped carry out an education program for birth control but also helped distribute contraceptives.

Life expectancy has risen dramatically since 1960.

Today, the vast network of government health centers set up at the province, district, commune and village levels provide the backbone of family planning services, though organizations like the Women's Union remain active. The government has a network of "collaborators" or social workers who go from village to village to provide counseling services. The government has also offered financial and other incentives to families using family planning.

"We offered medical support and exemption from certain responsibilities such as participation in public works," said Nguyen Van Giap, Vice Chairman of the People's Council in Tien Giang Province. "This has made it popular in urban areas." But he said that in rural areas, where the Catholic Church is influential, families still have as many as five or six children.

In recent years the government has expanded the focus of its family planning clinics to include a variety of health services. It is working to improve the quality of those services and stressing issues such as sexually transmitted diseases, adolescent sexuality and infertility, a growing problem never acknowledged before.

In general, knowledge about modern contraceptives is remarkably high, with 97 percent having heard of at least one method. Among Vietnamese couples of childbearing age, officials say 63.8 percent were using contraceptives in 1995, the last year for which figures are available. Of these, 36.9 percent preferred IUDs, 4.5 percent used condoms and 2.9 percent used the pill. Almost 80 percent of the contraceptives are supplied by the government through the health network, officials say.

Eight clinic staff members serve a population of 13,000.

Most health care professionals are on the government payroll, which makes it easier to coordinate policy and practice. Maternal and child health is the focus of the primary health care system, said Nguyen Duc Vy, Director of the Institute for the Protection of Mother and Newborn in Hanoi, which works to make health care accessible to women in the countryside.

The government has received much assistance in this area from the United Nations Population Fund (UNFPA), which has been involved in Vietnam since 1978, disbursing a total of $87 million.

The population agency is also involved in shifting emphasis away from contraception per se and toward broader health concerns. In the current budget cycle covering the years 1997-2000, around 70 percent of UNFPA's allocation of $24 million will go to what are called "reproductive health services," while 15 percent goes to advocacy and the rest to population and development strategies.

And UNFPA is helping the government extend programs to currently under-served populations such as ethnic minorities. There are more than 54 ethnic groups in Vietnam, although the Kinh, who live mainly in the cities and on the plains, account for almost 80 percent of the population. The ethnic minorities such as the Nung, Muonh, Hmong, Ede, Giarai and Thai live mainly in remote mountainous areas and highlands.

While the UN Population Fund used to be the only donor for population-related activities for the longest time, others have now entered the field. Sometimes that can lead to replication of programs and related problems. The World Bank is now into the distribution of the pill, for instance, something that the UNFPA has been doing for years. Except the new pill comes in different colors and with English instructions that the women cannot read.

Confused by the new colors they can no longer distinguish between the real pill and the iron supplements, causing unwanted pregnancies according to health workers.

"Certain painful efforts need to be made by the government to better coordinate the assistance given by various donors," said Nguyen Thi Mai Huong, the Population Fund's Assistant Representative in Hanoi.

The government also faces the tough task of improving the quality of services. Doctors and health workers, from the most advanced hospitals in Hanoi to the ramshackle clinics at the communes, speak of being overworked and seeing far too many patients, having to work with outdated equipment, inadequate supplies and infrastructure.

"With a staff of eight we serve a population of 13,000," said a tired-looking doctor in the tiny district hospital of Chau Thanh. Pointing to the broken-down wooden beds, the cracks in the walls and the pharmacy that consisted of a few shelves in an ill-ventilated tiny room, he said very simply, "We need more money."

Much remains to be done. While Vietnam's shift to a market economy has brought it economic growth, it needs even more money to bring its health and other social services up to modern standards. The government frankly admits that even though social expenditures have increased from 24 percent to 28 percent of total government spending, the gap between the demand for services and the supply remains large and critical in many areas.

"We can develop only if we have a stable population and a healthy one," said Dr. Nguyen Nang An, who is not only the director of a hospital in Hanoi but a member of parliament as well. "We are determined to improve our health care system, especially reproductive health for women. But you must remember we are a poor country. We've had some success, but we're still struggling to do better."

CAMBODIA: SCAVENGING FOR SURVIVAL

SATYA SIVARAMAN
September 1998

PHNOM PENH—To understand the tragedy of Cambodia's teeming underclass today, all one needs to do is take a deep look into the eyes of Souk Savath, a Phnom Penh street child. At 16 he looks just 10 because of malnutrition, eats discarded fruit from garbage bins for survival and longs to go to school, but "I need to feed my stomach," he says.

Even by Cambodia's dismal standards Souk's life is tough. It is a life, however, that is fast becoming typical of thousands of poor urban children who often come from a sad past in the rural areas and are now headed for a hopeless future in the city.

Forty percent of Cambodians live on less than $10 per month.

"It is a problem that is increasing," said Leonard De Vos, country representative of the United Nations Children's Fund (Unicef). "A few years ago there were only occasional children on the streets. Now it has become a phenomenon." According to De Vos the growth in the number of street children is a result of lack of care in the family, lack of income in the village and an attraction for the "big lights" of the city.

Government officials say these children are just a symptom of the country's overall economic backwardness, which itself is a product of decades of civil war and turmoil. According to Ngy Chan Pal, Undersecretary in Cambodia's Ministry of Rural Development, Cambodia's number-one priority at the moment is political stability, without which no other problem can be solved. "We need peace first," he said, alluding to the repeated eruptions of violence between the country's different political groupings.

Cambodia's fledgling nongovernmental sector acknowledges the need for peace and political stability but says these children should be a top priority for everybody. "The street children in Phnom Penh work in inhuman conditions and are at the very bottom of the Cambodian social ladder," said Shiva Kumar, adviser to the Community Sanitation and Recycling Organization (CSARO), a nongovernmental group that works with street children. "They should be given special attention."

Cambodia's desperate poverty—all agree—is a major contributing factor to the growing population of street children in Phnom Penh, which is estimated to have risen from 7,000 to 25,000 in the past five years. According to the United Nations Development Programme's Human Development Report, last year almost 40 percent of the Cambodian population lived below the poverty line, which is around $10 per month—making this Southeast Asian nation one of the 20 poorest in the world.

Children between the ages of 5 to 14 make up almost 30 percent of the total population and, although there are no exact data, at least 10 percent of them are believed to work as child laborers in harsh and unhygienic conditions for very little pay. According to estimates by the International Labor Organization (ILO), 60 percent of these working children do not attend school and seek employment only in order to supplement their households' income.

"Children are getting more vulnerable because family planning or child spacing practices are very limited in Cambodia, which means families are very big," said Hanneke Meijers, a gender specialist working with UN Development Programme. "This results in children moving out of households in order to support them financially." She added that in the Cambodian context many children leave their families because of domestic violence.

In Phnom Penh, where almost 71 percent of Cambodia's urban population lives, activities undertaken by street children include begging, cleaning cars, domestic work, scavenging, petty theft and even prostitution. Local groups estimate that there are between 10,000 to 15,000 child sex-workers in the Cambodian capital alone, a majority of them coerced by criminal gangs.

Also degrading is the work of scavenging, which involves large numbers of Cambodian street children. At the municipal rubbish dump at Stung Mean Chey on the outskirts of the Phnom Penh one can see scores of young children rummaging through garbage for cans, glass, plastic and paper—all to be sold for recycling.

"I would rather be a construction worker," said Huan, a 17-year-old who has been picking waste for the past two years. With the 2,000 riels (approximately 50 cents) he earns every day he feeds four younger brothers and sisters. His parents, farmers from the northwestern Cambodian province of Battambang, no longer work, for reasons he does not fully understand.

With the government too preoccupied with "macro issues," the only hope for children like Huan comes from some Cambodian NGOs that have taken up the task of directly targeting their problems. Some, like the Japan International Volunteers Center, work with government-run orphanages to improve their child-care work and cut the number of children on the streets. Others, like the US-based World Vision International, give financial incentives to families to get their children to stop picking waste or begging and go to school instead.

Yet another approach being tried out by CSARO is to organize street children who do waste picking to protect their rights and educate them about health and hygiene to obtain better prices for the waste they collect. Among the usual problems faced by waste pickers in Phnom Penh are injuries and infections while going through garbage, harassment by the police and criminal gangs, and low prices for the waste they sell to middlemen who resell it to recycling factories.

"We have started a center where children and women can drop in to take rest, obtain health services and counseling about obtaining the best prices for their waste," said Heng Yon Kora of CSARO. Based on similar experiments in South Asia, CSARO also plans to form an organization of waste pickers and get neighborhood associations to hire their services on a professional basis.

"For us the real issue is not just poverty but also respect and dignity of the labor that street children do," said Shiva Kumar, pointing out that it is time Cambodian society recognized and rewarded their contribution.

TANZANIA: A ROCKY ROAD OUT OF POVERTY

KYU-YOUNG LEE
February 1998

D AR ES SALAAM, Tanzania—In this, one of the five poorest countries in the world, almost half of the population, approximately 12 million people, live below the official poverty line—getting by on one dollar a day. And though in recent years the country's economy has shown signs of growth, people are skeptical whether that is enough to bring Tanzania out of its impoverished state.

It's not as if Tanzania lacks advantages. Unlike many of its neighbors in the Great Lakes section of Africa, it has suffered none of the ethnic chaos or bitter tribal rivalries that have led to bloodbaths and the displacement of large numbers of refugees—although many of those refugees have sought safety here. Nor has the country been involved in any recent wars. This is a tranquil country where the most serious disputes are over the bargaining for mangoes on a street corner or the bartering of a cow. But the reality is that, despite its political stability and its expanses of rich, arable land, Tanzania has not been able to wake from its slumber.

Buildings become darker as one travels inland from the dusty streets of Dar es Salaam to the countryside. Old burlap bags cover windows of shacks in the poorer areas. And when the rain comes, as it often does, its interminable drumming on the tin-roofed homes can be maddening.

But the land in Tanzania is rich, lush green, filled with banana and mango trees and fields of coffee, tobacco, sisal and many other tropical crops. Yet practically all labor is done by hand because the transportation of farm equipment is all but impossible on the uneven clay roads. In fact, 90 percent of all Tanzanians work in agriculture. And though the land has much to offer, because farming is so labor-intensive and vital infrastructure so lacking, it is more common to see villagers pushing a truck out of the mud than in the fields working.

Tanzanians give much of the credit for the region's stability to Julius K. Nyerere, the country's first President. Daudi Mwakawago, Tanzania's Ambassador to the United Nations, told The Earth Times, "His socialist programs created ethnic stability because he stressed that every tribe from the Masai, East Africa's most visible tribe, to the Bantu peoples, the majority of Tanzanians, learn Swahili to better communicate with each other."

On the other hand, some others charge that the country is languishing because of the decades of socialist programs instituted by Nyerere in 1961 after British colonial rule ended. Enamored of China's Communist system, he created the concept of the Ujaama villages, which were collectives set up by the government but run by the people who lived and worked in them.

But social costs were high, he said, and though political and ethnic stability flourished, the country's economy floundered. He said that poor infrastructure and the misuse of resources were the bane of Tanzania's development, deterring investment in this otherwise safe country. "To encourage foreign investment," Mwakawago said, "you need four things: trained manpower, capital, political stability and land. We only had the latter two." He added that money from Tanzania was flowing into the African liberation movements in Angola, Mozambique, Zimbabwe and South Africa in past decades, further draining the country's capital and leaving less for the needs of the burgeoning population at home.

Another legacy of the post-independence years is high population growth rates, which has adversely affected overall living standards. "During our socialist period we had very high population growth rates," said Ramadhan Swalehe, director of Tanzania's Population and Family Life Education Program, a government office. "The standards of living of the people gradually decreased and are now slightly down from 30 years ago."

That is bad and getting worse. But Tanzania's need for aid has always been great. According to the UN, Tanzania receives more than $1 billion in donor assistance annually, which amounts to about 30 percent of its gross national product. This percentage of aid is comparable to that of Uganda, Burundi and Haiti, which, unlike Tanzania, have had a history of political instability.

It has only been within the past decade or so that Tanzania's economy has risen above the red line, averaging 3.8 percent growth since 1985. The World Bank, however, estimates that even if the growth rate were to accelerate to 8 percent through the year 2000, 10 million Tanzanians would still be living below the poverty line.

The problem boils down to too little money for too many people.

"Population growth affects all areas of the economy and society," said Frederick T. Sumaye, Tanzania's Prime Minister, speaking at a recent awards ceremony organized by the Population Institute, a nongovernmental organization based in Washington. "Rapid population growth puts more strain and pressure on natural resources and other resources needed for sustainable development," he said. "The award given to us today is a reminder to us that we have to increase the momentum we have created in the area of family planning so that while we are putting much of our efforts into stimulating economic growth, these efforts are not thwarted by a population growth which is not manageable."

Today the country's population is growing at a rate of 2.8 percent per year, one of the highest in the world. Sumaye said that there is a clear relationship between his country's population growth rate and economic growth rate—unfortunately, he said, that relationship is inverse.

But things are slowly beginning to change, according to Mwakawago. "Look at our history," he said. "We have been a nation for only 30 years. This is a small period of time in the overall scope of a country's development." Indeed there are signs of progress, both in raising the economic indicators and lowering the country's fertility rate. Where women in the 1970s used to have approximately eight children apiece, they now have closer to six. Still, Mwakawago said, there is a long way to go.

Swalehe said that part of the reason for his country's high fertility rate is simply that women are uneducated. "In the past and even sometimes today," he said, "people believed there was no need to send a girl to school to get an education because once she was married she would end up in another home. It was considered a waste, so families preferred to use their limited resources to educate the boy at the expense of the girl."

"It's still hard to convince the men," said Marietha Hayuma, a worker for UMATI, a nongovernmental organization which promotes family planning in Tanzania. "Men's pride and tribal customs are still strong, but we will teach them." She said that increasing numbers of men were visiting her clinic, which is based in Arusha, a central point for most tourists because it is in the vicinity of popular national parks. She flipped through her brown leather log book, humming a song she said she had learned as a child. "They came in first with their wives," she said, pointing to signatures in the book, "but gradually they have started coming in alone, asking for contraceptives. They aren't so shy any more."

The introduction of concepts such as family planning has been met with resistance. "In every village, every town we have had to use new ideas to improve local economic conditions as an entry point to sell family planning," said Veronica Shao of UMATI.

"Even certain tribes like the Masai do not allow sex education to be taught to their children," said Veronica Shao of UMATI. "So at our youth centers, we have different classes for different tribal groups to respect the customs of each people."

On the periphery of Dar es Salaam, one of UMATI's youth centers is teaching mothers about family planning while struggling to raise enough money to be solvent. Inside the stone, white-washed walls of the complex, a score of children were singing nursery songs. The children wore blue and white checkered cotton shirts, slightly muddy from playing outside, and stood barefoot in single file. Most of them were the children of unwed young mothers, their teacher explained, but the children's shiny faces and bright smiles reflected the care they were receiving at this center.

'Women are ashamed to have abortions at clinics, but not because it is illegal.'

In Tanzania, as a matter of policy, girls who become pregnant are expelled from school. But at this youth center these young women and their children are embraced. The children's uniforms were made next door, where the youth center holds classes teaching the young women skills they will soon need to raise the children on their own. They receive training in tailoring and hotel management while, for a small fee, their children get a basic education at the day care center. Within a few months, though, this youth center will have to close its doors to the young women because its money has almost run out.

"We simply do not know what we can do," said Dr. S. J. Mamoya, a manager at the youth center. Looking around the center at the antique sewing machines, the chipped desks, television, VCR and, most importantly, the children, one could understand what a tremendous loss to the community the closing of this center would represent. Pregnant women would have few options other than to have abortions or raise their children with hardly enough money to feed themselves. Pamphlets and videotapes on sex education and reproductive health would no longer be distributed here.

With the closing of the center, chances are there would be be increasing numbers of unsafe abortions. Although abortion is illegal in Tanzania, the operation is performed regularly, local people say. "Women are ashamed to have abortions at clinics," said Swalehe, of the government's Population and Family Life Education Program, "not because it is illegal but because they are scrutinized by everyone in their village."

"When girls who become pregnant go to a youth center or a clinic," he said, "the status of the girl is first looked at. If she can marry the man and can afford to have the child, she is encouraged to have the baby. Otherwise she is directed to an abortion clinic. We would rather tell them where to get a safe abortion than have them risk their lives."

UMATI, the Family Planning Association of Tanzania, has three youth centers in the country. This one in Dar es Salaam is expected to close by the summer. When asked what might be done to keep it going, managers and counselors responded with blank looks. There was only one answer to their problems: more funds.

Mamoya said that the center reaches almost 5,000 children in the city. Through peer counseling, unwed mothers are taught about child care and sexual and reproductive health. The center's officials say that of the 300 mothers who participated in the classes in 1996, 200 now have jobs in tailoring and hotel management. "It costs around $4,000 a month to run this center," Mamoya said, "but our donors are pulling out." The main donor is the Swedish International Development Aid group, which has been funding the center since the mid 1980s. Its contract with the center ends this summer. Other centers in Tanzania have other funders, including the United Nations Population Fund, the International Planned Parenthood Foundation and other bilateral and multilateral groups. Those centers are still going strong, but the people running them understand that aid cannot keep flowing forever.

ZANZIBAR: RESTORING A CRUMBLING BEAUTY

ERIN TROWBRIDGE
April 1999

ZANZIBAR TOWN—The name alone bespeaks the magic. Zanzibar, even to those who can't quite say precisely where the island is, calls to mind a sense of an afternoon breeze, heavy with the scents of cloves, cardamom and cinnamon, and a harbor criss-crossed with dhow boats, the long, beaten wood hulls cutting through the water with their single canvas sails heavy and billowing in the wind.

This small island off the coast of Tanzania seems an allusion to all things exotic. Soft jasmine and fresh mangoes scent the morning air. The spices, hanging heavy from the rich green plants, come alive in the afternoon, doubly so after a rainstorm. It is the home of Swahili—a language part Bantu, part Arabic, part Hindi—and to this day is considered to be home to the purest form of the language spoken in East Africa.

Once the center of trade in the Indian Ocean, Zanzibar has been home to emperors, princesses, sheiks and prime ministers. The island has been colonized or coveted at one time or another by every nation from Portugal to Oman, by traders from Venice to Shanghai. After the 1963 coup, Zanzibar and Tanganyika, a mainland nation that had also recently gained independence from Britain, joined to form Tanzania. To this day, although the Zanzibari culture maintains a distinct presence, taste, sound and smell, it is a part of Tanzania.

Now, decades after the coup, Zanzibar is a crumbling beauty. The gold and brass hinges on the doors and balconies are tarnished, the turn of the century, limestone architecture fractured and eroding, but still, somehow, the magic lingers.

"Zanzibar has a tremendously rich history as a trade island," said Fatima Alloo, a writer who was born in Zanzibar and recently moved back to the island to help coordinate development and cultural programs. "From the beginning, we've been a merchant economy, an integral part of the Indian Ocean trade and dhow trade route. You can see through our architecture our heritage, how many different cultures, religions and nations have passed through and left a mark."

Indeed, a single stretch of road leading out of town bypasses a cross-section of history and development in less than a mile. Starting from the center of town, the crumbling (and some recently restored) buildings in the historic Stone Town bespeak Arabic design in their thin, high limestone facades and long, shaded alleyways, along with intricately carved and detailed teak balconies and balustrades added by the current Indian inhabitants.

When you move outside the Stone Town, the road widens, passing the mansions that once housed the British colonial officials. Farther along, stark, monotonous Bauhaus housing developments, uniform and sensible, hark back to the East German architects who came in after the coup as Zanzibar committed itself to socialist economic reform. Then, on the outskirts of town are the mud shanties, the kind that the poor of Zanzibar have been living in for centuries. The only consistent thing from one end of the road to the other is the fact that almost every building, every home, is in a state of dilapidation.

"There is a joke that there is no word for 'maintenance' in the Swahili dictionary," said Mohammed Bhaloo, another native Zanzibari who is now working for the Aga Khan Foundation on the island. "The story of Zanzibar as you see it now is a story of neglect. But we've now entered the phase of reclaiming our land, renewing our buildings. We had the colonization, we had the coup, we had the socialism, and now we're taking the next step."

The next step is prettying up Zanzibar, cleaning up the mess from decades of neglect as locals struggled to make ends meet. There is no question, said Bhaloo, that the same struggle carries on to this day, but now many officials and development workers believe that cleaning up and restoring the once glorious Zanzibar Town is actually much more than a cosmetic effort. It is, they say, a means of bringing dignity and pride back to a city for the benefit of the people who live there.

The other beneficiaries of the restorations will hopefully be the tourists, he said. Mainland Tanzania is currently enjoying a rapid increase in international tourism, thanks to the influx of safari-bound travelers tired of corruption in Kenya and sky-high prices in South Africa. Zanzibar, long a favorite vacation locale for Italians and Spaniards, is hosting more and more tours and overnight stop-overs as the mainland wins increasing acclaim for the richness of its safaris.

The thing with tourism, say many in the development field, is that it bolsters the local economy, and the environmental and architectural improvements it helps pay for can be enjoyed in part by the travelers, but year-round by the locals.

"You can't just give the tourists elegant hotels without giving the local people something to eat," said Fatima. "One of the clearest priorities here is that the redevelopment of the town is being done as much for the local people as for the tourists. Bringing jobs and higher standards of living is the goal of our tourist market, not making millions for Marriott."

One of the attractions that tourism officials are heralding in the developing world is precisely what they would have been deriding a decade ago: the lack of infrastructure. What it means to today's eco-friendly, culturally-sensitive tourist market is a chance to do the development right in the first place rather than having to go in and undo all the wrongs. In Zanzibar, there are no superhighways, no Marriotts, no Cancun-like lines of hotels blocking the beach.

Though the tourist amenities are few compared with other tropical islands, they are in strict accordance with and pay homage to the culture and traditions that surround them.

The Serena Hotel and Tomba Hotel, near one another just blocks from the main stretch of Stone Town, are both built in traditional Zanzibari style— open courtyards, airy walkways, mosquito-netted beds and antique furniture coming from all corners of the world.

The Aga Khan Foundation is integral in overseeing and helping to implement the changes needed to make Zanzibar a thing of beauty once again. One of the first tasks undertaken by the foundation's Trust for Culture has been the renovation and reopening of the Old Dispensary, a turn-of-the-century hospital and dispensary just across the road from the harbor. Now a glorious, sea-blue testimony to the designs of a 19th Century Indian architect, only a few years ago the building was a hollowed-out temporary shelter, its history not forgotten but not apparent either. Of the other 1,700 buildings in Stone Town, all have been declared by the government to be historical buildings and protected structures, but most are crumbling. Architects and builders, using money coming from the foundation and from donors throughout the world, work on the most critical homes and buildings first but plan to retouch all of the historic area.

"One of the biggest payoffs we've realized is that these are building skills and styles that had largely been forgotten," said Tony Steel, a mason working on the renovations of a local home and helping to train local workers. "We're working with local technical schools and teaching students this style of masonry. It preserves the building and gives them a greater advantage in the market as builders."

Though the buildings still creak and crumble, the glory of the past seems close at hand. The mix of cultures and traditions appears around every bend and curve on the cobblestoned streets of the Stone Town. Kuwaiti jewelers neighbor Pakistani spice shops. A mix of faces—long Arabic noses, dark African skin, fine South Asian hair—pass by, staring fixedly ahead. The smoky scent of za'atar, a Middle Eastern spice, drifts out from one shop and freshly ground cardamom from the next. In the night, bells from a Catholic Church ring out just as a muezzin from a nearby mosque begins to sing out over tinny loudspeakers and, from a Hindu temple near the sea, a shankh, a conch-shell, is blown to call to the gods. For a traveler the richness is there; whatever is lacking seems to fade into insignificance.

INDIA'S OTHER BOMBS

JACK FREEMAN
June 1998

International sanctions against the Indian government for its testing of five nuclear bombs in May 1998 have already cost India more than a billion dollars in development aid and credits. The United States, Germany, Japan, Britain, Denmark, the Netherlands, Norway and Sweden have all canceled bilateral development grants that were in the pipeline. And the World Bank wasted little time in freezing a $450 million loan intended to help build a modern electric power distribution system—something India needs desperately.

Critics of the international sanctions triggered by the A-bombs say that, although they are intended to punish India's government, their impact will be felt most harshly, not by the ruling class, but by India's poorest people—who are already among the most impoverished and deprived people on the planet. These critics argue that the cutbacks in international development assistance will do deadly harm to India's efforts to alleviate poverty and improve the lives of its people.

In India today, poverty and pollution are both stronger than ever.

But while nobody is claiming that bomb-protest cutbacks in aid will improve India's development prospects, the sad reality is that those prospects have already been devastated by two non-nuclear "bombs" of epic proportions. One is the country's so-called "population bomb"—in sheer numbers it has twice as many people living in poverty today as it had when it became independent more than half a century ago. The other is the disheartening way the Indian government's policies aimed at improving human development have consistently "bombed" and fizzled—so that the gap between the haves and have-nots continues to widen.

This double-whammy of overpopulation and poverty, some experts say, has done India's development far more harm—even when aid money was flowing freely, bringing in as much as $2.6 billion a year—than the new bomb-protest sanctions could possibly do.

The numbers (based on the most recent official reports) speak for themselves:

•More than half of all Indians—53 percent—live below the poverty line, defined as $1 a day;

•Roughly one-third of Indian adults—290 million people (the population of the US and Canada combined)—are illiterate; among women the illiteracy rate is 62 percent;

•In rural India, 90 percent of households have no access to any sanitary facilities; 60 percent have no electricity; nationwide, more than 171 million people have no access to safe drinking water;

•Although India has only one-third the land mass of the US, it has almost four times as many people; its population has doubled since 1961 and is growing by 19 million every year;

•India's fertility rate (the average number of children born per woman) has declined from around six at the time of independence to 3.5 today, but is still far above the "replacement" level of 2.1;

•Almost two-thirds—63 percent—of all Indian children under the age of 5 suffer from malnutrition.

•Other figures show that at least 25 million Indians are homeless, that India has only 4.4 doctors for every 10,000 people and that Indian schools have only one teacher for every 64 students.

Lurking behind the numbers are the realities of life in a society shadowed by deprivation: the miseries, frustrations and hopelessness of the masses of people held down by inequities.

But along with the human costs of this poverty/population "bomb," there are economic costs as well—and they are mounting. Experts at the UN estimate that India must build 10 million new housing units each year just to keep pace with its population growth, something it cannot possibly accomplish.

Economic pressures have kept the country from solving the environmental problems spawned by its rapid industrialization coupled with its deep poverty. And worker absenteeism caused by environment-linked illness is estimated to reduce the country's productivity by more than $10 billion each year.

At the UN-sponsored Earth Summit held in Rio de Janeiro in 1992, many a speaker quoted former Indian Prime Minister Indira Gandhi's observation that "poverty is the worst polluter"—and the corollary truth that environmental degradation makes life all the more difficult for the poor. But, leaving aside the chicken-or-egg question of which causes what, the reality is that, in India today, the poverty and the pollution are both stronger than ever.

The Earth Summit was not the only UN conference to deal with the complex poverty, population and development issues that India finds so intractable. The UN Conference on Social Development, held in Copenhagen in 1995, approved the "20:20 initiative," under which a donor country could allocate 20 percent of its aid money to "human priority" programs such as health and education while demanding that the receiving country spend at least 20 percent of its national budget on similar programs.

That initiative never really caught on anywhere after the conference delegates left Copenhagen, but for India such an arrangement would have been totally unthinkable. Even today, India spends only 11.9 percent of its national budget—scarcely more than half of the 20 percent target—on social services. (In contrast, the US spends 55 percent of its national budget on social services.)

The Fourth World Women's Conference, held in Beijing in 1995, stressed the need for gender equity. But, although India has a law allocating a certain percentage of seats in legislative bodies to women, in reality Indian women face serious discrimination throughout their lifetimes:

•Between their first and fifth birthdays, Indian girls have a 43 percent higher mortality rate than boys.

•As workers, Indian women earn only 35 percent as much as men.

•Women fill only 2.3 percent of India's administrative and managerial positions.

•Although 88 percent of pregnant women in India are anemic, when they give birth only 34 percent are attended by a doctor, nurse or midwife.

•The maternal mortality rate in India is 570 per 100,000 live births—roughly twice as high as for developing countries generally and four times as high as in neighboring Sri Lanka. Every year more than 100,000 Indian women die as a result of the complications of pregnancy.

(These figures are all for the country as a whole; in the poorer rural areas the statistics are even more appalling.)

The International Conference on Population and Development, held in Cairo in 1994, called upon the nations of the world to shift their emphasis away from numerical population targets and toward improving the overall health and status of women. It was a call that resonated with particular meaning in India, which in the past has tried a variety of target-based population control measures, including mass forced sterilizations of men and women in the 1970s.

"This period brought an enormous backlash that India is still recovering from," said Amit Battacharya, a technical adviser in social development at the United Nations. "People are still skeptical of the very word 'population.'"

Yet despite that history, surgical sterilization remains by far the most common form of contraception, used by 27 percent of women and 3.4 percent of men. Overall, the contraceptive prevalence rate is 41 percent. People working in the field say there are 30 million Indian women in need of family planning services who are not being served by current programs. Any cutbacks in international aid to India can only increase their numbers.

But money alone is not the answer either. As Khadija and Mahbub ul Haq point out in the newly published "Human Development in South Asia 1998" (Oxford University Press for the Human Development Centre), "Several poorer states in India have managed to achieve higher levels of education than their richer counterparts: Kerala, with a per capita income of $1,017. . .has a literacy rate of 90 percent, compared to 58 percent in Punjab, which has more than double the per capita income of Kerala."

The Haqs focus on education as the most critical need to solve the region's development problems, noting that, "In India, increasing average primary schooling of the work force by one year increased output by 23 percent." They also report: "In urban India, when mothers were uneducated, the child mortality rate was as high as 82 per thousand, but it dropped sharply to 34 per thousand when mothers were educated."

"Let us honestly recognize," writes the late Mahbub ul Haq, "that poverty is not merely a flu; it is more like a cancer. We cannot leave intact the model of development that produces persistent poverty and wistfully hope that we can take care of poverty downstream through limited income transfers or discrete poverty reduction programs...The real answer lies in changing the very model of development from traditional economic growth to human development, where human capabilities are built up and human opportunities enlarged, where people become the real agents and beneficiaries of economic growth..."

He cites the progress made toward the elimination of poverty by a variety of countries, including Malaysia, China, the Republic of Korea and Colombia, in the past two decades. "These countries," he writes, "restructured their models of development to generate pro-poor growth. Poverty was treated as a fundamental problem, requiring basic changes in the economic system, not mere cosmetic tinkering."

Or, in other words, there is more than one way to go "boom."

CHANDIGARH: STRETCHING THE LIMITS

VIR SINGH
May 1999

CHANDIGARH, India—For decades, this mid-size city in the foothills of the Himalayas has enjoyed a reputation as the country's most perfectly planned settlement. Its spartan, hulking gray buildings, broad avenues, large green spaces and clean, orderly neighborhoods defy popular images of urban India. Chandigarh's older areas, characterized by large sprawling homes, trimmed hedges and immaculate lawns, have even evoked comparisons with suburbs of American cities.

All of this is changing quickly, however, as rapid growth and increasing affluence are stretching the city past its limits. There is general agreement that it has grown much faster than planned and that decisions have to be made soon about how to accommodate even more people.

But as Chandigarh turns 50, planners and architects cannot seem to agree on how to respond to the challenge. While some professionals favor loosening up building codes to allow for more homes in this spacious city, most people say such a step would destroy the very character of the place. Unplanned growth has drawn Chandigarh, willy-nilly, into some of the predicaments facing other Indian cities. The population of the city and peripheral areas is 1.2 million, more than twice what was planned. Some 35 percent of its residents live in illegal settlements.

Built under the guidance of the French architect Le Corbusier 50 years ago, Chandigarh has rigid building and planning codes—laws that are vital for preserving the "special charm" of the place, say most architects, planners and civil servants who saw the city come up before their eyes. Several younger residents share this view. But an increasingly vocal minority is calling for change, asking that the laws be relaxed to meet the demands of a fast-growing population, especially the poor. These objectors, most of them architects, say there are basic flaws in Chandigarh's planning that have marginalized the nonsalaried classes—masons, carpenters, casual laborers and others who literally built the city and who continue to serve the city's more affluent residents.

"The buildings inspire me, the city does not," said Jaspreet Thakkar, a Chandigarh architect who says she misses the "large variety of people" she saw every day in faraway Bombay during her college days. "I walk through a street here and I see middle and upper-class people. I do not see the poor. Chandigarh does not reflect society, the world in which we live."

Such criticism is unwarranted, say Chandigarh loyalists who argue that it was the city's success that attracted jobless laborers and petty tradesmen from rural villages. They say Chandigarh has made substantial contributions to its citizens and to the development of architecture and town planning in India.

The idea for a new city came out of the bloody separation of Pakistan from India after the end of British colonial rule in 1947. The Indian part of the Punjab State no longer had a capital. Jawaharlal Nehru, the country's first prime minister, called for "a new town, symbolic of the freedom of India, unfettered by the traditions of the past . . . an expression of the nation's faith in the future."

The inter-communitarian violence that had claimed so many lives was still fresh on people's minds. So the new city could not reflect the influence of any one community. A modern style was needed, and the internationally known Corbusier fit the bill perfectly.

Ask people why Chandigarh was built and you get many answers. Older residents say the city was supposed to provide a sense of identity, not just to refugees from Pakistan but also to other Indians trying to find their place in a newly liberated nation. Architects hail the building of Chandigarh as the first comprehensive exercise in urban planning, which produced many generations of professionals who built other Indian cities. Ordinary citizens say they enjoy a "better quality of life" because of wide open spaces, greenery and the fact that water and electricity shortages, although getting worse, are not nearly so bad as elsewhere.

Chandigarh was planned to the last detail. It comprises a series of self-contained blocks, known as sectors, each with its own market, parks, schools, clinics and other services. Numerous regulations governing home building—such as what materials to use, the position of the gate and the height of the boundary wall—were laid down. Ironclad laws ensure that housing density in the older sectors—occupying about one-third of the city—cannot be increased, even though newer sectors are allowed to have many more homes.

As a result, just 6.2 percent of the people living in Chandigarh's legally developed areas occupy more than 30 percent of those lands, said Madhu

Sarin, an architect who has conducted numerous social surveys and is a member of the city's housing board.

Chandigarh was built on the principle that offices, homes and markets must be kept separate from each other in designated areas. Petty tradesmen such as barbers and cobblers were expected to rent stores in markets. But such an arrangement is impractical, says Sarin, because their incomes are far too modest for them to pay rent. And as for housing, those who planned the city did not make allowances for the poor. They apparently thought that, after Chandigarh was built, the laborers at construction sites would return to their villages. In subsequent years, these laborers' requests to city officials for housing credit plans fell on deaf ears. "Somewhere there is a statement that these people are not citizens, they do not have rights, they are not entitled," said Sarin.

These imbalances are expected to grow as Chandigarh continues to expand. The emergence of shantytowns has already transformed peripheral areas and some pockets inside the city. With increased urban migration, homelessness is on the rise and there is now a permanent "street population" found mainly in markets. Inadequate public transport, coupled with rising middle-class incomes, has brought a flood of new cars, scooters and motorbikes onto the streets. Chandigarh's avenues have a different look, now that several traffic circles have been replaced with decidedly less elegant traffic lights.

At a recent conference here involving architects and urban planners from around the world, one message came out loud and clear: Chandigarh must face up to the fact that rapid growth makes change inevitable, and that the city should act now to decide how it wants to change instead of being left with fewer choices later on. Indian President K.R. Narayanan underscored that message. "The city may have to see itself less and less as a brand-new experiment in urban planning," he said, "and more and more as an existing city… facing new problems and pressures it was not designed to cope with."

SECTION 5:
HEALTH AND
THE WELFARE
OF SOCIETIES

Statistics tell the devastating story of health concerns as related to population and human development. For just one example, in sub-Saharan Africa, one of the regions most desperately in need of constructive development, 60 percent of the world's 30 million people living with AIDS can be found. Ninety percent of the world's AIDS fatalities occur in Africa. These are only two of the statistics in C. Gerald Fraser's Earth Times article, "Uganda: The Orphans of AIDS."

This section also deals with the difficult and complicated relationships in many parts of the world between population, education, sanitation and health care—as the West sees these essential services on the one hand and, on the other, the often contradictory beliefs and practices of specific peoples. Thus, the ongoing pitched battles behind the scenes every day, now and then erupting in headlines, over the issues of contraception and female genital mutilation.

Even the effects of pollution on human health, or of global warming, spawn serious controversy, as requirements for industrial modernization are balanced against adverse effects on the physical health and psychological well-being of populations.

SECTION 5

HEALTH AND THE WELFARE OF SOCIETIES

THE 'BEST CONTRACEPTIVE' AND OTHER APPROACHES

GERARD PIEL

November 1993

World population growth is recognized in the official and academic discourse of the United States almost exclusively in terms of what contribution the country might make to "family planning program effort" in the developing countries. The literature has little to say about economic development in its relation to the change in the human condition that has reduced fertility to the zero-growth rate in the industrialized countries. It has still less to say about possible US contribution to the economic development that is already securing the same result in the developing countries. In part, this is concession to political reality; "foreign aid" comes close to last in national budgetary priorities. Discouragingly, after almost 20 years, it harks back also to the positions taken by the industrialized and the developing countries at the first United Nations conference on population, held in Bucharest in 1974.

There the parties of the first part opened the proceedings with the proffer of instruction in contraception and funding and supplies for its practice. They were astonished by the indignation with which the delegations from the developing countries responded. To charges of post-imperialist condescension and racism they could respond with indignation of their own. What nettled and required answer, however, was the claim by those delegations that "development is the best contraceptive."

The family planners had no adequate answer. Instead, they resorted to ad hominem argument at the same level as the charge of racism; they said the claim was a Marxist heresy. It is true that Karl Marx had disparaged "Parson" Malthus as blaming the poverty of the poor on their propensity to procreate. But in 1974, with the cold war in deep freeze, guilt by association sufficed to disqualify any claim so tainted from consideration in Washington. At the time, it did not help that the Soviet bloc endorsed the contraceptive virtues of economic development.

The 1974 conference had constructive outcomes nonetheless. The developing countries gave full cooperation to the World Fertility Survey, which found "a strong relationship between [developing] countries' recent fertility and the level of development and strength of family planning program effort." The Population Council in New York City, at the behest of its benefactor, John D. Rockefeller III, amplified the name of its quarterly journal; it has been "Population and Development" ever since.

Now there is more progress to report. In his address to the first meeting of the Commission on Sustainable Development on June 1993, Vice President Al Gore asked rhetorically: "Is population control only a problem of birth control?" Answering, "Of course not!" he recalled that Julius Nyerere, then President of Tanzania, had declared reduction of infant mortality to be "the most powerful contraceptive." Further, he quoted with approval the statement of an unnamed Keralese physician: "The most enduring contraception is female education." The more such contraceptives are identified, the firmer becomes the proposition that "development is the best contraceptive."

If all goes well, the Clinton-Gore administration may yet go beyond restoration of US Federal funding of the family planning enterprises conducted by the UN and US philanthropic organizations. That was suspended, of course, by the Reagan administration just in time to disgrace the US at the second UN population conference at Mexico City in 1984. This country may now join such civilized countries as Norway, Sweden, Denmark, France and Japan in allocating the promised 0.7 percent of the industrial world's GDP to accelerate the economic development of the now not-so-developing countries, in accordance with many commitments to do so. The latest was the commitment made by 172 nations to Agenda 21 at the UN Conference on Environment and Development at Rio de Janeiro in June 1992.

EGYPT'S FIGHT AGAINST FEMALE GENITAL MUTILATION

KYU-YOUNG LEE
October 1998

MAADI, Egypt—Even its name has sparked controversy. To the Egyptians it is known as "tahara," which loosely translates into "purity before God." But officially, among international bodies and governments trying to eradicate the practice, it is called female genital mutilation, or FGM for short. Dr. Mahmoud Karim, too, will call it FGM in conversation on the subject, but he prefers to define it specifically as the title of his recently published book, "Female Genital Mutilation: Circumcision," suggests.

Dr. Karim can be called a pioneer. Fifty years ago he started the first family planning center in Egypt with 2,000 intrauterine devices he acquired at a New York conference convened to teach doctors how to use the contraceptive. Ten years before that, his sister founded the Maadi Child Welfare Center. "My family was very much into social work," he said, "and helping the community around us from very early on." Now, at the age of 84, he has again taken up the fight in social work to eradicate a practice that has been scorned by the international community and many Egyptians as well.

Dr. Karim attributes most of his motivation for writing the book, which defines the practice and how to deal with it, to the press coverage that FGM sparked during the Cairo International Conference on Population and Development and since. "There seemed a point a few years ago when there was a negative article in a major newspaper every week," he said.

But Marie Asaad, coordinator of a task force to control FGM set into motion by Egypt's National Commission on Population and Development (NCPD), said she thinks the press coverage was counterproductive as well. "The Western media at a point really hurt our efforts to try to stop FGM," she said. Referring to a specific CNN report that aired during the Population Conference, she said, "It hurt people's pride. They asked themselves, 'Why should we stop doing this? Is it just because other countries are telling us it is bad?' It seemed like bullying tactics."

But many Egyptians concede that it was only after the 1994 Population Conference that Egyptians themselves realized how widespread FGM really was. The Egyptian demographic health survey in 1995 found that 97 percent of married women between the ages of 15 and 49 had experienced some form of FGM.

"Most cases, about 60 percent, involve the partial removal of the clitoris and the labia minora," said Dr. Karim. In his book he defines four different degrees of the practice, ranging from mere pricking of the genitalia to the most damaging form, which involves complete removal of the external genitalia and stitching the skin together. About 9 percent of all cases involve infibulation, in which the labia majora is completely removed.

"What the Western media did," Dr. Karim said, "was shock therapy. "You shock someone and you see if it has helped any. I believe it is up to us, the Egyptians, to understand it, nurture it and find the reasons why it is practiced and then try and stop it. That is the only way it can be stopped here."

Around 100 million women have undergone some form of female genital mutilation.

Why is it practiced? Dr. Karim says it is a matter of traditions and secrets. "Most people practice it in secret," he said. "That is why it took us so long to find the problem. Traditionally, almost 40 percent of mothers feel it should be done for ethical reasons or to discourage premarital sex."

FGM is also performed because of supposed religious dictates. As the Arabic name suggests, FGM is considered a form of cleanliness and being closer to God. "More than 30 percent of the people do it for religious reasons," said Dr. Karim. But leaders at Cairo's Al-Ahzar University, a center of Muslim theology, quickly denounced the practice and said it had no basis in Islam. The practice was also publicly condemned by Dr. Ismail Sallam, the Minister of Health and Population.

Dr. Karim is quick to point out that the practice is predominantly an African phenomenon, stretching through countries from the Mediterranean down through sub-Saharan Africa. It is not found in most other Arab Muslim countries, he said. And its history continues to be a mystery, some saying that the practice dates back to pharaonic times, others saying it came from abroad.

Approximately 100 million women have undergone some form of FGM and each year two million more women undergo the procedure.

"There is a direct correlation between education and prevalence of the practice," Dr. Karim said. "Among more highly educated people you won't find it done, or you may find the most benign forms."

The task force created by the NCPD and headed by Asaad has spear-headed Egypt's efforts to eradicate the practice—going to local communities and the source of the traditions, Asaad said, "Education and dialogue is what we need." Dr. Karim said. "You can't break old traditions within a few weeks. You have to go to each and every person and teach them the harmful nature of the practice."

Educating the public is one side but educating the people who perform FGM (including doctors) has been an ongoing and tricky process. Legislation which has been used to prosecute some doctors who perform FGM has forced mothers to take their daughters to underground surgeons, barbers and other untrained people. The Ministry and advocacy groups in the NCPD have made efforts to educate doctors not only to stop performing the procedure but also how to convince women of its needlessness.

Dr. Karim spends most of his time these days at Ain Shams University, where he teaches women's health and family planning. Ain Shams University is the first in Egypt to offer a degree in family planning. It seems Dr. Karim has been involved with a lot of firsts.

MEXICO: 'A LOT OF LIES' ABOUT SEX

ELIZABETH BRYANT

July 1996

MEXICO CITY—Humberto Garcia Vasquez was just following his calling as he handed out condoms at the Parque Popular Tezozomoc Azcapotzalco one brilliant July morning.

"When you buy condoms, always check the expiration date," the 24-year-old medical student told a throng of teens drawn from the park's basketball courts and verdant walks to listen to his impromptu presentation on safe sex.

Garcia, a volunteer for an adolescent-based nongovernmental organization, is among thousands of health experts and neighborhood volunteers that form the bedrock of a population program heralded as one of the best in the developing world.

Over the last 30 years, Mexico's annual population growth has tumbled from 7 percent to about 2 percent a year, according to local and international experts. Maternal and infant mortality rates have also dropped—thanks, officials say, to a public-private web of health and education programs that reaches from the sprawling inner-city clinics of Mexico City to remote mountain areas of Chiapas state.

This month, Mexico's Minister of Reproductive Health promised to deliver what many developing countries only dream about: to meet a target of 1.75 percent annual population growth by the century's close, and a 1.45 percent growth by 2005. It also prompted Nafis Sadik, UN Population Fund's Executive Director, to announce at an international population conference that the organization would cut funding to Mexico in order to help needier countries elsewhere.

But Mexico's population story has fallen short of a feel-good ending. More than half of the country's 94 million citizens are under 20 years old. The fueling of Mexico City's development by 16 million residents helps create classic big-city problems: bumper-to-bumper traffic that snarls major avenues, rural migrants who remain unemployed, and a choking smog that has earned this city notoriety worldwide.

Overpopulation's fallout makes its mark elsewhere, from environmental degradation in Chiapas to the thousands of illegal immigrants who flock to the US each year.

Too often, experts like Garcia say, private groups must still fill in the gaps when government programs fall short.

"The high school health programs say a lot of lies about sex," Garcia said, speaking through a translator about sexual education programs that begin in the fifth or sixth grades. "The older people don't want us to have sex, so they basically tell us not to have it."

Garcia works for CORA, a Mexico City-based nongovernmental organization (NGO) that offers adolescents a myriad of programs, from sex education to counseling about drug use and family violence. The organization's teen-based thrust began in 1978, said Director Marcos Velasco—more than a decade before the government launched its own initiatives. Today, however, the Health Ministry supports CORA through equipment, personnel and office space.

"One of the most important things about this program is that we go to where young people are," said Velasco of CORA's 70 field-based programs. "Because we know that young people often don't get to the hospitals and clinics."

If young people are Mexico's future, they help shape today's problems, the experts say. More than 40 percent of Mexicans with AIDS acquired the virus as teens, according to CORA statistics. Teens account for about 500,000 pregnancies in the country each year, not surprising since fewer than 30 percent of them use any form of contraception. Between 30 and 40 percent of Mexico's abortions are performed on teenage girls.

But Mexico's population problems stretch beyond adolescence. Illegal abortion is still a major cause of maternal mortality, and government officials admit a yawning gap between conditions in the towns and in the countryside. Rural contraceptive use is still low, and many families in these areas average seven or more children.

Naomi Vargas Baltazar and Julio Cesar Eliseo Leon, both 18, are precisely the kind of young people Mexican health experts hope to reach. Vargas has seven siblings; Eliseo comes from a family of nine. The couple began having sex eight months ago, but neither uses any birth control.

"I haven't really thought about it, but I guess I don't like the idea," said Vargas, speaking through an interpreter as she sat with her boyfriend at the

Dr. Manuel Cardenas Health Center in Mexico City, awaiting treatment for back problems.

Asked how many children she wanted, Vargas said two. "The economic situation is too difficult for more," she explained.

So how would she stop at two?

Vargas shrugged. "Let him take care of the problem," she said, pointing to her boyfriend.

Neither had heard about the Cardenas Center's array of family planning services, although the doctors here are supposed to give such information to their young patients. Birth control methods such as the pill and IUDs are available free of charge, along with information about ways to avoid pregnancy. As in virtually all other Latin American countries, abortions are illegal in Mexico, but male vasectomies are gaining a tenuous foothold. So far, the center has performed more than 800 vasectomies since the services began in 1993.

"It's been difficult to convince them," said Jose Oliver Marquez, the local director of health services, of potential male clients. "We know how famous Mexico machismo is."

Still, Francisco Xavier Altamira, 36, didn't need much convincing. After fathering five children from two separate marriages, Xavier called it quits, opting for a vasectomy. "I decided I had enough children," Xavier said, as he sat clutching his year-old son at the clinic.

Besides, the Cardenas Center has capitalized on a very special asset. The clinic sits on a main thoroughfare to the Basilica of the Virgin of Guadaloupe, one of the country's holiest shrines, which draws thousands of Mexican visitors each year.

"We get a lot of promotion," Oliver said with a grin. "There are many people from neighboring states who come to visit her. And they end up by visiting us."

BANGLADESH: SAVING LIVES WITH SUGAR AND SALT

JACK FREEMAN
October 1996

DHAKA, Bangladesh—The babies lie on their hospital beds, their tiny bodies limp and lifeless, filling row after row in the huge ward. They are all here for treatment of the same disease: diarrhea, which in this part of the world is a killer.

Some of the children clutch their middles, grimacing with pain at the cramps they are experiencing. Some have IV tubes pumping a life-giving saline solution into their veins. Some are nursing at their mothers' breasts, others merely clinging for comfort. Some are being spoon-fed thin gruel, or sipping a sugar-salt solution that can prevent life-threatening dehydration.

This is the scene in the hospital of the International Center for Diarrheal Disease Research, Bangladesh (ICDDR,B), formerly known as the Cholera Hospital.

A similar scene can be found in any other hospital in this country.

Diarrhea is a deadly problem here. The numbers don't tell the whole story but are frightening in themselves: By the time children in Bangladesh celebrate their fifth birthday, each one has, on average, suffered 18 bouts of severe diarrhea. And until recently, one Bangladeshi child out of every 15 was dying from a diarrheal disease before reaching that fifth birthday.

Bangladesh has 20 million children in that age group, and each year they suffer 75 million episodes of diarrhea. At the start of this decade these children were dying at the rate of 250,000 every year. And many who survived the disease suffered lasting harm in the form of stunted development.

Because of the effects of diarrheal disease, coupled with persistent and pandemic malnutrition (93 percent of children here are malnourished), Bangladesh is the only country in the world whose people, on average, are literally losing stature, becoming shorter over time.

The good news is that, although diarrhea remains endemic here, these days it is killing far fewer children. Recent statistics suggest that diarrhea-related deaths of children under five in Bangladesh have been reduced to 125,000 per year, which means that the country is four years ahead of schedule in achieving one of the key health goals it agreed, at the Children's Summit in 1990, to meet by the end of the century: reducing such deaths by half.

The bad news is that, despite this progress, 125,000 young Bangladeshi children are still dying every year because of diarrhea, and the doctors say virtually all of those deaths could be—and should be—prevented.

There is general agreement among government health officials, international development agencies and others that the key to reducing mortality has been the increasing public awareness and acceptance of the treatment known as oral rehydration therapy (ORT), giving patients dehydrated by diarrhea a specific quantity of a solution of sugar and salt to drink.

The formula for the oral rehydration solution (ORS) was developed and successfully tested here in Bangladesh, by doctors at ICDDR,B, in the late 1960s. Although a mixture of water, sugar and salt may not seem like high-powered technology, development of the formula was hailed by the British medical journal, The Lancet, as potentially the most important medical breakthrough of the century.

Among its other advantages, ORT is an incredibly inexpensive life-saver. A packet of the salts needed for one dose costs between 7 and 10 cents, and three doses are usually enough to get a patient out of danger. (In Bangladesh the packets are distributed by a social marketing organization set up initially by the US Agency for International Development to distribute contraceptives.)

Since the 1980s, ORT has been widely accepted and promoted by the World Health Organization (WHO) and, with particular vigor, by Unicef. Globally, according to Dr. Monica Sharma of Unicef, ORT is now saving more than one million lives every year. And by promoting the use of ORT, she told The Earth Times, Unicef is involved in the process of empowering people by putting a life-saving technology into their hands.

Over the last few years Unicef has been instrumental in organizing and coordinating a new drive to promote ORT in Bangladesh with the hope of saving even more lives. The drive, funded primarily through a grant of almost $6 million provided by the Dutch government, is getting under way this month. Its goal is to use virtually every means of communication to make sure that all the people of Bangladesh are ready, willing and able to administer ORT whenever it is needed—that is, in the words of Dr. Sharma, "to make

ORT a family habit, not just a medical intervention."

"Diarrheal control used to be a matter for health professionals," said Dr. Asib Nasim, who heads the government's program against the disease, "but it has now been turned into a societal movement."

Still, surveys taken by local health officials suggest that although 96 percent of people in Bangladesh know about the value of ORT, only 66 percent are using it—and only 45 percent are administering it properly. What people are most unclear about, it seems, is how to feed and care for children who are getting ORT.

Research conducted here in recent years has established that for the therapy to succeed, the patients must be given not only the ORS solution but as much other fluid as they can take, and they must also continue to be fed. According to some folk-medicine beliefs current here (and in many other parts of the world), food should be withheld from children with diarrhea—but doctors say such beliefs are not only wrong but dangerous.

Even though it has been well documented that ORT can save lives, getting people here to accept it has been an uphill battle from the start. Early

How a medical concern has been turned into a societal movement.

efforts to popularize the therapy focused on young mothers as the primary care-givers of the children at risk, but met with resistance. For one thing, it took a while to get the mothers to understand that ORT could save lives even though it did not stop the diarrhea. Another problem, it was discovered by field workers, was that decisions about whether to use the therapy were considered too important for women to make without consultation with the men in their families.

F. H. Abed, Executive Director of Bangladesh Rural Advancement Coalition (BRAC), the largest nongovernmental organization in Bangladesh (and possibly in the world, he says), told The Earth Times that early efforts to promote ORT also ran into difficulties because medical authorities insisted that the water for the solution had to be boiled and cooled before use to make sure it was free of disease-causing microorganisms. "In practical terms," he said, "that meant that the mother first had to gather firewood and build a fire—and if the child were sick in the middle of the night, treatment would have to be delayed until morning."

"To avoid such obstacles," he said, "it was decided to allow the use of unboiled water from tubewells."

Because of its huge grassroots organization, BRAC plays a key role in Bangladesh's ORT steering committee, along with Unicef and WHO, government health officials, the Grameen Bank and the Scouts. And it was the steering committee that organized the huge advertising and communication program to promote ORT that is now beginning.

The campaign includes a full range of multimedia messages on radio and television (developed by an advertising agency in India) along with printed pamphlets, brochures, posters and educational materials for use in schools. Special packages of materials have also been prepared for use by a variety of field workers and other influential people to get the message into the countryside.

Among the groups targeted in this face-to-face communication campaign are health and family planning workers and NGOs, licensed and unlicensed medical practitioners, schools, religious leaders and mosques, Scouts and Guides and even local postal workers.

The kits prepared for use by health workers in the field have built-in legs to turn them into makeshift tables. The kits prepared for the Scouts and Guides include stencils that allow them to reproduce the campaign's message on virtually any flat surface.

CHOKING PEOPLE IN ASIA

JAMES W. MICHAELS
March 1997

I was looking forward to visiting Shanghai's wonder-filled new museum and had reserved the last day of my business visit there last autumn for a bit of culture. I never got to the museum. A week of breathing the heavily polluted air of eastern China did me in. My last full day in Shanghai was spent in my hotel room. I returned to New York and read that pollution threatens India's magnificent Taj Mahal.

It is an all too common experience. Mexico City is one of my favorite spots on Earth, but I rarely go there these days: at my age I can't handle the bad air. My eyes water and I cough. I, of course, can pick up and go. Millions of people cannot. As an American who has traveled in Asia for more than half a century and who has many friends there, I'm thrilled to witness the dynamic economic development that is transforming ancient societies. However much one may yearn for the good old days, one does not want to return to the time when life expectancy was 40 years, when famines were frequent and chances for economic and social advancement were almost nonexistent. The picturesque nature of the old societies was paid for with appalling infant mortality.

Three cheers, then, for industrialization. China is telescoping into a few years the industrial and economic progress that took a century to accomplish in the West. Southeast Asia is fast leaving behind its bucolic past. India, preindustrial 50 years ago, has become a major producer of computer software. In parts of Asia, the grandchildren of rickshaw coolies are electronics engineers. China and India's emergence as industrial powers means a better life, not just for a privileged handful, but for a couple of billion people. No one who has witnessed the changes of recent years can believe that small is beautiful or that peasants are better off living in a state of nature.

In parts of Asia, the grandchildren of rickshaw coolies are electronics engineers.

But need we lose the Taj Mahal? Perhaps it is arrogant for someone who has come from an industrialized country with a high standard of living to suggest that India and Mexico and China and the rest of the modernizing countries should modify the pace of development in the interest of preserving the environment. But we must never forget that industrialization is not an end in itself, but rather a means of improving the living standards of the masses of people.

In this respect, healthy living conditions are as important as better nutrition, more leisure time and better medical care. Unless you pay heed to the environment, you extend life on one hand and shorten it on the other. You improve living standards and lower living conditions.

This is a question of democracy. Where ordinary people have a voice in the matter they are almost always willing to trade off a bit of economic growth against environmental amenities. The most democratic nations seem to be the ones paying the most attention to the environment. In Eastern Europe and the former Soviet Union, where the rulers cared little for public opinion, environmental conditions were deplorable. The successor governments are still trying to rid themselves of those stinking little Trabants that the Socialists fobbed off on their subjects in place of modern automobiles. By contrast, in New York and London, and in most of the industrial democracies, the air is more breathable than it was a quarter of a century ago.

We must never forget that industrialization is not an end in itself, but rather a means of improving the living standards of the masses of people.

Given the choice, ordinary people care about the environment. It is fair to say that a measure of democracy is the degree to which the rulers pay heed to this yearning.

Of course, you cannot have industry without accepting a certain amount of pollution, but experience in the West has shown that clean air and modern capitalism are not incompatible. There are plenty of ways to use market incentives sufficiently; we depend too much on command-and-control environmentalism. But it is absolutely clear that environmentalism and free-market capitalism can be friends.

Unfortunately, environmentalism has gotten something of a bad name from a handful of fanatics who literally try to stop progress. In the name of protecting the environment they try to thrust on the world some strange pantheistic vision. They put trees and rocks before people. But environmentalism needn't rest on the idea that man is a desecrater of God's Earth. It is defensible and desirable for what it can do for the human race.

The bad air that had my eyes watering in Shanghai reduces the productivity and shortens the lives of the inhabitants, who, unlike visitors, can't jet away. I'm willing to bet that in the long run you will get more efficient industrialization if you protect the environment as you go. Not only is sound environmentalism compatible with economic efficiency, it is a precondition for maximum efficiency.

In short, economic growth and sound environmental practices are not opposed. Quite the contrary, they supplement each other. Each contributes to a betterment in living standards. Too bad we don't have a statistical index that counts environmental improvement as an element in economic growth. It would go a long way in helping us get our priorities right.

EGYPT: THE CLINIC IS COMING TOMORROW

C. GERALD FRASER
September 1994

QENA, Egypt—Large red, blue, and green cloths hang over balcony railings and out of the windows of a modern, six-story, sand-colored apartment house on one side of an unpaved main street. Opposite is an older and dowdier structure to whose third-floor health clinic trek women and children for health services and family planning assistance.

It is in villages like this one, which clings, as most do in Egypt, to the banks of the Nile, that the national government is battling to win the war of development—a war partly fought by reducing the rate of population growth.

"If they have six or seven children it's a problem," said Qena's Governor, Mohamed Abdel Raheem Nafeh. "It's a problem for eating, a problem for educating." The Governor spoke to visitors in his large office with trophy cases full of plaques testifying to his good deeds.

"But now," he eased back and summed up, "it's changing." Small schools have been established to teach "ladies" to read and to train them for jobs. Unemployed university graduates have been put to work in adult education programs.

Qena, some 150 miles south of Cairo, with a population of 2.6 million, is a relatively poor Egyptian governorate—the equivalent of an American state—whose governor is a former major general appointed to his post by President Mubarak.

The Governor said the Qena population growth rate has gone from 3.38 percent in 1988 down to 2.3 percent. And to continue the drop he wants more mobile clinics.

Two mobile clinics roll around Qena, stopping in villages whose names are not on most maps and are otherwise devoid of medical facilities. These clinics on wheels came to Qena as part of "The Pilot Project for Family Planning and Maternal and Child Health Care in Naga Hammady." The clinics, large white Nissan vans, were provided in 1989 by the Japan International Cooperation Agency, which also sent along a nurse.

Also cooperating in sponsorship of the project was the government-owned Aluminum Company of Egypt, which has what amounts to a company town—factory, school and recreational facilities—in the village of Naga Hammady.

Now, the project is operated by an Egyptian doctor, two Egyptian nurses (one of whom went to Japan for training in the preparation and use of audio-visual materials) and several assistant nurses. One day before the clinic is scheduled to arrive, a small van cruises through the village blaring announcements about the next day's mobile clinic visit. The small van is equipped with a television set and video cassette recorder for show-and-tell sessions.

Clinic visits are not free. "We found out that anything free is not well respected by the client," said Dr. Mohamed el-Hawary, who is in charge of the clinic. The cost: one Egyptian pound, about 33 cents.

In Cairo, Waleed A. Alkateeb has the data on Egypt's struggle to promote family planning. The country has approximately 58 million people—"inside and outside" is the way it's phrased. "Outside" refers to the Gulf States, where many Egyptian men have gone for jobs, and to England, where 1,500 Egyptian medical doctors have gone to practice. By the year 2001, Alkateeb's figures indicate, Egypt's total population will be more than 67 million.

"One of the major problems this country is facing in development—in going forward into the 21st Century—is fertility," he said. "The fertility is eating up more resources than the country can muster and can develop. So the country cannot even keep pace with meeting the needs of the population. Every year we are adding 1.2 million people to the population pool—people who need social services, education, health services, roads, buildings. It's a major obstacle to development on the macro level."

Alkateeb ticked off what he considered three "obstacles" to development. The first is fertility, the second distribution. "All our people are at the delta, at the Nile," he said. "That hasn't changed since the pharaohs." Some 96 percent of Egypt's population lives on 4 percent of the land.

The third obstacle, he said, is the characteristics of the population—the educational level, literacy rate, unemployment and the status of women.

The good news, according to Alkateeb, is that "almost 100 percent of Egyptian men and women in the reproductive age [18 to 49 years] know about family planning." Most of these women, 63 percent, have used some method of contraception. And currently almost half of Egypt's women in their reproductive years, 47.6 percent, are using contraception.

Alkateeb, a health management consultant in Egypt's National

Population Center, is paid by the US Agency for International Development, a major supporter of Egyptian population programs. Other supporters are the United Nations Population Fund (UNFPA), Japan, the Netherlands and, lately, the European Union.

The multiplicity of donors can be as frustrating at times as it is useful. One must appease every donor, Alkateeb said, and sometimes one donor may want something done that conflicts with another donor's desires.

He said that the government is now seeking to place clinics offering quality service in deprived areas, rather than having clinics everywhere. Usually, clinics offer primary health care as well as family planning, he said, because many people will not go to a stand-alone family planning facility.

If a married woman visits a clinic, she does so usually with her husband's consent, Alkateeb said, even though she doesn't need his consent. In rural areas, he said, this is "problematic."

Abortion is a health issue, not a family planning issue, he said. "It is not in the national strategies." He also noted that there are no statistics and no references to premarital sex. "It's not recognized."

Those working in population appear to do so with the blessing of President Mubarak, who is said to mention population in practically every speech he makes. In 1986, Mubarak set up the National Population Council (NPC) to coordinate the country's population activities. The council is involved with technical assistance on one hand and, on the other, monitoring, reviewing and evaluating programs and activities.

Each of Egypt's 26 governorates has an NPC office and there are NPC offices in several ministries, including the one that deals with religion.

UGANDA: THE ORPHANS OF AIDS

C. GERALD FRASER
August 1998

KAMPALA, Uganda—A number of women here are writing books—memory books, they call them—for their sons and daughters. "We write down some memories for our children," said Scovia Kasolo, "because we don't expect to live." Kasolo is the treasurer of NACWOLA, the National Community of Women Living With AIDS, which has more than 50,000 members. Each child's book will describe the child's background, telling him or her about relatives and the significant things that happened when the child was growing up.

The mothers also want the book to help them "open up a dialogue with their children about their sero-status so that when they talk to their children the children will be supported to cope with future changes in case of the parents' death," according to the NACWOLA newsletter, "Positive Woman." In Uganda, authorities took public notice of AIDS in 1982. In urban areas it spread rapidly but has since declined somewhat. In rural areas, where most Ugandans live, the pandemic rose slowly but has remained at a high level. Practically every family has had a close or distant relative fall victim to HIV/AIDS. Doctors at the Uganda AIDS Commission told visitors recently that sub-Saharan Africa has 60 percent of the world's 30 million people living with AIDS. Africa "bears the heaviest burden of HIV," said Omwony Ojwok, the commission's director general. In Uganda, AIDS has raised the infant mortality rate and lowered life expectancy. For every 1,000 HIV mothers, 162 infants do not survive their first year. (The nation's overall infant mortality rate is 97 per 1,000 births.) Life expectancy has dropped from 50 years before the epidemic to between 40 and 43 years.

Sixty percent of Uganda's orphans are parentless because of AIDS. Ojwok said by the year 2000, 17 percent of the nation's children will be orphans. From 1991 to 1995, the percentage of all orphans below the age of 15 went from 9.9 to 12.9. AIDS has also created a significant number of households headed by children under age 16, he said. And beyond the dire economic consequences, he said, is "the aspect of stigma—still it is there." AIDS has also struck Uganda's labor force significantly. "We estimate that at least 10 percent of the labor force is HIV positive," Ojwok said. "A highly dangerous" situation, he added, is the fact that among professional categories—doctors, teachers, economists, architects—"about 24 percent of those tested randomly were HIV positive."

Dr. John Rwomushana is the commission's coordinator for health sector, HIV/AIDS research and development. Uganda has worked with the international community, he said, "in vaccine research, development and evaluation, including trials." He announced the start of a two-year "preventive trial" involving a French product, Alvac 205. Until 1986, the Uganda government was shy about openly dealing with the epidemic. Since then, however, Uganda has confronted the AIDS issue on all fronts. A keyword has been awareness, which seems to have led to behavioral changes. Women's groups like NACWOLA are working to both support women and empower them economically in order to enable them to "negotiate for safer sex with their male counterparts."

On the Mbale-Tororo Road, Edith Wakumire's Uganda Women Concern Ministry cares for AIDS widows and orphans. In the same geographical area, Salem (pronounced sah-lahm) Uganda also cares for widows and scores of orphans, teaching youngsters carpentry and tailoring and other skills so that they can earn a living when schooling ends. Also in Mbale, Connie Namono manages the regional office of AIDS Care, Education and Training, ACET, which received its first six months of funding from Unicef. Her staff of six talks to young people in and out of school about coping with love, lust and the risks of sex. Because HIV/AIDS can devastate a household, prevention work here is often linked with poverty reduction. And, for nongovernmental organizations involved in this work, in 1995, the United Nations Development Programme began a two-year, $12 million program for poverty reduction and tackling AIDS. Any positive aspects of the situation? The commission's director general says the AIDS infection rate is declining.

However, in addition to its devastating impact on African people, HIV/AIDS is bound to have a deleterious effect on the continent's overall population. Ninety percent of the world's AIDS fatalities occur in Africa. And the continent is locale of 70 percent of the world's persons with HIV. Ten percent of adults in several nations have the virus and life expectancy has dropped. Globally, population growth has declined due to falling fertility. But in Africa, US Bureau of Census demographers report, population growth will cease.

PROMOTING CONDOM USE TO FIGHT THE SPREAD OF AIDS

YASNA UBEROI
May 1999

Global use of condoms must be increased to 24 billion per year if we are to curb the spread of HIV/AIDS and other sexually transmitted infections (STIs), according to a new report published by the Johns Hopkins Population Information Program, "Closing the Condom Gap." This figure is approximately three to four times as high as current estimated condom use, six to nine billion condoms each year.

The estimate of 24 billion is based on research conducted by Johns Hopkins University in an effort to raise awareness of the consequences of rapidly spreading sexually transmitted infections.

The need for condoms continues to increase as more people become infected with HIV, the report says—some 16,000 more people every day. Globally, at least 33 million people are living with HIV/AIDS and another 14 million have died from the disease. Among the newly infected, six out of every 10 people who contract HIV are women, and many newborns get the virus from their infected mothers.

Efforts to increase condom use will reduce rates of HIV infection and, as a result, slow the spread of AIDS, the report says, noting that laboratory tests show the HIV virus cannot penetrate an intact latex condom.

In trying to analyze why more people don't use condoms, the authors of "Closing the Condom Gap," Robert Gardner, Richard Blackburn and Ushma Upadhyay, write, "Family planning programs usually focus on the contraceptive needs of married women, while much of the need for condoms is to prevent HIV/AIDS and other STIs among unmarried people, particularly youth."

The report cites research showing that 71 percent of the need for condoms is among sexually active unmarried men. Social norms often encourage men to take sexual risks such as visiting commercial sex workers, the report says, and women, because of traditional gender roles, often do not feel free to talk about sex or ask for condoms.

Misconceptions also play a role, the report says, noting that some people think they face little or no risk of pregnancy or STIs. Others know very little about condoms, do not like to use them, cannot afford to purchase them or cannot obtain them easily or without embarrassment.

To encourage condom use, the report suggests that community campaigns address issues of trust and communication between sexual partners and that condoms be made accessible in hotels, bars, grocery stores and vending machines, in addition to health clinics and pharmacies.

The report also makes a case for the cost-effectiveness of condoms as a method of disease prevention. The total US health care costs for treating STIs in 1994 was almost $17 billion. Each case of AIDS costs the US an estimated $100,000 to $200,000 in lifetime medical care expenditures. One study reveals that savings for US health care could be as high as $530 per condom when used by homosexual men having sex with multiple partners.

Additionally, the report says, "Making condoms more accessible, lowering their cost, promoting them more and helping to overcome social and personal obstacles to their use would save many lives and reduce the enormous consequences and costs of STIs and unintended pregnancies."

VIETNAM: FIGHTING TRADITIONAL TABOOS ON SEX

RESHMA PRAKASH
July 1998

HANOI—In a traditional society still largely bound by Confucian ethics of morality and modesty, it takes a lot of courage for a young girl to speak out publicly about adolescent sexuality.

But discussing such matters among friends some years ago, as young girls often do, made Nguyen Quynh Trang and her friends realize how little they knew and how difficult it was to get any accurate information about the topic from anyone else. For one thing, the subject was somewhat taboo. "Good" girls, after all, did not think about these things, let alone discuss them. And no one seemed willing to talk about the issue of sex and sexuality, or explain, except to impart a lecture on morals. There were hardly any books on the subject and no organization that considered it important enough to address.

"It's not just that young people want to know about sex, which they do," said Trang, now 24, "but they need to know about safe sex, the dangers of sexually transmitted diseases and how to cope with the emotional aspects of a relationship as well."

So Trang and a couple of friends decided to fill this need. Forming an organization called the Gender Education Group, they sought the help of one of Vietnam's largest and oldest nongovernmental organizations, the Women's Union, and, with a grant of $30,000 provided by the Canadian International Development Agency, embarked on a mission to write books that were not only informative but friendly and non-judgmental as well.

The project, known as Youth Write about Reproductive Health, involved group discussions and interviews with young people to ascertain their attitudes and where the gaps in information lay. The result, after more than a year of labor, was a book on reproductive health and sexuality that provides basic information on reproductive biology, birth control, AIDS and other sexually transmitted diseases, self esteem, and related topics. Smaller books on specific topics such as puberty, birth control and HIV/AIDS were also pro-duced.

Using cartoons and informal language, the books not only provide sim-ple, easy-to-understand information but debunk popular misconceptions as well.

The prejudices and attitudes of the young people interviewed for the study are similar to those expressed by young people everywhere, revealing the somewhat universal problem of misinformation.

"I don't like my boyfriend to use condoms—if you use a condom it's like the man is with a prostitute," said one female student. "It's not every time you have sex that you get pregnant. I read that in the newspaper." "If the man knows the way then you won't get pregnant," said another. "I hate all contra-ceptive methods," announced a male student. "I've heard they're both vulgar and indicate a lack of mutual respect."

Even though a lot of the boys interviewed said they were in favor of pre-marital sex, many of them still valued virginity in girls. "There is an advantage to sex before marriage because many couples have had to break up because of that," said one male student. But another pointed out that Vietnamese society is still reluctant to accept such matters. "I will easily break up with her if I know that the woman I love has lost her virginity," he said.

Some of the girls seemed to chaff at these gender biases. "I think the worst is when we have to seek the forgiveness of our husbands but we don't know anything about his virginity before he was with us," said one young woman. "It's really funny if he lost his morals, was unfaithful, but he still has the right to look down on us. And it's all because he's a man and we're women."

The issue of AIDS, not surprisingly, revealed confusion over methods of transmission. "If HIV can live in monkeys, then of course it can live in mosquitoes and I think maybe you can catch it—I'm very afraid," said one female technology student. Another male student said, "The semen enters the women's body, not the other way around. Women don't have semen, so it's very difficult to spread HIV to men." A male stu-dent expressed a common view that, "If you ejacu-late outside, then that's a better way of preventing HIV than condoms, especially since not all women

'If a young person wants to know about sex, he's already done something indecent.'

will accept it when they know you're using a condom. Especially when you love each other and haven't married yet, condoms seem coarse, unpoetic."

The study found that young men and women felt most comfortable talking to their friends, and not to their parents. As one student put it, "Adults always think that if a young person wants to know about sexuality then he's already done something indecent. They don't think that we want to know those things to avoid doing something bad." A young woman complained that her mother told her that children crawl out of the thigh. "I wonder why my mother had to say that," she asked. But friends can't always be relied on for sound information, they added, so books may be the best option for those too embarrassed to ask questions.

With the incidence of AIDS on the rise, and more young people forced to turn to abortion because of the social stigma attached to unmarried mothers, the need for sex education for young people grows by the day in Vietnam. It is estimated that there are about 163 abortions per 1,000 live births.

Trang's books have just been published and she is in the process of searching for distributors. She has approached some schools, but teachers so far haven't been very enthusiastic about the books. "Sex education in schools isn't really accepted," she said. "Obviously a lot of social attitudes need to change."

DOC SHARMA AND THE IMMIGRANT EXPERIENCE

ERIN TROWBRIDGE
October 1998

It's not your typical rags-to-riches story. Then again, not much about Doctor Samin K. Sharma is the run-of-the-mill kind of stuff. But to go from handing out chicken vindaloo to performing almost 1,000 angioplasties a year— well, that kind of blows all cliches out the window.

Sharma, once a delivery boy at an Indian restaurant on 37th Street making ends meet after arriving in the United States from India in 1983, is now the director of the Cardiac Catheterization Laboratory and Intervention at Mount Sinai's Cardiovascular Institute, one of the most successful, reputable catheterization laboratories in the country. And Sharma is one of the most respected and prolific doctors in his field. If you can catch him somewhere between his office, his research, his patients, his family or the catheterization lab, he'd be happy to give you a minute and tell you all about it.

To watch Sharma in his hospital office, a blur of energy darting from a phone call from a resident to dictating a letter to his secretary to the scrub room to prepare for the fourth angioplasty he's performed that day, one quickly realizes that, for someone dealing all day long with overstressed arteries, Sharma certainly does not exude the calm, Zen-like demeanor you'd expect from a man constantly confronting the dangers of stress and high-blood pressure.

"I'm just 41," said Sharma from his office on the fifth floor of Mount Sinai Hospital. "I've only just arrived at the top of my field, but I still have further to go. I want to gain more national respect and enlarge my international reputation in this field. Maybe after I'm 50 I'll start to slow down."

Even the mention of slowing down in terms of the number of hours he puts in at the office provokes a stormy unleashing of all the other kinds of research and product development he'd like to get into. Somehow, slowing down doesn't seem to be an option.

The area where Sharma has made the greatest strides, angioplasty, was not quite a decade old when he began working as a fellow at Mt. Sinai in 1988, and his influence on the field has resulted in many of the innovations and successes experts now see in this type of interventional therapy.

Before 1979, when Swiss doctor Andreas Gruntzig developed the technique, invasive bypass surgery that required cracking open the rib cage and cutting and removing major sections of the artery was the only interventional operation, and it was usually a last resort to be carried out after the patient had already had a heart attack.

Gruntzig had been working with a catheter inserted into an artery in the upper thigh and threaded up to the heart. With a micro-camera attached to the end of the catheter, cardiologists could view the damage to the arteries from the inside. Gruntzig realized that by using the very same technique, catheterization, a tiny balloon could be expanded inside the artery to push back the plaque that was blocking the flow of blood and causing the stress to the heart and arteries. And, just like that, the age of angioplasty was born.

"It's hard to describe just how invasive and traumatic bypass surgery is," said Dr. Jonathan D. Marmur, Assistant Professor of Medicine in Interventional Cardiology at the Mt. Sinai laboratory. "Before the advent of angioplasty, cardiology was a diagnostic field and medicinal therapy to lower blood pressure was the step before a bypass and a surgeon. Now, there's a middle ground between pills and surgery, where you have a minimally invasive procedure that can be quickly performed and prevent the heart attack and arterial stress that before meant hours of surgery and trauma."

Coronary heart disease is the leading killer in the US, afflicting 13.9 million people. Although bypass surgery, medicines and angioplasties have greatly enhanced survival rates, restenosis, the return of blockage in the arteries, remains a problem. Almost 40 percent of angioplasty patients redevelop blockages and must continue treatment. Lowering that percentage and developing alternative therapies is one of the leading priorities for the Mt. Sinai Cardiovascular Institute.

"Right now we're doing a lot of research and development with specifically two new fields of therapy: genetics and radiation," said Sharma. "We are a laboratory that deals with high-risk patients at a very high-volume level. We want to go into radiation treatment. Radiation is used in cancer treatment to kill the cells that produce the cancer. In cardiology, radiation used concurrently with angioplasty brings the restenosis rate down considerably. By the year 2000, this will be a laboratory for rotoblater angioplasties, radiation treatments and gene therapy."

The laboratory under Sharma's direction has already performed more than 3,000 catheterizations, including 900 angioplasties, just in the past nine months. Sharma works with four other doctors who make up the team of cardiologists working in the laboratory and insists that they maintain a high volume of patients.

"The American Heart Association has proven that the more procedures you do, the more skilled you become," said Sharma. "I won't let anyone here do less than 200 a year; that must be the minimum."

Asked whether that iron-fistedness creates hostility among his co-workers, Sharma replied, "At times I feel a bit of resentment. But at the same time, everyone knows that I've never been spoon-fed or coddled. I have high expectations and demands because I have respect for them and they for me. Forty percent of my patients are independent of Mt. Sinai; they are coming here just to have me perform the work. I think that is something to aspire to, not resent."

> *'Nothing prepared me for how amazing this lab and his work are.'*

The residents, fellows, nurses and secretaries working with Sharma are quick to concede that he's a tough boss, but just as quick to affirm that his model is one to aspire to rather than disdain.

"His drive and ambition lifts the level of the playing field," said Timothy Jayasundera, who works under Sharma on a fellowship in his post-residency training in interventional cardiology. "I had read his articles and knew his medical reputation, but nothing prepared me for how amazing this lab and his work are."

The lab is essentially a long corridor brimming with heavy, x-ray-proof lab coats, ceiling-high stacks of sterile catheters, charts, oxygen tanks and other equipment, with four small operating rooms branching off in different directions.

The doctors perform the angioplasties by inserting the catheter into the upper thigh, guiding it to the artery and then carrying out the procedure by watching the internal maneuvers on overhead monitors.

First, a high-powered rotoblater breaks down the plaque lining the artery wall. Then an inserted balloon presses the wall back into shape and, finally, a "stent," a tiny spring, is placed in the artery to maintain the restored form. On the screen, what looks like a small crook in a river suddenly disappears, and where the artery was once angled and bent, it will run straight and clean.

If all goes well, a doctor can be done with the actual angioplasty in less than 10 minutes. The patients remain awake throughout the procedure, asking questions and, at times, voicing their surprise at how quickly the threat of a heart attack has just been nipped and tucked away.

Sharma is efficient and even curt walking into the operating room, but the second he stands beside the patient his manner changes. He's warm and talkative, telling jokes and explaining, step by step, exactly what he's doing. The nurses and lab technicians working with him in the laboratory are quick to discuss this side of his professional demeanor—the calming way he has with patients, the simple explanations he's able to offer when someone doesn't understand. In the offices across from the laboratory, asked to discuss Sharma's drive and stamina, the people who work with him in the operating room highlight his warmth.

"I've never seen anyone so devoted to their patients," said Aileen Aponte, a registered nurse-practitioner. "He has excellent rapport with his patients and if there's anyone who utterly appreciates his devotion to his work, it is them."

Dr. Valentin Fuster, M.D., Ph.D., President of the American Heart Association and Director of the Zena and Michael A. Wiener Cardiovascular Institute at Mt. Sinai, stressed that this patient-driven care is one of the most significant features of the Institute. Acknowledging the astounding number of procedures performed at the catheterization laboratory, Fuster went on to say that although the clinic has many cases, it has the same feeling at 7 AM that it does at 10 PM because of the shifts and rest periods worked into the schedule.

'I've never seen anyone so devoted to their patients.'

Responsible for bringing Sharma to Mt. Sinai, Fuster also credits him with many of the successes and remembers first meeting Sharma and anticipating exactly that. "Within moments of meeting him, I knew he was a star," said Fuster. "He was ready to work with me in any capacity, and when he found that there were no residencies available, he said he would work for me for free."

For three months, that's just what Sharma did, asking only that he be given the same degree of consideration as the other residents for the angioplasty fellowship—a risky move for Sharma even though he had already been offered the chance to head the catheterization lab at Elmhurst Hospital.

"Soon after I became an attending physician, several doctors left to go into other fields," said Sharma. "Everyone was saying that the cath lab was going to go downhill and be phased out. Instead, we have increased the number of angioplasties performed here and gained enormous recognition for the

quality of our work. Since 1991 we have quadrupled the number of procedures."

Asked how much of the credit for the lab's success belongs to him,
Sharma pauses a second, gives a wry smile, and says, "Well, they do call it
'Sharma's Cath Lab,' and 50 percent of the angioplasties done here are done
by me."

His self-assurance can be daunting, but has certainly been integral to his
achieving such success in so little time.

Sharma immigrated to the US from India in 1983, after he had graduated from the medical program at the top of his class but, because of academic
politics, had been unfairly flunked during his residency. Working and studying
for a visa-qualifying exam in Pittsburgh and then New York, Sharma continued his medical studies and did his stint making food deliveries to pay the
rent. Settling into a better job working with an Indian jeweler, Sharma made a
diagnosis that would change his life.

The 42-year-old jeweler complained about headaches one day and, after
probing for more information, Sharma told him to have a CAT scan because
it sounded as if he had a tumor on the frontal lobe. A later visit to the doctor
proved Sharma correct and the jeweler invited him to come live with him and
act as his personal physician. He moved out of the apartment he shared with
three others in Long Island City and for one year he lived on the Upper East
Side, making $800 a month.

Sharma passed his medical exams and took his medical residency at
Beekman Hospital before coming to Mt. Sinai. Drive and ambition, he said,
made it possible for him to avoid getting weighed down in the difficulties a
new immigrant faces. Today, that immigrant experience figures quite promi-
nently in his work.

Recent studies in clinical cardiology journals have shown that Asian
Indians have the highest rates of coronary artery disease of any immigrant
ethnic group in the US. Sharma plans to incorporate research on the whys
and hows of this phenomenon into his work load.

"There are many hypothetical reasons why young Asian Indian men are
being afflicted," said Sharma. "Some say it's a high-fat diet, others say the
stress of such overly career-oriented people is the cause of the problems. But
the fact is, Indians living outside of the subcontinent are five times more likely
than other immigrants to have coronary artery disease. Sons living abroad are
dying before their fathers. This epidemic has not been given enough attention
and concern. I plan to change that."

Around the laboratory, Sharma has indeed gained the reputation of a champion of lost and forgotten causes. Taking on cases that other labs have turned away, Sharma is frequently called upon to meet, diagnose and treat people in the advanced stages of arterial disease.

On a recent afternoon, Sharma performed an angioplasty on a woman who had been turned away from two other catheterization labs. Given her history of two heart attacks and one bypass, the doctors had said there was nothing they could do. Sharma disagreed.

On the monitors above the operating table, the patient's arteries were cross-hatched and lined from the bypass. Sharma spent an hour performing the angioplasty, speaking quietly down to her as he explained step by step how the procedure was going.

"She was referred to me by word of mouth. I met her and scheduled the angioplasty for two days later," said Sharma. "Today is her wedding anniversary. I guess this can be her gift to her husband: no more heart attacks."

Sharma says it is the particularly risky cases that give the Mount Sinai Cardiovascular Institute an edge over many other hospitals. Throughout the medical community, the catheterization lab has a reputation for treating patients who have been denied care at other hospitals.

"Because we can carry out the procedures, in most cases so quickly, there is that element of immediate gratification," said Sharma. "This person came in with a clogged artery and only a 75 percent chance of surviving another bypass. Now she will go home with an open one. In this field you make an immediate difference in someone's life. That alone keeps my job constantly stimulating and rewarding. It keeps me waking up at 4 AM and working until 9 PM. I don't imagine that this could ever just be routine. Every case brings me a new challenge, and, really, there's nothing I like better."

Population and Development

FOLIO

The 1992 Rio Summit: Delegates made the connections between issues of poverty, population, environment, gender and human rights. The end result being the concept of 'sustainable development.'

Outside the museum of the Cambodia Killing Fields, a memorial to all the lives lost and the human rights violated during the long years of the country's civil war.

People and goods

- The total of all goods and services produced worldwide grew from $5 trillion in 1950 to $29 trillion in 1997, increasing more than twice as fast as the world population.

- Economic output per person rose from just over $1,900 in 1950 to almost $5,000 in 1997.

- In industrial nations growth has slowed to just about 2 percent a year during this decade, compared with almost 6 percent a year in developing nations.

- The fastest growing region from 1990 to 1997, Asia, averaged almost 8 percent annually.

- China led the Asian growth with an economy that has grown at almost 10 percent a year since 1990. Since 1980, China's economic output has doubled every eight years.

- Incomes have risen the most in developing nations where population growth has slowed the most. African countries, with population growth rates of almost 3 percent a year, have seen little increase in percapita income. (WorldWatch Institute)

- It is estimated that 10 million people in the world already have lost their jobs as a result of the deepening Asian financial crisis.

- The International Labor Organization estimates that 60 million people between the ages of 15 and 24 are looking for work.

- The World Bank estimates that 1.3 billion people live on less than $1 a day. That means that about one-fifth of the world's people have seen little improvement in their daily existence despite economic advances.

—ANNE SILVERSTEIN

Women are critical to sustainable farming practices.

LOUIS SILVERSTEIN

Jamshedpur, India: Poverty forces thousands of jobless people to comb the "slag" heaps outside the town for pieces of iron to sell to scrap dealers. Income? On a lucky day, the equivalent of two dollars.

Gourmet only: A fisherman in Guilin, China with tame fishing cormorants that catch fish that he can then sell to restaurants.

Rural Bangladesh: The most densely populated country in the world is also home to some of the most innovative and influential grassroots activists and organizations. Concepts like lending small sums to the poor and women to help them start up their own businesses flourish here.

Nafis Sadik, center, Executive Director of the United Nations Population Fund has been a pivotal figure in promoting issues of women's health around the world.

Figures in population: Jane Fonda, Nafis Sadik, Ted Turner.

PHOTOS: UNFPA

Water

■ *About 50 percent of the population in developing countries is suffering from diseases caused either directly by infection through the consumption of contaminated water or food, or indirectly by disease-carrying organisms, such as mosquitoes, that breed in water.*

■ *Unless action is stepped up, the number of people without*

access to safe water will increase to 2.3 billion by 2025.

■ *Twenty percent of the world's population in 30 countries face water shortages, a figure that will rise to 30 percent of the world's population, in 50 countries, by 2025, according to the UN. World Water Day is observed on March 22.*

■ *Every eight seconds, a child dies from a water-related disease.*

■ *Fifty percent of all people lack adequate sanitation.*

■ *Eighty percent of diseases in the developing world are caused by contaminated water.*

■ *Women and girls in developing countries spend more than 10 million person-years annually fetching water. (The UN Environment Programme)*

—ANNE SILVERSTEIN

In The Hague 1999: Florence Manguyu of Kenya, Hilary Rodham Clinton and Nicolaas Biegman of the Netherlands highlighted the progress made in the last years at the Cairo+5 review meeting.

Calcutta, India: In the aftermath of the Cairo and Rio conferences, development experts hone in on the housing and sanitation problems that come with urbanization.

Numbers that speak

ONLY 28.5 MILLION TONS

■ The number of fisherman worldwide, either wholly or partly commercial, has doubled since 1970. In that year, 13 million commercial fishermen took in 65 million tons of fish. In 1990, there were only 28.5 million fishermen but they produced 98 million tons of fish.

85 PERCENT

■ About 85 percent of the world's fishermen are in Asia, with the largest number in China.

12 MILLION

■ In many countries, fishing is a seasonal occupation, or a part-time job. In the early 1990s, about 12 million people were considered full-time fishermen; that is, 90 percent or more of their subsistence income came from fishing or large-scale aquaculture.

NO LONGER CHEAP

■ Approximately 35 percent of the 200 major marine animals harvested from the sea are showing declining yields. During the last 10 years, international seafood prices have risen almost 5 percent a year, with the result that a traditionally cheap source of protein has become less accessible to the poor. (Food and Agriculture Organization)

3.5 MILLION DEAD

■ An estimated 1.1 billion people use tobacco worldwide, and 3.5 million people die annually from tobacco-related causes.

Alcohol is estimated to cause about 750,000 deaths annually. (World Health Organization)

582,000

■ An estimated 582,000 women die each year in poor countries from pregnancy- related causes, compared with 4,000 women in developed countries.
■ Each year, about 7.6 million infants are stillborn or die in the first week of life.

9 OUT OF 10 BIRTHS

■ Nine out of 10 births occur in developing countries, where the number of people in their optimum reproductive years will double between 1995 and 2010.

50 MILLION ABORTIONS

■ About 50 million abortions are performed annually. Twenty million are performed under unsafe conditions by untrained providers in dirty and inadequately equipped places far from professional medical help.

$14 PER PERSON

■ Average annual spending on healthcare is estimated at about $14 per person in poor countries and $62 per person in middle-income countries. Half of these monies are from public funds. Health spending drops as low as $11 per person in China and goes above $1,800 per person in developed countries. (Population Reference Bureau)

—ANNE SILVERSTEIN

Nongovernmental activists at the 1995 Beijing Women's Conference throng to meetings in Huairou despite heavy rains. Tens of thousands of women attended.

Pranay Gupte (top row, right) in South Africa wrote of the gravity of the AIDS pandemic and its effect on this nation where it is estimated that nearly 500 people are infected with the AIDS virus each day

An editorial by Paula DiPerna in this section asks, "Where's the Money?" Less forthright allusions to money can be found in almost every official report and "document" coming out of recent international meetings. They include "official development assistance," "donor fatigue," "allocation of resources" and "fiscal priorities," all tributes to policy-makers' recognition of the bottom-line problem. At the watershed 1992 Earth Summit, 178 nations promised to provide 0.7 percent of their GNP for foreign aid. At

this point only a few countries—Denmark, Sweden, Norway and the Netherlands—have reached this figure. The United States contributes about 0.1 percent. The estimate at the 1994 Cairo Population Conference was that $17 billion in aid would be needed just for a reproductive health package in the year 2000. So far only one-third of this has been forthcoming.

Concerns over this shortfall from donor countries has led to wide discussion, finger-pointing and legitimate controversy. Some of the questions covered in this section relate to "moral imperatives." The Danes, for example, see foreign aid as help for world peace, but also as "the right thing to do." Other questions have to do with the equivocation of the United States on many of these issues and, not least, the awakening of the World Bank and International Monetary Fund to the human and social impact of their policies.

SECTION 6

MONEY AND THE INTERNATIONAL COMMUNITY

A 'MORAL IMPERATIVE' FOR DONORS

STEVEN W. SINDING
October 1994

I am dismayed to see that official development assistance has dropped in each of the last two years, suggesting a level of donor fatigue, or erosion of political support for international development assistance, that is extremely ominous. Unless development proceeds at a faster pace than it has over the past 30 to 40 years, particularly development that focuses on human resources and human development, the prospect of eventual global population stabilization will remain ephemeral. Until women have achieved true equality with men, until we begin to approach universal literacy and at least completion of secondary education, until we escape from subsistence agriculture as the economic base of the bulk of developing-country populations, there is no prospect that population stabilization can be achieved.

Again, there is both a moral imperative and, from a population perspective, a strategic necessity to invest in the Cairo menu of girls' education, reduced infant and young child mortality, reduced maternal mortality and the economic and social empowerment of women as essential dimensions of the development challenge. That is the population and reproductive policy package: enabling individuals to realize their reproductive goals through the provision of high quality, comprehensive reproductive health and family planning services, and investing in human development such that the need for and demand for children will soon approach replacement level.

There is both a moral imperative and, from a population perspective, a strategic necessity to invest in the Cairo menu of initiatives.

That is the package, but what will it cost? And can we afford it? Although there was considerable debate about the basis upon which the estimations were made, the Cairo Conference agreed that the price tag for the reproductive health package that the conference advocated would amount to some $17 billion in the year 2000, rising to approximately $21 billion by the year 2015. This estimate was based upon the present costs of family planning service delivery systems and what a projection of the costs of the reproductive health services that the conference called for: STD detection and treatment, HIV-AIDS programs, certain aspects of prenatal and postnatal care including delivery, prevention and treatment of infertility, prevention and management of consequences of abortion, safe motherhood activities, and so on. It also includes population policy and research work, including census and vital registration-related activities, demographic research and analysis, etc. In other words, it included most of what has conventionally been classified as population program activities and added to that the new reproductive health package.

There was considerable debate, particularly among the donor countries at Cairo, over these figures but subsequent analysis has tended to confirm their rough validity. I should say that these figures do not include the dimensions of the Cairo prescription that go beyond the reproductive health and population package. In other words, they do not include investments in female education, women's credit and economic empowerment programs, and so on. If they were included, the overall price tag would, of course, increase many fold.

Nobody knows exactly what is being spent to implement the Cairo package.

Cairo agreed that the burden sharing for this financial requirement should shift from the current three-quarters borne by developing countries and one-quarter borne by industrialized countries to a more equitable two-thirds by the developing countries and one-third by the industrialized countries. While this is a recommendation about which disagreement could occur, it means that more than $5 billion of the $17 billion projected for the year 2000 will need to be borne by the donor countries.

How are we doing in this regard? The answer, regrettably, is nobody knows just what is being spent. Data on donor expenditures for the Cairo package are extraordinarily difficult to pull together, particularly for recent years. The problems are in part definitional and in part the result of different accounting systems among the governments.

With all those caveats, it is clear that as we approach the year 2000, we are well short of what is needed. In 1994, the last year for which we have full data, 21 OECD members plus the European Union and the World Bank altogether committed $1.4 billion to population programs as defined by Cairo. In 1995, it appears, on the basis of incomplete information, that this number may have risen to $2 billion because a number of countries, including the United States, Japan and Germany, along with some small donors such as Australia,

Denmark, the United Kingdom, and the Netherlands, increased their contributions very substantially and it appears that World Bank lending for population and reproductive health also substantially increased in 1995. But 1995 looks like the high water mark. In 1995 total official development assistance (ODA) began to decline and, in 1996, it is clear that that trend has accelerated. In addition, the US, which has represented a very significant share of the total funding for such programs historically, severely cut not only its overall development assistance, but that portion of it committed to population and reproductive health. The prospects for 1997 may be equally grim.

The fact is that we, as a donor community, are providing only roughly a third of what the Cairo document calls for in the year 2000, and would have to substantially increase our annual expenditures to have any hope of meeting the year 2000 goal. Given the contemporary mood of voters and of governments, there is little ground for much optimism. UNFPA reports a significant decline in pledged contributions for the next fiscal year and there are other signs that the spirit and enthusiasm engendered by Cairo is already beginning to atrophy.

> *We, as a donor community, are providing roughly a third of what the Cairo document calls for in the year 2000, and would have to increase our annual expenditure.*

Unfortunately, no valid data are available from developing countries to estimate how well they are meeting the aggregate commitment of $17 billion. There are some very promising signs in countries such as India, several of the sub-Saharan African states, Pakistan and the Philippines of increased commitment to this sector, and certainly the rhetoric of international conferences and agreements has highly supported the Cairo orientation.

The Social Summit, the Beijing Women's Conference, the Human Rights Conference in Vienna, and even Habitat this year in Istanbul, have all included language that strongly reinforces the human development approach which was so prominent in the Cairo Program of Action, but I am nonetheless deeply worried that the breakthrough of Cairo and the enormous potential it represents for improvements in the human condition will founder on the shoals of precarious financial commitments.

While it is indisputably in the interest of both the industrialized and the developing countries to make the Cairo promise a reality, we appear as a community of nations to lack the will to implement the consensus we fought so long and hard to achieve. Cairo's program of action is truly a landmark document. It represents the first time in 25 years of international dispute and debate that the community of nations found common ground on an approach to one of the great issues facing humankind. What a tragedy it would be if we failed to make this promise a reality—a tragedy for millions of women around the world and for generations to come.

ETHIOPIA: A HELPING HAND IN BAD TIMES

LEYLA ALYANAK
April 1997

ADDIS ABABA, Ethiopia—In the inhospitable mountains of central Ethiopia, a rich man is one who has a stock of grain. Famine and drought are old acquaintances in this part of the world, and when the bad times come, people feel fortunate if they can eat one meal a day.

Demeke Abe fought in the Somali wars of the late Seventies and returned home to do what his father had done before him: become a weaver, producing yard upon yard of the richly bordered cloth local people wear every day of their lives. But Demeke is not a rich man, and he farms on the side. It is a precarious existence. As population grows, pressure on the land does too.

Adanach Dion is his neighbor. She spins cotton for a living, but when she can't make ends meet, she collects firewood and sells it. Life is hard with eight children and no husband, and disaster is often just around the corner.

When Demeke and Adanach need to invest a little money in their business, they turn to their new credit group, made up of small artisans like themselves, set up under the auspices of CPAR, Canadian Physicians for Aid and Relief.

"The project organizes people into groups of 10 to 15 who begin saving money," said Wondimu Zik, the project's monitoring and evaluation officer. "The group identifies activities for which it needs loans, such as weaving, spinning or petty trade. The project then lends them the money, usually very tiny amounts, at an interest rate of 10 percent a year." Private lenders charge 10 percent a month.

What makes these groups special is their mutual responsibility. If one member defaults, the entire group has to pay back the loan. Pressure is high and repayment rates are close to 100 percent.

Unlike what its name implies, CPAR is not a group of Canadian field doctors but a nongovernmental organization (NGO) in development working toward health in its broadest sense—including human well-being, environmental integrity and social justice. CPAR's work in five African and one Asian country was initially based on relief. In Angola, Uganda and Rwanda, it started in response to civil war. In the Philippines, involvement came with the eruption of Mount Pinatubo, and in Ethiopia it was the result of famine.

Like many NGOs, CPAR has shifted from relief work into development, working to bridge what aid workers like to call the "continuum from relief to development." The Ethiopian operation has become "indigenized," with only one mid-level staff member a Canadian.

Throughout Ethiopia, microcredit gives the poorest access to capital they are denied through normal channels because they lack collateral or regular income. Since CPAR works mainly in rural areas, another indigenous NGO, Good Shepherd Family Care Services, tries to ease poverty in the seething, stinking slums of the capital, Addis Ababa. Good Shepherd is the brainchild of two Ethiopian friends who decided to do something about the suffering of women and children in their country. In the poor parts of Addis, a third of households are headed by women, each with an average of five children. Not only are they mothers but they take on all household and many labor chores as well, just to feed their children.

Good Shepherd uses self-reliance as the basis for its work. By equipping women with new skills and entrepreneurial knowledge, it encourages them to start their own tiny, one-person businesses.

"You can train women but they may just go home and sit," said Nadia Waber, Good Shepherd's communications officer. "Few jobs are available. But if you give them small loans, they can do something with the money they have in their hands."

"The loans are only about 300 birr [$50]. We help the women decide the type of business they want, how to run it, and teach them to save money. They don't live hand-to-mouth any more."

Mulu Mekonnen received a small loan and started planting vegetables. "I have eight children and had almost no income," she said. "Now my children all go to school. They eat fresh vegetables from my garden, and I can meet their other needs with the money I get from selling vegetables."

In addition to providing microcredit, Good Shepherd runs a range of services from health care centers to sanitation and child sponsorship programs.

To both CPAR and Good Shepherd, giving people tools to help themselves is the key to the climb out of poverty.

BANGLADESH: A MATTER OF FREEDOM AND CONTROL

ERIN TROWBRIDGE
November 1997

DHAKA, Bangladesh—Nagma Bigum, 25, cupped her hand around her infant son's head and gingerly shushed his crying. Sitting on a bench inside the Maternity Health Clinic in the Azimpur district of the capital city with the infant and her 4-year-old daughter, she was waiting to be called into the clinic's rudimentary infirmary for the baby's immunization shots.

Nagma had come to the clinic, along with 30 other new mothers, not only for the shots but for checkups (for both mother and child) and to receive a supply of birth control pills. When asked whether she planned to have more children, her eyes opened wide and she snapped out an incredulous, "No!" She had six brothers and sisters growing up, she said, but she knows that large families are not only bad for Bangladesh but a sign of the past for Bangladeshi women. "I want to enjoy the freedom my mother didn't have," she said.

Women had children because husbands forced them to and they were ignorant of birth control.

Nagma's feelings are not uncommon. Though the terms "family planning" and "reproductive health" have, in developing nations, often carried the stigma of enforced child-bearing limits and of uninformed abortions, in this primarily Islamic country they mean nothing of the sort. Twenty-five years ago Bangladeshi women had, on average, seven children. Today that number has dropped to 3.3. "Women weren't having that many children out of sheer desire," said Jahanara Sobhani, director of Concerned Women, Bangladesh, a women's health care clinic in Dhaka. "When I started this clinic, I saw women who were having children either because their husbands forced them to and they were ignorant about birth control, or because the infant mortality rate was so high that they figured only a few would survive anyway. Now women know about contraception and the government has incorporated post-natal care into its family planning program. The infant mortality rate has dropped almost 50 percent. Women having so many kids today is irresponsible. They know that."

Though things have changed dramatically in the past few years, this nation is far from being in the clear. In fact, statistics say the worst is yet to come. With 2,166 people per square mile (836 per square kilometer), Bangladesh is still one of the most densely populated nations in the world. The size of the state of Wisconsin, it is home to 121 million people, almost half the population of the entire US. And with 43 percent of the population under the age of 15, this country will, in the next two decades, at least double its present population. According to the UN Population Fund (UNFPA), over the next 40 to 50 years Bangladesh can hope only to control its growth, not lower it. And with more than 78 percent of the people living on less than $1 a day, this spells disaster.

It is hard to say exactly how things got so bad in this lush nation. Mohammed Ali, Secretary for the Ministry of Health and Family Welfare, told The Earth Times that though the roots of this problem lay in a tradition that values fertility, Bangladesh's more recent history exacerbated the problem. "After the war for independence in 1971, we had a mass immigration. Our land is a very fertile delta. People came here from India and Pakistan to escape the desert. The geography of our nation was certainly seductive. But this, coupled with a cultural tradition that had no knowledge of family planning, led to our present state. We can come out of this only by educating people and providing the resources."

International donors, indigenous nongovernmental organizations and the Bangladeshi government have all developed programs to change the focus of population control in Bangladesh from mere distribution of contraceptives to client-centered family planning services. Informing, educating, providing ante- and post-natal care and immunizing newborns are the new priorities in reproductive health services in Bangladesh, and women like Nagma Bigum are the benefactors.

For many years family planning in Bangladesh meant door-to-door distribution of contraceptives, often without instruction in how to use them. Although population growth did begin to ease in the late 1980s, the government and nongovernmental organizations realized that education about family planning was imperative to ensure that the trend continued. Now, almost 50 percent of Bangladeshi women practice birth control, up from 8 percent in 1975, according to Bangladesh Demographic and Health Survey figures, but the purchase of contraceptives does not necessarily mean consistent and knowledgeable use.

"After [the UN International Conference on Population and Development in] Cairo, family planning and reproductive health services have taken on a client focus," said Althea Mulakala, Director of the Bangladesh Population and Health Consortium. "Now we concentrate on the information a woman is given along with her choice and consistent use of contraception. In the past, women were just handed the pill and told to take it. Sometimes, like right before Ramadan, women would load up on the pill so they wouldn't get their periods during the fast. With proper education we can avoid these misunderstandings, which ultimately end with unwanted pregnancies."

In Dhaka, where "marketing" still means going to the local green market, the women waiting outside a birth control center wear traditional saris and shalwar kameezes, but they request condoms and make appointments for Norplant implants with an assertiveness and familiarity that belie the reputation of the demure and passive Islamic woman.

"Twenty-five years ago this was unimaginable," said Rokeya Sultana, who heads the Concerned Women's birth control center. "I can feel the whole culture changing. When I first started this organization, I was considered a bad woman. My friends and I had to distribute birth control quietly from door to door. Now, women are proactive. They come to us."

Door-to-door delivery also made birth control an imposition and not a choice, say many health care providers. Clinics have sprouted up all over the countryside, as well as in the capital, that will provide home delivery of contraceptives but encourage women to come to them. The poster-lined halls bear slogans reminding women that the power of choice is theirs, and the furniture and fixtures around the clinics tell as much of an empowerment story as the women who use them.

The wooden benches, says Tajul Islam, Director of Public Affairs and Communications for a NGO called Bangladesh Rural Advancement Coalition, took years to arrive. "For so long women were ashamed to come to a family planning clinic and faced great scorn if they were seen," Islam said. "The greatest task at hand was simply making women comfortable enough to seek out birth control for themselves. Benches where they can sit and wait outside are a revolution of sorts. They mean that family planning is a choice that not only enhances an individual woman's life, but the future and culture of Bangladesh."

Bangladeshis have heard the information, seen the posters and read the pamphlets. They know poverty and landlessness cannot be reckoned with if the population keeps growing at its current rate. The cyclones and monsoons that for four months of the year tear through the river-crossed countryside, flooding the land and destroying the houses, keep the rural population in a constant state of redevelopment. Though the floods wash rich silt from the uplands down to the depleted soil and carry fish into landlocked areas, these offer little consolation.

While Dhaka is a home to a deeply entrenched urban poverty that forces hundreds of thousands to sleep in makeshift shanties lining the streets, the country's rural areas have their own form of poverty as well. "In rural areas, socio-economic indicators are pretty basic," said Am Sarder, Director of the Demographic Surveillance System at Matlab, a health care clinic in the swampy region of river villages in the south. "The three states of wealth—upper, middle and lower class—can be witnessed architecturally: brick, tin and thatched, respectively. The difference between tin and thatched is nil, and brick is simply too rare to count. That's how wealth and stability are measured outside of the city."

The goal of many maternal health clinics in the rural areas is to provide birth control and education and also to train mothers to identify their own and their children's health problems. With infant and child mortality rates still above nine percent in rural Bangladesh, access to health care is as significant a problem as overpopulation. As long as children die at this overwhelming rate, public health workers said, families will continue to have more and more children.

Matlab, which serves as the primary health center to more than 70 villages along the Gunti and Dhanagoda Rivers, teaches the local community workers, who daily venture out to serve 1,500 people, to recognize symptoms and instruct mothers on how to treat their children themselves.

Access to health care is as significant a problem as overpopulation.

"The idea is to have clinics close by that can provide emergency care and prevention, but to also have community workers who can identify the problem immediately," said Dr. Hafigar Rahman. "Women used to have to travel for two or three days just to see a doctor of any kind. In the 37 years the Matlab clinic has been here, we've been able to teach self-sufficiency in diagnosis and prevention so that the clinic can assist in emergency services and specialize in creating vaccines that will end many of the diseases that plague the people in this area."

In a nearby village, Aprajita Chakraborty, a Matlab community worker, lugs around an enormous red leather-bound register book filled with two years' documentation on each of the 1,370 villagers she visits once a month.

As she makes her way straight for the women to ask about their children and contraception use, the men congregate on the banks of a nearby pond, giggling nervously and glancing over their shoulders as the women ask questions in rapid-fire Bengla dotted with English words like "training," "condoms" and "pills."

The clinic workers learned long decades ago that the community women would talk freely only with female doctors, nurses and basic providers. In the time since, men have been relegated to the second-story administrative offices while women do all the field work, consultations, exams and social work on the clinic's ground floor.

"Unfortunately, the responsibility for diagnosis and care falls on the shoulders of the women" who visit the clinic, said Dr. Nurjahan Shelly at the Matlab clinic. "They are the primary contraceptive users and health care providers in the community." Birth control pills (taken by women) account for more than 90 percent of contraceptive use in Bangladesh, while condoms are used consistently by only 1 percent of men.

In both rural and urban clinics, doors boasting a "Vasectomy" sign are invariably shut and locked, with a fine layer of dust on the doorknob, while, a few feet away, women sit waiting for IUD insertion and pregnancy tests.

"When Henry Kissinger visited Bangladesh decades ago he called it hopeless, a 'basket case,'" said Musa Balla Silla, Acting Executive Director of the Partners in Population and Development Secretariat in Dhaka. "But in so little time, this country has shown its tenacity, its ability to change despite every adverse circumstance known to man. These are extraordinary people, not willing not back down."

The ball has started rolling and the momentum, it seems, will be impossible to stop. In clinics and homes around the country, women like Nagma discuss fervently and passionately the importance of controlling their lives. For them, if that leads to prosperity for Bangladesh, that is well and good. But for many of them, the simple power of family planning and control over their own bodies is a thrilling revelation. One that is not about to wear off any time soon.

JORDAN: FOR REFUGEES, THE HOMELAND AWAITS

ELIZABETH BRYANT
September 1996

BAQA'A REFUGEE CAMP, Jordan—Their dark canvas tents have given way to whitewashed cement houses and flourishing markets. Their stories of loss have faded as parents die and children grow up, and a fickle international spotlight turns to other crises. But their cause remains firmly etched in the minds of the thousands living here, Jordan's largest Palestinian refugee camp.

"Every minute we hope, we're dreaming we will return to our homeland," said Baqa'a resident Sara Kassem. "But it's hard when one has almost reached 40."

Since fleeing their homes in 1948, these Palestinians have been at the center of one of the largest unresolved refugee issues in modern history. First they set up makeshift lives in UN tents on the West Bank. When war erupted again in 1967, they fled again, this time to Jordan.

After spending several months in makeshift camps in the Jordan Valley, they settled in Baqa'a, a camp spread across the northern outskirts of Amman. Today, it is hard to realize that these streets packed with carts piled high with grapes, apples and steaming shawarma are any different from the other suburbs of the city.

But the residents and the Jordanian government know otherwise. "As long as the refugees remain, the camps remain," said Samir Ghawi, director of information for the Palestinian Affairs Department of the Jordanian government. "It all depends on a final solution."

Resolving their status is central to discussions now under way between Israel and the Palestinian Authority. The negotiations are due to begin this year and be completed by 1999.

More than 63,000 official refugees live in Baqa'a, according to UNRWA, the United National Relief and Works Agency for Palestinian Refugees, which has built houses, health clinics and schools for the camps. But that doesn't count the thousands of other Palestinians who have moved into

Baqa'a. These unofficial residents and their children boost population estimates to more than 100,000.

Some Palestinians have moved out of Baqa'a to other neighborhoods in Amman. Others have moved still farther, to the US and Saudi Arabia, sending remittances home to their families. Still others, like pharmacist Kassim Awad, have returned and set up flourishing businesses. But many remain in these free UN homes, poor and unemployed, clinging to scraps of memories and hopes for change.

Sara Kassem, a divorcee, lives here with her brother Ibrahim and her 12-year-old son in a spare, neatly kept two-room house. Outside, a grapevine flows across the tiny courtyard that is almost completely swallowed up by a tin shack. The shack once served as the Kassem family home, a step up from the tent the siblings moved into with their parents in 1968. But, aside from the extra space, the Kassems said, life hasn't gotten much better.

Ibrahim is unemployed, living on the last of his savings from years working in Saudi Arabia as a car electrician. When the family goes to the camp's clinic for medical treatment, they must sometimes wait for hours, Sara said—even for a bottle of aspirin. And classrooms at the UN school attended by Sara's son are often overcrowded.

Donor fatigue means longstanding problems like the Palestinian refugees may get overlooked.

The siblings fall back on memories of better times, recollections stitched together from stories told by parents now dead. A large grocery store in a West Bank town called Abassya. A prosperous life. Then, in 1948, war and flight. Then homes here and there. Now Baqa'a.

Why not elsewhere? The Kassems shake their heads. "It's either return to Abassya or stay here," Ibrahim said.

No ties bind Sara and Ibrahim to this place. Jordan is the only country in the Middle East that grants Palestinian refugees full citizenship and equal opportunities for jobs and social services. Those refugees interviewed said they were not discriminated against. But by staying in Baqa'a, many say, their children will remember they are children of refugees and their cause will remain on the international agenda.

Meanwhile, Baqa'a residents are trying to improve their lives. The Camp Services Committee, an all-male volunteer group of Baqa'a residents, is charged with the daily running of the camp, from patching up disputes to pitching for better services. The Jordanian Women's Federation, a nonprofit women's group made up of Palestinian and Jordanian volunteers, has set up job training programs for women and an after-school program for children.

The federation's Baqa'a office was bustling during a recent visit, with a sewing course for women being held in one room and a summer camp for children in another. Asked whether she wants to return to the West Bank, 9-year-old Esraa Salem nodded. "Of course," she said. "It's our land."

For Jordan, the refugees are neither temporary nor cheap. According to the government's Palestinian Affairs Department, Jordan spends some $300 million a year on the 300,000 Palestinian refugees living in the country. The refugee agency, UNRWA, spends more than $64 million on Jordan's refugees, out of its total $330 million budget for Palestinians living in all the camps in the Middle East—in Jordan, Lebanon, Syria, the West Bank and Gaza. Other international organizations, including Unicef and the US-based nonprofit agency CARE, also pour money into health care and other camp services.

UNRWA's expenditures have grown by 5 percent each year, and the organization currently faces a budget crunch, said William Lee, chief of UNRWA's New York office. "There is a certain donor fatigue in all human services worldwide," he said. "And longstanding humanitarian issues like the Palestinian refugees might be overlooked in light of others like Burundi or Somalia."

For refugees like Youssef Mousse Youssef, 25, waiting for a solution sometimes brings despair. Youssef has never visited his family's native town of Jericho, about a mile from the Jordanian border.

"Sometimes I feel I will never go back to my homeland," he said. "But our mothers tell our sons and daughters, 'You will be back. Maybe after a hundred years. But you will be back.'"

LOVELY GENEVA, A SECOND HOME FOR THE U.N.

JOHN CORRY
April 1997

The United Nations and Geneva are inseparably joined. It is hard to imagine one without the other. Bonn and other cities may draw off bits and pieces—the Secretariat of the Convention on Migratory Species, for example, or the UN Volunteers—but history, tradition and a general placidity make Geneva ideal for the care and feeding of bureaucrats. Besides, it abuts Lake Geneva and is overlooked by Mont Blanc, and France is only a local bus ride away. Why would the UN want to leave?

Critics, of course, say that Geneva is dull, even dour, although perhaps that is only because orderliness bores them. Geneva is very well managed. Everything has its place. Garbage is picked up, while buses run regularly, and streets feel safe, even though you seldom see police. The charge of dourness also seems unfair. Swiss humor, someone once said, is no laughing matter, but the Genevois are unfailingly polite and usually quite cheerful. Possibly the critics are misled by the weather. It is often gray.

January, for instance, had only 80 minutes of sunshine. But February was much nicer and March was almost glorious. The lakeside snack bars began to do brisk business, along with the various tour boats. Young families came out on bicycles and old-fashioned roller skates (in-line skates have not made it yet to Geneva) and the city seemed problem-free. Obviously it was not—no big city is—and Geneva has been having economic difficulties along with the rest of Switzerland.

When Bonn tried to lure the World Trade Organization away, Geneva offered inducements to keep it—work permits, for one thing, for delegates' spouses. That was no small concession. Unemployment in Switzerland is at a record 5.7 percent, and the economy is in a slump. Total growth since 1990 is less than 0.5 percent, and Switzerland is expected to record the slowest growth in the industrialized world this year and next.

Moreover, real estate prices have declined sharply and the fabled banking industry has suffered a crisis. Since 1990 about a third of all Swiss banks have disappeared, most saved from bankruptcy only by merging with larger institutions. At the same time, Swiss tolerance is being strained. The 5.7 percent unemployment rate—never more than 1 percent in previous recessions—is caused in large part by foreign workers.

When unemployment threatened in the past, Switzerland sent foreign workers home. In the early 1980s, however immigration laws were revised, allowing many of the foreign workers to stay on as long as they wanted. They now make up about 40 percent of the unemployed. Meanwhile, Switzerland is generous with unemployment benefits, paying 80 percent of a worker's previous salary for up to two years.

None of this is to suggest that Switzerland is facing disaster. Per capita income is still the highest in Europe, but clearly some strains are showing. Two years ago, demonstrations in Zurich against Swiss participation in European integration led to intervention by the riot police. Last year 15,000 farmers rallied in Bern, the capital, to protest cuts in agricultural subsidies. Then 35,000 public employees demonstrated against changes in work rules. Meanwhile, the army says it has studied the Los Angeles riots. Soldiers may soon be issued nightsticks and handcuffs for possible use in keeping the peace. The army has fired at Swiss citizens in the past: the last time in 1932 at a labor rally in Geneva.

Thus, Switzerland has at least some of the same problems that the 182 member states of the UN have. Geneva is not as trouble-free as it may seem. But, like Switzerland itself, it does not advertise its problems and practices discreetness in all things. Even vice, such as it is, is well-ordered. International travelers come and go in Geneva, most of them on expense accounts, and many of them self-indulgent. Escort services that advertise in French, English and German—"Services include visits in your hotel and business/private events," "Beautiful Eurasian and Indonesian Girls Available for Hourly Escorts," "You need some nice company for dinner, weekend or travel?"—cater to them and not to the Genevois. There are also transvestite night clubs with drag queens. At the low-rent end of all this is the street near the railroad station where less finicky visitors find prostitutes.

So Geneva in its way is deceptive: placid, bourgeois and bureaucratic on the one hand, and economically troubled and perhaps a bit kinky on the other. It is a little like the UN itself, although the UN is less able to hide its problems than is Geneva. Besides the World Trade Organization, the city is home to the International Labor Organization, World Health Organization,

UN High Commissioner for Refugees and some 20 other UN and intergovernmental agencies. It is also home to the International Red Cross and some 130 other international nongovernmental organizations.

One way or another, they all look to the Office of the United Nations at Geneva, better known as the Palais des Nations. It is located in a pleasant park of some 62 acres that was donated to Geneva in 1890, and it was erected between 1929 and 1936 for the old League of Nations. Its exterior was made of travertine from Italy and limestone from Switzerland, France and Sweden.

Time off with pay is hardly a human right.

The UN moved in after World War II, but as the UN grew from its original 51 members it also outgrew the original Palais. Construction of a new wing was begun in 1968; 700 offices and 10 conference rooms were added to the 886 offices and 22 conference rooms already in existence. The Palais also contains an impressive library, two museums, a bank, a post office and a small department store. More than 7,000 meetings are held there each year; some 25,000 delegates from all over the world attend them. Thousands of tourists also show up, and Palais tour guides all are required to speak three languages.

It is possible to fall in love with the Palais and all its works. The serious issues of our time—war and peace, disarmament, the suffering of refugees, hunger and disease—are talked about there, and often even acted on. Moreover, its dedicated secretariat of 1,900 work for a chronically cash-starved organization that has to answer to the conflicting and often frivolous and self-serving demands of the member states.

The frivolity has always been there. Often, it masquerades as high principle. The Universal Declaration of Human Rights, proclaimed by the General Assembly in 1948, for instance, solemnly holds that "everyone has the right to rest and leisure, including reasonable limitation of working hours and periodic holidays with pay." It also holds, as a human right, protection of the "moral and material interests resulting from any scientific, literary or artistic production" of which you are the author. But time off with pay is hardly a human right, and, desirable as it may be, neither is a good copyright law. There has been humbug at the UN from the beginning.

The Palais is a place of endless talk, interminable meetings and constant bickering. Pakistan and India distrust one another, for instance, and decline to sign a nonproliferation treaty or a test-ban treaty. They demand that the 61 nations at the Conference on Disarmament discuss a comprehensive treaty. The United States, in turn, denounces the Indian-Pakistani "high preachments" and calls the agenda for the disarmament conference "a disgrace."

Meanwhile, North Korea says that the "medieval fascist rule" in South Korea's "puppet" state has led to economic bankruptcy, widespread starvation and the highest suicide rate in the world. (At the same time, a UN team in North Korea is finding that people are foraging for edible grasses and roots.) Belarus denies charges of anti-Semitism, while Arab states once again assail Israel. Much of the bickering is routine, and the world pays little attention, although probably it should pay more.

The UN is always in crisis and, as one mid-level official put it, "The management stinks."

"They jerk you around," he insisted. "They can't keep you more than 11 months in a non-permanent position, so you work right up until then, and they lay you off for a month. Then you go back, and if there's nothing full-time, you might go on as a consultant.

"So you stick around, and try to get a post, and hope for a two-year contract, and then a five-year contract. But there's no real security, and if you're only on a one or two-month contract, you can't really live—you can't get your work papers from the Swiss. You end up sleeping on someone's couch or staying in a hotel. Many of the people in Human Rights, they're in hotels or on couches."

In fact, the Human Rights people in hotels or on couches were stranded in part because of tensions at the highest level of official power. Ayala Lasso, a former foreign minister for Ecuador, became the UN's High Commissioner of Human Rights in 1994 after Amnesty International and other rights groups lobbied the UN to create the position. Whether the Palais needed both an Assistant Secretary General for Human Rights and a High Commissioner for Human Rights was debatable and former Secretary General Boutros Boutros-Ghali opposed it.

But if Boutros-Ghali was on high ground, he soon lost it. Ayala Lasso and Ibrahima Fall, the Assistant Secretary General, did not get along. They argued over who was in charge. Long-time staff problems at the Center for Human Rights—low morale, inefficiency, low productivity—grew worse. Enter then, as a temporary remedy, the people who would have to sleep in hotels or on couches. Meanwhile, Boutros-Ghali made it clear he supported Fall over Ayala Lasso, and Fall made it clear he supported Boutros-Ghali. He campaigned for him when he sought reelection as Secretary General. Boutros-Ghali lost, of course, but shortly before he left office he extended Fall's contract for three years. One might think of it as a payoff.

In his farewell press conference at the Palais in March, Ayala Lasso insisted he never had a problem with Fall, the Assistant Secretary General for

Human Rights. It was unlikely that many of the correspondents believed him.

Despite its problems, a world without the UN is unthinkable. It is essential for global well-being. It is what it is—a large, bureaucratic organization with constant, competing pressures from its different constituencies. Many of its problems simply go with the territory. Its internecine squabbles cannot erase the hard work of the dedicated, gifted people who soldier on despite their burden.

At Ayala Lasso's farewell press conference, which he held just before he left Geneva to return to his old position as foreign minister of Ecuador, some of the 250 correspondents who cover the Palais were grilling him. One asked if he'd ever felt "political pressure" from any of the governments he investigated for rights abuses, and he replied with a magnificent evasion: "I have not received political pressures. Some governments have tried to achieve specific results."

Ayala Lasso had been under attack for not being assertive enough about rights abuses. As a correspondent noted, "Amnesty International said you didn't speak out."

"I am not convinced that simply speaking out is the best way of obtaining results," he replied. "We have a history of countries speaking out, UN institutions speaking out. I'm asking if the results obtained have been enough." In just one visit he got Cuba to ratify a convention against torture and free some political prisoners. "In the case of Cuba," he added drily, "we've had more than three decades of embargo, and I ask: Has that produced any results?"

RESTORING U.S. LEADERSHIP IN POPULATION POLICY

STEVEN W. SINDING

January 1993

For almost 20 years, from the early 1960s to the early 1980s, the United States played the central global leadership role on population. We were the first major donor country in this field and, among many other early accomplishments, our actions were instrumental in the formation of the UN Population Fund, the largest multilateral population donor agency.

But in 1984, at the Mexico City International Conference on Population, the US shocked the rest of the world and abandoned this leadership role by asserting that population is a "neutral factor" in the economic development equation, declaring our intention to defund any organization that cooperated with programs that offered abortion, and following through with the defunding of the largest international population organizations, the UN Population Fund and the International Planned Parenthood Federation.

The United States has provided more assistance to developing countries for population programs than all other donor countries combined, some $4.5 billion since 1965, and, despite losing its political leadership role after 1984, remains the largest single donor, currently providing some $325 million per year, or about 2.8 percent of the overall foreign assistance budget. In addition, the US has been the most effective and innovative donor agency, supporting groundbreaking research and action programs in the population and family planning field. Arguably, the US has been far and away the most important single force in bringing about what success has been achieved.

And there has been success. Since 1965, the average number of children per family in the developing world has fallen from more than six to slightly fewer than four—a decline of one-third but, more important, a fall halfway to replacement level: 2.1 children per woman. During the same time period, the percentage of women and men in the developing world using some form of contraception has risen from around 10 percent to just over 50 percent (in countries like the United States that are at or near replacement level fertility, use of contraception is normally around 75 percent because the balance of women are pregnant, want to become pregnant or are infertile). Thus, in the short space of 25 years or so, enormous progress has been made. There is reason for optimism.

But there is also great reason for alarm. Population growth continues at the high rate of almost 2 percent a year, a rate at which global population would double from the present 5.5 billion to 11 billion by 2065. More than 90 percent of this growth is occurring in the developing world. Present UN and World Bank projections are that, at present rates, the population will not stabilize until it has almost tripled, to 14-16 billion. The absolute number of people being added to the Earth's population is higher today than it has ever been before because, even though the rate of childbearing has declined, the numbers of women who are bearing children is at an all-time high. Thus, in order to avoid the frighteningly high numbers projected by the UN and the World Bank, we will have to do much better in the future than we have in the past in reducing family size.

Is population growth really a neutral factor, as the US government asserted in 1984? Almost no one thinks so. At the least, most analysts say, rapid population growth exacerbates problems.

The assertion that population growth is neutral as regards economic development is an outgrowth of analyses by neoclassical economists such as Julian Simon, who saw that some countries that have had the most rapid economic growth in recent years also had rapid demographic growth—at least during the take-off phase of their economic surge. What these analysts failed to see was that every one of these countries also had vigorous family planning programs that helped to accelerate the fertility decline that rapid economic growth stimulated, and that all of them invested heavily in the real basis of economic growth: human resources. But most of today's high-population-growth countries have an extremely difficult time saving enough resources to invest substantially in the human resources sectors. Thus, such basic and critical services as health and education are chronically underfunded, exacerbating the conditions of poverty and underdevelopment.

Most analysts argue that population growth is a direct cause of critically important environmental problems: soil erosion through over-cultivation of marginal lands, depletion of aquifers, deforestation, water pollution, urban crowding, habitat destruction and species extinction as human populations displace animal and plant communities, and so on. Other environmental problems such as air pollution, greenhouse emissions and ozone depletion are much more directly attributable to consumption patterns associated with wealth than to population growth, although population growth is not entirely unimportant in this equation.

High fertility also contributes directly to persistent health problems, particularly for women and young children. No factor is responsible for more deaths of mothers and children than too many births, too closely spaced, and births occurring too early or too late in their reproductive life spans. And no factor is more important to reducing infant mortality and assuring the survival of children than assuring the survival of their mothers.

Poverty, low education levels, poor health, high mortality, environmental degradation—all these are conditions that almost certainly would exist to some degree, even without high rates of population growth. But none would be as bad. The conditions of the developing world would almost certainly be better, including social and thus political stability, if population growth were slowed.

Survey data collected periodically makes it clear that a very large majority of Americans disagree with present US international population policy. They believe population growth is a problem and that the US foreign aid program should give high priority to addressing it.

But the US has been consistently out of step with the rest of the world on this always controversial issue. In the 1960s and early 1970s, we were seen by much of the developing world, as well as by Europe and the then socialist bloc, as too aggressively preoccupied with "population control," simplistic in our understanding of the causes of rapid population growth and, therefore, in our prescription for its alleviation: birth control. At the 1974 World Population Conference in Bucharest, the US was isolated and vilified by the community of nations. They saw us as wanting to throw pills and condoms at a situation that required much greater attention to the underlying problems that spawned high fertility: poverty, illiteracy and high infant mortality.

The US has been consistently out of step on the population issue.

The early extremism of the US image created problems that have bedeviled our efforts to this day. The Catholic Church, which has placed tremendous emphasis on overcoming the worst manifestations of poverty in the developing world, reacted very negatively to the US view and was inspired to mount a global campaign against it that eventually produced the Mexico City policy of 1984.

That policy, which was articulated as the official US position at the second global population conference, in the city that bears its name, shocked the world even more than the 1974 position at Bucharest had. Now, in an act of exquisite irony, the US was echoing the stance the Communist world had assumed at Bucharest: Development is the best contraceptive; population growth is vastly exaggerated as a problem.

The irony is that the resultant defunding of the UN population program and the largest and most effective international population organizations, rather than preventing abortions, probably caused many more to occur. The organizations that were defunded were not involved in abortion. Many were already precluded by preexisting US legislation—the Helms Amendment—from supporting abortion. But because their ability to provide voluntary family planning services was weakened, it is almost certain that abortion rates increased in many developing countries. The majority of the 500,000 maternal deaths that occur in the developing countries each year are the result of illegal abortion, which results from lack of access to good family planning services.

Purely voluntary family planning can take us a long way toward replacement-level fertility.

The US has also been blamed by many women's groups for encouraging governments to believe that their population problems were so serious that draconian control measures were required, including coercive sterilization and abortion. Whether true or not, there is a widespread view among feminists, most recently expressed in the NGO Forum at the 1992 Earth Summit in Rio, that the US is directly responsible for top-down population control programs in many developing countries that have put demographic targets ahead of concern for women's health. The result, they assert, has not only been coercion, but a more subtle dehumanization of women by poorly trained and inappropriately motivated field workers who treated them as mere contraceptive receptacles.

This complex and troubling political environment, which has frightened many other donor countries into retreat from population programs, exists at a time of extraordinary change in reproductive preferences. In the 1960s and early 1970s, our lack of knowledge about the demand for fertility regulation in the poor countries, and the assumption by many experts that only profound social and economic changes would alter fertility desires, led to a pessimism about the efficacy of voluntary family planning and produced the clumsy family planning programs of that era.

The remarkable series of global fertility surveys of the past nearly 20 years (sponsored principally by the US aid program) has revealed an unexpectedly high demand for contraception and family planning services. Careful analysis of these data by the Population Council and UN Population Fund reveals an extremely high level of "unmet need" for contraception. It is estimated that if all unmet need were satisfied tomorrow, the average number of children per family in the developing world would drop from just under four to around three, not replacement-level fertility but a giant stride forward.

What the surveys and the unexpected success of many developing country family planning programs in the past few years reveal is that purely voluntary family planning can carry the world a long way toward replacement-level fertility—and eventual population stabilization—in the next couple of decades. We must continue to work hard on the underlying problems that cause poor people to want large families—malnutrition and high infant mortality, illiteracy and subsistence agriculture.

Unless those problems are solved, the poorest and most disadvantaged will continue—quite rationally and in their own self-interest—to bear many children. But, at the same time that we attempt to alleviate the worst manifestations of poverty, we can also now take heart from the fact that voluntary family planning programs will produce dramatic results if we support them. Moreover, the better those programs are—the more they respond to women's health needs—the more effective they will be in demographic terms.

In 1989, the nations of the world met in Amsterdam to take a look at the population situation at the mid-point between the 1984 Mexico City conference and the 1994 International Conference on Population and Development in Cairo. Consensus was reached that expanding the provision of family planning services to meet demand is the number one population priority and that present resources are woefully inadequate. It has since been estimated by the World Bank and the UN that if global spending were doubled, from around $4.5 billion this year to $9 billion or $10 billion per year by the year 2000, present and projected demand for contraception could be met and real progress toward population stabilization would occur. Assuming the developing countries themselves could contribute half this amount (including commercial sales to individual couples), the remaining need for donor assistance would amount to some $4.5 billion-$5 billion, compared with today's level of around $2 billion. That $2 billion represents less than 1 percent of total foreign aid in the world today. Thus, doubling or even tripling the level would represent a practically insignificant shifting of resources on the part of the donor countries and multilateral agencies. Yet the impact on women's health, child survival and global sustainability would be enormous.

Renewing US leadership in population is important and appropriate for three reasons: our historic, if controversial, leadership role in this field; the absence of alternative leaders; and the tremendous body of experience and expertise the US possesses—a potential for positive change that is not being realized. These are the steps that are necessary:

1. Establish a rational and politically sound US posture on international population issues. The US must begin by overcoming its pariah-like position on population. It must overcome two dominant and somewhat contradictory images it projects: that of the demographic Pollyanna and anti-abortion fanatic (from the Mexico City conference); and that of the contraceptive-strewing, apocalypse-sounding Colossus of the North (from the Bucharest conference). A new administration and the need to prepare a new position for the 1994 Cairo conference present an opportunity to cast a challenging new, wise and yet moderate image.

Great care must be taken in how the new position is crafted because of our complicated and controversial history in this field. First, we should express the rationale for our concern about population in both micro and macro terms—in that order. In other words, we should say that our primary concern is to improve the well-being of the poorest and most disadvantaged people in the developing countries, most of all women, by helping them to overcome the worst ravages of poverty—illiteracy, poor health and nutrition and lack of employment—and, by helping them gain full control over reproduction, avoid recourse to abortion. Women throughout the world are crying out for help in having only the number of children they want, and we should be prepared to respond. By so doing, we would also be helping countries respond to the macro issue: too many people placing impossible pressures on fragile ecosystems and on overstressed social, economic and political structures.

Second, we should say that we do not see these two objectives as being contradictory: By helping individuals realize their reproductive goals, we would also be helping nations realize their demographic objectives. Whereas once it might have seemed that the demand for family planning was not sufficient to bring about rapid declines in birthrates, we now know that this demand, particularly among women, is sufficient so that its satisfaction would move us rapidly toward replacement fertility and population stabilization.

Such a posture would place us in a morally appropriate and politically unassailable position. It would acknowledge that development is an essential precondition of fertility decline, that family planning services must be focused on meeting the needs of the individual woman or couple, that effective contraception is a vastly preferable alternative to abortion, and that population growth is a global issue about which every country must be concerned.

2. Double direct aid for population activities from $300 to $600 million. If the world needs to double the resources going to population activities, and if the donor countries need to double their contributions, then certainly the United States can do no less. The funds would be well spent because the United States possesses the most professional and experienced staff to administer international population programs.

3. Immediately abandon the "Mexico City Policy" and resume funding for the UN Population Fund and the International Planned Parenthood Federation. The Mexico City Policy, and its corollary, the Kemp/Kasten/Helms amendment to the Foreign Assistance Act, were used by the administration to defund the above organizations on spurious abortion grounds. It would be a simple matter to jettison the policy. The amendment, which permitted a determination to defund the UN Population Fund on the grounds that it was actively participating in forced abortions in China, permits an alternative determination by the executive branch. Both the UN Fund and IPPF are essential to an effective global population effort.

> *The next eight to ten years will largely determine whether global population stabilizes or balloons.*

4. Press Europe and Japan, and the multilateral development banks, to substantially increase their funding for population activities. With the exception of Norway and Great Britain, none of the European countries exceeds two percent of development aid for population programs. Japan is at less than half of one percent, and the World Bank provides less than one percent of its lending for population. The regional development banks hardly mention the word. As the US regains a position of leadership in the field, and once it leads by example on the funding front, we should press the other donors hard to do their share. They say they are willing but they need help in identifying good programs to support. With our strong professional staff and extensive knowledge of the field, we can help them do so.

5. Support contraceptive research, including postconceptive methods. While the primary responsibility lies with the pharmaceutical industry, which, largely as a result of public policy, has more or less abandoned the contraceptive research field, there is much that government can do to encourage resumed private sector interest in this area. Most important will be a change in the general atmosphere regarding reproductive freedom and elimination of the climate of fear. But important steps can also be taken to remove more direct disincentives to research, such as extraordinarily high product liability

insurance rates. Beyond stimulating the domestic pharmaceutical industry, the US should again become a donor to the World Health Organization's excellent research program on human reproduction, from which it withdrew some years ago because WHO was sponsoring postconceptive research.

These five steps would turn back more than a decade of inaction and overcome more than two decades of controversy surrounding US activities in population. It would place the US at the forefront for the critical decade that lies ahead. What we as a global community do in the next eight to 10 years will largely determine whether global population stabilizes at 8-10 billion in the middle of the next century or continues to grow to 15 or 20 billion by the end of it. What happens to population will have an enormous impact on the sustainability of the planet itself in the 21st Century and beyond.

WHERE'S THE MONEY?

PAULA DiPERNA
April 1997

In 1992, the Earth Summit ended in an atmosphere of euphoria, but Ambassador Jamsheed Marker had something further to say. He raised the nameplate of his nation, Pakistan, then leading the Group of 77, and shared the triumphant mood. Marker had played a crucial role in negotiating the Summit's landmark consensus and had every reason to feel proud. But, elegantly and firmly, Marker also reminded the world that no real plan had been secured on a vital matter—how would the agreements be paid for? Financing, he noted, was being taken as a leap of faith.

Today, five years later, the question remains in the air. To help answer it, in early January the UN's Department of Policy Coordination and Sustainable Development convened the fourth of its annual expert meetings on Financing Agenda 21 (the set of recommendations that came out of the 1992 Rio Earth Summit) in Santiago de Chile, with the co-sponsorship of the governments of Chile and the Netherlands, and the cooperation of the Inter-American Development Bank and the Economic Commission for Latin America. Like its predecessors, the gathering intended to take stock of the financing situation and report to the Commission on Sustainable Development (CSD). This year's report will also, by extension, reach the General Assembly for the June 1997 five-year review of progress since the Earth Summit held in Rio de Janeiro. The status of financing is key, for it is likely to be the lens through which what has become known as the "spirit of Rio" will be seen as alive or dead.

Yet resolving the finance issue seems increasingly unlikely to ride on money itself. Rather, a subtle switch seems to have occurred over the last five years, so that the current financing message emphasizes better governance and appropriate policies rather than strict dollar amounts. Implicit is a shift from official development assistance (ODA) toward using private sector methods and market incentives to steer funds in the direction of sustainable development. In fact, given the heavy emphasis on alternatives to ODA, one senses the ODA model is being quietly abandoned—though not by developing countries, even as they too examine and implement alternatives.

In short, intellectual if not political energy seems to be drifting tacitly away from the task of raising new international financing toward concentrating on mobilizing existing resources.

It is the ODA stalemate that has provoked a hard look at the money pie. However, the new efficiency-oriented perspective could yield two distinctly different outcomes: Either it will reinforce the Rio consensus or act as acid on its fragile bonds.

The original price tag attached to the Rio agenda, though speculative, was nevertheless like the hoop to the basketball player—something to throw to: $625 billion per year for 10 years, including $125 billion—roughly double the amount of ODA at the time—to be provided by developed countries as assistance or concessional loans, and the rest to be redirected and squeezed from developing countries' national budgets. The basic Rio consensus hinged on the belief that new funding and pre-existing resources would move forward together.

However, as is now well known, ODA, at a total of $58.8 billion in 1995, has declined as a percentage of donor GNP by roughly one-fifth in three years, with only Denmark, Norway, the Netherlands and Sweden meeting the UN's recommended target of 0.7 percent.

The "Earth Increment," proposed by the late Lewis Preston, President of the World Bank in 1992, to add new monies for post-Rio projects to the Bank's International Development Assistance (IDA) fund, failed utterly. The Global Environmental Facility (GEF) secured $1.3 billion in truly new funding for its pilot phase, but its replenishment suffers chronic jeopardy.

Donor nations insist that their own national budget deficits must take priority, but also the very reputation of ODA has taken a fall. It's fashionable to argue that ODA cannot be convincingly correlated with economic growth or that ODA has too often been siphoned off to dubious infrastructure projects or to line the pockets of despots for private palaces or private armies that suppress opposition. It's said that "aid dependence" stalks too many countries, especially in Africa.

All these points are true to some extent, but as the United Nations Development Programme (UNDP) pointed out in its 1994 annual Human Development Report, for many years, instead of being targeted to the poorest nations, the bulk of ODA went to nations aligned with one or the other superpowers as part of the cold war seesaw, regardless of recipients' economic, social and environmental policies.

Still, as the Development Assistance Committee of the Organization for Economic Cooperation and Development (OECD) has pointed out, ODA has brought indisputable benefits and, for example, can be thanked for the fact that 1.4 billion of the world's poorest people gained access to clean water in the 1980s. There is, however, virtually no leadership in the donor countries, especially the United States, to expand the constituency in favor of foreign assistance. As a result one senses the waning of ODA as a staple of long-term progress, its value more in sporadic emergency relief than development.

At the Santiago meeting, Ron Lander of the Ministry of Foreign Affairs of the Netherlands declared that his country did not accept the decline of ODA as inevitable. Otherwise the gathering could report little encouraging on ODA, and the final report states, "Both donors and recipients need to reassert the primacy of the sustainable development goals of aid..."

But, after five years of aid stagnation, unless developed countries come to the June review with some sign of progress on the ODA front to offer, it's hard to imagine how the overall enthusiasm that prevailed at Rio can be recovered, for the spiritual compact between developed and developing nations that ODA represents will have been broken.

The ODA stalemate could also taint the atmosphere around the issue of mobilizing domestic resources, as a dizzying array of "market-based" tools— subsidy redeployment, shifting incentives, taxes, user charges and others— moves center-stage. Indeed, one might be tempted to characterize the current financing scene with a twist on the classic advertisement for a famous French perfume: Promise ODA but give market methods instead.

In fact, the market menu offers convincing success stories and many tantalizing "what-ifs." But the embrace of these methods, radical by some measures, requires a strong national commitment to change and capacity to confront and reconcile competing vested interests. This strength, while executed nationally, must draw staying power from the aura of international solidarity that made Rio a success in the first place, and which the ODA stalemate tends to extinguish.

The market can be stimulated so that the environmental and social are on par with economic goals.

For afoot is the implication that the free market can be stimulated to operate as it has never operated before—that is, with environmental and social consciousness on a par with economic goals. This three-dimensional capitalism would be a first, its new triangular form in theory a perfect fit with the trifaceted environmental, economic and social equity that is the goal of sustainable development.

High on the menu is the issue of rearrangement, removal and retargeting of subsidies deemed to undermine Agenda 21 implementation, especially overtly environmental aspects such as energy waste and chemical dependence in agriculture. Subsidy review could release from $500 billion to $1 trillion per year, according to various estimates, a veritable vein of gold waiting to be tapped. At Santiago, economic analyst Theodore Panayotou of the Harvard University Institute for International Development and others urged the replication of initiatives such as that undertaken by Indonesia on pesticides in the mid-1980s. Until then, to boost agricultural production, the government subsidized pesticide use—no doubt on advice from agrichemical advocates and companies at the time. By 1986, Indonesia was spending roughly 0.17 percent of GDP on these subsidies and represented 20 percent of the world market for rice insecticides.

Predictably, excess pesticide application ensued. The brown planthopper, a pest that destroys rice plants, then took over, since its natural predators were wiped out by the pesticide blanket. Major crop failures occurred throughout the country, compounded by water contamination in rural villages caused by pesticide runoff. But, reportedly, policies did not change until President Soeharto himself was persuaded to fly over dying rice fields in a helicopter and saw the extent of the problem with his own eyes.

Capitalist methods are explored without losing the socialist objectives of development.

Some pesticides were banned outright and subsidies were phased out, saving the government $100 million per year. Domestic pesticide production dropped by half, pesticide imports by one-third. Rice production, however, rose from 27 million metric tons in 1986 to 30 million metric tons in 1990.

According to Cyrillus Harinowo, Director of the Monetary Management Department of Bank Indonesia, the success continues to this day. In Santiago, he corroborated that the removal of pesticide subsidies "has been a big benefit in my country."

But, in general, how to disentangle the nightmarish spider web of unintended effects? During the Santiago discussion, Carl Greenidge, Deputy Secretary General of the African Caribbean Pacific Group (ACP), cited the recent case of Guyana. There, removal of subsidies on kerosene to reduce air pollution simply forced poor citizens to cut more fuelwood, mainly from mangrove forests, which are vital habitats for marine life and critical for coastline stability. "I'm not sure what was really gained by that subsidy removal in real life," Greenidge cautioned.

Juan Novara of the Mediterranean Foundation in Argentina offered a similar warning, citing the case of public transport in Buenos Aires. Zealous about subsidy removal, the Argentine government awarded a private concession to operate the city's public railway system, tied to reduced subsidies, saving itself $26 million from 1993 to 1995. But, Novara said, "This only made travel more expensive, put more people in their cars and made traffic worse."

These stories suggest that government policies matter more, not less, post-Rio, for how to fine-tune the subsidy issue—who, and how, to choose between kerosene and mangroves?

And, of course, what about shifting popular but questionable subsidies in the developed countries? According to Andre P. G. deMoor of the Institute for Public Expenditure in the Netherlands, subsidies for private road transportation range from $85 billion to $200 billion in the US, Japan and Germany alone, with another $335 billion in agricultural subsidies over all in OECD countries. European countries are torn between protecting their traditional small farmers, and the open market demands of the European Union.

Over all, how can nations retain "good subsidies"—those that favor research in renewable fuel sources, for example—or justify any subsidy at all, given World Trade Organization rules that push toward totally unsupported price mechanisms in the name of global economic competition?

Calibrating subsidies to better favor Agenda 21 is like trying to feed many threads through the eye of the same needle at the same time. Are today's leaders able to accomplish such precision, case by case? Will they need an intravenous infusion of courage to justify the new subsidy landscape to individual citizens? And will revenues saved in "bad" subsidies actually be shifted into "good" practices, such as environmental protection, education and health care, or will they simply be swallowed up by deficit reduction goals? And how will the public exert meaningful control? Should Ministers of Finance be renamed Ministers of Subsidy Replacement, for example, for the sake of transparency?

One senses too the subsidy discussion aimed mainly at developing countries, even though subsidies are rife in developed economies. And while developing countries, obviously, will reap their own benefits from reexamining ill-advised subsidies, as in the case of Indonesia and others, any quid pro quo or conditionality for loans or ODA tied to the subsidy issue could be politically explosive as the five-year review of Rio proceeds.

If there is gold to be unearthed in the subsidy hills, there's even more purportedly in the use of market-based instruments (MBIs), which place incentives and disincentives so as to encourage or discourage certain production and consumption patterns.

MBIs, like clarinets and violins, can play solo as well as ensemble. Generally, they intend to influence behavior with revenue as a byproduct. The main instruments include charges or taxes on emissions or pollutants, as well as on "inputs" such as energy or "outputs" such as electricity. Scenarios call for the trading of pollution and emissions rights, or raising prices on natural resources to truly reflect their market value and the long-term cost of their depletion. Most of these schemes have been discussed for decades, when environmental economics was considered a fringe science. Today the measures have become mainstream, and consultants globetrot constantly, attempting to convince governments to sample.

But, as Professor Anil Markandya, an economist at the University of Bath, admitted in Santiago, "It's one thing to push a button and see the MBI work out neatly in your computer model, and quite another to implement it in actual policy." For one thing, there is deep-seated worry about how MBIs might affect competitive standing, i.e., will additional costs to producers raise prices on products, making them less saleable? Markandya, however, believes most studies show that such fears are exaggerated.

A much-favored MBI is the emissions charge. In Sweden in the early 1990s, for example, as part of a broader package of charges, fees were levied on the sulphur content of coal, oil and peat used for fuel. As a result, noxious emissions declined, some sharply, and coal became the fuel of least desirability, triggering a switchover in demand to less polluting fuels. The government earned $137 million per year in the first two years of the program.

In Mauritania in late 1995, the government increased license fees for fishing in the nation's 200-mile economic zone and revenue was projected to rise from $27 to $83 million by the end of 1996. The increase in fees came as a response to overfishing and gross decline in fish stocks—commercial fishing in Mauritanian waters had not only been rapacious, it had been too cheap. Meanwhile higher revenue means that, theoretically at least, the government could afford to restrict fishing for a time, allowing fish stocks to attempt to recover. However, some local observers note an increase in illegal fishing, an inherent danger of higher fees.

In the US, research suggests that $2.8 billion per year could be generated annually by imposing market-based charges on such items as toxic releases and water effluent and better pricing of US Forest Service timber. Yet, in the clatter of Congressional budget debate, environmentally geared MBIs receive virtually no serious airing.

MBIs hold so much appeal that even Cuba is experimenting with them. Dr. Raul Garrido Vasquez of the Ministry of Science, Technology and

Environment explained in Santiago, "We want to use capitalist methods without losing the socialist objectives of development." For example, to achieve more energy efficiency in sugar production, a state-owned enterprise, a "tax" is being levied on the operating budget of sugar plant administrators if they exceed recommended energy use. This, of course, amounts to the government taxing itself, and lends a slightly surreal twinge to the concept of eco-charges.

"Yes, it's a kind of auto-tax," admitted Garrido laughingly, "but it works more as an efficiency incentive for the factory director." Cuba also has plans to establish a national environment fund to receive emissions taxes and charges levied on foreign investors and earmark them for reinvestment since, as in many countries, revenues earned from environmental policies otherwise disappear into the general budget.

A fascinating example of "monetizing"—that is, making money of—environmental factors comes from Colombia, according to Juan M. Ramirez, an analyst with Fedesarollo, a private research institution in Bogota. He told the Santiago gathering that when a hydroelectric plant called La Miel (The Honey), was planned for a forested area near Cali, the builders worried that sediment would build up behind the dam if soil washed off the hills where poor campesinos cut trees to expand their cattle pastures. A nongovernmental organization (NGO) called Herencia Verde (Green Heritage) brokered a deal whereby the local energy authorities make direct annual payments to the campesinos' cooperative, in return for their not cutting down trees, based on projected costs to hydroelectric operations if excessive sedimentation were to occur. Whether this will actually thwart deforestation and poverty in the long run remains to be seen, but the plan exemplifies how victims of environmental trade-offs can be compensated and a negative spiral avoided.

The MBI concept is rising in favor in Latin America, according to Ramirez, but he added assuredly, "It's only under pressure from NGOs that governments are moving in this direction."

Ronaldo Seroa da Motta of Brazil's Research Institute for Applied Economics also tempered optimism about MBIs, observing that "institutional fragility" remains a key barrier to their successful use despite scattered success stories. He cited overlap in legal jurisdictions and lack of communication between government agencies, with "environmentally harmful initiatives being approved with the exclusion of input from the environmental sector."

Then there's skepticism that the stated potential of MBIs can actually be realized. At Santiago it was suggested by several economists that by shifting from "command and control"—government-imposed requirements—to "least-cost" methods that include appropriate MBIs and allow industry to choose the most cost-effective abatement technology, India could cut the projected cost of reducing various air pollutants threefold, from $1.1 billion to $366 million. For China, the savings are even more staggering—from $4.7 billion to $494 million, or a tenfold reduction. But if such enormous gains are possible, why don't nations go full-throttle? Is it simply lack of familiarity with MBIs among government decision-makers, as some economists say? Or is it that harmonizing policy at the level that effective use of MBIs envisions is simply impossible as a practical matter, demanding unattainable and unprecedented policy integration?

Do market-based incentives require an impossible level of policy integration?

In Santiago, Ramon Lopez, of the Economics Department of the University of Chile and the University of Maryland, made a distinction crucial to understanding the realistic prospects of MBIs. Lopez suggested that, based on his survey of Latin America, profitable private-sector investments in the "brown" environment, covering energy and sanitation, have indeed begun to increase. This was true also in the "gray" environment, concerned with air and water pollution, he said. But when it comes to the "green" agenda, raw nature and natural resources, Lopez said, "Few investments in the protection or the truly sustainable exploitation of natural forests, aquatic natural habits and other rural resources are currently profitable from the individual-country perspective, and much fewer are privately profitable. It has been suggested that eco-tourism, genetic prospecting, non-timber forest extraction and other environmentally sound forest exploitation could be activities that are simultaneously environmentally benign and profitable. Unfortunately, these activities generally do not pass the profitability test except in cases of, for example, highly unique sites."

Lopez added: "The implication is that Latin American governments are as disposed to protect the green environment as the currently developed countries were 50 or 60 years ago." In other words, not very disposed.

This also means that MBIs can work only to the extent that natural resources can be exploited rather than held in reserve in perpetuity; or that some problems, like those in the "gray" and "brown" areas, have themselves reached such proportions that governments have become willing to pay virtually any price for remediation services, especially when faced with public pressure to solve intensifying sewage, air, congestion and water troubles.

It also means that unless a price can be affixed to a resource, it is unlikely to be protected for its own sake.

MBIs are not without what are called "dislocation effects." Though MBIs are often promoted as "win-win" situations, several participants at Santiago noted they can often actually be "win-win-lose." On their own, MBIs make no provision for losers, and it still remains for the state, or at least a public-private entity, to provide some ongoing cushion for those hurt by market shifts and ensuing economic streamlining. For example, according to Isaura Frondizi, Director of the Environment Department of the Brazilian Development Bank, "Green business is good for our bank, but while new investments may be eco-efficient on one side, they can drop jobs on the other."

To help neutralize this effect, she explained, the bank has had to lower its already low interest rates for environmental projects and demand that the borrower use the savings for worker retraining. Acknowledging the tricky counterpoint between economic and human factors, Markandya agreed that, "The balance of gainers and losers is possibly the most critical issue to be addressed in promoting any economic instrument." In fact, without provision for losers, MBIs have limited appeal for the average citizen and thus limited political sales appeal.

Perhaps the most idealistic item on the financing horizon is international taxation. Since Rio, the CSD and other bodies have pushed along various taxation proposals like heavy boulders in a wobbling wheelbarrow, but the principle received an energetic boost at the Santiago gathering.

The search for a socially, environmentally and fiscally responsible economic system is far from over.

Bernard P. Herber of the University of Arizona gave a comprehensive review of such concepts as the so-called Tobin tax on international currency transactions and a tax on international air transport. He cited the convincing precedent of the International Oil Pollution Compensation Fund, finalized in 1971, which compensates victims and indemnifies ship owners if damages from oil tanker spills within national waters exceed an owner's insurance coverage. Currently, 64 nations can draw from the fund, which is fed by an excise tax, called a contribution, paid on each ton of oil by oil refiners or others who receive oil into a nation.

Actually, a tax intended for international environmental improvement could certainly be collected and used nationally. For example, in 1992 the World Bank estimated that a surcharge of $10 per ton of carbon content of fossil fuels could generate $55 billion globally in the first year of operation, broken into national revenues based on consumption, such as $12 billion in the US or $90 million in Nigeria. Ultimately revenue would decline, of course, since the goal of the tax would be to discourage fossil fuel use to reduce carbon dioxide and other greenhouse gas emissions.

Acknowledging the daunting political debate implied, the Santiago gathering recommended in its final report that the CSD ask the World Bank and IMF to investigate the feasibility of "some form of international carbon tax," presumably modest but harmonized for national variations, and levied by all governments, with the governments retaining most of the earnings. With such a format, a small portion of revenue could also be earmarked to support global environmental management.

Another critical element of Rio financing had to do with how nations could avail themselves of available technologies they might not be able to afford. At last year's expert meeting on financing Agenda 21, held in Manila, Grant Ferrier, President of the California-based Environmental Business International, suggested an international technology transfer bank to finance environmental projects at the local level, to offset the fact that, "Substantial dollars are not flowing on behalf of sustainable development from private banks."

Such a technology transfer bank would use credits, guarantees and tax depreciation methods to nudge private capital to projects that do not promise early payoff and might carry financial risk, but are aimed at high-priority problems like soil erosion in Africa.

What is clear after five years of discussion of financing Rio is that countless economists, planners and analysts are focused on the problem, echoing decades of economic debate, theory and discussion. Free-market proposals are piling up, their pros and cons academically well dissected. Data stream across computer screens, and some real-life experiments are under way here and there, tempting nuggets of success. But can they add up to the broad financing shift needed without a fresh surge of global motivation? Will they answer the gnawing basic human needs at the heart of the Rio effort?

And how to weave detail-bound market manipulation into the carpet of free-wheeling foreign direct investment, running at $90 billion in 1995, most of it entirely unconscious of Agenda 21? If not through "command and control," then surely, at minimum, "coordinate and orient."

Ultimately, Agenda 21 tosses out the financial challenge of the century, for, although the cold war is over, the search for a socially, environmentally and fiscally responsible economic system is not.

Can the world capture the benefits of traditional economic growth in such an untraditional blend, while keeping life in the ODA ideal? Or will one approach hold the other hostage for so long that Agenda 21 will become merely a parenthesis in the history of our times?

In Rio a "Red Lane" was created on the public highways for UNCED attendees so they could bypass the usual traffic congestion. Perhaps the CSD should call for a "Red Lane" approach to financing, where the frontier of risk is extended, advances come more rapidly and nations rekindle their faith in one another—lest the spirit of Rio be lost forever in a vapor of ambitious, possibly great, but ultimately stillborn, ideas.

THE UNFULFILLED PROMISE OF RIO

JIM MacNEILL
June 1994

Ever since World War II, nations have struggled to adapt their notions of sovereignty and governance to the realities of economic interdependence, the coupling of local and national economies into a global system. It hasn't been easy, but the Bretton Woods institutions—the World Bank and the International Monetary Fund—the Organization for Economic Cooperation and Development (OECD)—and the G7 are evidence of serious intent and some success.

Nations must now struggle to adapt their notions of sovereignty and governance to the reality of an even more complex interdependence. The world's economic and the earth's ecological systems have become totally intermeshed. Their impact on one another is enormous, growing rapidly and could soon be decisive insofar as both economic development and human survival are concerned. Earth's signals on this are unmistakable. Take the hole in the protective ozone shield, or the warming of the Earth's climate. What are they, if not a form of feedback from the Earth's ecological system to the world's economic system? So is acid rain in Europe, soil degradation in Africa, deforestation in British Columbia and species loss in the Amazon.

The world's economic systems and the Earth's ecological systems are now totally and irreversibly interlocked—till death do them part. To ignore one system today is to jeopardize the other. This is the new reality of the late 20th century and it may well become the dominant reality of the new millennium. To quote President Bill Clinton, "If we do not find the vision and the leadership to defeat the unprecedented new security threats of global climate change, ozone depletion, habitat destruction and desertification, then those threats may well defeat us."

The 1992 Earth Summit in Rio demonstrated once again just how difficult it is for national leaders to address these threats. The optimists argue that they did the best they could and that their efforts have greatly increased the prospects for future action. The pessimists say that they engaged in nothing more than a grand, global photo-opportunity. Only time will tell who is right. Until then, should we err on the side of the optimists or the pessimists? We know that the politics of pessimism can be hopeless and self-fulfilling. We also know that the politics of optimism, especially the blind optimism that denies the objective evidence of our failure to act on politically awkward issues, can and often does reinforce the position of those who, for various reasons, are unwilling to act.

The brutal fact is that we don't have much time. Since mid-century, we have seen a relentless decade-by-decade growth in the frequency, scale and impact of environmental catastrophes—from famine in Africa, to shortened life expectancies in Eastern Europe and the former Soviet Union, to Chernobyl, accelerating loss of forests, massive loss of biodiversity, holes in the ozone layer and now, growing evidence of man-induced climate change. Rio did nothing to alter the policies that drive the sources of these disasters, so we have every reason to expect that they will continue to grow in frequency, scale and impact. Because of this, many optimists believe that it is only a matter of time before governments are forced to act. The pessimists ask: "When?" How many eco-disasters will it take to get governments to move from rhetoric to agreement, and from agreement to action? When they finally act, will it be possible to deal with the social, economic and political consequences of prolonged inaction? And will nature be able to mend in ways that preserve the planet as a habitat for the human species?

Optimists believe it is only a matter of time before governments are forced to act.

Let's take a look at the United Nations Conference on Environment and Development (UNCED) for some clues in answering these questions. Let's look at its successes and failures and ask: "Are these issues within the political reach of governments? Can they adapt their notions of sovereignty and governance in time? And when can we expect action?"

In December 1989, thirty months before UNCED, the UN General Assembly agreed to convene a Conference that would address some of the most fundamental issues facing humankind, as recommended by the Brundtland Commission. The agenda came to include the population explosion, wasteful consumption patterns and the growing disparities between the rich and the poor. It recognized the rapid decline of soil, land, forests, fish and fresh water resources per capita. It called for conventions to stem the threats of global warming and sea level rise and the loss of biodiversity. It accepted the need for reforms in the economically and ecologically perverse ways that governments now intervene in the market. It acknowledged the links between environmental degradation and global security. And it conceded the need for a range of measures to reshape and strengthen international institutions for an age of total interdependence.

In politics, a day or a month can seem like a century. Between December 1989, when the General Assembly decided to convene the conference and June 1992, when the President of Brazil welcomed the delegates to Rio, the international politics of environment experienced a total reversal. In December 1989, the world was still enjoying the longest period of economic growth since 1945. It was celebrating the end of the Cold War and looking forward to a "peace dividend," with military spending to be channeled into international development, the protection of the environment and the building of a durable peace. Political pressure to act on environmental issues had been growing for a number of years.

An upsurge in environmental awareness especially among business and opinion leaders helped, as did the rapid growth of environmental activism. By 1988, the pressure in most OECD countries was so intense that leader after leader found it convenient, if not necessary, to undergo a public baptism as a "born-again environmentalist." US President George Bush declared himself an "environmental President" before the election cameras in Boston Harbor. Canadian Prime Minister Brian Mulroney took the oath in the presence of Norwegian Prime Minister Gro Harlem Brundtland before hundreds of scientists and opinion leaders assembled at the International Conference on the Atmosphere in Toronto. UK Prime Minister Margaret Thatcher went green before a meeting of the Royal Society in London. Before the end of the year, German Chancellor Helmut Kohl, French President Francois Mitterand, Japanese Prime Minister Kaifu and many other leaders also found themselves on the road to their environmental Damascus.

The pressure to stop talking and start acting on the environment continued through 1990. In the Netherlands, a government fell on an environmental issue. And a UN poll found that public concerns about the environment were at the highest levels ever recorded in the South as well as the North. This poll pressure transformed the G7 Summits in Paris (1989) and Toronto (1990), both of which produced long declarations devoted largely to the environment and sustainable development.

Unfortunately, this political clamor for environmental action could not be sustained through the buildup to Rio. By June 4, 1992, when UN Secretary General Boutros Boutros-Ghali opened the Summit, the economic and geopolitical situation had been transformed. Instead of economic buoyancy,

North America was experiencing economic recession and the highest levels of unemployment since the 1930s. A buoyant economy may not be a precondition for action on environmental issues, but a depressed economy creates a markedly unfavorable climate. An economic recession can and usually does produce an "environmental recession," as it did beginning in 1991. Environmental concerns took second and then third place to economic and social concerns. This did not go unnoticed in Washington and Ottawa. And, by early 1992, the "environmental recession" was lapping at the shores of both Europe and Japan.

The South takes its environmental temperature from the North. Although the level of awareness is growing in developing countries, it translates into quite a different set of concerns. Ever since the 1972 UN Conference on the Human Environment in Stockholm, the Western industrialized countries have been chiefly concerned about pollution problems, and many have tended to view the environment problem and the pollution problem as one and the same thing. Developing countries do not agree. In their view, underdevelopment is a much more serious environmental problem than pollution. During the Stockholm debates in 1972, Prime Minister Indira Gandhi of India captured this view with her famous phrase: "Poverty is the worst pollutant."

In the two decades since Stockholm, pollution has become a serious problem in many developing countries. Even so, their leaders continue to place a much greater stress on the political imperatives of rapid economic development to satisfy the needs and aspirations of their exploding populations. Nations like Brazil, China, India and Indonesia know that their future impact on the global environment is so huge that no international accord on any of the strategic issues like climate change, deforestation and species loss can succeed without their full cooperation. They feel that they should be able to trade their participation in new international environmental arrangements against Western agreement to address their issues of catchup economic development. As a group, their number one goal is to reverse the huge flow of resources from the poorer to the richer countries—a levy that now exceeds $100 billion per year. Beyond that, they want to address debt reduction, trade access, technology transfer and bilateral and multilateral financial assistance. And, of course, they want reforms to the international system that will give them more power.

While the emerging giants of the South have a few clear objectives, the same cannot be said of Russia, or of any of the nations of the former Soviet Union. Nor can it be said of the new nations of Eastern and Central Europe.

In Rio, their leaders spoke at length about the environmental-cum-economic catastrophe that glasnost had uncovered. They left the impression that they would like to clean up some of the worst environmental legacies of the communist system. But they were not at all clear about the priority they could or would give to this task. As with developing countries, action on their environmental priorities, to the extent that they had any, appeared to depend almost entirely on Western largesse.

By 1992, the West was also absorbed by the aftermath of a major conflict in the Gulf and transfixed by the rise of tribal nationalism and the horror of ethnic cleansing in the states of the former Yugoslavia. The situation in the countries of the former Soviet Union appeared ever more threatening with a crisis in governance interacting dangerously with a breakdown of the economic system and the rise of ethnic and cultural conflicts. The convulsions in Somalia and South Africa reinforced the public's preoccupation with the immediate and gave rise to calls for short-term measures to cope with a growing agenda of crisis. Thus, world leaders were convened to an Earth Summit and asked to address some of the toughest issues ever placed before an international conference at a time of global economic recession and increasingly uncertain and unstable geopolitical conditions.

Those from the key industrialized countries of the OECD knew that these priorities would require additional resources at a time when their electorates were in no mood to assume any new burdens. They also knew that they could not avoid the new priorities pressing in from Eastern and Central Europe, including Russia. Moreover, a number of them were about to go to the polls. The United States was affected by all of these events. Given its dominant position in the new world order, and led by a President who, even in the best of times, was convinced that the environment was the enemy of the economy, this proved to be very bad news for the Summit.

In spite of this, and thanks largely to the superb political skills of Secretary General Maurice F. Strong—a Canadian who had also served as Secretary General of the 1972 Stockholm Conference—the event was a political success. It brought together the largest array of world leaders ever assembled in a Summit. It brought forth a new generation of leaders within industry and it marshaled the resources of the scientific and business communities in an unprecedented way. It signaled the arrival of nongovernmental organizations as a new force in international diplomacy. It generated enormous publicity and raised the level of public awareness in the South and East as well the North, at least momentarily.

Less significantly, perhaps, most leaders went home feeling that they had gained more in short-term domestic support than they had lost. This was true, apparently, even of President Bush. Under fire from the US media for gutting the climate convention and for refusing to sign the biodiversity convention, he was reported to have felt that in protecting American values and the "American Way of Life" (which, he insisted, were not up for negotiation), he had come out on top with the key domestic constituencies on which he depended to win the forthcoming election. The Republican Convention in July 1992, with its virulent anti-environment rhetoric, gave him every reason to believe that this assessment was correct. His subsequent defeat, however, by a Democratic ticket that included then Senator Albert Gore—whom Bush disparagingly called "ozone man" during the 1992 campaign—may have given him pause to wonder.

The Summit's political success, unfortunately, was not reflected in substantive results. It's true that the Summiteers and the governments they led were able to agree on broad goals. And they were able to agree on new processes to continue talking. But when it came to hard commitments to reverse the dismal trends that had brought them to Rio, they failed totally. They received waves of applause for their global display of good intentions. They left nothing unsaid and everything undone.

To be positive, the Summit did produce five major agreements: the Rio Declaration; an Agenda 21, with 40 chapters; a Statement of Principles on forests; and two conventions, one on climate change and one on biodiversity. In the Rio Declaration, Agenda 21 and the Forest Principles, leaders adopted some new and potentially more sustainable directions for change. In the conventions, they adopted two broad frameworks for future negotiations. Throughout all the documents, they promised repeatedly to increase monitoring, to undertake more research and to submit reports on national performance on a voluntary basis. Leaders also agreed to establish a new UN Commission on Sustainable Development and various other processes to continue talking and negotiating. All of this offered some promise of action in the future, if not today. As Barbara Ward, the British writer on development, used to say, "We have a duty to hope."

It's easy for politicians to embrace environmental platitudes in the guise of principle.

But I can't resist one observation. It comes from more than three decades as a key advisor to governments at bilateral, regional and global meetings on the environment. I have been struck repeatedly by the fact that leaders always find it easy to embrace environmental platitudes in the guise of principles and then support continuing processes of conferences, studies and negotiations in the guise of action. As a political strategy, it's a proven success. As a strategy for environmental protection or sustainable development, it's a proven failure.

Still, leaders almost always get away with it. It seems to appeal to their dominant majorities who seek the nourishment of "feel good environmentalism" that doesn't threaten their own little cocoons. Rio was no exception. The documents are studded with the words "should" and "may"—until they deal with the establishment of new processes to continue talking. Then the tone changes. Instead of "may," we read "will." Thus, a Commission on Sustainable Development "will" be established. A conference on fisheries "will" be held. And so on. No one would argue, of course, that these processes are not needed. Rome was not built in a day and a transition to more sustainable forms of development cannot be mapped out and agreed at any one conference. It's an ongoing challenge. But, international agreements to establish continuing processes to talk and negotiate are not substitutes for action.

Though necessary, agreements to continue to talk and negotiate are not substitutes for action.

The sad fact is that Rio's bottom line was written in red ink. One will comb the text of these agreements in vain to find a clause, a phrase, a word, or even a bracketed punctuation mark, in which the assembled heads of state and government commit themselves to actually do something to alter the trends underlying the issues that brought them to Rio. Again, to be positive, they did agree that national governments "should" or "may" take certain actions on a voluntary basis. But agreeing that nations should or may do something is vastly different from agreeing that nations "will" do something.

At the end of the Summit, Maurice Strong observed that the road from Rio will be longer and more challenging than the road to Rio. Indeed it will. Just about everything that needs to be done remains to be agreed to and implemented. Perhaps the biggest failure, even of the rhetorical process, was the unwillingness of the assembled leaders to deal with three of the most serious threats to the global environment: overpopulation, overconsumption and poverty.

Demographers tell us that the world's population, now 6 billion, is likely to double within the next 40 years, with all the associated social, economic and ecological pressures. There was a lot of denial about this in Rio, but there is no getting around the fact that global sustainability depends on a significant and rapid reduction in high rates of population growth. The issue, of course, is not simply one of numbers. A child born in a rich, industrialized country places a much greater burden on the planet, by consuming more, than one born in a poor country. So sustainability also depends on a rapid reduction in certain forms of consumption—fossil fuels, for example. The industrialized world found that development along with education and the empowerment of women is the best means of population control. These processes are also at work in some developing countries and they have met with some success. But development and empowerment alone are not sufficient. Without access to the means of birth control, nations with high levels of development and empowerment will continue to have high birth rates.

During the 1990s, unless things change, over three billion young people—about equal to the world's population in 1960—will have entered their childbearing years, mostly without access to dependable means of birth control. Nafis Sadik, executive director of the United Nations Population Fund (UNFPA), says she could use an additional $2 billion right now to provide access to birth control measures to 300 million women who are educated, empowered and want to use them. In spite of this, some rich countries have been reducing rather than increasing their contributions to population programs. At the same time, some European countries spend billions in support of national fertility programs. It's not the money we lack, it's the political will to make the stabilization of human population a priority.

Rio could not deal effectively with this question. Thanks to an unholy alliance between the Holy See and several fundamentalist Muslim States, aided and abetted by the White House, the Rio consensus on population moved the world community backwards.

Reducing high rates of population growth cannot be separated from reducing high levels of mass poverty. Rio was not able to deal with this question either. The income gap between the rich and the poor, the powerful and the powerless, is wide and growing wider. "In 1960," according to UNDP's recent Human Development Report, "the richest 20 percent of the world's population had incomes 30 times greater than the poorest 20 percent. By 1990, the richest 20 percent were 60 times greater." That's the gap between countries. It's even worse within countries, especially the poorer countries. "The richest 20 percent get at least 150 times more than the poorest 20 percent."

This income gap translates directly into a consumption gap. With less than 20 percent of the world's population, the West consumes nearly 70 percent of the world's goods. The poorer countries, with nearly 80 percent of the world's population, are left with about 30 percent of its product. They get it both ways: they feed our affluence and they often suffer the initial and most severe effects of our effluence. It's an unjust world and I fear that the situation will continue to get worse before it gets even worse.

At Rio, leaders stated, time and again, that a reduction in third world poverty and a transition to more sustainable forms of development depended on reducing the debt burden, improving terms of trade, including unstable commodity prices, reducing protectionism in developed market economies, and increasing flows of aid. No one disagreed. But, unfortunately, Rio was not a turning point on any of these issues.

When the preparations for Rio began, three major international conventions were under negotiation—a world climate convention, a convention to conserve biodiversity and a world forestry convention. The convention on forests was abandoned in favor of a Statement of Principles, but the negotiations for the climate and biodiversity conventions bore a certain type of fruit—all skin and no pulp. During the negotiations on climate and biodiversity, governments pursued two types of framework conventions.

The first was "empty." It was marked by declarations of good intentions concerning measures to limit climate change, but it was devoid of any binding commitments to reduce greenhouse gas emissions. The second was "substantive." It was marked by firm commitments to reduce greenhouse gas emissions with targets and timetables, as well as agreed means of financing the measures needed in developing countries. Both promised more monitoring and research, greater information exchange, and the possible transfer of technology, as well as a mechanism for continuing consultations.

A number of countries initially favored a substantive convention. The European Community, Japan and Canada not only supported the long-term goal of stabilizing greenhouse gases in the atmosphere, they supported clear targets and timetables to get there, beginning with rolling back CO_2 emissions to 1990 levels by the year 2000. President Bush and his White House staff were vehemently opposed. Backed by the Arab OPEC states and some other oil-producing countries, and major segments of the world's carbon industry, they waged a strong campaign against both targets and timetables. Their spokespersons made exaggerated claims of enormous costs that would bankrupt the petroleum industry and impoverish the oil-producing states. They started a growth industry in scare metaphors. At the final negotiating session in New York in April 1992, governments opted for an empty convention. Europe, Japan and Canada gave up their demand for targets and timetables in exchange for a promise by Bush to attend the Summit—probably the worst bargain ever made in the history of international environmental negotiations.

Maurice Strong stated repeatedly that he would resist putting anything but meaningful, or substantive, conventions before the Summit. On biodiversity, he never had the option. Negotiations began in Madrid in July 1991. The sessions were arduous, marked by heated debates which quickly divided the delegates along North/South lines. By late 1992, it was clear that the choice was between an extremely weak framework convention or none at all. The results confirmed that prognosis. The convention adopted in Rio sets out a number of important principles concerning conservation, access to genetic resources, technology transfer and financing, but it does not commit any party to act to reduce the loss of biodiversity.

It must be admitted that leaders have always found it virtually impossible to resist empty framework conventions on the environment. They are easy to negotiate, being little more than a wish list. They are politically very attractive. They don't commit leaders to actions that would upset the comfortable power structures of which they are a part and on which they depend. Signing an empty framework convention is little like an author signing a contract with a publisher on the basis of a table of contents and a statement of good intentions to have the text written (perhaps by somebody else) at some later date. I call them "NIMTOO" conventions—"not in my term of office." With them, today's leaders can gain enormous political credit at no political cost. The temptation is irresistible.

More than 150 governments signed both conventions in Rio. While most leaders returned home waving the conventions as evidence of their commitment and even success in securing a safer planetary home for present and future generations, some were clearly disappointed. In signing the conventions, they recognized their weaknesses, referred to them as "first steps" on a long road, and called for early efforts to strengthen them. Strengthening the climate convention will not be easy. It would involve amendments to include the targets and timetables rejected on the road to Rio, as well as firm commitments to finance the incremental costs of participation by developing countries.

If and when the Clinton Administration decides to propose such amendments, it will be interesting to observe how other states respond. There is more than a little evidence to suggest that the strong positions taken by Australia, Canada, and certain member states of the European Community on the road to Rio owed much to their confidence that the Bush

Administration would never agree to them. They were able to fight the good fight and win the applause of their environmental communities without frightening their carbon industries. As for nations like Brazil, China, India and Indonesia, they know that their future impact on the global environment is so huge that no international accord on climate change can succeed without their full cooperation. They will almost certainly want to trade their support for any amendments that commit them to real action for Western agreement to address the issues that concern them most: debt reduction, for example, as well as trade access, technology transfer and bilateral and multilateral financial assistance. The domestic and international politics of climate change are completely intertwined —perhaps fatally so.

The same is true of amendments to strengthen the biodiversity convention, which President Clinton signed at a ceremony on the White House lawn on Earth Day. Without the full participation of those tropical states that control the richest remaining treasures of genetic resources, the convention will be meaningless. And when the major industries engaged in bioprospecting and genetic modification get their lobbies organized, Western leaders may find the political costs of action greater than they care to bear.

If population, consumption and poverty were the greatest failures of the Summit, financing the Rio package was the greatest disappointment. The debate was bitter, with battle lines separating rich and poor, North and South. Unfortunately, the whole debate on financing got off on the wrong foot in December 1989, during the General Assembly debate on the resolution to convene the conference. Rather than adopt the Brundtland Commission's sustainable development agenda, which integrated environmental with economic issues, governments retained the two separate agendas of environmental protection and business-as-usual economic development. According to these agendas, the choices are stark. Societies may improve their environment or grow their economies, but not both. Companies can reduce their impact on the environment or increase their profits, but not both. It's a tradeoff. If we want a clean environment, we have to destroy the economy. If we want a robust economy, we have to destroy the environment.

These two agendas polarized the debate. Environmental protection was seen as the "Northern," and economic development as the "Southern," agenda. What was intended as environment *and* development quickly became environment *or* development, the negative-sum game of the 70s, in which there are no winners, only losers. Given the need to choose between environment and development, the finance issue was easily—and fatally—framed. Developing countries need all the investment they can attract for development. If the North asks them to add environmental protection to development projects, the North will have to provide the "new and additional" resources required. Having accepted environment and development as two separate agendas, Northern governments also accepted the concept of "new and additional" resources, at least in principle. But when the time came to ante up, they could not follow through.

Development assistance has acquired a bad odor in many OECD countries, for good reasons as well as bad. In addition, prevailing doctrines coupled with economic recession favored reducing public expenditures in most of these countries, especially in those areas that do not offend sensitive groups of voters. Foreign aid topped the list. The Rio Conference Secretariat estimated that the costs of implementing Agenda 21 could amount to a staggering $625 billion per year, of which one quarter would come from the richer countries. At a pre-Rio meeting in London, the Brundtland Commission suggested that a minimum of $12 billion would have to be put on the table to make the Conference a success. Even with the aid of creative bookkeeping, Western leaders offered less than 10 percent of that.

There ought to be a statute of limitations on the number of times governments can use the same commitment to get themselves off a political hook.

The hidden agenda for much of the finance debate was to find a way out that would not be interpreted as failure. The late Canadian Prime Minister and Nobel prizewinner Lester B. Pearson's target for development assistance came to the rescue—once again. Western governments again took the oath and agreed to meet the target of 0.7 percent of GNP by the year 2000 "or as soon as possible thereafter." This commitment was first made in 1964 and has been repeated several times since. There ought to be a statute of limitations on the number of times governments can use the same commitment to get themselves off a political hook. On returning home from Rio, most Western leaders once again forgot their oath. They cut development assistance and they diverted much of what remained from the South to Eastern Europe, Russia and the nations of the former Soviet Union.

Throughout the bitter debate on "new and additional" resources, both developed and developing governments were able to divert attention from the ways they now spend their "old and traditional" resources. Western countries lead in rhetoric about the free market; they also lead in systems of incentives, including production and export subsidies, that distort the market, a prime example being agriculture. Agricultural subsidies in OECD now cost taxpayers and consumers over $300 billion a year. They encourage overproduction, market gluts, export subsidies and trade wars. They also underwrite a fast drawdown of our most basic farm capital—soils, woods and water—not only in the North, but also in the South, where we dump our surpluses and undermine their agriculture. We have them in energy: enormous coal subsidies in Europe, over $40 billion a year in subsidies for conventional forms of energy in the US, perhaps $4 billion in subsidies for fossil fuels in Canada.

These subsidies tilt the playing field in favor of fossil fuels, result in more acid rain and global warming, and penalize efficiency and renewables. Developing countries are similarly burdened. They spend over $200 billion a year on energy subsidies, according to the World Bank. In addition, both developed and developing countries provide huge subsidies which encourage deforestation and species loss, overfishing and the overuse of water for irrigation. These and other incentives are economically perverse, ecologically destructive and trade distorting—sometimes all at the same time.

I have worked with more than 50 governments and I have never met a politician prepared to give up the right to promise grants and subsidies of all kinds for any purpose. If we must have subsidy systems—and I fear we must—we have to design and deploy them in ways that encourage more sustainable forms of development. We could reduce energy subsidies, for example, and redeploy the balance in ways that encourage conservation and end use efficiency and that discourage fuels that lead to acid rain and global warming. We could reduce agricultural subsidies and redeploy the balance in ways that sustain farm income and encourage farmers to engage in sustainable agricultural practices. And so on. Far from being a drag on the economy, these reforms would relieve public budgets of an enormous burden and release resources for other purposes.

Environmental trends are becoming a major force that could alter the foundation of the international political system in the coming decades. Some will result in changes that are sudden and dramatic, like the Antarctic ozone hole. Others will result in changes that are slow and underreported, but nevertheless profound and irreversible, like the projected flooding of coastal areas from sea-level rise, and the growing volume of environmental refugees crossing national borders. Still others will simply grow in intensity until conflict becomes unavoidable, like the deteriorating population-land ratio in parts of Asia, and the population-water ratio in parts of the Middle East and North Africa. History is full of examples of nations fighting to gain control of, or to stop another nation from gaining control of, raw materials, energy supplies, water supplies, sea passages, and other key environmental resources.

The drive to gain or to protect access to scarce energy and other resources is often described as a major motive underlying the foreign policies of states, especially in the industrialized world. This type of conflict is likely to increase as certain resources become scarcer, and as competition for them grows. The oil wars, in fact, have begun. The water wars may not be far behind—and then conflicts stemming from the consequences of soil loss, forest loss, higher global temperatures and rising sea levels. A number of leaders recognized these new threats in Rio and indicated that they were prepared to address them. When or how they appear on national security agendas depends on a number of factors, however, especially the rapidly changing geopolitical situation.

The world's response to these issues will depend increasingly on leadership from one capital, Washington. Rio confirmed that the United States, as the world's only military superpower, and as its dominant economy, has been given an effective veto on international environmental policy. Clinton's Earth Day speech on April 22, 1993 was designed to set the Administration's course. In the delivered version, he committed the United States to scale back carbon emissions to 1990 levels by the year 2000. Observers noted, however, that he made the commitment without any specifics.

Will the Clinton Administration—in its remaining years in office—provide the needed world leadership on these issues? In November 1992, expectations were high. But the environmental establishment sees no real direction, few real gains and much inconsistency and fence straddling. Jay Hare, the head of the National Wildlife Federation, summed up their reaction succinctly: "What started out as a love affair between the environmental community and the new administration is turning out to be more like date rape."

The challenges ahead are enormous. If one judges by Rio, it could be a long time before the international institutional and political system catches up with the new global reality of economic and ecological interdependence. The problems that brought the heads of state to the Earth Summit are still with us and growing worse every day. Let us hope that it does not take another ozone hole, or something even worse, to enable leaders to shift from rhetoric to action. But don't bet on it.

RIO: 'AH, I REMEMBER IT WELL'

RICHARD F. SHEPARD

June 1997

It was a time of hope, a time of awareness. The very title Earth Summit seized the imagination. Not just of the veteran greens, those who had gone about the Earth, like Jeremiah, shouting warnings that the world as we know it was coming to an end. For years, these had been the global eccentrics, who made the ordinary folks who saw the sun rise and the moon set each day wonder, "What are these nuts yammering about?"

No, until 1992, the year of the Earth Summit, the environmentalists had yet to fire the imagination of the public, that vast, shadowy mass of world citizenry on whose good will governments live or die, whose ideas are molded by those in charge and rarely erupt until long after the thought, the popular thought, had jelled.

That time arrived in the spring of '92. Oh, there had been work, serious study of serious concerns for decades and an educated body of environmental opinion had been cultivated by works such as Rachel Carson's "Silent Spring." That spring of '92 was anything but silent. Environmental concern, worry about human effect upon the globe and the subsequent effect of the global deterioration on humans suddenly caught the popular fancy.

When we told friends that we were going to Rio de Janeiro to cover the Earth Summit for the newly-born Earth Times, created initially for just such an event, we were the envy of those who a month earlier could not have cared less about clear-cutting or holes in the ozone. Environment became the darling of the news media and infected all those within touching distance of broadcasting or publishing. Children told their parents, in that dry season in New York, to conserve water at the tap. Even kids, it seemed—especially kids—were worried about the future of their Earth. There were even Earth Summit T-shirts, and you can't get down to grass roots any deeper than that.

Rio was a magical city, if magic may be applied to any place that was tenanted by 9,000 journalists, each of them sending home stories about the 30,000 people who were meeting there, come to influence the 178 nations that were to decide the ecological fate of the world at this oversize United Nations gathering. Of these delegations, 108 were headed by the chief executives of their governments, ranging from Fidel Castro and George Bush to the President of the Marshall Islands, who allowed that this would be an education for his small waterlogged South Pacific republic, which was still wet behind the ears in diplomatic affairs.

The United Nations had met so often on thousands of other issues that affected the lives of millions. There had been consideration of disarmament, pollution, of bellicose relations between member states. Interesting but not the stuff of dreams. The Earth Summit promised a better world, with a specific blueprint. The Earth Summit fired the world with hope.

Here in Rio, the deserts would be pushed back. The oceans would recede. The firmament would be returned to salutary conditions. Poverty would be outlawed. Population would be modified.

In short, nature—that of the world and of man—would be put on a strict regimen by those heads of state, so many of them, more than at any other congregation until that time. They would be guided by the thousands of nongovernmental organizations, the workhorse NGOs that had the knowhow.

The Earth Summit promised a better world, with a specific blueprint.

All this caught the fancy of the media. The Earth Summit took on the dimensions of a World's Series. As the limousines hurtled by in Copacabana, which was under heavily armed guard and probably safer for passersby than it had been for years, as the dignitaries marched over red carpets into their assigned hotels, there was a feeling of power. Back home, the public received daily reports of who was doing what at the Earth Summit. There were features about unique experiments in family planning in faroff places, about the Japanese initiative to sort out their garbage, about the aspirations of unofficial hangers-on to make their voices heard in the holy of holies at Rio Centro, where the Earth Summit was being enacted.

President Bush arrived toward the end of the summit. By that time, cracks were showing. The expected announcement of mammoth aid by Japan was not heard, perhaps because the country's head of government was not allowed to give his five-minute address to the assembly over television, because the others had all come to Rio to deliver their comments live. Nobody wanted to be the bad guy and even countries that would not, at least to date, ratify decisions to better the world, agreed in their votes to sign these resolutions.

"What will Bush do?" This was the question put to all Americans by those who hoped that, somehow, the arrival of the chief executive of the last remaining superpower would put the final Good Housekeeping seal of approval on the deliberations. President Bush arrived in a frenzy of reception at a hotel down the coast from crowded Copacabana, into a resort that was rumored to have been booked by a Saudi representative who was traveling with his usual retinue of sisters, cousins, wives, aunts and servitors. Our leader brought himself and the boys and girls on the bus.

Agenda 21, like most great documents, is honored in word and ignored in deed.

His press retinue filled two rooms at the hotel and they watched him over the small screen as he delivered his message at Rio Centro, several miles to the south. Tape recorders whirred, pens glided over paper and those of us who were by now grizzled veterans of Rio wondered why so many of them, dozens and dozens, had to accompany him to watch him on television as the American public was doing at the same time back home.

Bush put a damper on the runaway enthusiasm. The American position was one of extreme caution. Some commitments were made, but it was a grudging performance and we could see that hope was being dashed among delegates like the surf that broke along the Atlantic shore. The vision, the hope that carried us and the world to Rio, evaporated into the familiar push-and-shove of workaday politics.

Perhaps this would have been the case even without the Bush presence. To be sure, there was enough basic disagreement on who should give what, between the North and the South, the haves and the have-nots. Agenda 21 was a wonderful outline and is a powerful reminder of what could be done to redeem the 21st Century, for which it was named. Like most great documents, it is honored in word and ignored in deed.

This November, the nations of the world again meet, this time in the United Nations itself and, here in New York, they will assess what has been done since the Earth Summit. Some things have gotten better, even as some things have gotten worse.

This time around, hope does not have the great press it had five years ago, but then again that public has become accustomed to an ecological face. We are segregating our garbage, we are worried about toxic levels and, outside of the United Nations chambers, who can smoke in public any more?

The Earth Summit's formal title was the United Nations Conference on

Environment and Development, which we acronym-happy scribes quickly abridged to UNCED. As the wits used to say, there was a lot to be said for UNCED, but this week we will see if there remains anything that should be unsaid.

IN THE UNITED STATES, INDUCING YAWNS

MICHAEL LITTLEJOHNS
March 1999

Some time in October 1999, our Earth's population is projected to top six billion, twice what it was in 1960 and an increase of a billion people in just the last dozen years. As if those numbers are not already awesome enough, Nafis Sadik, head of the United Nations Population Fund and the foremost authority on the subject in the UN system, predicts no letup until the end of the next century. It's small consolation that after about 3.4 billion more people are added by 2050, the growth rate may slow from a race to a trot. We say awesome, but the phenomenon seems to have left the mainstream media curiously unawed. A recent review of a hefty batch of press clippings as well as media Web sites turned up precious little population news of commentary. Alas, this newspaper is an all too lonely voice.

Should political wrangling about 'abortion' issues continue to hold family planning funding hostage?

It is the custom nowadays to add "sustainable development" to the thematic title of many UN conferences, reflecting the organizations emphasis on helping (cooperating with, in the current language of political correctness) developing nations in their fight against a trio of age-old evils: poverty, disease and ignorance. Conquering these ills is hard enough; it is infinitely harder where population growth has gotten out of hand, as in several countries where multiple births are the norm. As recently as 1995, developing countries accounted for 73 percent of global population. If anything has changed since then, it is surely not for the better.

Yet in the United States, talk of family planning often induces a yawn or, worse, negative reactions. (As for abortion, more later.) Until quite recently, even the authorities in Japan raised all sorts of excuses not to approve the birth control pill. In a famously male-dominated society and it was less surprising when those same bureaucrats took only about six months after its introduction to decide in favor of Viagra.

Dr. Sadik has often said that abortion is not a favored form of birth control and denied charges by American ideologues that her agency funds involuntary abortions in China.

Such denials are not enough for Representative Christopher Smith, Republican of New Jersey, who forced the addition of irrelevant language on abortion to a bill to authorize payment of hundreds of millions in US arrears to the UN. Invoking principle, President Clinton vetoed the measure. October 12, designated by the UN as "The Day of Six Billion"—coincidentally, just after the start of a new fiscal year—would be a fine time for Smith & Co. to back off, while sparing a few million also for UNFPA, which can never have too much money to carry out the tasks it performs so well against considerable odds, and for which there is so much need.

SHOULD WE CHANGE OUR FINANCIAL ARCHITECTURE?

FLORA LEWIS
October 1998

PARIS—Some slight improvement in statistics, a small Federal Reserve reduction in interest rates and a sunny, agreeable European summit two months before the launch of the euro have suddenly changed the tone. From warnings of global financial meltdown, the talk has shifted to cautious optimism that the worst has passed and the system will right itself without further great damage.

In itself, this is a tribute to what there is of an international financial "architecture," to use the going phrase for the complex of rules and agreements affecting the market. Enough confidence exists in the willingness and ability of the world's financial authorities to cooperate against potential disaster that the temptation to panic was averted. Enough was learned from 1929 to 1933 to make clear what shouldn't be done, what would only make things worse, and how to seek improvement.

This was the purpose of the 1944 Bretton Woods agreement, which set up the World Bank and the International Monetary Fund to launch reconstruction after World War II and fight off any renewal of the Great Depression. It worked so well that the world's economy has multiplied fantastically and international exchanges have reached an unimagined level, beyond the capacity of any government to manage. That very success plus the technology that obliterated time and space in financial transactions have brought new problems.

That is the logic behind the calls for a new international architecture, a new Bretton Woods to take account of what has changed and draw up new rules and procedures to accommodate changes. It is a straightforward idea, but in this period of post-cold war market idolatry it is running into some ideological barricades.

The reluctant argue that governments should have no mandate to interfere in the market because governments are always worse at running things. The issue is tied to the question of globalization—whether that is a bad or a good idea, whether countries should expose themselves to the open currents and benefit from them or try to build dikes. It is a false question, and in fact involves not the ideology of a (hypothetically) free market but how best to manage it.

There is no mature economy that doesn't regulate banks, oversee stock markets, assure fiduciary responsibility and provide certain safeguards. But these are all national undertakings. Beyond the Bretton Woods provisions and certain useful requirements established by the Bank of International Settlements in Basel in the wake of the Depression, there are no international rule-makers and referees.

The near collapse of Connecticut-based Long Term Credit Management (LTCM) is a dramatic example of how the challenge has changed. A hedge fund, LTCM engaged in sophisticated, computer-based speculation with highly leveraged funds. That is, it borrowed some $100 billion on the basis of a little more than $3 billion in assets it managed to collect and made bad bets with money it did not have.

Beyond Bretton Woods there are no international financial rule-makers and referees.

In the national market, margin requirements and borrowing limits would have made such enormity of loss impossible. But rules didn't apply in the international market, and because the managers of the fund were glittering Wall Street stars who had turned out huge profits in the past, investors didn't ask the usual questions. Because the losses could have brought down important banks and caused a chain reaction, the Federal Reserve stepped in to prevent bankruptcy by persuading a group of big private banks and funds to bail out LTCM. This was a necessary remedy but not a cure for the disease.

Theoretical free-marketeers object to this kind of intervention because it reduces the constraint they call "moral hazard"—that is, it limits the risk side of the risk/profit calculation. But the banks and funds agreed because they also could have been badly hurt if they had to write off the bad debts.

There are a number of ways to reduce the dilemma, other than by directly supervising hedge funds or through the banks and companies that invest in them. That is the preference of New York's Federal Reserve President William McDonough. A conference needs to be called to study and discuss the possibilities. The Basel BIS has set up a working group on the issue, which is a start.

It wouldn't be necessary to create new institutions or some supernatural watchman to implement the rules once they are agreed. That can be left to the national authorities so long as they can all be sure that they are working together, on a common guideline.

There are other aspects of the system to be reviewed, including IMF policies that have been blamed for cruel economic destruction by demanding excessive austerity from countries that have indulged excessively. Some separation of the international flow of investment capital and sudden speculative tidal waves that ruin even flourishing economies has been suggested. Chile, for example, taxes incoming short-term funds to discourage both exaggerated lending and borrowing, an approach that has worked and can be copied.

The crisis has already caused enormous pain in a number of countries, and it could have been headed off. If it seems to be winding down now, this is not the time to avoid the planning and organizing for the future that can help prevent a recurrence. When the trouble looked bleakest, there was an insistence that immediate measures had to be considered first and the needed strategic thinking was deferred.

It shouldn't be. No economies, however thriving and important, can insulate themselves from the ravaging storms of loose capital when it panics, nor do without the benefits of productive and balancing capital flows. They can make the game less dangerous.

YEMEN: DESIGNING DEVELOPMENT

RESHMA PRAKASH
November 1998

SANA'A, Yemen—Eveline Herfkens is out to change the way the Netherlands administers development aid. As her country's new Minister for Development Cooperation, Herfkens wants the Netherlands aid program to be leaner, more efficient—fewer countries, perhaps fewer projects; a concentration on quality and impact not dissipated over too many countries. She traveled to this Middle East country to spell out some of her ideas.

"Dutch aid covers 85 countries and 15 themes," Herfkens told The Earth Times during her trip. "We can't manage so much efficiently. We're not the World Bank with a staff of 10,000. It's a question of institutional capacity. Our aid needs to be more focused. The parliament will discuss bringing down the list of countries receiving bilateral aid this December."

But first, the Minister said, she needs to ascertain that aid works. The Netherlands is one of the biggest donors in the world with 0.8 percent of its gross national product—$3.25 billion—going toward official development assistance. Only Denmark, Sweden and Norway devote more of their GNP to development aid. An overwhelming majority of the Dutch public supports aid. But, ironically, every year fewer and fewer people seem to think that it works. Herfkens wanted to see a success story for her first official country visit. She sought a prime exhibit for her case that aid should go to places and projects where the Dutch can make a difference. She selected Yemen.

And so, in October, on the 20th anniversary of the start of Dutch aid to Yemen, Herfkens embarked on a whirlwind tour of the country. Her every move and word were recorded and scrutinized by both local and Dutch media. Everywhere she went she was accompanied by scores of officials in vans, Land Rovers and white Mercedes. White and blue security cars with sirens blaring led the 10-vehicle convoy at breakneck speed, bulldozing through the countryside, scattering people and vehicles aside. In three hectic days, Herfkens went from Sana'a, the capital, to the areas where Dutch aid is concentrated—the mountainous region of Dhamar and the town of Rada and then further to the dry, remote interiors of the country, to Ataq and the tiny village of Yashbum in the Shabwah governorate. Some areas she visited were so remote they could be reached only by helicopter. There was brief stop in Aden, the beautiful port city on the Gulf of Aden, to have lunch with Ali Abdallah Seleh, the President of Yemen.

Each day's blistering pace started early in the morning as she toured premises, listened to presentations, waded through statistics, questioned aid workers, spoke to people benefiting from the project and received many presents. They ranged from simple bouquets of flowers, to beautifully hand-embroidered scarves made by local women, to exquisitely worked silver jewelry. Photographers and television crews struggled through the milling crowds, anxious not to miss that perfect shot. Reporters scribbled into their notebooks, straining against the din of raised voices to hear what Herfkens was saying, or urgently drew aside people for quotes as to how the projects were doing.

This is the legendary land once ruled by the Queen of Sheba and an important stop on the ancient frankincense and myrrh trade route. There are places here that seem as though they've been untouched since the Prophet Mohammed himself walked through the land preaching his new faith. A bird's-eye view from a helicopter reveals a harsh, rugged land. There are few sources of water and isolated little hamlets lie strung out below mountains. Lone tire tracks in the dust make do as roads. Cactus and a few thorny shrubs struggle to grow among the rocks.

Yemen is a poor country, one of the poorest in the world, with per capita income of $300, say Dutch officials. Adult literacy is 56 percent, but even lower than that for women. Only 38 percent of the people have access to health care. The fertility rate, the number of children born to the average woman in her lifetime, is 7.5. Yemen has hardly been a darling of the international aid community. Its biggest donor, Kuwait, and some Western and Arab donors canceled their aid programs when Yemen came out on the wrong side of the Gulf War in 1991.

But Yemen has had a 20-year aid relationship with the Dutch. It began with North Yemen in 1978, when the country was still divided between the North and South, and extended to the whole country when it was unified in 1990. Starting with approximately $16 million, Netherlands' aid has increased to around $54 million in 1997, making it Yemen's largest bilateral donor. The bulk of Dutch aid supports various social projects, particularly those in the health, water, education and agriculture sectors. In 1997, this amounted to around $25.7 million. Balance-of-payment support accounted for $8 million, while approximately $19.8 million was in the form of soft loans for development related export activity.

"I'm here as part of a secret agenda," said Herfkens before a large gathering of Yemeni and Dutch officials in Sana'a. "I want to show that aid works." Citing poverty, good policy and good governance as the criteria for deciding which countries are to be recipients of Dutch aid, she said that Yemen fits the criteria. The government had conducted fair and free elections and was meeting World Bank and International Monetary Fund guidelines for good economic policy, she said. There was no fear that Dutch aid for Yemen would be cut.

Herfkens visited a number of the projects funded by Dutch assistance and at every stop she wanted to know one thing—to what extent was the local community involved in the projects? "Too many times," she told this reporter, "aid officials make the mistake of not trusting the local people. All projects have to build in a role for local authorities, allow them to make mistakes and learn from them."

At every opportunity she stressed that projects have to be self-sustaining, suggesting that Dutch aid was not a bottomless pit, that projects had to learn to stand on their own after a while. "There's got to be a timetable for how long the Dutch will be actively involved," she added. "There are some projects that have been hanging around for decades. That is not development that is sustainable."

Development should go beyond aid, she said, and the success of development aid should be

The success of development aid should be judged by how well a country manages without it.

judged by how well a country manages without it. Judged by that criteria, she said, she feels that the Seed Potato Company she visited in Dhamar is a success. The Dutch have put almost $2 million into this project, which supplies high-quality seeds to farmers. The aim is to promote food sufficiency and broaden the food base of Yemen. She nodded approvingly when told that the potato company will be the first public entity to be privatized in Yemen by 1999-2000, and that the process was well under way. "That's precisely what should happen," she said, beaming. "We should get out and let the local sector take over."

On a mostly deserted and winding road through the mountains of Dhamar, she insisted on making an unscheduled stop. Heading toward a cluster of houses, the convoy of cars veered off the main road onto a bumpy dirt path, raising a cloud of dust. Nabil Shaiban, director general of the technical bureau of Yemen's Ministry of Planning and Development, explained that the houses were part of an emergency housing project built by international donors to accommodate people displaced by the big earthquake of 1982. It had been a terrible disaster, leaving thousands dead and thousands more with no shelter. Herfkens had visited Yemen then and she recalled now that a mile away one could smell decomposing bodies that authorities had not been able to clear from the rubble. Donors spent millions building new houses for the local people.

"They got it all wrong," said Herfkens to a Dutch television reporter as the cameras rolled. "Here is a project that failed." She went on to say that the donors had rushed ahead with the project without bothering to ask local people what kind of houses they wanted to live in. As a result, the houses turned out to be too small for the typical Yemeni family, which has six children. The women didn't like the houses because they didn't have high compound walls that guaranteed their privacy. The houses had remained unoccupied for years. It may beg the question as to why Yemen's government hadn't intervened. "You don't ask for relief or emergency aid and then be picky about it," said Shaiban drily.

The houses stood alien and conspicuous, surrounded by fragmented patches of dry field. It was after the harvest season and the people had extracted what little they could from the rocky, dry earth. In the distance, one could see traditional houses, but they can be missed by the careless eye. These are tall houses of mud and stone, motley brown with small dark windows, nestling in the mountains and blending right in. They're part of the landscape, these ancient multi-rises, and have been for centuries.

POPULATION AND THE POLITICS OF TRADE

SUSAN J. TOLCHIN
May 1993

"Nouveau colonialism." You heard it here first. It's the new trade politics, of the '90s, another powerful undertow tugging at delegates to a meeting on population held at the United Nations. Whether it's called "structural adjustment," "protectionism," or "tied aid," it will pack quite a wallop, particularly for developing countries.

Trade and aid have always been wrapped up in each other; if not actually married, they've at least always gone steady. The "apple amendments" tied to US human rights legislation in the 1970s compelled the purchase of apples from the state of Washington. Don't ask why; what's important is that the law bore even more fruit with the political support of the late Senator Henry "Scoop" Jackson, Democrat of Washington state.

The Marshall Plan's image of munificence belied the markets it created for US businesses.

Understandably, recipients of "tied aid" criticize its wastefulness. A delegate from a North African nation talked about US foreign aid for a water treatment plant that was technologically too sophisticated for its engineers to maintain, and required more power and energy than was currently feasible. "Equipment sold by the Netherlands would have better suited our needs, but we were forced to buy the US equipment," remarked the representative. As a result, the plant was used for a very short time, after which it became useless. But foreign aid has never been an altruistic exercise; it would be impossible politically if it were. The Marshall Plan's image of munificence belied the markets it created for US business; so much so, in fact, that by the late 1960s, the Europeans complained of an "American [economic] invasion."

In contrast to the developing nations, Europe started with an industrial base. What the rest of the world worries about is the dependence created by too many aid projects geared to the short-term—instead of aid intended to generate infrastructure and industrial capability. "Every third world country has its own technological needs," said another delegate. "We don't invent our own technologies because of our dependence on others."

In spite of its great promise, technology is often seen in a threatening light by developing nations. It means that their countries, many of them with economies designed for colonial needs, will become less and less relevant as the world "progresses." The Caribbean sugar economies, for example, cannot readily convert to semiconductor manufacture; and what promise does a future in tourism alone hold in an uncertain economic climate—with fewer tourist dollars?

Now for trade protectionism which serves as an umbrella for many policies, good and bad, all with a sore need for some intelligent sorting out. Here, too, the weak suffer. The US can't get Japan to buy its rice, even with a $50 million trade deficit, but it can compel smaller, weaker countries to purchase the products Japan won't touch. Trade protectionism from the European Community and the US will increase, as those nations' trade deficits expand, while trade protectionism in Japan is a way of life, changing to be sure, but at a glacial pace.

"Free trade means less work," said a delegate from the newly-formed Southern group, referring to a variety of "market-opening devices," designed by the North to sell its products.

Policies inflicted on the developing world from multilateral organizations like the World Bank and the International Monetary Fund are also viewed with a jaundiced eye. Take "structural adjustment policies," which have "all but destroyed our health and educational services," according to Peggy Antrobus, a leading grassroots activist. "The gains of the 1970s have all been reversed," she added.

One wonders just what the rationale—other than political—lies behind some of these policies. Will privatizing water, for example, create more incentive, make people work harder, and make them place a higher value on water?

In effect, the bureaucrats in these agencies want to "teach people to fish; not give them the fish." But tied aid, structural adjustment policies, and "market opening" devices often prevent diversification in developing nations, because they prevent capacity building—in effect, the ability to buy the fishing rod. Telling a country it needs a hospital, when it really needs a road to the market to sell products, produce hard currency and build its own hospital is the nouveau colonialism—with the US all too often in the uncomfortable position of the mother country.

SECTION 7:
THE CONFERENCE
IN CAIRO

The great UN conferences on social themes of the 1990s have spawned many critics: "Too much talk, too much money, too ambitious, too narrow, too exclusive, too broad" are some of the criticisms. The Population Conference in Cairo in 1994, however, was not only the largest in the number of participants, but was also without question, one of the most successful. The Earth Times published a daily newspaper in Cairo, as it has

done at all the major UN conferences on social issues. Special reports, some reprinted here, stress the controversial nature of some of the deliberations, with the divisive issues of abortion, contraception and family planning holding center stage. The great achievement of the Conference was that a consensus was actually achieved, and language hammered out on these issues, so that giant steps were indeed taken in population and the interrelated fields of education, family health, and the empowerment of women. The specific positive initiatives directly attributable to Cairo are many. The work of the South-South initiative—called the Partners in Population and Development—and the encouragement of population education efforts in Indonesia, the extensive efforts concerning reproductive health in Egypt and other developing countries, and the platform provided for the following women's conference in Beijing in 1995—these can certainly be traced to achievements in Cairo. Much publicity surrounded gifts made by Bill Gates and Ted Turner specifically aimed at population efforts. This, too, was a direct result of Cairo.

SECTION 7

THE CONFERENCE IN CAIRO

THE LARGEST INTERNATIONAL CONFERENCE EVER

JACK FREEMAN
September 1994

CAIRO—Down to its very last moments, the International Conference on Population and Development kept making news and making history.

During the closing session of the Plenary, in the soaring space of Cheops Hall, the Program of Action was adopted by acclamation. And the Vatican's delegate took the floor to state that, for the first time in history, the Vatican was prepared to endorse the consensus of a population conference—at least partially.

In recognition of the momentous event, Nafis Sadik, Secretary General of the Cairo Conference, told delegates: "You should not be modest about your achievements." She added: "Compared with any earlier document on population and development, this program of action is detailed in its analysis, specific in its objectives, precise in its recommendations and transparent in its methodology.

"In our field, it represents a quantum leap to a higher state of energy," Sadik said as delegates applauded. She praised the conference's hosts— Egypt's President Hosni Mubarak and Population Minister Maher Mahran in particular—and she complimented the delegates for their long, often arduous and ultimately successful deliberations under the chairmanship of Fred Sai of Ghana.

Dr. Mahran characterized the Cairo conference as "a turning point for humanity."

"Agreement has been reached while respecting the diversity of viewpoints," the minister said. The adoption of the Program of Action, he said, "will make a major difference in the quality of life of the world community living today and for the happiness of future generations."

His statement ended not only the nine-day conference but a three-year process that included three preparatory meetings in New York and scores of regional and local gatherings at which representatives of governments and nongovernmental organizations made significant suggestions for inclusion in the Program of Action.

Monsignor Renato Martino of the Holy See told the Plenary that his delegation wished "to associate itself with this consensus [on the Program of Action] in a partial manner compatible with its own position, without prejudicing its own position with regard to some sections." Those sections included Chapters 7, 8 and 12 through 16.

Several delegations, mostly from Islamic and Latin American nations, took the floor to register their reservations about the text of the Program of Action. Most of the reservations spoke of countries' desire to disassociate themselves from concepts in the text that they felt went against their laws, religions or cultures—even though the text itself states clearly that countries are not obliged to implement recommendations that they feel violate their laws, religions or cultures.

The Program of Action stressed the balance between population and sustainable development.

Among the delegations voicing reservations were: Iran, Libya, Yemen, El Salvador, Malta, Yemen, Peru, Ecuador, Argentina, the Dominican Republic, Nicaragua, Honduras, Guatemala, Paraguay and Brunei.

Despite the reservations, at 4:30 PM Dr. Maher Mahran asked from the chair whether the Plenary wished to adopt the Program of Action. There were no objections and so the text was adopted by acclamation, touching off thunderous applause. The adoption means that it will be presented to the General Assembly in New York in October.

Many delegates praised the Program of Action, particularly its elaboration of new concepts such as reproductive health and reproductive rights and its endorsement of women's empowerment.

Tunisia lauded the program's stress on the "balance between population and sustainable development, in the context of religion and culture."

Belize's delegate suggested that even though governments are not bound to follow every recommendation of the Program of Action, the conference's efforts could well "have normative or juridical importance. Perhaps our labor," he said, "will help the poor to inherit the Earth."

Cameroon suggested that the document should be "not just a beautiful volume for our libraries, but a reference book" that will be consulted often to help produce results.

Australia's delegate noted that: "The nations of the world have put women, women's rights, women's health and the empowerment of women at the center of the global agenda." He also pointed out that this Cairo Conference was the largest international conference ever held.

In her concluding statement, Secretary General Sadik hailed its achievements as "historic." She added: "Thanks to the media, it has already drawn the interest of people worldwide." More than 4,000 journalists registered to cover the Cairo Conference.

She said the Program of Action was a document that the delegates could be proud of, adding, "I wish you the greatest success in its implementation."

THE MEANING OF THE HISTORIC CAIRO CONSENSUS

JYOTI SHANKAR SINGH
September 1997

At the concluding session of the International Conference on Population and Development (ICPD) on September 13, 1994, Dr. Nafis Sadik, Secretary General of the conference, expressed the view that women's issues and concerns had taken the center stage at Cairo and the advance registered there on reproductive health and reproductive rights issues would contribute significantly to the empowerment of women. Millions of words that have been written since—explaining and analyzing what was new and significant in the ICPD Program of Action, particularly on reproductive health and reproductive rights—broadly confirm and support this view.

I remember reading a very perceptive story published in The Far Eastern Economic Review the week after Cairo, which said: "Ultimately the message of Cairo was that women's empowerment is essential to the alleviation of poverty and population stabilization." Commenting on the experience of many developing countries, the story pointed out that higher literacy, better health and slower population growth are the best basis for economic development, and that none of these aims can be achieved without involving women as actors and agents as well as beneficiaries.

It is within this larger perspective that we should look at the major achievements of the conference in the areas of reproductive health and reproductive rights:

•For the first time, a far-reaching, comprehensive definition of reproductive health was negotiated and approved by 179 UN member countries at a global intergovernmental conference. Though it is based on a "working definition" used previously by the World Health Organization (WHO), it incorporated significant revisions of many of the concepts included in the working definition and added new ones. There is clear and unambiguous recognition of "the right of men and women to be informed and to have access to safe, effective, affordable and acceptable methods of family planning of their choice." It also allows them access to "other methods of their choice for regulation of fertility which are not against the law." This would obviously include access to abortion in countries where it is legal.

Cairo's definition of reproductive health has been embraced by an increasing number of countries in all parts of the world. At the same time, it is being used by WHO, UN Population Fund (UNFPA) and a whole host of other intergovernmental and nongovernmental organizations to reformulate and update their program priorities and strategies. Attempts made by a small group of countries to water it down at subsequent UN conferences proved unsuccessful. The definition remained intact in the Platform for Action adopted at the Fourth World Conference on Women (Beijing) and in the recommendations of the Social Summit (Copenhagen), Habitat II (Istanbul) and the World Food Conference (Rome).

It is interesting to note that while the Holy See does not fully endorse the Cairo's texts on reproductive health and reproductive rights, it has ended up supporting the inclusion of these texts in the recommendations of all subsequent UN conferences, in preference to other formulations offered. While its opposition to abortion remains unwavering, it also seems to have eased its stance on modern or "artificial" contraception. A news dispatch in The Times (London) of March 3, 1997 says the Pontifical Council for the Family has issued a new handbook for priests recommending that "Catholics who admit using the pill, the sheath or other forms of contraception should be given absolution, even if they carry out the 'sin' repeatedly, as long as each time that they confess they are penitent and make a commitment 'not to fall again into sin.'" The Church thus seems to acknowledge the reality that a vast majority of Catholics in Europe, North America and Latin America are already using modern contraceptive methods.

Cairo did not delve into two delicate questions, and neither did any of the other UN conferences: What is the relationship between "the rights of individuals and couples" and their responsibilities; and how is the disagreement to be resolved if there is a disagreement between a man and a woman on the number and spacing of children? These questions concern the most intimate and personal aspects of human relationships, and serious attempts to discuss them have led to extremely difficult ethical, moral and social dilemmas. Perhaps that is why nobody has been able so far to articulate widely acceptable answers. While a debate on these questions will no doubt continue, it can be said that Cairo has significantly changed and broadened the concept of rights and choices in the area of reproductive health for both men and women.

•The Cairo Conference clearly spelled out the linkage between family planning and other reproductive health activities. This was achieved during the process through a series of negotiations aimed at confidence building and evolution of a common understanding of the issues involved among three distinct groups—supporters of "vertical" family planning programs, supporters of fully integrated programs in the health and medical professions, and feminist groups that were proponents of a "quality of care" approach. In the post-Cairo period some supporters of family planning have argued that family planning should not be neglected when advocating the broad reproductive health approach. At the other end of the spectrum, several women's groups have expressed apprehension that the approach adopted at Cairo would not really be put into practice in many countries because of political or religious opposition, lack of political commitment or lack of resources.

I read recently a declaration issued by the Eighth International Women's Health meeting, in Rio in March 1997, which presents the view that "in many countries what is occurring is a narrow interpretation of the Cairo and Beijing resolutions, the implementation of vertical models, and the renaming of pre-existing and newly launched family planning programs as reproductive health" (The Earth Times, 1-15 April 1997). The countries being criticized would probably argue, with some justification, that it is impossible to change family planning programs into reproductive health programs overnight and that, given the limitations of infrastructure and resources, they have no option but to adopt an incremental approach to integrating family planning with other reproductive health services. This would also appear to be the general approach favored by UNFPA. I would agree, at the same time, that it will be important for NGOs, women's groups and other actors in civil society to keep the spotlight on how this process of integration and expansion is working or not working. This would help ensure that rhetoric is followed by real action.

•The Cairo conference accepted a quantitative goal for delivery of reproductive health services to "all individuals of appropriate ages as soon as possible and no later than the year 2015." At the same time, it specified qualitative goals aimed at improving the quality of family planning and other reproductive health services. It also provided a set of fairly precise estimates for mobilization of domestic and international resources that would be needed to realize these goals. Chapter XIII of the Program of Action listed estimated program costs under four major categories—family planning services, other reproductive health services, prevention of sexually transmitted diseases including HIV/AIDS, and basic research, data and policy analysis. These will come to $17.0 billion in the year 2000, $18.5 billion in 2005, $20.5 billion in 2010 and $21.7 billion in 2015. Up to two thirds of the estimated costs are expected to be met by the developing countries themselves, while one third is expected to be provided by external sources.

A recent study by UNFPA indicates that developing countries are contributing $7.5 billion toward the $11.3 billion target by the year 2000. While their contributions seem to be on track, the contributions from donor countries do not seem to be increasing at the same pace. These contributions increased dramatically during 1993-1995, but there was no significant increase in the overall amount in 1996, and the indications are that international population assistance has reached a plateau. How to mobilize the additional resources needed to implement Cairo's goals remains a major challenge before the international community.

•The conference signaled the unequivocal acceptance by the international community of the notion that targets and quotas should not be used for delivery of family planning services and that coercion in any form is unacceptable. Principle 8 in Chapter II stated that "reproductive health care programs should provide the widest range of services without any form of coercion." Further on, Paragraph 7.12 said, "Demographic goals, while legitimately the subject of government development strategies, should not be imposed on family planning providers in the form of targets or quotas for the recruitment of clients." This statement has already had a profound impact on the thinking of the government of India, which in April 1996 abolished the nationwide system of targets for family planning providers and replaced it with a system of monitoring performance-based indicators.

> *The conference signaled that targets and quotas, if they are the basis for coercion, are unacceptable.*

•A new definition of reproductive rights was adopted, going well beyond the formulation adopted by the World Population Conference (Bucharest, 1974) on the rights of "couples and individuals." Though many governments participating in the process at Cairo continued to insist that no new rights were being formulated, the inclusion in paragraph 7.3 of "the right to attain the highest standard of sexual and reproductive health" was highly significant. Acceptance of the concept of sexual health, and various specific references to "sexuality," "human sexuality" and "high-risk sexual behavior" that are to be found throughout the Program of Action brought in the notion that procreation is not the sole purpose of sexual relations and that human beings, including adolescents, need to be fully aware of the implications and consequences of various kinds of sexual behavior. The Cairo Conference broke the taboo on open and frank discussion of sex-related topics at intergovernmental forums.

•The role and responsibilities of men in sexual and gender relations, use of contraceptives and parenting were strongly emphasized throughout the Program of Action. In a section of Chapter IV titled "Male Responsibilities and Participation," the conference recommended that "special efforts should be made to emphasize men's shared responsibility and promote their active involvement in responsible parenthood, sexual and reproductive behavior, including family planning; prenatal, maternal and child health; prevention of sexually transmitted diseases, including HIV; prevention of unwanted and high-risk pregnancies; shared control and contribution to family income; children's education, health and nutrition; and recognition and promotion of the equal value of children of both sexes."

•The Cairo conference crystallized the international community's growing concern about the pandemic of HIV/AIDS. "Prevention of Human Immunodeficiency Virus (HIV)" is addressed in Chapter VII, and an entire section in Chapter VIII is devoted to HIV/AIDS. On moral and religious grounds, the Holy See and several UN member countries emphasized the importance of voluntary sexual abstinence in HIV/AIDS prevention; and while this was given appropriate recognition in the Program of Action, the conference called for urgent national and international action in the fight against the pandemic of HIV/AIDS by providing information, counseling and condoms and drugs. Paragraph 8.35 says, "Responsible sexual behavior, including voluntary sexual abstinence, for the prevention of HIV infection should be promoted and included in education and information programs. Condoms and drugs for the prevention and treatment of sexually transmitted diseases should be made widely available and affordable and should be included in all essential drug lists. Effective action should be taken to further control the quality of blood products and equipment decontamination."

The most ambitious global undertaking on HIV/AIDS prevention is the Joint United Nations Program on HIV/AIDS (UNAIDS), established soon after the Cairo conference under the joint sponsorship of the UN Development Programme, Unicef, UNFPA, the World Bank, UNESCO and World Health Organization. The strategic plan of this program, which was developed over 1995-1996 and is now being put into operation, incorporated all the relevant objectives and recommendations of the Cairo conference.

•While reiterating the position taken at Mexico City that abortion should not be regarded as a method of family planning, the Cairo conference went far beyond the Mexico City population conference by assigning high priority to action on unsafe abortion as "a major health concern." The Mexico City conference had urged governments "to take appropriate steps to help women avoid abortion, which in no case should be promoted as a method of family planning, and whenever possible, provide for the humane treatment and counseling of women who have had recourse to abortion." Instead of asking for "appropriate steps," the Cairo conference urged that recourse to abortion be reduced "through expanded and improved family planning services" and that women should have access to "quality services for the management of complications arising from abortion. . .in all cases" and not "whenever possible." Paragraph 7.6, which listed reproductive health services to be provided in the context of primary health care, included among these services "abortion as specified in paragraph 8.25." In practice, this would mean improving the quality of services and facilities so as to ensure safe abortion in countries where abortion is permitted by law.

•The conference emphasized the need to give particular attention to the sexual and reproductive health needs of adolescents. In a separate section on adolescents in Chapter VII, it called for urgent action on a whole range of issues in this area, while recognizing the rights, duties and responsibilities of parents and guardians. The chapter included a key phrase asking countries to ensure "that the programs and attitudes of health-care providers do not restrict the access of adolescents to appropriate services and the information they need, including on sexually transmitted diseases and sexual abuse." Going further, one of the following paragraphs urged governments, in collaboration with nongovernmental organizations, "to meet the special needs of adolescents and to establish appropriate programs to respond to those needs."

While provision of information and services to unmarried adolescents and young people remains a touchy and sensitive subject in a number of countries with Catholic and Islamic traditions, even these countries recognized at the conference the need to pay special attention to the real problems facing adolescents in the areas of sexual and reproductive behavior. The challenge before these and other developing countries is what they are going to do specifically, apart from engaging in moral exhortation.

•Accepting the argument that a large number of maternal deaths are caused by pregnancy-related complications, the conference linked maternal mortality to other issues relating to family planning, women's health and safe motherhood. It called upon countries to "strive to effect significant reductions in maternal mortality by the year 2015" and for provision of adequate maternal health services within the framework of primary health care. Safe motherhood was not to be regarded henceforth as a unique initiative but as an activity closely related to family planning and other reproductive health services. Paragraph 8.26 stated, "Programs to reduce maternal morbidity and mortality should include information and reproductive health services, including family planning services. In order to reduce high-risk pregnancies, maternal health and safe motherhood programs should include counseling and family planning information."

Cairo will be remembered for the clear links it established between women's right to choose and their empowerment.

This is not a complete listing of Cairo's achievements. Cairo broke new ground in many other areas. While emphasizing the integral interrelationship between population and development, it underscored the importance and urgency of instituting and implementing population policies and programs that seek to meet the needs of individual men and women. It endorsed a holistic view of social development and a whole range of quantitative and qualitative goals covering health care, education—particularly for girls—and a complement of legal and social measures aimed at promoting gender equality. It gave full and unequivocal support to the concept of "partnership" between governments and civil society. But above all, it will be remembered for the clear links it established between women's right to choose and their empowerment.

THE SILENT 'D' WORD AT CAIRO

BELLA S. ABZUG
September 1994

Post-Cairo, let us give due praise to the women from all over the world who came together to achieve a remarkable victory in transforming language, policies and, hopefully, attitudes. The narrow vision "population control" approach expressed in rigid numerical demographics and the traditional approach of seeking to control the female half of the world's population were overcome in the realistic and forward-looking document that was approved by 180 United Nations member nations. Instead of "control" the key word became "empowerment."

Recognized at long last was the centrality of women's empowerment to achieving sustainable development—the important but too often silent "D" word in the Cairo document. The elimination of political, economic, legal and social discrimination against women was recognized as a prerequisite to a country's achieving success in eradicating poverty or attaining other development goals. The Cairo Program of Action spells out the case for promoting gender equity, including increased economic activity for women, wider educational opportunities for all—especially for girls—comprehensive and integrated primary health care and broad access to sexual and reproductive health services, including the widest range of non-coercive family planning services.

Instead of 'control' the key word became 'empowerment.'

Despite the dominating press coverage of the Vatican's diehard opposition to family planning, reproductive rights and safe, legal abortion, and even condom use to protect against HIV/AIDS, the real news was the emergence of women as an international, effective and courageous force—the "messengers of change," as I called them at the final meeting of the Women's Caucus in Cairo. Congratulations are due to the thousands of women who came to Cairo and to the women and girls whose messages they brought with them. Among those who came from the South and North were experienced women activists and tacticians, indigenous women and women from towns, villages and rural communities, some of whom had never been away from home before.

The Women's Caucus document heading into Cairo was the product of more than 400 nongovernmental organizations from 62 countries. Throughout the preparatory process leading to Cairo, hundreds of women NGOs participated in the Women's Caucus.

As in the aftermath of every UN conference, the final determination of success lies in implementation of commitments made by the UN, its international agencies and governments. Women activists will network around the world to monitor implementation as well as violations of the agreements made in Cairo.

The strategies proposed by the Women's Caucus and Post-Cairo Task Force include monitoring UN General Assembly discussions on funding and resource allocations of the Cairo Program of Action. Close scrutiny will also be focused on how major multilateral, bilateral and nongovernmental institutions dealing with population policies (e.g. The World Bank, US Agency for International Development, UNFPA, International Planned Parenthood Federation, etc.) allocate their resources and the extent to which they integrate women's health and development needs into their programs.

WHAT I SAW FROM THE CHAIRMAN'S SEAT

MAHER MAHRAN, M.D.
September 1994

CAIRO—At 6:00 PM Cairo time on Tuesday, September 13, 1994, I declared the end of this historical meeting. It was a happy end for a long, protracted delivery, but both the mother and the baby were safe and healthy.

Apart from the discussions and views on different chapters and beyond fighting over the insertion and removal of brackets, I could see many significant things happening:

I could see the meeting of different cultures as members of the global society involved in serious talks about the future of their planet with great concern.

I could see the dialogue between different religions and politics within the frame of ethics and mutual respect in spite of different views on matters concerning reproductive issues.

I could see clearly the world community's caring for morality and moral issues and for the integrity of the family.

I saw the resolve of many participants to defend their views in a democratic way. It was not a conference where superpowers tried to impose their views by using arm-twisting techniques.

I saw for the first time the flexibility of the Vatican in accepting the document—an attitude which saw its delegation leaving Cairo winning instead of losing.

I saw how the world society acted positively when they discussed the future of our children and coming generations in spite of political differences. The performance of Iran was a model when its delegation collaborated with Egypt's delegation and the rest of the Muslim world to solve some controversial issues—not by refusal, but by better understanding and reconciliation.

I saw the keen interest in South-South cooperation in the 5th meeting of "Together," a project which Egypt, Indonesia, Mexico and Zimbabwe started in 1993 in Bellagio, Italy, with the guidance of the Rockefeller Foundation.

I saw Africa very clearly in this conference the great will of its countries to participate in this major event; the welcoming of South Africa by the world community after its rebirth as a democratic state.

I could see the unanimous triumph of family planning as an inbuilt component of socio-economic development.

I saw clearly the enthusiastic responses of the rich toward the poor and the commitment to implement programs for human development, probably for the first time in United Nations meetings.

I saw new nongovernmental organizations successfully take on a great sense of responsibility. I was very happy that we gave NGOs the same services provided by Egypt to the UN governmental meeting. Within the NGO meeting I saw a good representation of African and South American delegations, which added to their success.

I witnessed the Global Parliamentarians for Population and Development meeting as a concomitant event with the Cairo conference, which recommended the establishment of national committees to pave the way for establishing an African Parliamentarian Forum for Population and Development.

The Cairo conference was a successful beginning but the real success will be measured by how we rise to the challenge we have in front of us to implement the recommendations.

In Egypt, the Ministry of Population has started to work by establishing a task force with subcommittees with the following responsibilities:

• To review the document and select the recommendations needed for Egypt—to Egyptianize the document.

• To prepare the preliminary projects.

• To seek the necessary funds.

We decided that the governmental departments, NGOs and the private sector should work hand in hand to solve our population problems using the recommendations of Cairo.

WHAT WAS MISSING FROM CAIRO

NICOLAAS H. BIEGMAN
November 1994

Now that some time has passed since the International Conference on Population and Development (ICPD) in Cairo, it is becoming easier to look through the fog of "values" that obscured our view somewhat at ICPD and to evaluate the Cairo process as a whole, as well as the results we have achieved. In fact, we have come back to the clarity that appeared at the Preparatory Committee meeting in April 1994: an overwhelming worldwide consensus on the urgency of the population problem and on the need and the responsibility to tackle it in a decent manner.

Except for some issues marginal to the focus of ICPD, there was no specific "Southern" or "Northern" approach, and this made the conference an outstanding exception to the ever-lengthening series of big United Nations gatherings. This was partly because the magnitude and the urgency of the problem were clear to everyone, and partly because the problem of finance was solved very intelligently. Experts provided the estimates of what was needed and their figures were included in the Cairo Program of Action. "South" and "North" agreed without much of a discussion on a global cost-sharing on the basis for two (South) to one (North).

Also absent was the old controversy between ecologists ("The population explosion has to be contained no matter how . . . ") and feminists ("Women used to be told to produce sons for the armies; now they are told to stop reproducing; let them decide for themselves").

The magic rested on the recently established knowledge that, regardless of the measure of development of the countries concerned, there is an unmet need for family planning which could be estimated at hundreds of millions of couples and individuals worldwide. Meeting this unmet need would be more effective than any number of coercive top-down family planning programs. Moreover, there was a generally shared opinion that this would work best within a framework of improved reproductive health services, and that the status of the women involved had to be enhanced, especially through education, in order for them to be able to make a free choice and to defend it.

All this meant that "the basic right of couples and individuals to decide freely and responsibly the number and timing of their children, and to have the information, education and means to do so" had, at last, been put at center-stage. The right had been recognized as the basis of each country's population policy. What was needed now was to provide the education and information and, as a component of a wider reproductive health system, the means.

Cairo recognized the need to provide education to women, to emphasize health issues and to create economic opportunities for advancement.

Now technically this can be done. But will the necessary finance be found, and as a prerequisite for finding the finance, will population remain high enough on the priority lists of recipients and donors? What with the UN family rushing from conference to conference and from summit to summit, this is not a certain thing at all.

What I dread is that the coming 10 years could see under-prioritizing and under-funding of population and population-related activities, and consequent failure to realize a sufficient lowering of fertility rates.

In that case, the next population conference, presumably to be held in 2004, would again be confronted by a controversy. Some of those who now believe that the problem can be faced on the basis of free choice might then come back to the coercive approach, even though the successes of that approach have been few and far between in the past. Moreover, and more importantly than having a controversial conference, we would have lost the opportunity to stabilize the population of our ever-smaller world at a level that could still be ecologically sustainable.

During the next few years we must combine finance, technique and management to realize Cairo's Program of Action. In doing so we will also lay the basis for effectively addressing the subject matter of those numerous other UN conferences that are bound to take place.

A UNITED NATIONS SUCCESS STORY

NAFIS SADIK. M.D.
October 1994

Holding meetings is not usually rated as one of the United Nations' successes, but perhaps it should be. At its best, the United Nations process provides a forum for discussion on a matter of global concern; leads the international debate; finds a consensus on what the problem is and what should be done; and then stimulates action, collectively and in each country. It often takes many meetings and many years—but the success of the process stands among the solid achievements of the system in the last half-century.

Fifty years ago marked the end of a vast conflict: social upheaval, famine and war were part of the normal order of things. People hoped for peace in their own corner of the world; few people hoped for more than that. Over the last 50 years we have learned that peace is not divisible: we live, for better or worse, in one world.

The global discussions, debates and action over the last 50 years have shown us a vision of a better future, a world without war, or want, or daily violence. It is a distant vision and one that will be hard to turn into reality; but our successes have shown us that the possibility exists.

One of the great successes of the United Nations process of discussion into action has been in focusing attention on social as well as economic development. Health, education and the equality and empowerment of women are recognized today as the basis for any successful, peaceful society.

The debate on population shows the process at work. Population was one of the first issues taken up by the United Nations in 1945; but it took almost 25 years of discussion before the world community agreed on the need for action. One result of the discussion was UNFPA, the United Nations Population Fund, which celebrated its 25th anniversary last year. UNFPA's role has been to assist developing countries to find solutions for their population problems and to raise awareness about the place of population in development.

The debate has been carried on at every level, from the local community to the international community, during the whole of UNFPA's life. Its progress has been marked by a series of international population conferences which started in 1974 and culminated in the International Conference on Population and Development (ICPD) last year in Cairo, the most successful conference of its kind in United Nations history. It was a landmark in the history of international discussion and action in the field of social development.

After 20 years of sometimes heated discussion and always delicate negotiations, the ICPD has successfully integrated population with the parallel discussions on poverty, the environment, human rights, health, education and the status of women. Population issues are now seen to be inseparable from these other concerns, and vice versa. The ICPD showed that action on population is essential for success—but it also showed that we will succeed in stabilizing world population growth only if population policies are part of an all-out effort to end poverty, protect human rights, improve health and education, and secure equality and equity for women.

The ICPD reached agreement in all of these areas and adopted a concise and explicit Program of Action to help make the consensus a practical reality. The Program of Action is firmly centered on the rights and aspirations of the individual human being.

The Program recognizes that bringing women into the mainstream of development is an important end in itself and a key to improving the quality of life of everyone: there can be no sustainable human development without the full and equal participation of women. Gender equality and equity, therefore, are emphasized throughout the Program of Action. For the first time, the empowerment of women is acknowledged as a cornerstone of national and international population and development policies.

The Cairo conference introduced a new concept: "reproductive health." During the lifetime of UNFPA the use of family planning has risen from about 10 percent to 58 percent of couples worldwide, and fertility rates and family size have declined accordingly. The Program of Action looks beyond family planning and fertility toward a comprehensive view in which family planning is part of the wider context of reproductive health, and reproductive health is seen as an essential part of primary health care. This is central to the conference's true claim to landmark status: that it puts people before numbers.

The Program of Action represents thousands of hours of drafting, negotiating and consensus building by citizens and governments—and women played a key role in this process. Women's efforts were largely responsible for the acknowledgment that gender equity and equality are essential to sustainable development and to improving reproductive health. Women's NGOs achieved this success by serving in broad-based groups, many of which had never worked together before.

Women researchers influenced the ICPD process with important new research into women's lives. This research was made possible by women moving into decision-making positions in government, social services, academic institutions, funding organizations and NGOs.

Women are also acting to ensure that the Program of Action moves from words to reality. The NGOs accredited at ICPD included women's groups from all over the world.

In 1995, Cairo has already had an impact—at Beijing. The Fourth World Conference on Women agreed that the agreements reached in Cairo should not be reopened, and the Beijing Conference endorsed and even strengthened key recommendations of ICPD.

There can be no sustainable development without equal participation of women.

The true impact of the Cairo consensus, however, will be measured in how well it is understood and responded to at the national level. Many countries have issued "popular" versions of the Program of Action so that the message of Cairo is more widely available, and in a number of countries educational versions have been published for use in schools.

National committees set up to prepare for the conference have transformed themselves into "implementation committees" and have begun to work out country strategies. "Cairo" is a process which began well before the conference and will continue into the future, changing the way everyone looks at and responds to population issues.

In some countries, actions are already under way to restructure institutions in line with the Program of Action recommendations.

Nongovernmental organizations are undertaking activities in dozens of countries. Community organizations, medical associations, scientific institutes, family planning associations, churches, women's groups, youth associations, labor organizations, mothers' leagues and a variety of others are advocating and working towards implementing the Program of Action.

The discussion goes on. To ensure a coordinated response within the UN system, I have been asked by the Secretary General to convene and chair an Inter-Agency Task Force on the Implementation of the ICPD Program of Action.

As a result of our discussions at UNFPA, we have made changes in our institutional structures, policy guidelines, operating procedures and collaborative activities. We have, for example, established new guidelines for reproductive health and begun work on a system for countries to establish their reproductive health status as a basis for future action. UNFPA is committed to expanding our partnership with NGOs and to creating an environment in which this relationship can grow. An NGO Advisory Committee has been established to advise UNFPA on various matters related to our policies, programs and advocacy strategies.

"All those meetings" have produced a transformation in the way that population issues are discussed. They have paved the way for national commitment and action. More than that, they have made a start in changing the lives of women and men around the world. Now for the next 50 years.

HOW WOMEN FARED AFTER CAIRO

BHARATI SADASIVAM
June 1999

In the five years since governments adopted the landmark Program of Action at the Cairo International Conference on Population and Development (ICPD), the enabling environment essential to fulfill its promises has come under severe attack from a range of forces. Globalization and fiscal austerity policies have cut public spending and services without denting the debt burden of poor countries. Economic reform policies have led the governments of rich and poor countries alike to withdraw from their role as primary providers of social services. In the world's poorest countries, spending on health and education is minuscule compared with debt repayments. In most of these countries, family planning and reproductive health programs remain heavily dependent on donor aid, for which the current outlook is less than promising.

The Asian economic crisis has led to drastic cuts in social spending. This has especially victimized women and children.

The Cairo conference estimated that $17 billion would be needed by 2,000 to cover core programs identified in Cairo. Donor countries have delivered only $2 billion of their share of roughly $6 billion. Donor countries are also far from achieving the ICPD goal of devoting 4 percent of their official development assistance to family planning and reproductive health. Among developing countries, just a few large countries account for most resource flows. Overshadowing the issue of lack of funds are economic crises, precipitated by the unregulated flow of transnational capital. The Asian financial crisis has led to drastic cuts in social sector spending in countries in the region that have long invested strongly in health and education. Coupled with precipitous devaluation of national currencies, this has placed food, medicines and other essentials beyond the reach of large sections of populations. In Indonesia malnutrition among women and children is sharply on the rise. In Japan the economic crisis has spawned a growing category of new poor who are not covered by any form of health insurance.

The reports in the Women's Environment and Development Organization's survey "Risks, Rights and Reforms: A 50-Country Survey of Government Actions Five Years After the International Conference on Population and Development" (March 1999) add to accumulating global evidence of the erosion of equity and rights-based approaches in health as a result of the economic environment. At the same time, they attest to the efforts of individual countries to advance the goals of the Program of Action under difficult political and social conditions. Twenty-eight countries, for example, report that reproductive health is an explicit part of national health policy. Public health systems provide cancer screening services for women in Australia, Brazil, Chile, Costa Rica, Mexico, New Zealand and the US. HIV/AIDS prevention and treatment are part of reproductive health services in Germany, Korea and Senegal. Adolescent sex and health education programs are a priority in Cuba, Germany and Jamaica. Free primary health care for women and children under six years is a cornerstone of South Africa's reproductive health policy.

In the majority of countries, it is women activists who have been catalysts of change. Through tireless campaigns and coalition-building, they have wrested victories in some of the most contested areas in the Program of Action, such as reproductive and sexual rights, adolescent sexual health and education, and harmful traditional practices. In the process, women's organizations have often taken on responsibilities that governments have been unwilling or unable to handle.

All respondents cite economic reforms as major constraints in implementing the ICPD program. In particular, health sector reform, designed by the World Bank and other donors, is emerging as a challenge to expansion of reproductive health services. Many reform measures, while promising greater accountability of health systems, have in fact eroded equity of access. Moreover, like other adjustment policies in the social sector, health sector reform has defined efficiency without taking into account the enormous human cost of coping strategies adopted by the poor, women in particular.

Seventy percent of countries cite cost constraints as resulting in several adverse health consequences for women. In Botswana, where one in four people is infected with HIV, pregnant women who are HIV-positive can receive the drug AZT free of charge only during the third trimester. Forty-four per cent of countries report cuts in public health services. Budget squeezes that lead to the closing of public hospitals or their offering curtailed services particularly affect women because they are the only institutions that provide reliable care with equipment and staff for quality obstetric-gynecological services. In Peru reforms have increased the number of health centers but more than halved the number of public hospitals in the last six years. In Russia, budget cuts have forced closure of hospitals in rural areas and cutbacks in emergency obstetric services.

Nongovernmental organizations in every region of the world report that conservative forces in various guises, predominantly religious, represent key obstacles to the advancement of Cairo's goals. Adolescent sex education is under attack from the Catholic hierarchy and other conservative forces in Australia, Chile, Costa Rica and Mexico, to name a few. These are also among the countries where sexual activity begins early and teen pregnancy rates are unusually high. The vast majority of countries surveyed are far from fulfilling the Paragraph 8.25 recommendation that "in all cases, women should have access to quality services for the management of complications arising from abortion."

Industrial chemicals and other toxins in the environment are taking a massive toll on the health of women globally.

Even in countries where abortion is permitted by law to save a woman's life, women can be denied the procedure by doctors and other health care providers on religious grounds. They also have to endure humiliating and time-consuming formalities at the hands of the police, courts and other bureaucratic bodies, often with fatal consequences. Activists in Argentina, Botswana, Nicaragua and Peru report these trends. In the US, since 1993 there have been seven murders of doctors and workers in abortion clinics and 14 attempted murders. In Norway, the Christian Democrats in the governing coalition are seeking to restrict the 1978 law on abortion on demand, creating new fears of a rightward shift.

The Program of Action highlights the links between increasing population, environmental changes and sustainable development. Women are often those who are most sensitive to changes in the environment because they are in closest contact with the home and the land and they are the first line of defense when the family system is threatened. The drive for increased productivity has led to more and more women filling jobs in labor-intensive industries. Industrial chemicals and other toxins in the environment are taking a massive toll on the health of women around the world, through both occupational and residential exposures.

Eighty-two percent of countries report on occupational health hazards faced by women. In Poland, the upper Silesian Industrial Zone, designated an "ecological disaster area," is characterized by high cancer and infant mortality rates and lowered birthrates. Forty-four percent of countries report reproductive health disorders as a result of chemical exposures in the workplace and other occupational hazards. Women carpet weavers in Iran, flower workers in Colombia, shoe industry workers in Italy and makers of chemical fiber carpets in China show evidence of complex symptoms including menstrual disorders, stillbirths, miscarriages or impaired birth weight due to exposures to various chemical mixtures. In Eastern European countries such as the Ukraine, women with long-term pesticide exposure report high rates of reproductive health problems including fibromyomas and inflammations of the uterus.

Industrial sites are often too close to where the poor live. This raises concerns about environmental justice, including class and race discrimination. In South Africa the poorest women have the greatest exposures to disease and toxins and suffer poor quality water and sanitation. Fifty-two percent of countries link rising rates of breast and other cancers to environmental problems. In the US and Canada, high rates of breast cancer—and activism by grassroots women's groups—have impelled governments to fund new studies to explore environmental links to the disease.

Environmental devastation from uranium mining, nuclear energy and nuclear weapons production has taken a tremendous toll on women's health. In Chelyabinsk, Russia, where radiation is twice that of Chernobyl because of a nuclear accident in 1957, cancer incidence has since increased by 21 percent and birth defects by 25 percent. While compensation for damage from nuclear testing and mapping of health effects has occurred in some regions such as Southern Australia, most countries have no effective response. There is still not enough recognition among governments of the effects of environmental degradation on health. Prudent precautionary principles call for efforts to prevent harm by avoiding suspect risks, even where scientific evidence on these risks is still evolving. Instead, official response continues to focus on those few risks where the human evidence is overwhelming.

In most countries, it's women who have been catalysts of social change. Cairo was a great inspiration for women.

Five years after ICPD, it is clear that incremental progress toward the Cairo goals is possible, given political will and the presence of an informed and active civil society pushing for change. Reproductive health is now part of official lexicon, policies and programs. The emergence of new partnerships between governments, NGOs, international actors and the private sector has enabled creative collaborations and promoted rights-based approaches.

Women's health advocates have won recognition of the fact that structural adjustment and other economic reforms must be responsive to gender and environmental concerns.

In the wake of the profound economic and human crisis in Asia, the new climate of caution and introspection in the international financial institutions opens up critical space for women activists to renegotiate neo-liberal policies that have long ignored gender implications.

BILL GATES AND HIS BILLIONS

ROBERT L. SCHIFFER
February 1999

THE HAGUE—The news that Bill Gates and his wife Melinda were donating $2.2 billion to be used largely for population and health-related projects worldwide electrified what, for all their importance, had up to then been a fairly pedestrian series of advance meetings leading up to The Hague International Forum in February 1999. It was the perfect prelude to the appearance of First Lady Hillary Rodham Clinton at the Forum.

The excitement generated is not likely to wear off before the Forum's central concern: the Special Session of the UN General Assembly, scheduled for June 1999, devoted to what has happened in the five years since the 1994 International Conference on Population and Development (ICPD) in Cairo. With his donation, believed to be the largest of its kind ever made by a living philanthropist, the Microsoft chairman, and pioneer in computer software and operating systems, moves into a class by himself. His public-spirited gesture could not have come at a better time.

The donation, in Microsoft stock, will go to the William H. Gates Foundation, a family foundation, which will now have a total endowment of $4.2 billion. Suzanne Cluett, Associate Director of the foundation, and Dr. Gordon Perkin, Adviser, in The Hague to attend the Forum, told The Earth Times that the foundation will invite selected organizations, such as the United Nations Population Fund (UNFPA), to submit proposals. A previous grant to UNFPA, they said, helped fund The Hague Forum.

Although the Forum will not be a negotiating or policy-making session, it is inevitable that the dark cloud of insufficient funding for the ICPD Program of Action will overhang its deliberations. In short, the big unanswered question here is: Where will the money come from to pay for all that must be done if the promise of Cairo is to be fulfilled?

The delegates to Cairo agreed that their Program of Action would cost $17 billion a year by the turn of the century. That figure, less than one week's global spending on armaments, was to rise to $21.7 billion by 2015. The ICPD delegates further agreed that one third of the price tag was to be borne by the donor countries and two thirds by the developing countries; but donor country contributions have been declining and now stand at less than half the target figure, far behind what they should be, according to a recent report issued by Population Action International in Washington, DC.

Where does that leave the ICPD Program of Action? The UNFPA has warned that shortfalls in promised assistance to developing countries will result in at least 120 million additional unwanted pregnancies, 49 million abortions, five million deaths of infants and children, and 65,000 maternal deaths over the period 1995-2000.

The decline in donor country support has nonetheless continued, aggravated by such unanticipated actions as the defunding of UNFPA by a Republican-dominated US Congress, a loss of $25 million. The Clinton administration, however, has announced it will move to reinstate this amount in the President's fiscal year 2000 budget, but the proposal must first be passed by the same House that rejected it last time around.

By itself, of course, no grant made possible by the Gates donation will solve the basic funding problem confronting the ICPD Program of Action. It is no substitute—no foundation grant is—for governments' living up to their Cairo commitments.

BEHIND THE DOORS: THE FIVE-YEAR REVIEW

NICOLE SCHWAB
March 1999

At the Cairo International Conference on Population and Development (ICPD), held in 1994 under the auspices of the United Nations, the international community agreed on a program of action in the field of population and development for the next 20 years. Cairo's program marked a major shift away from population policies based on numerical goals toward policies meeting the needs of individual women, men and adolescents.

It called, among other things, for the empowerment of women; a reduction of infant, child and maternal mortality; and the provision of universal access to education and to a full range of reproductive health care and family planning services.

Five years after Cairo, the UN was supposed to meet again to review how nations were implementing these recommendations. This process included an International Forum held in The Hague in February 1999, followed by a PrepCom—or preparatory committee of the Commission on Population and Development—in March 1999. The process to review the implementation of the Cairo program, and identify successes, failures and future needs, was to culminate in a special session of the UN General Assembly in June 1999. The purpose of these initial meetings was to prepare a document recommending future actions in the field of population and development that could be presented to that special session. However, despite long negotiations and late-night working sessions, the PrepCom did not find sufficient time—and, some would argue, sufficient will—to reach agreement on the complete text.

Anwarul K. Chowdhury, Bangladesh's Permanent Representative to the United Nations, who chaired the PrepCom, had prepared a draft document. Chowdhury stressed that the draft was about "further implementation" of the Cairo program of action, not "further dilution" or "further interpretation." The draft served as a basis for the long negotiations that extended into the early hours of the morning for two consecutive days. Despite its long hours, though, the working group failed to complete its review of the draft working paper in the time allotted to it.

The PrepCom ran out of time for several reasons: The Group of 77—a coalition of 133 developing countries—and China, required additional time for negotiations within its own group; negotiations were interrupted by a three-day weekend; and debate on certain issues lasted far longer than expected.

To preclude renegotiation of controversial issues that had been resolved in Cairo, the draft used language agreed to in Cairo and made frequent references to specific paragraphs of the Cairo text. Despite these precautions and the initial consensus that programs negotiated in Cairo would not be renegotiated, many participants in the PrepCom insisted on revisiting the most controversial passages of the Cairo text. Paragraphs dealing with adolescents, emergency contraception, the family, and reproductive rights were among those most hotly debated.

The negotiations took on a complex dynamic because several members of the Group of 77 and China entered the negotiations independently, with new positions not discussed in the separate G77 negotiations. Under these conditions, said the representative from Guyana. "It becomes very difficult to hold consensus."

Many representatives of nongovernmental organizations (NGOs) expressed outrage at the outcome of the PrepCom and accused the delegates of renegotiating Cairo and watering down the draft working paper. A group of NGOs protested in front of the main conference room, brandishing bright pink "G77 Minus 7" flyers—a reference to the number of dissenting countries—and urging delegates to move the discussions forward.

"While there has been significant progress in reproductive health programs around the world over the past five years, a number of obstructionist delegates are debating principles already agreed to by 170 countries in Cairo," said Katherine Hall Martinez of the Center for Reproductive Law and Policy.

Several delegates said they did not appreciate the NGO demonstration or statements made by NGOs during the PrepCom and called NGO representation at the PrepCom "one-sided." The Nigerian delegate said that NGOs' "ultra-liberal views are an abomination to many countries."

A number of delegations also voiced disappointment with the outcome of the PrepCom. "Are we here to repeat what Cairo said?" asked the Mexican delegate. "Or are we going to move forward?" Another veteran UN observer said: "Even if the language is watered down, the ideas remain." He suggested that even though the conference moved at a snail's pace, this was nothing unexpected.

Chowdhury was more optimistic. He told The Earth Times that the PrepCom "made good progress given the constraints of time" and was successful in addressing and dealing with the substantive issues. By the end of the PrepCom, delegates had reached agreement on 43 of the 79 paragraphs included in the working draft, with nine additional paragraphs discussed but temporarily set aside. Chowdhury said that the mandate of the PrepCom was to prepare a document for the special session and that about 70 percent of that task had been accomplished.

The draft prepared by Chowdhury calls on countries to achieve specific benchmarks that were not part of the Cairo Program of Action. These include targets for access to and choice of family planning and contraceptive methods; a decrease in maternal mortality; and a decrease in the prevalence of HIV/AIDS. The working document also stresses the needs of adolescents and proposes that 20 percent of reproductive health programs be earmarked for adolescents.

Diplomatic negotiations are almost always delicate, and certainly what happened at the United Nations was no exception. But a look behind the scenes suggested that often much fuss was made over the Cairo Program of Action by parties for whom political theater seemed of greater consequence than arriving at a consensus.

PARTNERSHIPS AFTER CAIRO

MUSA BALLA SILLA
November 1998

DHAKA, Bangladesh—Cooperation between developing countries—through South-South activities—is a deliberate and increasingly important element of a worldwide strategy to improve reproductive health and family planning.

The Partners in Population and Development (Partners) was launched in Cairo at the same time that the ICPD Program of Action was ratified by consensus by 179 countries from around the world at the International Conference on Population and Development (ICPD).

The Partners' aim, as set out in Cairo, was to gain a broader view of one another's programs by sharing and adapting successful initiatives and strategies, leading to deeper understanding of the strengths and weaknesses from both sides. Such candid sharing of experience is possible in a South-to-South setting of mutual trust, respect, and openness.

The Partners continue to be guided by a clear goal—the expansion and improvement of reproductive health services that will enable all couples to have only wanted children, all children to be born in healthy circumstances, all women to avoid unwanted pregnancies and to give birth in health and safety, and all adolescents and adult men to help prevent the harmful consequences of unsafe or irresponsible sexual activity.

These services constitute the basis of what, since Cairo, has been popularly referred to as "reproductive health programs." Under the Cairo Program of Action, reproductive health services are not only a basic human right but, in addition, "if seen in terms of wanted and healthy babies and children who can be properly and lovingly cared for by healthy parents," they are something much more concrete: Reproductive health programs serve to ensure the health and survival of families and the future of generations to come.

The tasks mandated by the ICPD and its Program of Action are immense but, fortunately, many organizations, institutions and agencies are engaged in carrying them out, using different modalities. In response to the urgent call at

Cairo for intensified South-to-South collaboration as a key modality for implementing the ICPD, 10 developing countries which had acquired a high level of expertise in various areas of reproductive health decided to form an international alliance—Partners—for the explicit purpose of sharing this expertise among themselves and with other developing countries.

The founding members were Bangladesh, Colombia, Egypt, Indonesia, Kenya, Mexico, Morocco, Thailand, Tunisia and Zimbabwe. Since then, China, India, Pakistan and Uganda have joined, broadening the reach of Partners to more than half of the world's population. Partners was established on the premise that scarce resources need to be pooled and shared for maximum cost-effectiveness. It is rational and economically sound to share success stories as well as failures and to disseminate best practices.

Supporters of Partners will see a high pay-off from its activities because already-existing investments in one country can be brought to bear on similar problems faced by other developing countries. Because the Partner countries have benefitted from years of investments in population, health and education, they have the political leadership and technical knowhow for developing successful programs and projects. They have proven their dedication and competence, but they still need continued donor commitment to long-term collaborations between Partners and other developing countries. Only through such long-term partnerships between North and South will it be possible to bring the commitments made at the ICPD to fruition.

The struggle to help provide quality reproductive health care to the poor and to ensure each couple's right to freely determine the number and spacing of their children—and to have the information and the means to do so—is a worthy cause for all of us involved.

Partners is not the only organization promoting South-to-South exchanges. The others, however, are usually in the form of single projects or represent only a South-to-South dimension added onto an existing program. They tend to take the form of study tours or short-term exchanges of skills, and they are usually initiated and driven by donor countries.

Partners in Population and Development, however, takes a completely different approach. Partners represents the political will of its developing-country members to move ahead in reproductive health and family planning in a concerted manner by learning from each other through long-term partnerships and by sharing their experiences and successes with other interested countries and collaborators.

Partners has learned that having expertise does not necessarily go hand-in-hand with having the capacity to share that expertise. Therefore, Partners aims at creating the kind of permanent structures that allow for sustained, effective and efficient interaction among its members and with other developing countries.

Partners provides a new basis for making significant contributions to the realization of the ICPD program. In light of the determination of its member countries to improve reproductive health and family planning in a self-initiated and sustained manner. Partners is a small and flexible organization which is burdened neither by a cumbersome bureaucracy nor by the administrative responsibilities of direct implementation. The organization can, therefore, respond quickly.

Partners provides a climate of mutual trust, respect and openness, which places it in a unique position to address culturally sensitive subjects. Partners' members have proven that they are willing to commit their own resources to help improve capacities, not only within their own borders but also in other developing countries.

The organization provides a climate of mutual trust, respect and openness, which places it in a unique position to address culturally sensitive subjects.

Without duplicating the efforts of other organizations, Partners operates in a fully transparent fashion and documents its activities carefully in full recognition of its obligations to be accountable. Partners is clearly focused on four priority areas of the ICPD program, namely:

•integration of family planning and reproductive health services and the establishment of reproductive health structures;

•promotion and integration of programs to prevent and treat sexually transmitted diseases, including HIV/AIDS, within reproductive health structures;

•provision of family planning and reproductive health services aimed at the special needs of male and female adolescents;

•reduction of maternal mortality and morbidity.

In all of these areas, Partners pays careful attention to the crosscutting issues of women's empowerment and the roles of religion and culture.

In addition to the uniqueness of its mission, mandate and structure, several other factors contribute to the "value added" of Partners.

Partners develops programs and projects which the countries themselves desire. This invariably brings the kind of political commitment that is prerequisite to sustainability. Since Partners' board members usually are the highest-ranking officials in their countries' health or related ministries, they can easily dialogue with counterparts in other countries. Because of their high place-ment, Partners' board members not only possess knowledge of their countries' needs and opportunities, but they are also in the best position to facilitate action. Through its board members, Partners is most advantageously placed to impact on policy improvement—another crucial element for developing successful programs.

Partners does not deal with governments alone. In fact, it is the only South-to-South organization that is pursuing a strategy for integrating govern-mental and nongovernmental structures in the reproductive health field. Partners strives to engage the whole spectrum of civil society—from research and training institutions to the private sector—in forming partnerships to impact on the sexual and reproductive health of the poor.

By working through Partners, donors access systems of partnerships among various segments of society. Partners is in a unique position to address culturally highly sensitive issues, such as the involvement of religious leaders in reproductive health programs or adolescents' sexual and reproductive rights—still considered taboos in many societies. Such areas do not lend themselves easily to direct involvement by agencies from the North.

Partners is a membership organization which was born from the desire to make maximum use of the resources located in the South and to become more self-reliant. Though the annual membership fees are modest($20,000), Partner countries are making substantial contributions in kind. For example, they send professionals to other countries to provide special technical assis-tance, and several countries have pledged a number of fellowships for training candidates from other countries.

Partners' Strategic Plan shows that the member countries themselves are the primary target for increasing the funding base. However, for the near future it would be unrealistic to expect that developing countries would be able to achieve the targets set at ICPD without any external assistance. Partners will therefore continue to require funding support for its activities in 28 developing countries: Mali, Senegal, Niger, Mauritania, Tanzania, Kenya, Uganda, Nigeria, Zimbabwe, Peru, Panama, Dominican Republic, Ecuador, Colombia, Mexico, Bangladesh, China, Pakistan, India, Nepal, Vietnam, Indonesia, Malaysia, Thailand, Egypt, Tunisia, Morocco and Algeria.

While keeping the long-term goal of self-reliance in mind, Partners seeks to engage in long-term partnerships with funding agencies, foundations and private sector firms that share the organization's philosophy and its commit-ment to make quality reproductive health care and family planning services available to all, particularly to the poor and to adolescents.

Partners already enjoys the confidence of several donor agencies with which it collaborates: the European Commission, UK, the World Bank, UNFPA, The Rockefeller Foundation, the David and Lucile Packard Foundation, the William and Flora Hewlett Foundation, and The William H. Gates Foundation.

By funding Partners, contributors to the program can be sure that there is high return on their investments.

The benefits will be mutual. For all the reasons described above, Partners offers donors many substantial advantages that cannot be matched by any other organization. By funding Partners, contributors to the program can be sure that there is high return on their investments. Partners' member countries have already made significant investments to improve the quality of life of their citizens; what they seek now is to share the benefits of those investments and make them accessible to a wider audience for maximum cost-effectiveness. As they work together to disseminate information on successes, failures, best practices and research results, they greatly reduce unnecessary duplication and thus make sure that scarce resources are directed toward ventures that promise the highest return.

SECTION 8:
BEHIND
THE NUMBERS

326

The last few years have seen dramatic turnarounds—including the collapse of the Soviet Union and the Communist bloc, the end of apartheid and the rise of democracy in South Africa—causing reassessments that affect development and population policies in many ways, some very specific: For example, the International Monetary Fund's help to

the former Soviet Union territories; opening up of South African investment opportunities; and stirrings of social healing in Kosovo's neighbor, Bosnia.

In addition, there are private stirrings and notable projects that are interesting in themselves and point the way for private enterprise in cultural

and development fields to take some of the burden from diminishing public funds. Some of these enterprises are even commercially viable, as Pranay Gupte's article on the work of the Aga Khan Foundation spells out. In India, A. M. Rosenthal, frankly partisan about a land where he began his Pulitzer Prize-winning career as a foreign correspondent for The New York Times, sees positive stirrings where others see only the dark side of poverty and official ineptitude.

SECTION 8

BEHIND THE NUMBERS

HIGH ADVENTURE IN INDIA

A. M. ROSENTHAL
June 1997

When I was young, and writing from India, I embraced the gift of each day. Each day was filled with sound and movement, with thought and action, with delighted awareness of the present, hope for the future and the sense of the rolling of history.

I did not go to India in search of my soul but just to be a foreign correspondent. But somehow, from the beginning, I understood in India, as never before, that virtue lies in rushing toward each day with its joys and adventures and even its pain, and that the only real sin is demeaning God's gift of each day by turning away.

How India taught me this I cannot entirely say. But when I think of my four reporting years there, I see myself surrounded by people and motion and color and joys and horrors and kindly friends, by heat, rain and scent of dung and of the marigold, snow on the mountain, muck in the village, anger, laughter, elegance, decay.

I knew what was happening to me, this acute realization of the day as a gift. And I ran forward and seized what I could.

I thought, well, if I ever come back someday, a long time from now, it will be different, it won't be so full of zest; India and I will be older and drier.

But I did go back, a half-dozen journeys, after I had lost, for long periods, the virtue of joy in the day—and each time I found that India and I were both young again, together.

Now, how can this be? When I tell my friends about my love for India, they say, but how about caste and filth and poverty and stench and disease, riot and death?

Yes, I tell them, of course, of course. But that is not all of India, and it is the rest, I say, the huge infinite variety of the rest, that lifted my heart and still does.

It is the sense of color and dash in the dress of every Rajasthani woman brick-carrier. It is the music everywhere, the dozen different countries and the races and religions roiling in the one India. It is the warmth of the people you meet who are so kind, so loving, the adventure in travel and the still-existing greatest adventure—the Indian adventure in freedom.

So please understand that I really do know all the bad things about India, but you will not find many of them here, for this is a letter of loving thanks for the gift of the day.

All India is an itinerary. Mine always starts in New Delhi simply because it was home for so long—or at least the base from which I kept wandering about the subcontinent.

I am, of course, a man of enormous self-control and concealment of emotion. So it was not until the wheels of the airplane had touched down on one of my recent visits that I pounded my colleague on the back and shouted, "India, India, India!"

This was his first visit to India and he peered out of the window at this great country I was presenting to him, saw an airstrip and nodded amiably enough. I assured him that even more wonders lay in store.

There was something I was waiting for and I rushed out of the airport to find it. There it was, after just a few moments. India at night—the sharp scent of charcoal burning in hundreds of roadside fires of the migrant workers mixed with the aroma, half real, half a memory, of the sweet flower that Indians call Raat ki Rani—Queen of the Night. If you know India at all, you can close your eyes and be home.

Open them in the morning and there are the great red sandstone government buildings built by the British to celebrate their own sense of power. The British Raj is gone, but the buildings remain—imperial, self-satisfied, historic in their Mogul style, very Indian in the memory of history, very Indian in the celebration of national glory and pomp.

This grand sense of theater and drama is everywhere in India, not simply for tourists but for Indians as well.

What buildings like that need is what India gives them—magnificent mounted lancers on guard every day, the motionless beasts of the camel corps on the bulwarks on national days, huge pipers and drummers whenever there is an excuse for a parade, thousands of oil lamps outlining each balcony and turret at holiday time.

This grand sense of theater and drama is everywhere in India, not simply for tourists but for India and out of India. Houses are lighted for religious festivals and weddings, lighted with oil lamps, with garish electric bulb strings and with delicate little lights glowing from tree branches—princess lights, they call them.

There is theater in the magnificent military bands at the Gateway to India on Bombay's waterfront, in the bracelets of barefoot women in Calcutta, in cymbals banged and gods paraded ceaselessly in the holy city of Benares, in the starched turbans of government servants and even in the white homespun caps Indian politicians love to wear at election time to show their undying devotion to Mahatma Gandhi, as they climb into their chauffeured cars.

Sometimes it is cold in India, sometimes terribly hot, often dry, sometimes rainy. It doesn't matter all that much.

Just go somewhere, anywhere. India is alive all year, and all India is worth visiting one month or another if you don't just look but open your pores.

There is a place called Gulmarg in Kashmir, to which I try to go often. I ride a pony up a trail to a high meadow and the meadow is full of flowers and above the meadow are more mountains, beyond, touched by snow, always.

It is high and pure and clean and cold, and although I have actually ridden in Gulmarg only twice in my life, I go there often in my dreams and at times of deep pleasure. I know it well, and I never wish to see a photograph or drawing of it, because it is painted in my mind, my own sweet lovely meadow in Gulmarg.

Jawaharlal Nehru, who was Prime Minister of India when I lived there, wrote a book I took everywhere with me in my years of travel in the country. It was called "The Discovery of India." To me, the title meant that India was a perpetual discovery, too large to be known entirely but always available for one more journey, one more discovery.

Sometimes you discover India for yourself by yourself, as I discovered Gulmarg. Sometimes another person helps discover it for you.

I had been to Chandni Chowk, the bazaar quarter of the Old City of Delhi, dozens of times. But I really discovered it only on my last visit because of my colleague's own eye and interest.

I had not discovered Chandni Chowk in any of my previous visits because I had disliked it so—smelly, dirty streets, beggars, open drains—that I saw it only as a whole, an unpleasant whole, never separately. But on this visit my friend insisted on going back several times, and I saw it new. I realized that the crowded streets, the hundreds upon hundreds of stalls of cloth sellers and jewelers and spice merchants, were distinct, each of them, with its salesmen, gofers, hawkers. Suddenly the streets were not a mass but separate, hustling porters and businessmen, running, carrying, moving, buying, selling.

Each person, each movement, each noise and sensation was separate but, together, quite as real and as powerful as the red sandstone buildings and the mounted lancers.

The discovery lay in the sorting out of individuals and sensations. The sandalwood from the incense, the fried sweets from the spices. The noise was deafening. But there was discovery selecting out of the sounds the whine of motorcycles, the shouting of pedestrians, the clop of horses, the screech of machinery in a second-story factory.

Suddenly, and for the first time, I was comfortable in Chandni Chowk because I was experiencing it as did the people who lived there, separately, face by face, sound by sound.

I discovered Gulmarg in my first year in India; I discovered ancient Varanasi—it is known throughout most of the world still as Benares—more than a quarter-century later.

I wrote to a friend on a postcard: "My God, India at last! It has taken me almost 30 years of involvement with this country to get to the heart of India."

Indians call this holy city on the Ganges the navel of the world, and for all Hinduism it is. They call it the mother of cities, the mother of us all, the city of light. It is Jerusalem.

It is Jerusalem with smelly streets, huge crowds, cow dung everywhere, shrieking horns. It gives you a headache, until you suddenly realize where you are. You are in the very center of a religious experience, a day-long, everyday religious experience. The city, creature of the passion of prayer and belief, is the wild and deep inner heart of Hinduism.

Hundreds of temples can be found—up winding bazaar streets, in the middle of roads, around corners, huge temples and small wayside altars. All India is here to worship, to pray and dance. Small Bengalis, Madrasis plump with the southern coconut-oil cooking, northwesterners with faces like mountainsides—each group in its own section, its own tumbledown hostelries. Separate by night, all jumbled together by day in Varanasi.

There is a fierceness of devotion, but there is also a kind of jolliness that I did not expect. The bazaars are full of children's toys, wooden dolls and bracelets, and everybody seems to have at least one child for whom to buy a trinket.

I thought once that Hindus came to Varanasi to die, to be cremated and to have their ashes thrown into the Ganges. But most people come here to pray and see and live and believe. The religion is the reality, the only reality, and they live in it and then they die in it. But mostly they live in it.

Varanasi bounces and shrieks and smells. There are crazy monkeys that jump all over the temples and snatch garlands from around people's necks. It is wild and alive and, while you are there, there is no other place.

We saw the sun rise over the Ganges and we saw the people wash and pray. At one time I did so want to squat on the steps of the ghats and feel the Ganges, at least just touch it. I restrained myself, which I now regret.

I did not bathe in the Ganges, but will always revisit, rediscover Varanasi, just as I will always, every trip, rediscover Calcutta.

Calcutta is worth the visit, just for the statistics. All Bengalis seem to love numbers, and we had a guide who was the best Calcutta statistician I've ever met. He had a number for everything. There were 40,500 rickshaw drivers in Calcutta, exactly 180,000 people slept on the street, 30 tons of spit were spat every day and 18,500 cows roamed the streets, along with no fewer than 72,000 pigs.

Once he told me that 80 percent of India's budget went to national defense. When I mildly questioned that, he shrugged. So it wasn't 80 percent, maybe some other figure, but a figure anyway.

Of course, everybody knows that Calcutta is the worst city in the world, only it isn't. It's bad enough, all right, it's dirty and hungry and diseased. But I would take the action and vitality, the movement and the yearning and the hunger for knowledge and the humor and the wild melee of commerce any day over some of the drab and dreary cities of Eastern Europe and the former Soviet Union, or the lifeless creations of the architects like Islamabad in Pakistan and Brasilia in Brazil.

Calcutta is many things, of course—students in coffeehouses, radical mobs and a whole quarter given over to making clay gods, worshipped just one day a year and then thriftily destroyed, so that good fruit and nuts won't have to be fed to them all year round.

There's the municipal government, not quite in collapse, open sewers and moldering buildings.

But mostly it is bazaars. Fruit bazaars, vegetable bazaars, Hindu bazaars and Muslim bazaars, bazaars for cloth and gold and flowers and meat and car parts and stolen goods, whole vast cities of bazaars jammed ankle-deep in straw and bouncing, bouncing, bouncing all day long. Push, hustle, buy, sell, push, hustle. It isn't neat and it isn't clean, but it surely is alive.

The lovely valley of Kashmir and its streams are India, and so are the sweeps of beaches of the south and the Himalayas of the north. But so is Calcutta and so is Bombay, across the subcontinent. It is to the cities that villagers by the millions come in search of work and a taste of a better life.

About 10 PM the day we arrived in Bombay, I took a walk around near the hotel with William K. Stevens, who was then The New York Times's correspondent in India. There was something on the pavement.

"Is that a person?" Stevens asked me. I looked and started. "Well, I don't know," I said.

Perhaps that says more about Bombay than anything else I can think of—a nice capsule-size symbol. Around the corner from a great hotel that sells silk and gold and jewelry in its shops, a bundle of rags that might or might not be a person, who might or might not be alive.

Calcutta is mostly poor and shabby, middle-class at best, a vast busy tatter of a city. But Bombay is power—Arab princes, skyscrapers, hotels, big business deals, billions of rupees, drugs, oil, machinery, industry, women in saris slung low about their hips, handsome men, money, money, money.

And everywhere the unending shantytowns, hundreds of thousands of people poured into town looking for work, being born, living, loving, next to those hotels filled with men and women of gold and silk.

Do the people in the hotels and the apartment buildings along the beaches see the people in the shantytowns they pass every day?

I am not really sure. I will have to return to discover. After all, I never really stopped to find out whether the bundle in the street was a person or not a person, alive or dead.

In India you can discover a lot about yourself, but I suppose that is true everywhere. It was in a village that I discovered again what meant most to me about India. The colleague with whom I was traveling—Arthur Ochs Sulzberger, then the Publisher of The Times and now chairman-emeritus of The Times Company—likes villages. He had a notion that he might find out more about India in villages than in garden parties or even politicians' offices. So we saw villages in Rajasthan, in the Punjab, in Bengal, in Goa, in Uttar Pradesh, and we even saw one near New Delhi.

We walked into the village near Delhi and it looked pretty good to me, —compared to the villages I had seen years earlier in the same area.

It was clean, it had some sewers, there was farm machinery to be seen, children had real clothes, not just rags; there were some roads and the courtyards were swept and neat.

We stopped to talk. We strolled about, and people were open and friendly. There was a handsome farmer of about 50 with a quick wit and a curly gray moustache.

We asked him how crops were, and he said, terrible, awful, ghastly, a misery. I have heard these same words from farmers all over the world, and for all I know crops are always terrible, awful, ghastly. Then we asked him about what he thought of Indira Gandhi, then Prime Minister, and her government, headquartered just 20 or so miles away. This time he really got enthusiastic with distaste—terrible, awful, corrupt, inefficient, uncaring, nobody here would ever vote for her. He waited while Stevens got it all down, including his name, and we said goodbye.

A moment later I stood still outside the village and asked my colleagues where else could that happen—in what few countries in the world could a peasant denounce his own government and its leaders and spell out his name. In China, in Eastern Europe, in the Soviet Union, the very idea of listening to such questions—let alone answering them—would strike terror. They could not be asked or answered in most of Asia, in almost all the Middle East or Africa or in many countries of Latin America. But in a village outside New Delhi, a farmer with bright eyes, a curly moustache and a keen sense of himself said exactly what he thought about his Prime Minister and her government.

There were a few years when Mrs. Gandhi tried to eliminate the political democracy her father and his generation had created in India, but she failed. She was thrown out by the voters, then brought back by them out of disgust with her successors. She died a victim of India's terrible religious passions. I believe that farmer will go right on talking his heart about any Indian ruler because he has this idea that he lives in a free country.

We used to call that kind of thing—free politics, a free society, in a poverty-stricken country struggling upward—the great adventure. It still is. And that is still what means most about India to me, more than all the bazaars, all the great cities, more even than the flowers in the lovely meadow of Gulmarg.

The night we left India, I had a dream that I saw Nehru, whom I had admired. He shook my hand and said, "How are you, Abe?" and I thought, now isn't that warm of him to remember my first name after all these years.

Mrs. Gandhi was standing nearby, and I kissed her on the nose. How nice, I thought, to kiss the Prime Minister on her nose.

When I awoke I realized with a thrill of pleasure that the plane to London did not leave till very late that night. So I had ahead of me one more day in India, one more gift.

IRAN'S OTHER REVOLUTION

PRANAY GUPTE
December 1997

During the last two decades, Iran has loomed large in my life. My only son was born in 1979, the year of the revolution that toppled the Iranian monarchy and ushered in an Islamic theocracy. Iran was my first assignment as a foreign correspondent for The New York Times that same year. I was thoroughly enchanted by Persia's people and culture. I was hooked by its history. Persepolis, Mashad, Hamadan, Shiraz, Tabriz—I visited them all, these magical places. I was enthralled by the idea of reporting on international affairs—I still am—and Iran provided a glorious, if exhausting, introduction.

When I first went to Iran, in those early months of the Islamic revolution, I sought out ordinary people all over the country, listening to diverse voices in a textured, multilayered land, visiting with them in hovel and hacienda alike, partaking of their hospitality—eating chello kabab made out of succulent lamb, enjoying taftoon, the clay-baked bread that melts in one's mouth, and drinking endless cups of chai, the strong tea that Iranians consume with sugar cubes held between their tongue and teeth.

The soundtrack of those conversations and the aromas of those meals still linger in my mind, and I have often replayed in my private moments the warm generosity of Iranians as I explored Persia from Azerbaijan to Zahedan, stopping in obscure villages and towns, roaming through teeming cities, reporting on a nation in tumult and transition. Over the years I stayed in touch with many of the Iranians I met in those early months; some left their country in despair, some became casualties of a revolution that began to devour its own.

That early period in Iran was a wondrous time for me, filled with discovery of a new land and a new culture. I was, after all, a freshly minted foreign correspondent for one of the world's most prestigious newspapers, and here I was covering the biggest story around. It wasn't an auspicious time for Iran, however. There was economic chaos and political terror as the Islamic militants who seized control of this oil-rich nation dismantled the ambitious

Western-style development projects of Shah Mohammed Reza Pahlavi. It was also a time of deep antagonism between Iran and the United States because of the hostage crisis: Islamic radicals had overrun the US Embassy in Teheran and taken 52 American diplomats as hostages (they were freed only after 444 days, during which the presidency of Jimmy Carter was doomed and Ronald Reagan came to occupy center stage). It was a time when Washington was frequently and publicly denounced as the "Great Satan" by Ayatollah Ruhollah Khomeini, the spiritual "father" of the Iranian revolution. Soon there would be an eight-year war with neighboring Iraq, initiated by Iraq over a dispute concerning the Shatt al-Arab waterway, and I would return to Iran to cover that senseless conflict in which more than a million people perished. For ordinary Iranians, swept up first by the tide of revolution and then pushed into a wrenching war that affected every sector of society, it was a time of profound uncertainty.

It was by talking with the everyday people of Iran that I gained some understanding of the confusing dynamics of the Islamic revolution of 1979, which ended the monarchy and ushered in the theocracy that has controlled Iran ever since. It's doubtful, of course, that any outsider can fully grasp the complexities of Persian culture—especially not in the relatively short bursts of time that journalists are permitted in government-controlled systems such as Iran's; the eddies and cross-currents of contemporary Iranian society have their source in antiquity, and journalistic newcomers run the risk of not only being hopeless neophytes but also naive. But on the assumption that the best interpreters of Iranian society would be Iranians themselves—as opposed to, say, foreign diplomats, the favorite sources of visiting correspondents—I turned to common people. By welcoming me into their homes and opening up on a variety of issues, ordinary Iranians provided me special insights into their extraordinary society even as it was being battered by turbulent forces both within and outside their country. Talking is the national pastime here, as in many developing countries. A young reporter could scarcely ask for more.

My fascination with Persia and its people continued after my last visit in 1980. I was frustrated at being unable to continue covering Iran's tumultuous political, economic and social story. The country became a pariah in the West, especially after a fatwa—a religious death sentence—was pronounced on Salman Rushdie, the Indo-British novelist who'd allegedly blasphemed the Prophet Mohammed in his novel "The Satanic Verses." For many outsiders, Iran conjured up visions of weapons of mass destruction, which the US said the Islamic regime was developing. What also came to mind was Iran's undercutting of the Arab-Israeli peace process and its support for extremist Islamic movements in the Middle East and elsewhere. The mullahs were suspected of being behind terrorist attacks in Lebanon and in several European cities. There were reports of kangaroo courts and mass executions of the Islamic regime's perceived opponents in Teheran's notorious Evin Prison. Western organizations such as Amnesty International and Human Rights Watch frequently issued reports citing gross violations of human rights and persecution of religious minorities in Iran.

Not surprisingly, Teheran's theocrats felt that the world's media were biased against them. And so Iran became inaccessible to most journalists as its Islamic revolution unfolded. In Persian, the word for journalist is the same as for spy. Even a journalist of Indian origin was presumably suspect, notwithstanding the traditional friendship between Iran and India, and I found that a visa was impossible to obtain.

From the outside, I often wondered: Had the Iranian revolution become as malevolent as portrayed in the West? What had happened to the social justice that the Islamic militants had promised to their brethren who had lived under the tyranny of the Shah? Now that the Shah's big-ticket development projects had been mothballed, what were the mullahs doing with Iran's annual oil revenues of $15 billion? I wanted to see for myself the changes in the country. With 70 million people, Iran was too big to ignore; with the world's second-largest reserves of natural gas and fourth-largest reserves of crude oil, it was too important not to cover from inside. But how?

In Persian, the word for journalist is the same as for spy.

I had heard that there was "another" revolution going on in Iran, one that promoted family planning, literacy and health care. According to United Nations statistics, there was now 100 percent enrollment of primary-school-age students in the country's 25 provinces. Shortly before his death on June 4, 1989, Ayatollah Khomeini authorized a national "dialogue" on population after he was persuaded that the country's population growth rate was galloping out of control and straining the economic and social fabric. "Dialogue" was code for authorizing a renewed family planning movement; the ayatollah may have been an autocrat but he understood the politics of demography: No country, however wealthy, could accommodate a rapidly growing cohort of young, restless and unemployed people without endangering long-term domestic stability.

In the years since Khomeini's death, Iran's theocracy has pushed family planning so extensively that the country's population growth rate has almost been halved to under two percent annually. Condoms, birth control pills and intra-uterine devices are freely available. With the blessings of the clergy, there are now pre-marriage counseling classes for both men and women— these, in fact, are compulsory before couples can be legally married. In Teheran and elsewhere, physicians like Dr. Fereidoon Forouhary offer vasec- tomy services; clients include even the most observant of Muslim men. Infant mortality rates—usually a telling sign of the state of sustainable develop- ment—have also fallen dramatically, as have maternal mortality rates. Basic health care is widely available because the number of physicians graduating from medical schools each year has increased from 667 in 1979—the year of the revolution—to 4,500 now; in 1979 there were just nine medical schools in Iran and now there are 39. A vast network of community health workers, known as behvarz, has also been mobilized around the country.

I had heard about the Literacy Movement Organization, aimed at adults and run largely by volunteers. Its campaign has been astonishingly successful, raising Iran's literacy rate to almost 90 percent—certainly among the highest in the developing world. In Isfahan province, for instance, more than 70,000 adults—mostly women—are enrolled in free literacy classes in which they receive up to 500 hours of instruction from community volunteers. More than two million Iranians are signed up in such classes nationally. Barely 20 years ago, the literacy rate was under 40 percent.

So when an opportunity presented itself to cover an international confer- ence in Teheran, I rushed to apply for a visa. I was no longer with The New York Times; I was editor and publisher of The Earth Times, whose journalis- tic universe encompassed environment, development and current affairs. Iran's "social revolution" would be right up the newspaper's alley. Much to my surprise, the Iranian Foreign Ministry granted my visa within 24 hours. I was off to Persia. So what if my visa was valid for only a week? After 17 years of doing time elsewhere, eight days in Iran seemed time enough. It would be a different Iran that I would be visiting, of course, and quite possibly a different society. But I would be in Persia again.

It is impossible for any visiting reporter to adequately comprehend rapid changes in a society as complex as Iran's, with its 17 different nationalities and ethnic groups, its 66,000 villages, its mix of social gentility and political volatil- ity, its traditions of hospitality and deep-rooted tribal feuds. But for the reporter who is willing to invest time and effort in traveling and meeting everyday people, Iran can offer intriguing insights into how an ancient nation is struggling with the demands of modernization. It was a different Iran I encountered, but it was the same Persia.

• • •

Ziba Abbasi remembers the last time she saw her husband. She had a terrifying feeling that she would not see him alive again. It was a sunny September day in Isfahan, and her husband Mehdi Sharifian, a 34-year-old Iranian army colonel, was leaving home for Khoramshahr, the region where his country and Iraq had fought an eight-year war. "I told him not to go," Ziba said, "I told him that he had already been in battle eight years. Why now? Why go back again?" But Colonel Sharifian said, "I must go because it is my duty."

By most conventional standards, the colonel would already have been deemed to have discharged his duty well. He had served on the front for the entire duration of the Iran-Iraq war, which ended inconclusively in 1988 after more than a million casualties on both sides. He had been decorated many times for bravery. He had risen in the ranks. He was considered a model officer by his superiors not only on account of his military record but also because of the long hours he put in as a community-service volunteer. But Colonel Sharifian had a personal obsession: He would frequently return to the battle zone to search for the missing remains of Iranian soldiers. He embarked on this latest trip, in September 1997, because of appeals from mothers of Isfahan-area soldiers he had known. The women had beseeched him to look for their sons. "He told me that he had no choice but to oblige," his wife said.

Two days after Colonel Sharifian left home, Ziba Abbasi was informed by the Iranian military that her husband had been killed by a landmine.

I met Ziba at the martyrs' cemetery in Isfahan a few weeks after her husband's death. It was a Friday afternoon and thousands of people had come to pay their respects to their departed ones. There were women in black chadors, the tent-like outer robes that Iranian women wear in public; children scurried about; old men wandered among gravestones that were neatly arranged on a succession of slopes of a craggy hill known as Seyed Mohammad. The shouts of children at play, the wailing of bereaved women and the passage of a mild breeze through the tree-dotted cemetery—the mix of all these seemed strange and disorienting.

Beyond the cemetery was the sprawling campus of Isfahan Technology University, and in the distance I could see a huge bill board with a painting of the late Ayatollah Khomeini, the cleric who masterminded Iran's Islamic revolution in 1979 and who vowed to fight Iraq to the finish after Saddam Hussein, the Iraqi strongman, invaded Iran in 1980. At the base of Seyed Mohammad Hill was a mosque, its blue-and-gold exterior glistening in the sunlight. Photographs of dead soldiers—called shahids, or martyrs—were placed before many graves. Red flags were strung on kadj, stubby pine trees.

Families sat on intricately woven carpets; on the carpets were bowls containing apples, dates and bananas, which passers-by were invited to share in the Iranian custom of hospitality.

I felt like an intruder bursting into the private grief of people I hadn't known. But as I spoke with Ziba Abbasi and her family it became clear that I wasn't being treated as a stranger. She sat on a brown carpet next to her husband's grave, surrounded by her three children, Zahera, a 6-year-old daughter; Ahmad Sharifi, a 3-year-old son; and a 13-month-old girl, Marzieh. "I remember my husband as a kind and gentle man," Ziba said, in translated Farsi. "I have nothing to complain about. Life was good with him. But I always warned him about going to the battlefield. He never listened. And now he is gone forever."

What now? "I cannot do anything except be patient," Ziba said. "I have his children. I must raise them with what he has left behind." As she spoke, little Ahmad Sharifi raised a water bottle to his father's photograph, placing its mouth on the colonel's lips. Did the boy know that his father was dead? "He knows only that his father has gone away," Ziba said. The picture of the colonel was in black-and-white, and it showed a strong face with deep-set eyes and curly black hair, a neatly trimmed beard, and a uniform, and just a hint of a smile on the lips that Ahmad Sharifi had tried to touch with his water bottle.

> *I felt like an intruder bursting into the private grief of people I hadn't known.*

Ziba's father-in-law, Ali Sharifian, was present at the cemetery as was his wife, Ezad Mirdamadi. "He was a man of strong character," the dead colonel's father said of his son. "He was always kind. I have three other sons and they all looked to their brother for strength. He was always the one to solve problems in the family. All families have problems, you understand." His wife was sobbing loudly. Ziba's brother, a tall young man named Rasool Abbasi, took me aside. "She is only 27 years old," he said of his sister. "What kind of a life is she now going to have, with three small children and a husband who is dead?"

As I left the cemetery, I thought about the time I had last visited Iran. I was taken to Behesht Zahara, a cemetery outside Teheran, by an elderly couple I'd met. They had lost their two sons in the initial stages of the Iraq-Iran war. All around me were gravestones of young men who had died in the war and of many other Iranians who had died in earlier years at the hands of the Shah's dreaded secret police, the Savak. That was 17 years ago. I had come to this Middle East country then as a correspondent to cover the very war in which Colonel Sharifian had fought. Ziba Abbasi told me that her husband had spent most of his tours of duty in the southwest part of the country—a region that I knew well. Had I ever met the colonel? It seemed unlikely—he must have been just 17 then and probably a foot soldier—it was so long ago and I wouldn't have remembered even if I had run into him in the battle zone. Now I was in Iran as a peacetime visitor, but the war still touched the lives of everyday people almost a decade after it had formally ended. The guns had ceased blazing, but men like Colonel Mehdi Sharifian were still dying. Iran would honor them as shahids, of course, but what consolation was that for a 27-year-old woman who was left with three small children to raise on her own?

• • •

The turbaned man in a flowing brown cloak went up to shoppers in a food store in Teheran. "How do you find prices these days?" he asked. The shoppers vied with one another to respond, but they all had one clear message for the questioner: Inflation was hurting urban Iranians. Why, said one woman, a small chicken—barely enough for her husband and two children—cost almost 12,000 rials, the equivalent of $4. The bespectacled turbaned man took notes and moved on to another shopper much in the manner of an American retail politician working a crowd.

"When are things going to improve?" a woman asked him, echoing the sentiment of her fellow shoppers.

"Soon, I promise," the turbaned man said with a soft smile.

The man happened to be the new President of the Islamic Republic of Iran, Syed Mohammed Khatami, a moderate 54-year-old cleric. He was elected in May 1997 in a stunning landslide over Parliament Speaker Ali Akbar Nateq-Nouri, who had been favored by the hardline theocracy controlling most public institutions in this country; to everyone's surprise, including his own, Khatami received 20 million of the 29 million votes cast.

Hojjatoleslam Khatami took office in August and at once signaled his willingness to soften the harsh public face of Iran's government—making such dramatic moves as appointing a US-educated immunologist, Dr. Masoumeh Ebtekar, as Iran's first-ever woman Vice President. Among the Western-oriented intelligentsia here there was hope that the new President would be able to end the two-decade-long hostility against the US and, if not restore diplomatic ties, at least soften the poisonous rhetoric aimed at Washington, which many clerics here still ridicule as the "Great Satan." There was even hope that Iran would be able to renew trade ties with America in order to purchase computers, Boeing aircraft and much-needed oil technology.

It is obviously too early to say whether these hopes are misplaced. Politics may make strange bedfellows, but politics doesn't change overnight—not in a place like Iran, where no political parties are formally permitted to exist. After all, relations between Iran and the US have been poor since the 1979 storming by Iranian militants of the US Embassy in Teheran and the incarceration of the hostages. There is the contention of the Clinton Administration that Iran finances international terrorism, particularly aimed against Israel—an accusation that Iranian officials predictably deny. Human rights groups in the West charge that Iran continues to persecute its religious minorities and also perceived opponents of the Teheran regime.

Politics may make strange bedfellows, but politics doesn't change overnight, not in a place like Iran.

And now there is the rift between Washington and the European Union over the new $2 billion deal under which Total, the French energy company, will develop the South Pars natural gas field in Iran, which—with 21 trillion cubic meters—has the world's second-biggest gas reserves after Russia's. Total's partners in the venture are Gazprom, Russia's gas conglomerate, and Petronas, Malaysia's state oil company. The consortium is taking advantage of a 1994 US ban that prohibits American firms from doing business with Iran, the biggest buyer of foreign goods and technology in the Middle East. Too bad for the Americans, because the Iranians are actively scouting for builders of oil and gas pipelines, offering contracts that could exceed $25 billion over the next few years.

It is also premature to speculate whether Khatami will be able to deliver on his election promises to improve the domestic economy, permit freedom of expression, allow greater economic opportunities for women, legalize political parties and introduce elections for local governments and municipalities. Although Khatami is opposed to the hardline policies of the ayatollahs, his main challenge will be governance—whether, even as a popularly elected President, he will be allowed by the theocratic establishment to chart more liberal policies in foreign affairs, economics and trade.

Khatami may represent the human face of Iran's government, but not for a moment does anyone here believe that the real authority doesn't rest with shadowy Shiite ayatollahs who see themselves as the heirs of the late Ayatollah Ruhollah Khomeini.

Khomeini, of course, was the spiritual founder of revolutionary Iran. One sign of the continuing preeminence of the theocracy: Buildings all over Iran are still festooned with huge paintings of Khomeini and his successor,

Ayatollah Ali Khamenei. Khatami's face is visible only on posters left over from this year's campaign.

Still, to a foreign correspondent returning to Iran 17 years after having covered the hostage crisis and the Iran-Iraq war, it is clear that across this land people are increasingly hopeful about the prospects for change. Gone from the streets are the scowling pasdaran, the Kalashnikov-toting "revolutionary guards" who often arrested women simply because hair showed on their forehead under the traditional head-to-toe chadors and hijabs that all women are required to wear. Gone, too, are the gaudy slogans on posters condemning the US. Here and there one spots satellite dishes, which are officially banned. And even though no public dancing is permitted, Iranian homes often resonate with private gaiety. (One evening, I was invited to a dinner party at the home of an international aid official. I was introduced to several beautiful women in Western attire. One of them said, "Don't you recognize me?" I was puzzled. Then she gave me her name. It was a woman whom I'd met that very morning in a Teheran office, but then she wore a chador that concealed her features. Now, in an elegant evening dress, she was a different person entirely.)

Teheran and other places such as Isfahan are, to be sure, crowded and often chaotic. But they can no longer be called drab, a word that came to mind most frequently during my previous visits to Iran in 1979 and 1980. Boutiques are stocked with the latest fashions from Paris and Milan; electronic stores carry Sony television sets, even IBM and Apple computers (smuggled from Dubai); confectioneries feature Swiss chocolates and some bakeries pride themselves on offering bread as savory as can be found in France (although the overwhelming favorite remains the taftoon); Swatch and Rolex watches are available in large stores; and the tree-lined streets of Teheran are clogged with cars and vans made by Peugeot and Mitsubishi. Businessmen and top clergymen ride in Mercedes sedans. Gasoline costs barely 25 cents a gallon. Evin Prison on the slopes of Alborz Mountain in North Teheran—where so many executions took place during the Shah's time and certainly after the revolution—is being torn down; a park is being planned for the site. (An Iranian companion told me: "I'll never go into that park—just think of how many ghosts will be floating there.")

The 42-year-old mayor of Teheran, Gholamhussein Karbaschi, is wryly referred to by some Teheran residents as the "Giuliani of Teheran"—after New York's Mayor Rudolph Giuliani. Why? Because, like his American counterpart, the mayor is an activist who emphasizes the lowering of crime and the greening of urban areas. New parks are being created and there are signs everywhere urging residents to mind their civic manners; in fact, Teheran has become one of the cleanest cities you might see anywhere. There is a construction boom here and in other cities, especially in pricey high-rise apartment blocks. And even if rents are high in cities such as Teheran, housing is affordable in smaller towns, where municipally subsidized residential developments seem to be sprouting every day.

Hotels in Teheran no longer carry a foreign imprint—which is to say that the old Grand Hyatt is now the Grand Azadi, the Intercontinental (a favorite of journalists during the 1979 revolution) is now the Laleh, and so on. Foreigners continue to be welcomed at these establishments but they may sometimes have to pay more than they had expected. For example, single

After long years of economic hardship, there is good economic news.

rooms at the Grand Azadi ordinarily go for $70; when I came to Teheran in October, though, the rate had been jacked up to $140. Why? Because the Grand Azadi was where the World Health Organization (WHO) was hosting an international conference, and participants found it convenient to stay at the hotel. The liveliest place was the lobby, of course, where you could buy a slice of delicious chocolate cake and rich coffee for under $2 (which was still twice the price charged at cafes elsewhere in Teheran).

President Khatami turned up to inaugurate the WHO meeting and urged the international community to freshly study Iran's domestic efforts to promote health, education and literacy. Some in the audience read into his speech a subtext: that Iran was inviting greater foreign participation in its efforts to push sustainable human development. I was struck by how much at ease Khatami seemed and how accessible he was to delegates.

Khatami's presence at events such as UN meetings, trade conventions and on television partly explains the relaxed mood in Iran these days. After long years of economic hardship spawned by the early throes of the Islamic revolution and by the Iran-Iraq war, there is even good economic news: Iran has registered a $7.5 billion trade surplus for 1996. That, of course, is mainly due to the fact that Iran is the largest exporter of crude oil in the Middle East after Saudi Arabia, selling an average of 2.5 million barrels a day. Iran exported $22 million worth of oil last year, mostly to Japan and Europe, and imported about $15 billion worth of goods. Moreover, according to the Iranian Central Bank, the country's foreign debt has fallen from $22 billion in 1996 to $16 billion now.

Not far from my hotel was the site of the 23rd Teheran International

Trade Fair. It attracted 1,100 companies from 78 countries, along with almost 3,000 Iranian companies. The trade fair was held on a sprawling site on the slopes of the Alborz hills of northern Teheran. There was a bewildering assortment of displays of electrical household appliances, furniture, computers, automobiles, video equipment, movie cameras, textile machinery, teas, coffees, printing presses, paints, refrigerators, edible oils. Nothing from America, everything from Europe and various third world nations such as India and Pakistan.

"Iran is a growing market for us," Erik Højbjerg, deputy director of Hempel Marine Paints of Denmark, told me. "Politics aside, this is too important a market to ignore. Seventy million people is a big market by any standards." His company, one of the world's biggest manufacturers of paints for ships and tankers, has a virtual lock on the Iranian market. Too bad for the Americans, he seemed to suggest—with a smile, of course.

President Khatami showed up for the opening ceremonies at the trade fair. Speaking in Farsi, the national language, he called for fresh foreign investment in Iran and for technology transfers. "If we are able to develop our scientific, economic and technical ties with other countries and bond the interests of nations, then politicians will also be forced to adapt their own demands to the people's interests," he said. Again, words that suggested an interest in opening up Iran's market to more countries.

I got the impression that Iranians would like the United States to be among those countries. The US remains, as one Iranian told me, "the invisible guest" here. The Europeans are way ahead in the selling game here, even though they cluck their tongues sympathetically whenever Washington raises the question of Iran's alleged financing of international terrorism. As it was during the Shah's time, Germany is the chief supplier of industrial and communications products to Iran, with Siemens AG, Daimler-Benz and Alcatel all doing robust business. Italy has a steel mill in Isfahan; France sells food and the French automobile maker PSA Peugeot Citroen last year resumed sales of Peugeot 405 kits to its Iranian partner Iran Khodro for local assembly after a one-year break over debt disputes.

The US remains, as one Iranian told me, 'the invisible guest' in this country.

The Asians are also flourishing in Iran. Japan helps build power stations and dams. Top Japanese companies such as Nissan, Mitsubishi and Ishikawajima are here in full force, and Japanese cars compete with French and German cars for supremacy in the streets. South Korea's Daewoo

Corporation assembles cars in Iran.

Europe's growing trade with Iran is especially intriguing in view of the fact that not one of the European Union countries currently has an ambassador in Teheran. The EU asked its envoys home after a dispute last year that was sparked when Bonn accused Iran of being behind a bombing in Germany. The EU says it is willing to dispatch ambassadors again but that the German envoy must be the first to re-enter Iran; the Iranians say he must be the last in line.

Despite the US trade embargo, Iran is doing just fine with the help of the Europeans, who don't mind tweaking Washington's nose. Still, Iran continues to be watched warily by much of the international community. A recent report to the United Nations General Assembly by Maurice Danby Copithorne, a special investigator, said that the number of people executed in Iran doubled between 1995 and 1996 and may double again in 1997. But he provided no figures other than quoting reports in the Iranian media that 137 people had been executed between January and September this year. In Iran, crimes such as adultery, murder and robbery are punishable by death;

Despite the US trade embargo, Iran is doing just fine with the help of European companies.

Iran has consistently denied that its Islamic judicial system is capricious, and Iranian officials have often blamed human rights allegations on the cultural biases of Western observers.

• • •

My visit to Iran coincided with that of Nafis Sadik, Executive Director of the United Nations Population Fund (UNFPA). The Iranians were obviously pleased that she had come: UNFPA is about the only multilateral organization offering any sort of meaningful assistance to the Iranians for population and development work. It doesn't offer much money—barely $5 million each year for about 15 projects—nowhere near the $500 million of its own funds that Iran spends annually on health, education and social development. But at least the UNFPA money is a sign that the outside world hasn't entirely shut out Iran when it comes to development aid. (More than half of the $45 million or so that Iran receives annually from UN and its international agencies goes toward helping the two million refugees from neighboring Afghanistan and Iraq who have camped in Iran.)

Dr. Sadik had come to Teheran to attend the same health conference which I'd planned to cover. But clearly the highlight of her trip was her meeting with newly elected President Mohammed Khatami.

When she met with the soft-spoken President in Teheran, he said to her, according to Dr. Sadik: "I am hoping that Iran will be able to channel 10 percent of our arms expenditure into family planning and population projects." Ten percent? That could easily translate into $400 million annually. Dr. Sadik told me that she was startled because this wasn't just a newly elected political figure speaking; Khatami was, after all, a cleric, a representative of fundamentalist Shiite Islam, a religion widely perceived to have priorities other than birth control.

"I mean, he said that a few times," Dr. Sadik told me. "He talked about the importance of population programs, of reproductive health. He also said he hoped more and more women would occupy public positions in Iran—and positions of importance at that."

One woman whom Khatami elevated to the position of vice president—making her the highest ranking woman in Iran—is Dr. Masoumeh Ebtekar. She is a US-educated immunologist and one of 14 women elected to the 270-member majlis, the national parliament. As one of six vice presidents in Khatami's cabinet, Dr. Ebtekar is also in charge of environmental protection. I met the Vice President in her modest office in the Environment Ministry.

There was a computer at her desk, a healthy ficus on one side, and a well polished conference table made out of oak. An aide offered tea and delicious grapes and apples. When I pointed to the fruit, the chador-clad Vice President said: "Do you know that more than 40 percent of our agricultural products are directly produced by women?" In rural areas, she said, growing literacy had contributed to increased employment opportunities for women.

I asked Dr. Ebtekar whether she saw herself as a role model for contemporary Iranian women. After all, she was the first woman to rise so high in government. Even during the Shah's time—supposedly a more liberal era—there had been no woman in a comparable position.

"This has come as a natural event," the Vice President said, speaking so softly that I had to strain to hear her. "There is a basic development in our society where women are coming up in terms of education, in terms of political and social participation in general. So my becoming vice president is a result of both a natural consequence of developments and of a request on behalf of women that they want to have a more determining role in decision-making in our society. And in that sense I feel that, well, there's a lot of responsibility on my shoulders right now in terms of being the first woman appointed to a major decision-making position in the country.

"Also, my portfolio is environment, a very serious issue in Iran right now," Dr. Ebtekar continued. "Environmental issues are considered as basic infrastructural issues. They involve many complexities. So I feel that's a heavy responsibility." Among the things she is emphasizing is a campaign to ban smoking in public buildings and another campaign to persuade women—especially young women—to quit smoking.

Was she receiving adequate political support from her colleagues in government? The Vice President said: "Sometimes we see in different countries where women are coming into decision-making positions that there's no backing, no genuine development in that line. But in Iran, thank God, we can say that a genuine commitment exists to support women. That in turn makes things much better in decision-making circles. I feel that there is a great deal of support among both the political elite and my colleagues in the ministry and outside. There is genuine support for women's participation and presence in decision-making."

'What we're searching for is not ideology but sustainable solutions to social and economic problems...'

As Iranian politics go, Dr. Ebtekar and President Khatami are considered moderates. Both are undoubtedly sincere in their desire to improve the lot of everyday Iranians whose per-capita income—notwithstanding Iran's oil wealth—remains below $2,000 a year. Cities such as Teheran may be bustling with commerce, but they also contain slums. And rural poverty has by no means been fully eradicated. In view of Iran's emphasis on social development, to what did the Vice President feel the outside world should be paying more attention?

"You must judge Iran by what we are accomplishing in social development—in education, in family planning, in dealing with the environment," Dr. Ebtekar told me. "What we're searching for is not ideology but sustainable solutions to social and economic problems. It's not enough to have laws—we've got to implement them better."

Then she spoke critically of the foreign media. "The media have never come to terms with the realities in Iran," the Vice President said. "They always took a very biased stance in the face of the developments that occurred here. They could have made efforts to better understand the position of Ayatollah Khomeini as a religious and political leader—that he had made it clear that religion and Islam were no obstacle to women's advancement. The only difference between Islam and maybe other ways of thought and lifestyles is that Islam provides a framework where the woman's dignity is not compromised by her social activity. She is not abused, she is not exploited, but she is considered as a human being with human dignity. Also, her role in the family is not degraded. In Islam, the family itself is not undermined as a cornerstone of human development and education for the future generations. In the model we've tried to follow in Iran, the family is considered a very basic issue; it's the sacred center for human growth and development. And these are maybe the basic aspects of our social development in terms of women's issues."

"What happens in the East is not well understood in the West," Vice President Ebtekar continued. "Maybe the foreign media should take a more careful look at what we're trying to do in Iran in human development. Maybe the outside world is fixated on political developments and doesn't care much about our efforts to promote human development. And we feel that it's time to change that. I think that after people get an opportunity to see what we've accomplished here, they can decide for themselves what really has happened—what the values and developments have really been in Iran."

• • •

Implicit in what Vice President Ebtekar said to me was the fact that much of Iran's contemporary ethos has been shaped by Shia theology. The opposition to Shah Mohammed Reza Pahlavi was spearheaded by Ayatollah Ruhollah al-Musavi al-Khomeini, who lived in exile first in Najaf, Iraq—the burial place of Shiite Islam's first Imam, Ali—and then in Neauphle-le-Château, France. Khomeini had been banished by the Shah because of his intractable opposition to Westernization and his hatred of the monarchy.

From abroad Khomeini and his minions steadily mobilized Iranians through cassettes that were smuggled into Iran and distributed clandestinely, through pamphlets and books, and through messages injected into homilies delivered by the ulema—the Muslim priesthood—during Friday services at mosques all across the country. While Iran's Westernized elite may still insist that the Shah's "liberal" regime wasn't that unpopular, ordinary Iranians did not want the monarchy to continue.

What is now widely called the Iranian "revolution" was actually a 13-month phenomenon that started on February 7, 1978, when the Shah's troops fired on rioters in the holy city of Qom, Khomeini's spiritual home. About 100 people, most of them seminary students, were killed in what started as a protest against a scurrilous article that the Shah's supporters had planted exactly a month earlier in the newspaper Ettelaat. It charged, not so subtly, that the septuagenarian Khomeini engaged in deviant sexual practices and that he was also a British agent. Soon after the shooting, anti-Shah sentiment spread across the country. The monarch's soldiers were increasingly being ordered to fire into crowds at pro-Khomeini rallies. But the demonstrations

escalated, as did the violence. By various estimates, more than 15,000 peo-
ple—mostly innocent civilians—were killed in the 12 months preceding
January 16, 1979, when the Shah and his wife, Empress Farah, fled Iran for
Egypt.

Khomeini returned to Iran on February 1, 1979. He set about re-estab-
lishing the twin pillars which had dominated Iranian society for hundreds of
years: the Shia Muslim hierarchy and the bazaar merchants. It was the
bazaaris who bankrolled much of Khomeini's revolution; they had resented
the Western-style development schemes of the Shah and welcomed the arrival
of a more conservative state under Khomeini. Just how rigidly conservative
Iran would soon become was something that the bazaaris—or anyone else—
could hardly have anticipated.

There are few reminders in Iran these days of the 1978-79 revolution.
The billboards along the six-lane highway from Teheran to Qom, which once
denounced the United States, now caution drivers against speeding and urge
motorists to fasten their seat belts. Qom itself seems like just another dusty,
chaotic Iranian city, with a plethora of mosques and a warren of bazaars
where vendors offer sohan—a chewy nougat filled with pistachios—trinkets
and color pictures of Iranian leaders. The main street, Kheyabun-e Inam
Khomeini, is usually packed with mullahs and seminary students, in their
flowing brown and black tunics, neat white shirts and turbans. Near some of
the mosques are rows of bookstores offering scholarly tomes in Persian on
every aspect of Islamic theology. Fatemeh, sister of Emam Reza (whose
shrine is in another holy city, Mashad), is buried here; the golden cupola of
her 9th Century tomb is dazzling. The nearby Majid-e-Jame, with its intricate
mosaic and blue tiles, reflects the high style of the Safavid period, when architecture and the fine arts flourished in Persia.

Qom is the seat of Iran's powerful clergy, a center of theology and political intrigue. To the outside world, Iran's Shiite clergy often seems like an
homogeneous establishment, unified in its opposition to the United States
and determined to root out Westernization within Iran. But the clergy are far
from united on most major issues of governance and development, and
increasingly their leadership during the post-Revolution years is being questioned by ordinary Iranians, who accuse them of incompetence and corruption. As a result, a key debate that is shaping up in Iran today revolves around
whether Islamic values should be further imposed—by force, if necessary—or
whether Iranians should be afforded more of the civic rights and freedoms
spelled out in the 1979 Constitution.

Iran's power structure and the role of the ayatollahs is still evolving. Few outsiders have access to theocratic decision-making, and the occasional interviews granted by religious figures here scarcely shed light on the mullahs' thinking. I was impressed, however, by a recent paper by Bijan Khajehpour of the Petroleum Finance Company of Washington, DC, in which he carefully outlines how the Islamic theocracy rose to pre-eminence in Iran.

During the revolutionary period leading up to the toppling of Shah Mohammed Reza Pahlevi in 1979, the main clergy association was the Jame-e Rohaniyat-e Mobarez, the Society of Combatant Clergy. It mobilized a vast network of religious figures within Iran and also tapped Iranian exiles to help finance the anti-monarchy movement.

Following the fall of the Shah in 1979, the clergy and their supporters split into what can be characterized as three factions: conservative, moderate and leftist. The conservatives sought to forcefully impose Islamic values on all sections of Iranian society and pushed the notion of the "divine right" of the clergy to rule without any questioning of their leadership.

The main organizations in the conservative camp are: Jame-e Rohaniyat-e Mobarez (the Society of Combatant Clergy), Jamiyat-e Motakefeh Eslami (Society of Islamic Coalition)

> *The struggle for the ideological heart of Iran continues.*

and various organizations that call themselves Tashakkolhay-e Hamsou (United Institutions). The moderates rallied around Hashemi Rafsanjani, former speaker of the 270-member Majlis, or Parliament, and later President of the country. They advocated an open and liberal domestic cultural policy and the pursuit of economic liberalization, including greater trade with the West. The chief organization of this faction, consisting of clerics and technocrats, is Kargozaran-e Sazandegi (Executives of Construction).

The leftists in Iran are actually the most hardline faction among the clerics, calling for continued hostility toward the US and Britain—although their harsh rhetoric seems to have softened since 1992, when they were beaten badly by the conservatives in the parliamentary election. The main organizations of the leftists are Majma-e Rouhaniyoun-e Mobarez (Association of Combatant Clergy) and the Organization of Mujahedin of Islamic Revolution.

Although President Mohammed Khatami—a cleric himself and a founder-member of the Majma-e Rouhaniyoun-e Mobarez (Association of Combatant Clergy)—is the highest publicly elected official in Iran, there are four religious centers of powers he must deal with, and whose cooperation he needs. The highest authority in Iran is Ayatollah Ali Khamenei, who became the country's "Leader of the Revolution" upon the death of Ayatollah Khomeini in June 1989. (The Iranian Constitution requires that the nation's "Leader" have the rank of an ayatollah.) Then there is the Assembly of Experts, the highest leadership organ in the Islamic regime, which consists of 83 top clerics—elected by public vote—who have the right to ratify government appointments.

The 12-member Guardian Council is the religious supreme court in Iran, entrusted with approving all laws passed by the Parliament. Finally, there is the Majma-e Tashkhiss-e Maslahat-e Nezam, the 26-member Expediency Council, which is headed by former President Rafsanjani; it mediates between the Guardian Council and the disputatious Parliament. Because of Rafsanjani's enormous clout and popularity, the Expediency Council is widely thought to be growing in power—and its members seem inclined toward greater liberalization of the economy, greater freedom for ordinary Iranians, and overtures to the US.

Although President Khatami is clearly seeking to diversify his power base by encouraging civil-society organizations to contribute toward policy-making, in the short run the Iranian clergy will continue to enjoy high influence. The clergy of Shia Islam has four ranks: Hojjatoleslam, or student of preliminary theological studies; Hojjatoleslam val Moslemin, student of advanced theological studies; Ayatollah, one who has completed the most advanced theological studies; and Grand Ayatollah, one who has presented his Resaleh, or thesis, in theological studies and who has followers of his own thesis and ideas. It is estimated that there are more than 2 million clergy in Iran of all ranks.

In addition to the clergy, President Khatami must deal with other centers of power. They are: the judiciary; the army; the Pasdaran or Revolutionary Guards; the National Security Council; the hugely wealthy public foundations such as Bonyad-e Mostazafin va Janbazan (Foundation of the Deprived and the War Veterans) and the Bonyad-e 15 Khordad, which placed a bounty of $2.5 million on the Indo-British writer, Salman Rushdie, because he allegedly blasphemed the Prophet Mohammed in "The Satanic Verses." There is also the constituency of the rich bazaaris, the traders and merchants who helped finance Khomeini's revolution.

And there is the Astan-e Ghods-e Razawi, the most important Shia shrine in Iran, the mausoleum of Imam Reza in Mashad in eastern Iran. The institution runs Iran's largest province, Khorassan, and has great political clout around the country.

It was in Mashad that a landmark seminar on population was organized by the Ministry of Health and Medical Education in 1988. A ceasefire had just been reached with Iraq, bringing eight years of a debilitating war to an inconclusive end. The ministry had been concerned over the findings of the 1986 national census which showed that between 1977 and 1986 Iran had added 16 million people; annual population growth was at an unsustainable rate of 3.2 percent. After the ceasefire, the ministry quietly initiated a series of discussions on Iran's population problem. Ayatollah Khomeini then approved a national "dialogue" on the subject—in effect approving an accelerated family planning program.

Surprising fact: Family planning is widely accepted in theocratic Iran.

Dr. Kamel Shadpour of the Ministry of Health and Medical Education recalls that the Mashad seminar was the first national gathering at which sensitive population issues were discussed after the 1979 revolution. "It was a breakthrough," Dr. Shadpour told me in his Teheran office, which was lined with books and reports and had a long blackboard in the fashion of a classroom. "The seminar enabled the government to renew a national family planning program after a hiatus of almost a decade."

The Mashad seminar was attended by top government officials, including many cabinet members. Participants recommended that the government should come up with a comprehensive family planning program in order to slow down the country's population growth rate. A United Nations document notes that the first indication of the government's "firm commitment to recognize family planning and fertility regulation as an official policy" was the incorporation of a strong population component in the First Five-Year Development Plan of 1989-1993. The plan called for lowering the annual population growth rate to 2.9 percent.

A senior international official based in Teheran told me: "Let me tell you that back in 1990, when the UN got involved seriously in family planning here, if you would say to somebody that you were running a population program in Iran, they would laugh at you. They would say that you would never succeed within an Islamic setting because this is very much a controversial issue. The Prophet had sayings to the effect that it was better to have more children. But we began telling the government that if they wanted to reduce some of the economic difficulties facing the country then they simply had to do something about the population situation. And they agreed."

If the Mashad seminar in 1988 was a watershed in Iran's family planning history, the UN's "World Population Day" in 1992 was no less significant. On that day various cabinet ministers attended a ceremony in Teheran during which they spoke about the need to widen health care and population services. But the speech that everyone noticed was made by Ayatollah Makaran, then the head of the Qom Theological Seminary. He said that what was attributed to the Prophet and the Koran about large families was not quite relevant instruction for contemporary times.

"There should be flexibility and we should be able to make some interpretation of our own," the Ayatollah said. While it was commendable that Iran should be a big nation, he continued, it was hardly advisable that Iran be populated by poor and illiterate citizens. "I believe that Islam is very right to say that it's good to have more children because children are assets," the theologian said. "But what kind of a life are we going to give our children? We must think of that. If you pay attention to the teachings of Islam, you will see that our religion calls for the betterment of people's lives."

'We have understood that in order to be meaningful, development must translate into social justice.'

The Iranian government proceeded carefully. It persuaded various ministries to develop new programs emphasizing health care, education, housing and food security. A family planning component was worked into each of these programs. Special priority was given to establishing medical schools and widening basic health care.

"The Iranians have learned how to build partnerships among different communities and constituencies," UNFPA's Nafis Sadik told me. "That, combined with the rapid development of health services and the blessings of the religious leaders, has accounted for the success of family planning here." By 1996, Iran had lowered its annual population growth rate to under two percent. The Second Five-Year Development Plan (1995-1999) emphasizes coordination among various ministries in the social sector and among various nongovernmental organizations. Such coordination is aimed at firmly establishing population as a key element in Iran's sustainable development programs.

"In Iran," Dr. Shadpour of the Ministry of Health and Medical Education told me, "development isn't just a nice catchy slogan. We have understood that in order to be meaningful, development must translate into social justice."

Dr. Shadpour's concern is underscored by the fact that, notwithstanding the relative calm of Iran today, the years ahead are likely to impose fresh pressures on the country's ability to cope with the demands for jobs, housing and better health care. That is because 50 percent of the country's population is under 20 years of age—which means that a huge cohort of men and women are about to enter the child-bearing age. In Iran, girls are legally permitted to marry at 15 and, while the authorities are encouraging people to marry later, old customs aren't easily eradicated.

This means that the number of people being added to Iran's population each year will grow from 1 million today to almost twice that figure in another five years. Though almost 50 percent of Iran's current annual budget of $63 billion is allocated to social services—with $100 million for family planning and reproductive health—population growth will almost surely render even this formidable expenditure wholly inadequate.

• • •

I was intrigued by the fact that the country's religious leaders had come around to supporting family planning. After all, wasn't family planning against Islamic traditions?

I posed that question one morning to Seyed Ali Fouladi, a local mullah in Isfahan. He was visiting the Sajad Health Center, a neatly organized facility that offered services such as contraception instruction, vasectomies and Norplant implants for women. For some reason I was startled by the mullah's youth; he couldn't have been much more than 30. He wore a white turban, brown cape, white shirt and an olive-green tunic. His white-stockinged feet were enveloped by brown slippers.

"We favor small families because we simply couldn't adequately educate large families," the mullah said. "And our religion calls for an educated public."

Did he encounter resistance from his parishioners? Not at all, the mullah said. "I often quote from the Koran," he said, "and I say that people should have only as many children as they can afford to properly take care of. Children are a precious treasure and parents are obligated to enhance the value of every birth."

I asked Fouladi whether his youth was an advantage when he discussed population issues. "Certainly," he said. "The older mullahs often experience a generation gap."

We were talking in a room that was filled with a number of women volunteers. They all wore chadors or the hijab, also a black cloak. I asked the mullah about the role of women in promoting development.

"There's no difference in the role assigned to men and women," the mullah said. "Both have a responsibility to serve the community."

I asked one of the volunteers, Zahra Taherian, about what she saw as her "responsibility." She was just 19, possessed a high school diploma, and worked three days a week with families in the Isfahan area. She focused on promoting better hygiene, better nutrition for children, and on persuading women to have small families.

"I like health issues," Zahra said. "This work enables me to stay within our culture and religion. The Koran says that we must help our neighbors. What I'm doing is something very concrete and specific." Fouladi, the mullah, said: "The mosques encourage young people to serve the community."

Zahra told me that her mother had worked as a volunteer during the Iraq-Iran war and that this "was an inspiration for me." Her father, a worker at a sugar factory, supported her decision to become a community volunteer. Was the fact that Zahra was young and single a disadvantage when dealing with married women? "Not at all," Zahra said. "This way I can also relate to these mothers' daughters."

'I'm glad to have played a role in their decision not to have more children. Five was enough.'

Zahra has been a volunteer for about two years now. Shahla Nazenan, a mother of two children, has been a behvarz or volunteer for more than five years. "I always like to be out there to help," she said. "When I see a family struggling to support 10 children, I instinctively think, 'How are these kids going to be properly raised?'" Her work involves explaining contraceptive methods to local mothers and persuading them to come for regular checkups at facilities such as the Sajad Health Center, which is run by the local municipality.

Another community volunteer, Susan Jozdani, told me of a recent encounter with a 17-year-old woman. "This woman already had five children," Susan said. "I decided that I was going to speak to her husband about the situation." Now both husband and wife come to the Sajad Health Center for regular counseling on family planning—and for contraceptives. "I'm glad to have played a role in their decision not to have more children. Five was enough."

• • •

I had been brought to the Sajad Health Center by Morteza Mehdizadeh, a biochemist, and Shahrebanou Nematollahi, a family welfare worker, both with long experience in public health in the Isfahan region. I had a vague feeling that I'd met them somewhere, and then it occurred to me that they seemed so much like many grassroots social workers I had encountered in Iran—dedicated, hardworking and probably not very well paid.

Their concerns had less to do with money than with persuading mothers to bring their children to community clinics for proper growth monitoring;

vaccinations; family health counseling; and offering proper education on contraceptives.

"National plans finally boil down to how individuals can be provided proper services in their communities," Mehdizadeh said. "I always ask myself, 'How am I discharging my responsibility toward the community?' I think people who are in public service must give more thought to serving people."

Nematollahi, who was covered with a chador, said: "I think the behvarz, our volunteers, are good examples of people who help out in their communities without any expectations of reward." She told me about a foreign consultant who came to Isfahan recently to assess local health programs for the UN. He was astonished by the long hours put in by unpaid workers. "Why do you do this?" he asked the women volunteers. One woman, echoing a general sentiment, said: "We do it for God—and we do this for ourselves." This is the kind of feeling one encounters all over Iran; religious devotion is deep rooted among everyday people, especially in villages and small towns.

Nematollahi said: "I really believe that God has a sort of secret camera. You know, I get the feeling that He is watching over me. I try and not forget this. So when people come to me and ask for something, or phone me for some favor for their children—even if it's difficult for me I always try to do my best to respond. That doesn't mean that I always succeed, of course, but at least I can say truthfully that I try and help my community."

That morning at the Sajad Health Center, I hadn't felt very well. I had been on the road continuously for several days immediately upon arrival in Iran and hadn't been able to overcome my jet lag. The center's head, Dr. Ali Mazaheri, checked my blood pressure, and pronounced it normal. His assistant, Dr. Maryam Shareghi, offered to give me medication for my headache, which an aide brought immediately.

Dr. Shareghi told me that facilities such as the Sajad Health Center not only served local communities, they also gathered research data for the Ministry of Health and Medical Education. The data involved matters such as the prevalence of contraceptive use and unmet demand for family planning services. The Ministry, after studying such data from the country's 25 provinces, was able to ascertain where additional resources and personnel were needed. As Dr. Shareghi explained this, I remembered the voluminous files and wall charts in the office of Dr. Shadpour at the Ministry's headquarters in Teheran. "Public health is probably more extensively studied and documented in Iran than anywhere else in the developing world," Dr. Shadpour had said. At the Sajad Health Center, Dr. Shareghi and Dr. Mazaheri took me to their computer room where a chador-wrapped young woman, Adeleh

Shokoohi, worked on inputting data that would be transmitted electronically to Teheran.

That same morning, I observed Dr. Shareghi implant a contraceptive called Norplant in the arm of Soraya Karamynia, a local housewife and mother of a 4-year-old boy. I thanked the patient for permitting me to be present during the implant, and I asked how she felt about the procedure. "I feel comfortable now," she said. "If there are no side-effects, I might even recommend this to my friends. I see no shame in birth control." Time and again during my Iran journey, I was struck by how open women were about their reproductive health, how matter-of-factly they discussed sensitive issues such as contraception, and how concerned they seemed to be about the relationship between family size and community welfare. And some Westerners called this a backward society?

By assigning young doctors to clinics in different parts of the country, the notion of nationhood was reinforced.

In addition to myself and a nurse, two physicians, Dr. Firozeh Mousavi Nasab and Dr. Rebrya Sakeni, were present during the Norplant implant on Soraya Karamynia. The doctors had come from neighboring towns, Khomeinishahr and Arak respectively, on a special mission: they were to be understudies to Dr. Shareghi for several weeks. I thought that the idea of two male physicians working under a female doctor was sufficient evidence that when it came to science and the professions, there certainly didn't seem to be inequality among the sexes in contemporary Iran.

I asked the physicians how they felt about their assignment. They smiled goodnaturedly. Dr. Firozeh Mousavi Nasab said: "Medicine is neutral. We have come here to learn." This kind of professional mobility is actually encouraged by the health authorities on the grounds that by assigning young doctors to clinics in different parts of the country, the notion of nationhood was reinforced.

•••

That same day, I went to a family counseling center with Morteza Mehdizadeh and Shahrebanou Nematollahi. Couples are now required to attend premarital counseling sessions on family planning, and only after being issued a certificate attesting to their attendance are they permitted to marry. At this center, located in the chenar-tree dotted compound of a modern hospital, a woman named Ayhdas Fahari was seated in a waiting room. She looked to be about 60, and I puzzled by her presence.

Was she getting married? And what would be her interest in family planning? Fahari gave me a huge grin. "I'm the mother of the bride," she said. "My daughter is upstairs attending the class. I wish I had this opportunity when I was getting married. I wish I had learned about family planning. I would not have had five children, maybe just three."

"Do you have such classes in America?" she asked me. "You should."

I asked Fahari what she wished for her daughter, Badul Abedi. "Of course I wish for her a good life," she said. "I wish that her husband treats her well. And I hope she doesn't have more than one or two children at most."

Upstairs, the daughter was in a class of about 50 young women, a typical class that is offered daily by Sahar Heidari. The teacher told me that in addition to the three-hour class, her "students" could reach her anytime by phone. Heidari also works as a midwife in Isfahan so she's in a position to help some of her students after they have been married.

I asked Badul Abedi to identify herself, and she shyly raised her hand. What was she learning in this class?

"About contraception and hygiene," she replied without hesitation. "This is very useful for me."

In an adjoining room, a number of young men were attending a similar counseling session. One young man, who identified himself as only Ali, said he was a theology student. He was to be married within a week.

"This class was an eye-opener for me because I learned a lot about AIDS," he said. He added that the "curriculum" also involved a lecture on respecting the rights and feelings of women.

"Our mullahs urge us to attend these classes," Ali said. "They say that if we become better aware of social issues, we will be able to raise our families better."

After walking out of the counseling class, I was invited for refreshments. In Iran, even a brief visit to a government office or someone's business elicits a glass of tea and a plate of fruits and walnuts; no family will offer anything less than a full meal, whatever the time of day. Morteza Mehdizadeh and Shahrebanou Nematollahi insisted that I accompany them for lunch at the cafeteria of their headquarters. An elaborate meal was rolled out: lamb kababs, saffron, taftoon, and delicious hot tea. When I apologized that I could not eat the meat because I had converted to a vegetarian diet for health reasons, Mehdizadeh dashed off to the kitchen. Within minutes he returned with a waiter who carried a huge bowl of rich yogurt that was laced with saffron, raisins and pine nuts. It was-

'If we become better aware of social issues, we will raise our families better.' The mullahs teach this.

n't a dish designed for a dieter but I couldn't help devouring it.

• • •

As I drove around Isfahan and its environs, I strained to see signs of the kind of grinding poverty I had encountered in Iran when I first visited this country in 1979. There was little such evidence any longer, but this still remained a poor nation in terms of its development status. The per capita income is under $2,000. At the heart of Iran's economic worries are two key factors: the fact that 50 percent of its population of 70 million is under 20 years of age; and the rapid urbanization that has afflicted already large cities such as Teheran, the capital, Isfahan, Hamadan and Mashad. What this means is that Iran is going to have to come up with more and more funds to promote economic growth—to generate jobs, create new housing and provide social infrastructure.

Where will the funds come from? Oil and natural-gas revenues, which currently amount to $18 billion annually, account for more than 80 percent of Iran's overall foreign-exchange earnings. (In 1996, Iran's oil exports amounted to $15.4 billion out of a total export figure of $20 billion, the balance being revenues from mostly agricultural products.) So, in the foreseeable future, the petroleum and energy sector will continue to be the mainstay of the country's economy.

But Iran's oil sector is in pressing need of investment and technology. Julia Nanay, director of the Washington-based Petroleum Finance Company, says that if Iran doesn't invest around $7 billion annually in upgrading its oil and natural-gas sector, it seriously risks losing its export capability.

"As OPEC's largest producer after Saudi Arabia, Iran has a special role to play but it's in the context of a largely irrelevant organization," says Nanay. Of the 74 million barrels a day of total estimated world oil demand for 1997, OPEC producers will satisfy less than 40 percent. World demand for oil is expected to rise to nearly 105 million barrels a day by 2015, according to the Energy Information Agency.

Will Iran (and other OPEC countries) be able to meet such demand without "busting quotas"? As a growing number of non-OPEC producers continues to flood the market, OPEC is feeling the squeeze.

Iran's oil production was around six million barrels a day prior to the the fall of Shah Mohammed Reza Pahlevi in 1979. The current figure is around 3.7 million barrels a day, most of it from onshore fields that are badly in need of upgrading; the government wants to increase daily oil production to 4.5 million barrels by 2000. Offshore production has increased in the last two years by 200,000 barrels a day to 550,000 barrels. Iran's current oil reserves are 88 billion barrels, and its goal is to increase offshore production to a million barrels a day by 2000—but that is going to require foreign investment.

Iran's new Oil Minister Bijan Namdar Zanganeh may be strengthening ties with his Gulf neighbors and fellow OPEC members Saudi Arabia, Kuwait and the United Arab Emirates but they already belong to the camp of "quota adherers." It may be too late to bring OPEC's "quota busters" (such as Venezuela) to heel. In the end, Zanganeh may find it even in his own interest to let the revenue imperative govern and toss quota adherence out the window, says Nanay.

Iran also has the world's second largest natural gas reserves, after Russia, or 740 trillion cubic feet; it accounts for 47 percent of the gas reserves in the Middle East and for about 14 percent of the world's total gas reserves, says Nanay. It finds that gas is increasingly important to its neighbors, which lack reserves and production facilities—and therefore need to import. So it is positioning itself as a prime supplier.

Who were the real losers in this, the Iranians or the Americans?

According to the Petroleum Finance Company, Iran's plans call for an increase in gas production from 2.7 trillion cubic feet in 1995 to 4.7 trillion cubic feet by 2000. The government wants to reduce the growth in oil consumption so as to free up more oil for export—and is therefore committed to gas substitution. However, gas needs pipelines for transportation not only for exports but also to connect into the existing (and aging) national grid—and here again, Iran needs foreign investment.

Since US policy forbids American firms from entering into contracts involving Iranian gas, it's the Europeans who've emerged as the key players in lucrative deals. But Iran clearly prefers American technology and marketing expertise, which for now it's going to have to do without. Too bad, because Iran right now has nearly $10 billion in foreign-exchange reserves, and it is looking for ways to spend that money on improving its oil and gas industries.

The huge refinery outside Isfahan made me think of opportunities lost. Who were the real losers in this, the Iranians or the Americans?

• • •

While oil may account for the bulk of Iran's revenues and therefore qualifies it—in the jargon of most journalists, at least—as an "oil rich" nation, the country's economy has had a mixed record of performance before and since the 1979 revolution. In addition to oil and natural gas, natural resources include iron ore, copper, lead, zinc, chromite and gold. The infrastructure—roads, power supply, transportation—is quite modern. A recent UN report says: "This country has a huge potential for economic prosperity due to its educated and able population, its natural resources, its well-developed infrastructure in roads, communications, social services and its geographical position. This potential has not yet been fully realized."

Part of the problem of sustainable economic development stems from the enormous strains placed by the influx of refugees from neighboring countries experiencing internal conflict—Afghanistan, Iraq, Azerbaijan and Armenia. The lawlessness in Afghanistan has made that country the world's largest producer of opium and its derivatives. As a result, Iran must channel tens of millions of dollars into fighting drug trafficking—money that can be surely used for social development. Moreover, the prolonged friction between Iran and the US, and the US embargo on trade with Iran, has affected this country's ability to more expansively tap international capital markets.

Iran has tremendous potential for sustainable economic growth. But the right policies are needed.

Economists in Iran fret about the employment situation. With more than a million men and women graduating from Iranian universities each year, there simply aren't enough jobs going around.

The lucky ones often tend to be those fluent in English and in Western knowhow. Morteza Hassani is a case in point.

He is 28 years old, stocky, and single. He just graduated from the University of Tehran ("Daneshgahe Tehran") with honors in mechanical engineering. Just getting into university in Iran is a huge challenge, Morteza explained, because some 2 million students graduate from Iranian high schools each year and there are places for only 300,000.

In order to obtain a bachelor's degree, Morteza had to earn 140 credits over four years. Of these, 32 credits were required to be in Islamic Studies. He opted to learn English. Why English? Because it proved useful to him as he moonlighted as a night receptionist at the Raamtin Hotel in Teheran, earning money that would supplement his two brothers' income and pay the rent for the small apartment they shared. Because many guests at the hotel were visiting diplomats and aid workers, Morteza soon found himself in demand not only for his knowledge of local conditions: an entrepreneur at heart, he decided that he would give informal tours around Teheran to visitors. Cost: the equivalent of $5 per hour, but a nice sum in Iranian rials.

English also proved useful when it came to getting a job. A consortium of European construction companies needed a mechanical engineer specializing in pipes and circuits. Morteza proved to be the man. But it was his fluency in English, he says, that nailed down the job.

"People outside sometimes think that we live insulated lives in Iran," Morteza said. "Not true. The revolution is settling down, and young people are giving more and more thought to their careers, what role they can play in national development."

One of his brothers, Mostapha, is among those who decided to play his own special role in another sector of Iran's economy. An agricultural engineer, he returned home to Hamadan—about 300 miles from Teheran—to help his father, Abdei, run the family's 40-hectare farm. The farm, which produced wheat and beans, had been languishing on account of outmoded equipment and growing techniques. Mostapha helped turn things around, securing bank loans for new equipment and reorganizing farm production. Now the farm yields more than 50 tons of wheat each year, and the Hassani family is prosperous.

Some things, of course, never change. "My parents are putting pressure on me to get married," said Morteza. A proposal was recently received from an eligible girl's family, Morteza met her, and now they plan to get married in a couple of months.

"I know that unemployment is high among young people," he said, referring to the 30 percent unemployment rate nationally. "But I've been fortunate. I just wish others were as fortunate as I am."

• • •

As much as university and school education, adult literacy is being emphasized in Iran these days. One morning, I went to the Isfahan headquarters of the Literacy Movement Organization (LMO). It was a four-story building located in a large compound not far from the Zayande Rud river. I was taken to meet Abdullah Akbarzadeh, a stout, bearded man who wore a light-blue suit and no tie.

'With a literacy rate of barely 50 percent, how could our people grow culturally?'

Akbarzadeh appeared wary at first. Journalists did not ordinarily visit the LMO, a deeply conservative organization. Then an aide brought in a large plate of grapes and peaches, and tea, which got our conversation going amicably. Akbarzadeh was armed with statistics about the increasing literacy among the non-schoolgoing public: in Isfahan province, which contains 4.5 million people, there was 87 percent literacy.

More than 66,000 people, mostly women who had not had the chance to be formally educated, were now enrolled in his organization's free program.

Barely 20 years ago, he said, the literacy rate was just 50 percent.

"Our revolution was a revolution of values," he said, "and we wanted our people to grow culturally within an Islamic context. That meant we had to reach adults who'd not received a formal education. With a literacy rate of barely 50 percent, how could our people grow culturally?"

Akbarzadeh explained that the LMO was entrusted with developing a national program to accelerate literacy. The idea was to offer adults the means to achieve the equivalent of fifth grade literacy. In order to achieve this literacy status, a typical adult needed to attend 200 hours of "preliminary" instruction, a "completing class" of 278 hours, and a "finishing class" of 486 hours. Individuals frequently continued their education at local schools after graduating from LMO facilities, Akbarzadeh said. In particular, the program emphasized female literacy.

I asked to visit some LMO classes, and we jumped into a Mitsubishi van and headed toward Shahin Shahr, a small community about 25 miles from Isfahan.

As we drove through Isfahan's crowded streets, past mosques resplendent with blue tiles and gold cupolas, fountains in traffic islands, and pleasant gardens where roses bloomed, Akbarzadeh talked about how the literacy program focused not simply on grammar and syntax but also on getting people to understand issues such as everyday economics, religious teachings, and healthcare. Participants were taught about child-rearing and how communications within families could be improved.

'Our religion says that it is our duty to acquire knowledge...But you have to be able to read for that.'

"Because people saw an immediate benefit in all this, we have been able to sustain their interest in our programs," Akbarzadeh said. "Our religion says that it is our duty to acquire knowledge. I urge people to look for knowledge from birth to death. But you have to be able to read for that."

"Also," he continued, "making people literate means that they can integrate better into society. You may continue to have disparities in income. But at least the gaps will close among people when it comes to the ability to acquire knowledge."

During our car ride, Akbarzadeh expressed concern that foreigners viewed Iran only in the context of its theocratic politics and not its "other revolution." He quoted from Ayatollah Khomeini: "We hope that the human race will grow to the point when all guns will be converted into pencils." I said that the outside world's perception was that Iran was determined to export Islamic militancy.

"Why do Americans hate us?" Akbarzadeh asked. "What can be done to make Americans understand us better?"

Americans don't necessarily hate Iranians, I said, it was just that there were major differences in political ideas that were probably irreconcilable.

"Nothing is irreconcilable," Akbarzadeh said, not entirely with conviction.

We arrived in Shahin Shahr, a neat town with one-and-two-story buildings, broad roads lined with plane trees. The LMO's classes were held during the mornings for women so they could return home before their children. The classes were organized in assorted mosques, primary schools and community centers.

One of LMO's literacy centers was in the Rafsanjani School. It was a bright sunny day as we got out of the Mitsubishi van, and I immediately felt the dry heat. Boys were playing soccer in the school yard, and I wondered how many of their mothers were studying inside.

We were greeted by the teacher, Irandocht Sourani, a woman in her 20s, who explained that like all teachers in the national literacy program, she was a volunteer.

"I do this in the hope that I can somehow change people's lives," she said. Like other teachers, she was recruited by the Ministry of Education, which offers incentives such as fully paid graduate-level education after a certain number of years as a LMO teacher.

An elderly woman named Fatemah Khousari was among two dozen women attending a class taught by Irandocht Sourani.

At her age, why did Fatemah bother with the literacy program? "This way I can finally read the Koran," Fatemah said, referring to Islam's Holy Book. "This way I don't need any mullah to interpret the Koran. I can also help my grandchildren with their homework. I feel much more useful this way."

Another student, a young housewife named Ezat Mousafic, said: "Before I started to learn to read, my eyes were closed. I now realize how much I had missed out. My relationship with my four children has also improved. I can understand them better."

She said that she'd heard about the literacy program on a local radio station. "They said all those who were illiterate could attend free of charge," Mousafic said. "That was the first time I thought of myself as an illiterate. I didn't like that word, so I decided to do something about the situation. And here I am." Ezat Mousafic was a woman who lived in modest circumstances but she certainly articulated a determination to break out of what she perceived to be an unacceptable situation.

Every day during my eight days in Iran I met other women like her. Whether it was acquiring formal education or learning more about family planning, they seemed eager to embrace a new idea or concept, something that would bring tangible benefits to their lives and to those of their families. And I was struck by their willingness to talk about their lives in a thoughtful manner to someone they had never met before. They rarely hesitated to pinpoint what they saw as their problems.

• • •

"Iranian women want to be part of the nation's social development," Dr. Vahid Marsousi, an obstetrician and gynecologist, told me in Teheran. "They are struggling for greater opportunities in education, in employment. That's not a problem in the cities for the most part, but in the rural areas the situation needs to be improved considerably."

In addition to being a physician, Dr. Vahid is a member of the Majlis, the 270-member Parliament, and her responsibility is to oversee social legislation. Not long ago, for example, the Majlis approved seven new bills concerning children's rights and issues such as maternity leave for working women (which was increased from two months to four). Another accomplishment that she cited was legislation that resulted in mothers being allowed to breast-feed their babies during work hours (employers are required to pay the salary for one hour a day of breast-feeding time). The Majlis also ruled that women must be given more judicial appointments. In all of these matters, Dr. Vahid was a key player.

She received me at her clinic in a residential neighborhood of Teheran. It was 8 o'clock in the evening, and it had been a long day for her: the Majlis was in session and Dr. Vahid had also been seeing patients. In fact, the last of her patients was leaving just as I arrived. Dr. Vahid wore traditional attire. On her desk were two red roses, and on the wall behind her desk was a picture of Ayatollah Khomeini. A female aide offered an orange beverage as we talked.

"It is not enough to talk about male-female equality," Dr. Vahid said. "We need to promote this concept more vigorously in all areas of life. I believe in activist legislation." She pointed out that the wives of male parliamentarians were frequently contacted by her to persuade them to influence their husbands on social legislation. She was the driving force behind the establishment of a special 15-member parliamentary committee on women and children.

"Our task is to seek greater empowerment of women," Dr. Vahid told me. "We need to get more women into jobs that pay better, jobs that have more responsibility." She pointed out that since the 1979 revolution, significant gains had indeed been made by women in some fields: at medical universities, 35 percent of teachers and more than 50 percent of students are female. Women also account for more than 20 percent of the faculty at other universities. Dr. Vahid said she has also focused on the private sector's role concerning social development; she frequently calls on companies to hire more women.

> *'Officials in Iran are not as unenlightened as some outsiders may think.'*

Dr. Vahid has been married for the last 19 years to an architect; they have a 15-year-old son. A product of the Iranian academic system, she also studied in France and is fluent in French and English, besides her native Farsi. I asked her why she decided to run for parliament.

"As a doctor I always understood that I had a responsibility toward my community and nation." she said. "As an obstetrician and gynecologist, I had a special responsibility toward women. It was important for me to work toward the promotion of women's causes in Iran, and I always believed that family planning was extremely important—as was getting more women into better economic situations. Parliament is a good place to speak out on these issues—you have a national platform. People—especially men—see that women can be as strong and capable as men."

Any surprises in the parliament? Dr. Vahid smiled. Then she told me that she was surprised by the overwhelming support for the legislation on women's and children's rights. "Officials in Iran aren't as unenlightened as some outsiders may think," she added, still with a smile.

In addition to her work as a parliamentarian and a physician, Dr. Vahid is also active in a number of nongovernmental organizations. The fact that NGOs existed at all in Iran surprised me, and I conveyed that to Dr. Vahid.

"This shouldn't be surprising," she said. "The revolution itself was a grassroots phenomenon. I focus on women's NGOs, which are becoming increasingly energetic in family planning and education. All of this is in the national interest."

• • •

During my visit to Iran, the men and women at the UNFPA's Teheran office were extraordinarily generous with their time and thoughts. Some of them suspended their own off-hour plans in order to help me reach people in Teheran and elsewhere. These staffers were concerned that I obtain correct information and statistics and often went out of their way to get me up-to-date facts and figures. But the Iranian nationals insisted that I shouldn't use their names or photographs. The UNFPA country representative, Xu Shu-Yun of China—a kindly, softspoken man who was quite solicitous of my well-being—arranged for me to visit several projects that were supported by the international agency.

At any given time, I found out, more than two dozen such projects in population and reproductive-health were being assisted by UNFPA. A country document prepared for UNFPA's Executive Board states that "the main challenge for the government is to ensure that the achievements in social fields remain sustainable."

Notwithstanding the oil income, about 17 percent of the population remains mired in poverty, according to UN estimates. "Presently, all social services are being provided universally through generous government subsidies," the UNFPA document says. "With the decline in the real value of the oil income, new initiatives of financing social and infrastructural services as well as targeting the poor would be needed." UN policy calls for supporting Iran's social development policies and also promoting environmental protection programs.

The NGOs that Dr. Vahid had mentioned are also receiving support from UNFPA and from the United Nations Development Programme. Increasingly, the international development system is paying attention to Iran's work in gender issues and health-care—although, apart from the modest UN assistance, Iran gets little by way of bilateral help for its sustainable development programs.

I could not but help feel that global geopolitics frequently penalized worthy development programs. That is not to say that issues such as terrorism and weapons of mass destruction need not be addressed, but how much awareness was there of the fact that Iran was already signatory to the nuclear nonproliferation treaty, to another banning chemical weapons, and to virtually every environmental covenant that exists?

After my visits to grassroots projects, I also found myself thinking: Iran should really permit more independent observers—including, of course, journalists—to visit these programs. People such as Dr. Vahid and local volunteers could tell Iran's social development story far more persuasively than anything contained in official brochures.

Everywhere I went, there were articulate, committed Iranians who clearly cared enough about issues such as community health and family planning to devote long hours each day to volunteer work. One morning I drove with Dr.

Safieh Shahriari-Afshar to the Namju neighborhood in East Teheran, a quiet area of narrow streets and neat three-and-four-story buildings, to see for myself the sheer time and energy contributed by such volunteers, often physicians who might be earning respectable sums had they been full-time in private practice. Whether it's called nation-building or simply commitment, a visitor finds such work quite impressive.

At the Namju Health Center, Dr. Rosa Ranjbar Motlagh, a young physician, supervised a staff of a dozen other physicians and nurses. All graduates of medical schools in Iran are required to perform two years of national service.

What, specifically, did she do at the health center? "Everything," Dr. Motlagh said with a smile. That meant examining 50 women and children daily; it meant ensuring that there were enough vaccines for the children; it meant working with the 40 community volunteers who assisted the center; it meant updating the growth charts of local children (the charts were kept in alphabetical order in blue-coded files); and it meant overseeing premarital counseling classes for men and women.

> *For physicians in family planning centers, it is especially important to win the confidence of their patients.*

"Communication is important in this line of work," the doctor said. "Especially when it comes to issues like family planning in a conservative society, it is so important to build trust. The eye-to-eye contact with community residents helps build that trust. They know we would never violate their confidence in us."

As she spoke, a young couple walked in with their daughter. The father, Mostafa Davoodi, was an engineer; his wife, Fahime Esmikhani was a teacher; their girl, Diba Davoodi, was just nine months old. What brought them to the Namju Health Center? "The convenience," Davoodi said, "this place is very near my home." His wife added: "I feel comfortable with the staff."

Dr. Shahrzari-Afshar, a gynecologist, spoke to me about the need to upgrade the quality of healthcare in the country. "We've reached the stage where health services are widely available, as are family planning services," she said. "Now the challenge is to refine these services, and to reach those people for whom family planning still isn't accessible." She also seemed quite firm in her belief that more Iranian men needed to be sensitized about family planning.

Were Iranian men becoming more sensitized? I posed the question to Dr. Fereidoon Forouhari, who ran the Shahid Jafari Center, not far from the

Namju facility. "Of course, just look around you," he said.

At this center, men showed up for "no-scalpel" vasectomy. There were elaborate pre-vasectomy instruction charts on the procedure, and videos about vasectomy. Soft music was piped through hidden speakers. I asked a man named Mohammed Ruhiani, a cloth seller, why he chose to be vasectomized.

"I already have six children, and that was enough," he said. "I consulted my wife before coming here."

Dr. Forouhari told me that Ruhiani was among nearly 13,000 men who had come to the center for vasectomy in the last four years. The center also offered special courses for physicians, and some 180 doctors from different parts of the country had already "graduated" from the facility.

The center offered more than vasectomy. There was an audio-test section, (where I got hearing tested). There was a laboratory for blood tests. There was a day-care center, where Zahra Alinejad taught nursery rhymes to children, and Leila Alinejad cooked a savory meal. There was a ward where Norplant was injected into women seeking contraceptives. And there was a family counselling department. All around me there was a cheerful, clean ambiance.

I told Dr. Forouhari that his center was as good as I'd seen anywhere. He seemed pleased at this, and said, "We try."

• • •

On my last night in Iran, I walked along the banks of Isfahan's Zayande Rud river. Old brick-and-stone bridges spanned the river; some of them dated back to the 17th Century when Shah Abbas created his charming city of gardens and monuments here. There were a number of teahouses under the arches. Men sat smoking the hubble-bubble, the traditional Middle Eastern water pipe. Couples walked along the river, holding hands. There were a few paddle boats on the river. It was the mesmerizing hour of twilight and a soft breeze made the leaves of the plane trees rustle.

A magical place with a magical history. One is overwhelmed by the warmth and generosity of Iran's people.

It was a clear night, as most nights are in Iran, and the sky was studded with stars. I would be off to Teheran by car the next morning; from Teheran it would be a long plane ride to Europe and onward to New York. My eight days in Iran were up. Time to go home halfway around the world.

As I walked along Isfahan's river, along the grassy banks now bathed in the light from old lampposts, I reflected on the people I'd met and the places I'd seen on this visit and on previous trips. How long had it been since my first time in Iran? Just 18 years. Not even a drop in the bucket of time when you measure Persia's long history. I thought about the turbulence of recent times, of the hopes of ordinary Iranians, of their fears, of how people had welcomed me into their homes and made me feel less of a stranger. Besides its warm people, what was it about Iran that made one so attached to the place? Its poetry? Its art? Its architecture? All of these things mattered, of course, but there was one other thing, too. Not for one moment, anywhere in Iran, had I ever felt like a foreigner.

> *Not for one moment, anywhere in Iran, had I ever felt like a foreigner.*

I stood on the Pol-e-Khaju bridge and thought about how much history this place had witnessed and about the opportunities I'd received to glimpse a bit of what was happening in this extraordinary land. Would the system liberalize, as the West hoped? Would there be more freedoms for ordinary Iranians? Would they be free from the terrors of political radicalization? Would Iran open up more fully to visitors from abroad? Would there be a rapprochement with the United States? Would Iran once again take its rightful place in the comity of nations and not be perceived as a pariah? What about human rights? Would Iran be able to sustain its momentum in family planning, literacy and health care or would resources be diverted toward new militarization?

Could Iran really expect economic and political cooperation from the United States as long as there remained the suspicion that it sponsored terrorism overseas? Impossible to say what would happen politically in Iran, difficult to predict what sort of future for Iran's "other revolution." So many questions, so few certainties.

Most journalists go through periods of introspection after an assignment, and it isn't uncommon to wonder what one has missed, what one would have done differently. Standing on the banks of Zayande Rud River, lines from T. S. Eliot's "The Dry Salvages" came to mind:

> *We had the experience, but missed the meaning,*
> *And approach to the meaning restores the experience*
> *In a different form...*

Isfahan was a strange place to recall Eliot. Maybe Persia's Hafez or Firdaus would have been more appropriate—except that the American-born poet's words were easily recalled. But in that moment I thought about that very first journey to Iran and how my heart had missed a beat when I saw the twinkling lights of Teheran as my plane descended. I thought about the frenzied crowds outside the American Embassy, about the hostage crisis, about covering Iran still in the throes of its Islamic revolution as the last vestiges of Pahlavi rule were stripped away.

I thought about all the people I had met and become close to, about their homes and about the companionship, the food and lodging they offered to a stranger in their midst. How long had it been since that first visit to Iran? Just 18 years? But on this bittersweet evening in Isfahan, on the eve of yet another departure from this land of magic and painful history, I felt that I had known Persia during more than just one lifetime. And perhaps I had.

A PEOPLE'S PARK IN CAIRO

RABYA NIZAM
May 1999

CAIRO—In the drab and dusty climate of Cairo, where everything seems to be covered with a film of grit blowing in from the desert, greenery is scarce and hard to find—but that is changing.

Plans for an innovative new park in the heart of old Cairo promise to brighten the lives of the people living here. Proposed by the Aga Khan, the spiritual leader and Imam of Ismaili Muslims, as a gift for the people of Cairo, the park is expected to provide a much-needed green lung for the overcrowded metropolis.

The gift, to be known as the al-Azhar Park, was first proposed to the First Lady of Egypt, Suzanne Mubarak, in the mid-1980s. And in 1984, the Aga Khan Cultural Services-Egypt (AKCS), the Trust's local organization, was established to implement the construction of the 70-acre (32-hectare) park on the barren Darassa site, which was contributed by the Governate of Cairo.

The site is centrally located between the eastern edge of the Fatimid city and the Mamluk "City of the Dead," an area filled with tombs, many of which are full of life—occupied by squatter families.

When it is completed, the al-Azhar Park will be Cairo's largest open public space. Improving the barren site is also expected to benefit the residential areas adjacent to the park, which also serve as home to several mosques and other historic structures, including the 12th Century Ayubbid city wall.

In the past, according to AKCS, the limited funds available from the government for preservation work were directed mainly toward the conservation of pharaonic monuments. But the structures in the neighborhood of the new park were allowed to decay and are now in serious need of conservation and rehabilitation.

With an estimated construction budget of $10 million, the al-Azhar Park is expected to take at least four to five years to build.

In a city dogged by urban problems of pollution, traffic, congestion and the emergence of shantytowns behind five-star hotels, a park on such a scale would be a welcome addition to the city's landscape.

Standing on the park site, one can see breath taking panoramic views of Cairo and monuments like Saladin's Citadel, the Blue Mosque, the al-Azhar Mosque and university and, far in the distance but visible on a clear day when the smog and pollution allow, the pyramids.

"There certainly isn't another spot where you can stop and have a vista of Islamic Cairo while being in a lovely setting," said Tom Kessinger, General Manager of the Trust.

The formerly barren site is currently under construction using both highly expensive modern equipment and the much less costly manual labor of local residents. Bulldozers and enormous soil separation machines work alongside workers transporting stones, soil and other materials on their heads, from one end of the park to the other. The hope is that once the park is finished, these local people will play a role in running and maintaining it.

Eventually, a number of income-producing activities will also be introduced into the neighborhood to provide furnishings and services for the park, said Kessinger.

What is making the task of building the park difficult, said Stefano Bianca, Director of the Historic Cities Support Program, the Trust program overseeing the park project, is that its site is filled with rubble. According to the historians working on the project, the land had been used as a rubbish dump for centuries. Walking through it, one stumbles across old car tires, soiled diapers, medical waste, dead animals—and also broken pottery, cooking utensils and other valuable artifacts of past and possibly ancient civilizations.

Bianca said that one of the main reasons the site was selected is that it was the last large open space in the crowded inner city of Cairo. AKCS has drawn up plans for the park which would transform the barren site into outdoor recreational spaces including a children's play area, game fields, gardens, a coffeeshop and cultural and educational facilities. Beautifying the area with greenery and landscaping would also make it more appealing to adjacent residents, the students of the nearby al-Azhar University, international visitors and the general public, AKCS says.

The Trust has already started an on-site nursery and a desert nursery to start growing the trees, plants and flowers that will be used for landscaping the park once it is completed.

Expressing concern that a state-of-the-art park might attract a lot of private investment that would in turn cause uncontrolled development in the surrounding area of Darb al-Ahmar, Kessinger said that unless this develop-ment is held in check and properly channeled through a conscious planning effort, both local residents and their businesses would be forced out of the area. "Currently, there are not even the basic facilities like running water or a proper sewage system," said Kessinger. "We'd like to see all of that develop without there being a massive change in who lives there," he added.

"Our biggest worry is that if you don't have an overall development plan for this area, several generations will undergo some profound gentrification once we get started," said Kessinger. He added that houses that are now of almost no value would suddenly be overlooking a multi-million-dollar park.

This concern led the Trust to expand its activities into the surrounding neighborhood. "The project presented a unique opportunity to serve as a cat-alyst for the old city rehabilitation," said Bianca, adding that by embarking on a number of spin-off projects, it would improve the living conditions on the fringe area of the old city in al-Darb-al-Ahmar.

THE AGA KHAN: VENTURE CAPITALIST TO THE POOR

PRANAY GUPTE
June 1999

Prince Karim, Aga Khan IV, is one of the world's wealthiest men and a seasoned philanthropist, but he's no longer just giving his millions away in third-world countries. The spiritual leader of 15 million Ismaili Shia Muslims, spread over 25 nations, the Aga Khan is changing the face of global philanthropy through the Aga Khan Development Network which consists of institutions fostering economic, social and cultural development. The Aga Khan Fund for Economic Development takes equity in small-scale and large enterprises in order to spur economic development at the grassroots and lessen what he calls "aid dependence." In the process, he's making everyday people more affluent—or at least more self-reliant—in many developing countries, including basket cases such as Tanzania, Pakistan and Tajikistan that don't hold much hope of otherwise attracting high-profile foreign investors.

In this era of globalization, when developing countries often seek overseas investment for mammoth industrial projects, the Aga Khan is encouraging the expansion of small-scale enterprises as a way out of the economic malaise afflicting many emerging societies. "My sense is that at the present time there's an increasing opportunity to achieve results," the Aga Khan said in an interview. "And my sense is also that people in developing countries want new ways to address the question of their economic and social well-being. What we're saying through the Aga Khan Development Network is that the era of giveaways is gone. This is a time to enhance self-reliance, for grassroots groups to generate profits and use money for promoting social good."

The international media, especially British tabloids, have long highlighted his glittery lifestyle—racehorses, Alpine skiing and collecting silver. His private life, however, is considerably less colorful than this tabloid image, and in extensive conversations with the 62-year-old Aga Khan what emerged is his increasing focus on changing lives through socially conscious capitalism.

Prince Karim is astonishingly well acquainted with minute details of such enterprises. He cites the success of his Network's cooperative and mainstream banks in India; he points to hotel and printing industries in Pakistan and to power-generation and emerging banking facilities in Tajikistan; he talks enthusiastically about leather tanneries, agriculture and packaging in Kenya and about plastic and jute bag manufacturing in Côte d'Ivoire.

Hundreds of thousands of jobs are being created in these and other countries, with a minimum of the bureaucratic interference long favored by third-world governments and international aid agencies in the name of illusory concepts like "sustainable development."

The Aga Khan is impatient with bureaucracies and the jargon they spew. "Essentially our network has been people-driven, not dogma-driven," he said at his home in Gouvieux, outside Paris. "The only thing that we are concerned with in the Network is improvement of the quality of life of people. And insofar as those goals are achieved, then I think that our initiatives would be considered positive. Now, development is such a multiple process that others will have other approaches to this. The new area we're looking at now is culture as an area of development, for instance. That's another issue that's been in the cards for some years. But these are things which actually come from the field. They don't come from bureaucrats sitting at headquarters and dreaming up projects."

The Aga Khan's approach to development is, very simply stated, to encourage and enable the less fortunate to take care of their own futures. While the Aga Khan Development Network does indeed disburse significant sums every year—$150 million, including $85 million in outright grants this year, a high proportion of spending is directed to small but appropriate and highly effective grassroots projects. Through the economic development agencies of the Network—financial institutions, insurance companies, manufacturing companies, tourist organizations, among others—as well as through the social development institutions, the Aga Khan seeks to establish working partnerships with local groups and encourages third-world societies to move on from the culture of dependency that has long been fostered by the postwar international development movement.

He sees people as the most valuable resource in the development process—a seemingly obvious matter but one that the Aga Khan complains is often overlooked by the behemoths of the aid industry. Communities across South and Central Asia and Africa are encouraged and assisted "in the context of their individual cultural, economic and physical environments," as the

Aga Khan puts it, "to assume responsibility for actions which lead to long-term improvement in their health, their education, their incomes and their environment." The Network's activities, therefore, focus largely on areas such as primary health care, early childhood and female education, the development of income generation opportunities, the provision of clean water, cultivation of vegetables and marketable plants, and the upgrading of shelter in rural as well as urban areas.

But it's not old-fashioned philanthropy that seizes his imagination any longer. One of the questions he poses to his associates is: How do you define happiness for deprived people? It's a fairly simplistic question, but it's quite a shrewd question nonetheless. The Aga Khan tells of the time when he was visiting the remote provinces of northern Pakistan a few years ago. The infrastructure was bad, the education system was bad, but at least the locals had their own land. He stopped to talk with a girl of about 11 and asked, "Where do you see your future? What would you like to be doing?" She said, "I'd like to be a doctor and come back here as a doctor." Last year an associate of the Aga Khan went to the same village, in the shadow of the mighty Karakoram Mountains, and asked the same question of a girl of similar age. This time she said she wanted to be a pilot.

Through expedited education programs, local people in conservative Muslim areas have been given hope. Female children can now aspire to a life beyond the kitchen; their parents are being sufficiently challenged to realize that progress doesn't happen by osmosis but by cracking open inhibiting traditional customs that have held women back from contributing to economic development.

The Aga Khan's concern for the poor is rooted in the social conscience of Ismaili Muslims' traditionally liberal brand of Islam and its ethic of compassion for the vulnerable in society. He has—in the 42 years since he became Imam—encouraged fresh thinking in approaches to development, defining the concept of the "enabling environment," emphasizing the role of the private sector, working with communities to develop self-reliance, while always seeking to reduce, and eventually eliminate, dependency by ensuring long-term sustainability.

The Network's activities seek to complement those of national governments and multilateral agencies. The Aga Khan's commitment has a long-term perspective. It is a commitment that reaches far beyond the Ismaili Community and the agencies of the Aga Khan Development Network, accompanied as it is by a concern for the strengthening of civil societies, the building of capacity and the enhancement of the contribution by the wider community of citizens' organizations.

The Aga Khan Development Network disburses some $150 million into third-world enterprises each year; the Aga Khan Fund for Economic Development (AKFED) has assets of more than $1 billion, and in 1998 AKFED's specific investment figure for equity investment in third world small-scale enterprises was $65 million.

One of his priorities is to make these enterprises self-sufficient without continuous inputs, either from his own pocket or from other donors such as the OECD countries. And his aim is to turn these communities away from this dependency culture and into something which comes from within themselves. The Aga Khan's Network, mainly through the Fund, takes equity in the projects of small-scale entrepreneurs so that they can generate money for themselves and the Network. The Fund pays dividends to its external shareholders, reinvests and, indeed, is increasingly funding social development programs: For example, the Aga Khan recently undertook a major rehabilitation of schools in Uganda that were returned to his Network by the government; the schools had been seized by dictator Idi Amin Dada in the early 1970s and had become dilapidated. And the Aga Khan has been doing all this without abandoning the ethos that has characterized his Ismaili Muslim community for a thousand years—social service to all, regardless of religion.

The Frigoken Company is a good example of this approach. It was established in 1994 in Kenya—where there's been an Ismaili community for a century—to assist non-Ismaili local African farmers to grow and can beans and export them to European supermarket chains. A typical Kenyan farmer has an average plot of about one-seventh of an acre (600 square meters), of which a third is marked to grow beans for the market while the remaining land is used to cultivate subsistence crops such as corn and cassava. The Aga Khan-funded company provided seeds, fertilizers and crop expertise that enabled the farmers to increase yields and also cultivate crops on a year-round basis.

In five years, the number of farmers associated with the company has grown from 100 to 20,000. The company's success has meant that the number of local schools has grown, and also health clinics in what were once deprived rural areas. Local population growth rates have fallen, as have infant mortality rates. Frigoken's revenues this year will exceed $12 million. The Aga Khan's initial investment of barely $5 million has not been repaid, but his network gets substantial income each year from the Kenyan company.

In the former Soviet republic of Tajikistan, the Aga Khan is focusing on promoting agriculture and agribusinesses—not through the old collectivist communes and cooperatives but through giving loans to farmers and entrepreneurs. In the last three years more than 600 loans ranging from the equivalent of $100 to $5,000 have been given. As a result, a new entrepreneurial class of shoemakers, pharmacists and shopkeepers is springing up, in addition to farmers who can take pride in owning their land and not slaving for some faceless state bureaucracy.

Tourism is another success story for the Aga Khan, particularly in Kenya and Tanzania, where the Network's Tourism Promotion Services Inc. (TPS) is traded on local stock exchanges. Aga Khan-funded companies have built three lodges in Kenyan game parks and reserves and on the Mombasa coast. In 1997-98, the company added three new lodges and a luxury tented camp in Tanzania's fabled Serengeti game reserve and a major hotel on the island of Zanzibar. The Network also tied up with local entrepreneurs in developing tourism in Pakistan.

And then there's banking and finance. Longstanding ventures such as the Jubilee Insurance Company in Nairobi have been successfully replicated in neighboring Uganda and Tanzania. The Diamond Trust, a banking company, now trades on the Nairobi Stock Exchange. In India, the Aga Khan started the Development Cooperative Bank (DCR), which was originally a grassroots cooperative bank for the Ismaili community, but has gone way beyond the roots of the community now. Three years ago, the DCB was the first cooperative bank in India to be converted to a private sector commercial bank, giving shareholder status to its 55,000 customers.

Complementing AKFED's work in economic development, the other agencies of the Aga Khan Development Network pursue the Aga Khan's commitment to the other facets of the development process he sees as critical for healthy societies. The Aga Khan Foundation has established an innovative rural development program in Northern Pakistan that has been highly praised in an independent evaluation conducted by The World Bank and is being replicated by AKF in the mountainous areas of Tajikistan and in Kenya, and elsewhere by others. The Aga Khan University in Karachi is the first private autonomous university in Pakistan. At present, it consists of a medical school, nursing school and a professional development center for teachers. The majority of its students are women, and women make up more than thirty percent of the staff, remarkable numbers for that part of the world. Another of AKU's resources is the location on its campus of the Aga Khan University Hospital, one of a series of world class hospitals operated by the Aga Khan Health Services located in places like Nairobi and Dar-es-Salaam.

The Aga Khan is also a pioneer in arguing that culture, and particularly architecture, is central to genuine development and meeting the pressures created by globalization. The Aga Khan Award for Architecture, in existence for twenty years, seeks out, rewards and publicizes innovative building and restoration projects in the Islamic World to encourage building that meets contemporary needs and yet is meaningful to people. The Award and the other programs of the Aga Khan Trust for Culture—the Historic Cities Program and the Education Program—restore historic buildings and public spaces for reuse, and train architectural professionals for work in the Muslim world. The Trust's largest grantee is the Aga Khan Program for Islamic Architecture at Harvard and MIT established in 1979.

What of the future? The Aga Khan says that his emphasis on pushing rural development will be increased. "The next Imam will then decide how he wishes to handle the issues," he says. "But it is the continuum which is at the back of my mind, which in a sense affects the way I look at things. And that's why, perhaps, my time dimension appears different from what it might be for other people. If I have to wait 12, 15, 20 years to achieve goals which I think are important, I will wait 12, 15 or 20 years."

Whoever his successor is, the Aga Khan is confident that the emphasis on promoting entrepreneurship in the third world will continue. He is ensuring that his two sons and daughter are immersed in entrepreneurial developmentalism. Prince Rahim is Executive Director of the Fund for Economic Development. Prince Hussein is involved in the Trust for Culture. Princess Zahra looks after the Network's health and education programs, with a particular emphasis on the concerns of women. At the same time, the Aga Khan has also set up a small think-tank within his Secretariat to advise him on how to refine ways of meeting global economic and social challenges.

At 62, Prince Karim is still a relatively young man; there's clearly a recognition on his part that he's in it for the long haul and that his programs speak for themselves. He's the leader of the Ismaili community until the day he dies. So, in that sense, he has the luxury of being able to have a long-term view. When asked how much of a visionary he thought he was, the Aga Khan smiled and slipped away from the question, saying instead: "In the last 42 years, I would say a lot of work has been done and there is some clarity ahead. Whether that clarity will be validated by time, I don't know. But what I can tell you is that I have a higher level of comfort today than I would have had four decades ago."

MINORITIES AND CULTURAL IDENTITY

RAHUL SINGH
April 1999

On April 13, 1999, all roads led to Anandpur Sahib, a small, sleepy town in the north Indian state of Punjab, in the foothills of the Himalayas. More than five million people were there on that day, most of them Sikhs, to celebrate the 300th anniversary of the founding of the "Khalsa," which means the "pure." On a day called Baisakhi, when the harvesting of wheat—the staple crop of the Punjabis—traditionally starts, exactly 300 years ago, in 1699, Guru Gobind Singh, the last of the ten Sikh Gurus, assembled his followers at Anandpur Sahib. He performed an initiation ceremony whose details have been described in a variety of ways.

One widely accepted version, which has certain parallels with the story about Abraham and Isaac in the Old Testament, says the Guru asked for volunteers to sacrifice themselves. Five sprang forward. He took one of them to a room and returned with his sword covered with blood. Similarly he took the rest, one by one, into the room, returning with the blood-covered sword. In reality, he was just testing their courage and devotion, as his sword was covered not with human blood but with the blood of a newly slaughtered goat.

The five disciples were then made to sit, side by side, while the Guru poured water into a vessel and added refined sugar to it. This he stirred with a double-edged dagger and made them drink the liquid, thus anointing them. They came from different Hindu castes and the ceremony was meant to signify that henceforth the Sikhs would not differentiate between castes, as the Hindus did, but would be one family.

He called them the "panj piyarey" (the five beloved ones) and named the fighting Sikh fraternity the "Khalsa." The Khalsa were told that their last name would be Singh (lion) and that they must observe the five "Ks": "kesh" (not to cut the hair or beard), "kangha" (to carry a comb in the hair), "kuchha" (to wear underpants, as a sign of cleanliness), "kara" (to wear a steel bangle) and "kirpan" (to carry a dagger, to indicate their martial tradition).

Thus Guru Gobind Singh gave the Sikhs their distinctive appearance of beards and turbans. Though quite a few Sikhs have given up these symbols and "modernized" themselves—by cutting their hair and not having a beard—even the so-called modern or unorthodox Sikhs remain fiercely proud of their religion and traditions.

Why does Sikhism matter? Not only because it is a vibrant religion and a way of life. Sikhs are a distinctive minority whose contribution to India's economic, political and cultural history has been enormous. Notwithstanding the problems caused by separatists in Punjab state, Sikhs have coexisted harmoniously with India's Hindu majority over the centuries. Such coexistence offers valuable lessons in pluralism to developing societies everywhere.

Guru Gobind Singh was the last in a line of 10 Sikh Gurus. The founder of the religion was Guru Nanak, born in 1469, more than 200 years earlier, and actually named Nanak Chand. The two major religions in the Indian subcontinent then were Hinduism and Islam (Buddhism, after having been dominant earlier, had gone into retreat). Nanak attempted to bring the two together by picking what he felt were the best traits of both, while rejecting the worst. He started his quest with the simple statement, "There is no Hindu, there is no Muslim." He preached love, tolerance and the abolition of meaningless rituals.

Once he saw some Hindus throwing water in the direction of the sun. "What are you doing?" he asked them.

"We are offering water to our dead ancestors," came the reply.

Nanak, promptly started sprinkling water in a different direction. When asked what he was doing, he answered, "I am watering my fields. If you can send water to your ancestors in heaven, surely I can send it to my village!"

Nanak's followers came to be known as Sikhs, the Punjabi form of the Sanskrit word, shishya, or disciple.

Nanak was followed by nine more Gurus. Though Nanak had preached pacifism, continued persecution of the Sikhs by some of the Muslim Mughal kings, who ruled over the Indian subcontinent at the time, turned the Sikhs militant, culminating in Guru Gobind Singh. He declared that he was the last in the line of Gurus and that henceforth only the Guru Granth Sahib, the holy book of the Sikhs which had been compiled by an earlier Sikh Guru containing the teachings of the various Gurus, should be worshipped. There was to be no idolatry, as in Hinduism.

The Sikhs as a community reached their apogee towards the end of the 18th Century, during the rule of the Sikh king, Maharaja Ranjit Singh, whose kingdom comprised much of present-day Pakistan, Kashmir and large parts of the Indian states of Himachal Pradesh and Punjab as well. One of Ranjit

Singh's generals even made an unsuccessful incursion into Tibet.

Soon after Ranjit Singh's death, the British, who had already been in India for more than half a century, moved against the Sikhs, their last major opponents for domination of India. In a series of fiercely contested battles, the Sikhs were finally defeated. But the British, admiring their great valor and fighting skills, quickly incorporated them into their own army, which they served with outstanding distinction. During the Second World War, 30 percent of the officers in the Indian armed forces and 25 percent of the soldiers were Sikhs. The only Indian officer to have won the Victoria Cross, the highest award for gallantry in battle given by the British army, was a Sikh, Prem Bhagat (he won it for clearing German mines in North Africa during the Second World War).

Sikhs constitute just 1.6 percent of the population, but play a disproportionate role in Indian society.

When the Indian subcontinent was partitioned into India and Pakistan in 1947, amidst terrible bloodshed and suffering, almost half the Sikhs found themselves in West Punjab, in what was to become part of West Pakistan. Many of them had to leave their homes and all their possessions before coming to India. They arrived destitute—penniless and dispirited. Yet in a remarkably short time, they lifted themselves up by their bootstraps and prospered.

Large tracts of jungle in what is known as the terrai region, a heavily forested and inhospitable area of the state of Uttar Pradesh, were given to Sikh refugees from Pakistan. They cleared the jungles, dug wells and planted crops, converting a wilderness into one of the most fertile areas of the country. Likewise, Sikh refugees sent to the largely desert state of Rajasthan changed land that had been barren for centuries into rich fields of wheat and sugar cane. The "Green Revolution," perhaps independent India's outstanding economic achievement, which made India self-sufficient in food and banished mass famines from the country, was almost entirely the result of the hard work and enterprise of Sikh farmers.

Because of their distinctive appearance, most people imagine that Sikhs are more numerous than they actually are. Surprisingly, Sikhs number only around 16 million out of a total Indian population of close to a billion. In other words, they constitute just 1.6 percent of the population. Yet they play a role which is disproportionate to their numbers

In sports, Sikhs have carried off a great many of the gold medals India has won in international meets. Runner Milkha Singh is recognized as the greatest athlete India has produced. The record he set in the 1960 Rome Olympics in the 400 meters race was broken only last year. His son, Chiranjeev, is India's finest golfer. In cricket, Bishen Singh Bedi is widely considered to be one of the world's best leg-spinners ever.

Sikhs have also shown great enterprise in traveling outside India and becoming successful. Large numbers of them are in Canada (notably Vancouver and Toronto), the US, Britain, Southeast Asia (particularly Thailand), East Africa and South Africa.

Perhaps the Sikhs' biggest crisis came in the decade between 1984 and 1995. An obscure preacher, Jarnail Singh Bhindranwale, rose to prominence and managed to capture the imagination of quite a few Sikhs who felt their religion was under threat. He holed himself up in the Golden Temple, the holiest shrine of the Sikhs, in the Punjab city of Amritsar, along with some armed terrorists.

The government sent in the army. Hundreds were killed in the two-day battle—soldiers, terrorists and innocent pilgrims. Four months later, Prime Minister Indira Gandhi, who had ordered the army action, was gunned down in her garden by two of her Sikh bodyguards. Anti-Sikh riots erupted in the Capital, New Delhi, and elsewhere. Around 4,000 Sikhs were butchered. This, in turn, led to renewed Sikh terrorism.

It was a dark period for the people of the Sikh community. But they emerged from it, as they had from similar crises in the past, undaunted and unbowed, their magnificent traits firmly intact. Today they are once again very much part of the Indian mainstream and most of the terrorists are either dead or rehabilitated. They have not allowed themselves to be hindered by their minority status; instead, Sikhs, through their extraordinary efforts in economics and politics, have had a disproportionate—and positive—impact on all of India.

Farming, soldiering, athletic skills, business enterprise, pride and immense resilience seem to come naturally to Sikhs. How come? Nobody seems to know, but it must have something to do with their religion, the defining moment of which took place 300 years ago at the town of Anandpur Sahib.

BOSNIA: A BITTERSWEET RETURN

RESHMA PRAKASH
January 1999

SARAJEVO, Bosnia-Herzegovina—Winter's here in the Balkans, blinding white and biting cold, and deceptive. For the snow blanketing the roads and homes softens the shattered remains of war—mortar-gouged concrete, bullet-ridden walls, collapsed roofs, rubble, gutted shells of homes in deserted villages.

The guns are now silent and the fighting's stopped. There were no windows left intact when the war ended in 1995, people say, but the glass panes are back now. The gaping holes are no longer covered by yellow and blue plastic sheeting. There are signs of construction everywhere. Homes are being rebuilt, the electricity's on line, the phones are working, the water's running, produce is in the market and the people who fled the fighting are trickling back.

"The best part of being back is that I'm finally in my own country again," said Cakic Milsad, who was a refugee in Germany for six years but who has now returned to the town of Bosanska Krupa, 18 miles from the town he lived in before the war. "I was treated well and had a lot of friends in Dresden, but it wasn't home. I was so homesick."

Milsad is one of the estimated 1.3 million people who fled their homes as old ethnic tensions tore the former communist state of Yugoslavia apart into five independent states, resulting in one of this century's worst cases of "ethnic cleansing."

Milsad, a Muslim, said he was imprisoned and tortured by Serbian troops for five days during the war. The presence of United Nations forces near his village probably saved his life, he says, but it didn't prevent him and as many as 18,000 other people from being put into trucks and forced out of the region. Although he and his family eventually found refuge in Germany, as a refugee he couldn't work and his whole family—wife, son and parents—were dependent on the social security assistance provided by the German government.

The people were good to him, he says, but the six long years he spent without work made him feel useless. It wasn't just the cessation of fighting that drew him back. It was the promise of a job. He now works as an occupational safety expert for a lumber company that manufactures wooden products.

"The country needs to bring professionals like these back," said Frances Sullivan Michaels, Chief Mission for the International Organization for Migration (IOM) in Sarajevo.

"You need more than just bricks and mortar when you talk about rebuilding the country and the economy," she said. "You need flesh and blood. Professionals like doctors and engineers and teachers are the ones who really need to come back. They're the ones with a vested interest for the long term. But qualified people are the very ones who will find it easier to find jobs abroad. What they need are inducements to come back. They need the guarantee of a job offer and equipment to work with, a place to live. That's where we try to help."

IOM has two programs intended to facilitate the return of qualified professionals like Milsad who live as refugees in other countries. One, known as the Return of Qualified Nationals Program (RQN), has been operational since 1996. It has as its target the placement of 1,000 highly qualified Bosnian professionals whose skills IOM says are necessary for the reconstruction and development of the country. The program reached its midway mark in September 1998 with the placement of 500 people. IOM performs the service of putting these refugees, or "candidates" as they're called, in touch with prospective employers and provides a travel allowance and limited housing assistance for them and their families. On the other end, employers are also given certain incentives to hire refugees in the form of a one-year limited subsidy for each person hired through RQN. The employer can also sit down with the candidate and decide what equipment is needed, for which IOM will pay. In a country that's struggling to get back on its feet, it's an incentive that works.

"Why would we not hire someone through IOM?" said the owner of a factory who had recently hired an economist. "She was qualified and, besides, we could get the money and equipment."

The second IOM program is called the Economic Revitalization and Employment Generation Program and is funded by the European Union. It is similar to the RQN program except that it combines the placement of qualified professionals with the physical rehabilitation of places such as schools, hospitals and health centers.

When the fighting in Bosnia-Herzegovina came to an end with the signing of the Dayton Peace Agreement in December 1995, international agencies identified the return of refugees to their homes—whether they had fled to foreign countries or were displaced within the territory of the former Yugoslavia—as one of the most important tasks facing this region. It was hoped that 1998 would be the "year of minority returns," but international agencies monitoring the situation now admit that the numbers have fallen far short of their expectations.

During the first two years of the peace process the focus was on the supposedly easier task of returning Bosnians to their homes in areas controlled by their ethnic brethren. Even then, the numbers were not very impressive. Although there were more than 1.3 million refugees and one million internally displaced people by the end of the war, according to the International Crisis Group, by mid-1997 only about 250,000 had returned home—almost exclusively to areas where they belonged to the majority group. A target of 20,000 minority returns was set for 1998 for Sarajevo, the capital of Bosnia, which was supposed to function as a model of coexistence and tolerance. As the year ended, though, fewer than 2,000 people had returned.

International agencies have faced criticism for accepting the results of ethnic cleansing.

International agencies have not been happy with the rate of minority returns. They have faced some criticism for accepting, de facto, the results of ethnic cleansing. On the other hand, the local people who stayed through the war, either because they didn't want to leave or because they didn't have any money to bribe their way out, sometimes resent international agencies for helping those who fled to return. They feel that those who left abandoned their people and country at a time of need and that international agencies are wrongly rewarding this abandonment by giving people money to come back.

The ethnic cleansing and massive shifts in population have created a bitter choice for people wanting to return—they can either return to their previous homes and run the deadly risk of belonging to a minority or give up any claim on their homes and relocate to a totally new area where they could belong to an ethnic majority.

Milsad says he's happy to be back, but what he leaves unsaid is that he cannot return to his house or the town he used to live in any more because he would be a member of the minority community there. The village he used to live in before the war now belongs to Republika Srbska, a Serb-controlled entity. But he's as close to home as he could be. Bosanska Krupa, the town he's now relocated to, is only about 18 miles from his old village.

Like so many of the people who have made their way back to Bosnia, Milsad has no house of his own to move into and has had to depend on the kindness of strangers and family. His family has squeezed into a room in his employer's house, but he's not sure how long he can continue staying there. Because he has no documents to prove that he used to own his old home, and with the backlog of people waiting to receive apartments, it will be a while before he will be given a place to live by the municipal authorities. When that happens, it's likely that the place will have been heavily damaged by the war. Milsad says he's been left with no savings, but plans to repair and renovate the house with a housing subsidy from IOM.

He spoke, almost in passing, of his old friends and neighbors with whom he's lost contact.

"No one from my old place has called to find out how I'm doing," he said quietly. "No one who left has gone back there."

Author's Note: In spring 1999, Serbian troop action in Kosovo, Yugoslavia, forced a massive exodus of refugees into neighboring countries. Serbian atrocities elicited military action by member-countries of NATO. The parallels between Kosovo and Bosnia were startling. As international mediators began their search for agreement on the elements of a peace settlement for Kosovo, including as a priority item the repatriation of refugees, the global community could only hope that they would learn from what has happened with minority returns in Bosnia.

PUSHING GOOD GOVERNANCE

FRANK VOGL
June 1999

The international debate on formulating effective development strategies will be absorbed in the immediate years ahead by the issue of how to secure public sector and private sector good governance.

People across the world are fed up with corruption (as defined as the abuse of public office for private gain). They are angry about the greed of politicians as poverty grows. They are bitter that vast sums of international finance can move out of their countries with lightning speed and leave economic carnage behind. Public protests, opinion surveys and media stories from across much of the developing world show that the general public is distrustful of major corporations that seem ever more dominant, yet opaque and poorly regulated.

Public pressures for good governance are gathering momentum. International organizations—official ones like the United Nations, the OECD and the World Bank and a growing number of nongovernmental organizations (NGOs)—are responding. In the last few years the leaders of these institutions have given many speeches, inspired important international conventions and formulated promising initiatives.

The stage is now set for a series of far-reaching programs, which have the potential of improving the prospects for economic growth in many parts of the world. The scripts have largely been written, the actors selected and the play is beginning. This will be a drama in many acts that will unfold slowly. The issues are complex, the approaches to be pursued need to be tested and refined, and the stakes are high.

Good governance embraces negatives and positives. It involves efforts:
- to fight corruption by public officials (who annually steal tens of billions of dollars);
- to criminalize the payment of bribes by international corporations; and,
- to ensure that publicly traded enterprises and financial institutions abide by clear rules and regulations that serve the public interest.

Good governance efforts also seek to find constructive ways to encourage the private sector to play far greater roles in contributing to social development.

These are huge challenges. Corruption has decimated the Russian economy. It has prompted massive waste of scarce foreign exchange across most of Africa. It has been at the heart of economic and political crises across most of Asia, from the downfall of governments in Pakistan, India, Indonesia and the Philippines, to high-profile trials in South Korea, China and Vietnam. Presidents have been impeached for corruption in Latin America, where opinion polls show rising public concern about this critical problem.

Securing good governance in the private sector is no less a challenge. In the heyday of foreign aid in the 1960s and 1970s it was the conventional wisdom at bilateral and multilateral aid agencies that the public sector would solve almost all problems. The private formal sectors of the developing economies were small, foreign direct investment was tiny and, as the Latin American debt crisis highlighted, foreign financial relations were precarious.

> *Corruption has been at the heart of economic and political crises in many countries.*

Everything has changed. Now the private sector is widely seen as the engine of development growth. But can it be controlled to curb bribery habits? Can it be encouraged to unleash positive forces for greater employment, better education and health care, fair and sound labor benefits, enlightened environmental management and transparency with regard to consumers, regulators and shareholders?

Countries from Uganda to South Korea now have stock markets and rising numbers of publicly traded domestic companies but feeble regulatory systems. Almost all developing countries, plus those in transition in Eastern Europe, now attract foreign direct investment (FDI) from the world's transnational corporations (net FDI to these countries has gone from just about $6 billion per year in 1980 to more than $100 billion today). Often it appears to the citizens of these countries that these firms are far more powerful than governments.

International finance has exploded. Net external financing of the leading 30 emerging market economies (from foreign banking lenders and from investors) has gone from $70 billion in 1980 to a record $320 billion in 1996 (the Asian crisis subsequently saw a pullback). Banking systems in many developing countries, and across the former Soviet Union, are under-capitalized, timidly controlled and often poorly managed.

These issues will be tackled in unique ways country-by-country, but the pressures for reform and for progress are universal. The prospects for constructive action are good, for three reasons:

• These are initiatives that will have formidable public backing, which makes them popular causes for political leaders in democracies;

• NGOs are working at national and international levels to strengthen pressures in these areas and they are being influential in the capitals of the leading industrial countries; and

• These are not expensive initiatives—these are not aid program areas that require huge new allocations of foreign assistance cash.

We are at base camp and an Everest of corrupt dealings has yet to be scaled. But even climbing to base camp is an achievement. A handful of years ago the corruption issue was not on the agenda; now NGOs and international organizations are rapidly evolving programs and initiatives. The challenge is to mobilize the political leadership and public support behind national integrity programs. Key elements must include clean and fair elections, public statements of personal assets by government leaders and decent pay for public officials. In addition, programs in increasing numbers of countries are now shaping up around five areas. Expertise is being mobilized and it is probable that momentum will gather in each of the following:

• Securing and enforcing laws that enable the investigation and public disclosure of government actions, laws and law enforcement to secure freedom of information, freedom of speech and freedom of the press.

• Enforcement of existing laws that deal with corruption. This demands the building of systems of independent judges and public prosecutors (independent of political control and pressure).

• Ending corrupt public financing and opening the books to public scrutiny—establishing parliamentary oversight systems plus independent government auditing departments.

• Building systems to enforce environmental regulation, involving the monitoring of actions by officials in this area and curbing the widespread corruption that takes place.

• Making transparent the systems of public procurement and contracting and customs services which will require creating effective independent monitoring in every aspect of government revenue collection and contracting.

The Asian financial crisis exposed the inadequacies of regulation of publicly traded corporations and the lack of influence that many stakeholders have in the ways in which major corporations operate in developing countries.

This has prompted a host of diverse initiatives, which are reflected in part in recently approved OECD Principles of Corporate Governance, which focus on:

- the rights of shareholders;
- the equitable treatment of shareholders;
- the role of stakeholders;
- disclosure and transparency; and
- the responsibilities of the board.

The World Bank and the IMF will be making it a priority to translate the principles into practice by assisting scores of regulatory authorities in developing countries to build effective, modern, corporate governance systems.

At the same time, civil society organizations and a growing number of international organizations (as well as some enlightened transnational corporations) are pushing hard for businesses to recognize they have responsibilities beyond the narrowly defined generation of profits. They have responsibilities to all their stakeholders, from the shareholders that invest, to the employees who labor, to the customers who buy and to the local communities where factories are located. We will be seeing this recognition translated to an increasing degree into national and international actions to secure constructive corporate behavior.

Corporations are learning they have responsibilities beyond the bottom line.

One example is the OECD Anti-Bribery Convention, which was ratified in February 1999 and which makes it a criminal offense in many leading industrial countries now for corporations to pay bribes abroad. In Germany, for example, it was the case that corporations paying bribes abroad did not have to fear prosecution in Germany, while they could deduct the foreign bribes from their taxes. German laws have been changed.

Actions are likely in many areas to improve corporate behavior and secure corporate contributions to social and economic development. Areas that will see action include: strengthening compliance with governmental rules, regulations and laws; introducing standard US-type corporate gender equality and other personnel ethics standards around the world; securing sound human rights behavior by business; embracing ethical workplace conditions, including protections for child labor; enhancing corporate compliance with rising environmental standards; strengthening business transparency and respect for free-market competitive systems (including anti-trust regulation).

The good governance agenda is large indeed. But imagine the benefits if this bold program is implemented. Today there are schools and hospitals that are not being built because government officials are putting budget funds in their own Swiss bank accounts. Today, journalists are being killed or libeled into silence in scores of countries, while judges and public prosecutors are forced to turn a blind eye to criminal behavior by powerful politicians and business leaders. Today, children in many poor countries are working in Dickensian conditions, while businesses are often treating female employees as second-class citizens.

Today the full potential of the economies of many developing countries, and the productive skills of the peoples of these countries, are undermined by the lack of decent governance by government and business. This has been widely recognized; coming years will see major changes and improvements.

THE LITTLE RED SCHOOLHOUSE

AUDREY RONNING TOPPING
November 1997

Recently I was surprised by a phone call from the interior of China. It was the headmaster of the Number One Middle School in Hubei Province. He invited me and my family to come to China to celebrate the 100th anniversary of the Hung Wen Middle School that my grandfather, the Reverend Halvor N. Ronning, had founded when he was a Lutheran minister with the China Inland Mission during the last years of the Manchu (Qing) Dynasty.

I had to tell him that we could not arrange it on such short notice but promised to come next October. Wu said they would celebrate it every year. He asked me to write an early history of the school because the records had been lost during the Civil War. I gathered the following story from treasured old letters. It is a story of courage and determination that proves the old adage that great things begin with one small step.

Grandfather began building the Hung Wen Middle School in 1894 in the town of Xiangfan but it was not officially founded until 1897. He started the school with his wife (my grandmother) Hannah Rorem and his sister, Thea, because they fervently believed that all children should have the opportunity to be enlightened intellectually as well as spiritually. "Schools," wrote grandfather, "are just as important as churches."

As supervisor of the mission, grandfather, with the help of a dozen Chinese workmen, built a two-room brick school house: one room for boys, whom he would teach himself, and one for girls, to be supervised by Hannah and Thea. They soon discovered that it was easier said than done.

During June and July of 1894 they hung posters on the town bulletin boards announcing the opening of free schools for all children regardless of sex or social standing, which was hitherto unheard of. There had never been a girls' school in Xiangfan. The missionaries visited local families and urged them to send their children to the school, which was to open on August 1, 1894. Books and materials would be furnished by the mission.

They invited the officials and gentry of Xiangfan to the mission for tea and discussions in hopes of gaining their support. Reverend Ronning explained that reading and writing would be taught first in Chinese and then English. He pointed out that the merit system established by Confucius was to be highly recommended but that it usually allowed for only one boy in a family or one boy in a whole village to be educated whereas his school was for the average child.

He reminded them that during the Tang Dynasty, when China was at the height of glory, girls had the same opportunity for education as boys. He explained that Hannah and Thea wanted to restore the educational opportunities that girls enjoyed during that period. The elite group, according to a letter written by Halvor to his brother Nils, "listened with an air of apathetic indifference which seems to veil the inner feelings of most polished Chinese gentlemen." He was soon to discover their real feelings.

At 6 o'clock on the morning of August 1, 1894, Ronning dressed smartly in the black mandarin scholar's robe tailored to fit his tall frame. Then he carefully placed a long black queue attached to a satin skullcap over his wavy fair hair and set out for his new schoolhouse with long, purposeful strides.

This was before my father, Chester, who 25 years later became headmaster at the same school, was born. At that time, the Ronnings had one son, Nelius, who was too young to attend school, and a 10-year-old Chinese son, Peter, whom Halvor had rescued from jail. Peter was a starving orphan who had been caught stealing food. Reverend Ronning held the reluctant Peter firmly by the hand and dragged him to school. Halvor was full of enthusiasm but it was not a very auspicious beginning.

'I found one small ragged urchin sitting on the school steps. That was all! Just one!'

"When I came to the schoolhouse," he later wrote, "I found one small ragged urchin sitting on the steps. That was all! Just one! Two with Peter. However, I welcomed the child warmly and carried on classes as if I had a full house. The two children, Peter and the urchin, whom I called John, seemed to enjoy it greatly. The next day the boy came back with a friend who looked so bedraggled and frightened I had to laugh. That was a mistake. I scared him away and Peter had to run after him. So now there were three. I taught them how to count. The boys learned quickly and seemed proud of themselves. They left smiling and spread the good word. The next day there were five. That's what we call progress, isn't it?

"The boys arrive at school between six and seven in the morning, go home at noon and then study and read until it is dark. All the children read aloud, all together at the top of their voices, just as in Norway in days of old. It is a deafening noise, so it is almost impossible to be near the classroom. Soon we shall introduce more modern methods."

Grandfather wore his Chinese robe and false queue in the hopes that he would not be too conspicuous. But with his height, blue eyes and big nose he was always spotted. One day while he was shopping, a crowd began to follow him. Suddenly they became a mob. Shouting "yang kuei! foreign devil!" they chased him up the street to the mission compound. The gatekeeper heard the noise and, unaware that Ronning was involved, barred the gate. Seeing the gate closed, Halvor, who had been an athlete in Norway before he became an American missionary, made a desperate leap up the seven-foot wall

> *An old Chinese saying went, 'If women all take to reading, what will the men do?'*

around the mission compound. As he scrambled up the rocks, a ruffian grabbed his queue and yanked it off, together with his skullcap. The angry mob suddenly began to laugh at this alien who sat straddling the wall with his short hair blowing in the wind. The man who had snatched the queue now stared at the object in his hand, apparently suspecting some evil foreign magic, and quickly carried the dangling braid to the gatekeeper. Halvor descended from the wall on the inside, stepped to the open gate and thanked the frightened man for returning his precious queue. He placed the cap back on his head and, taking advantage of his unexpected audience, explained that he wore it because he was a teacher. He then invited them to send their children to his school and to visit him another time when they were not in such a hurry.

While Halvor was making progress, Hannah and Thea were despondent. Theirs was to be the first girls' school in the interior of China but, in spite of their earnest campaigning, not a single girl had appeared on the first day. Obviously the citizens of Xiangfan had been shocked at the very thought of educating girls, which was not surprising considering the history of women in China. Educating females was a revolutionary and frightening idea. Women, they knew, were necessary for the proliferation of the species but inferior by nature. The sages stressed the danger of educating women or letting them go about freely, lest they gain the upper hand.

There are two "old sayings" that reveal the attitudes at that time. "At the bottom of every trouble there is a woman," and, "If women take to reading, what will men do?"

With this way of thinking brainwashed into the minds of the Chinese for centuries, it is no wonder that my grandparents had a difficult time getting girls to go to school. Customs regarding women were even more restrictive in China's interior than in the coastal cities. Beggars, servants and the poorest peasants were often freer than the upper classes, among whom it was considered cause for divorce if a woman dared to venture alone on the streets. If called upon to go on an errand without her husband, she had to ride a mule or travel in a curtained sedan chair. If she did go out with her husband she was obliged to walk three paces behind.

As it happened, the first girl student in the Ronning school was not a member of the gentry but a 10-year-old girl whom Hannah and Thea bought at the slave market for a few silver dollars. It was unusual to find a girl for sale who had bound feet for it was only the privileged classes that perpetrated that horror upon their little girls. The servant class and peasants let the feet grow normally so they could do the work expected of them. They could only deduce that the girl must have been orphaned or kidnapped. The slave girl was hysterical with fear and the pain in her tightly bound feet.

When they arrived back at the mission Hannah and Thea unwrapped the two layers of filthy rags that bound the child's feet. She screamed in agony as the blood suddenly rushed to her toes. They lowered her feet into a bucket of warm water with soothing oils. The child sighed in relief, but Hannah and Thea were horrified beyond belief. "We saw with our own eyes what the Chinese call 'killing the feet,'" wrote Hannah in a letter to mission headquarters in Minnesota imploring them to send funds for a hospital.

"The smell was quite revolting but we tried not to notice. Her poor feet had been forced into line with the leg and the toes doubled under the soles of the feet. The big toes had been forced crooked to overlap the others. The bandages had been applied with a cruel amount of pressure. The child's feet were blue and the skin cracked and indented where the circulation had been completely cut off. Fortunately she was not yet permanently crippled as her young bones are still soft. It must be the cruelest custom ever inflicted by man. Mothers sleep with sticks, which they use to beat the child if she disturbs the household with her wails and if that doesn't work they sometimes lock her in an outhouse. The little girls are often in such pain that their mothers give them opium to stifle the pain. We are told that the pain lets up after three years, but many of the girls die of gangrene or shock before that. Some go mad and others become opium addicts. When they grow up they are crippled for life. They get no exercise because they can only walk on their heels with the knees stiff. The muscles of the calf never develop and the lower legs are like broomsticks with drooping folds of skin. But, thank God, our little girl will not suffer this. She will recover in time and we will do everything we can to give her a good education in our girls' school. Halvor baptized her and we have named her Sarah.

Both Hannah and Thea wrote often about the cruelties of foot binding. Why? why? why? they always asked. "What induces a mother to impose such suffering upon a daughter?" agonized Hannah.

"How my heart aches for all these little Chinese girls. When I think of myself in Iowa at the glorious age of 10, running and leaping on a horse and galloping over the fields and jumping the creeks, and these poor children have no freedom at all and can barely walk.

"I cannot imagine that the Chinese men find it attractive but they say it is so. They call these hideously crippled feet 'golden lilies.' The ultimate disgrace for a middle class family is for their daughter not to get a husband, and no man will marry a girl with natural feet. I think it is also a means to control the women and to make sure they cannot run away. Now I see that we must first unbind the minds before we can unbind the feet."

'Now I see that we must first unbind the minds before we can unbind the feet.'

Three days after Sarah was adopted and sent to school, another 10-year-old girl was brought to the mission by her father, Chou Fu-yen, who was a well-off gentleman in the salt trade. He was a Christian who had been converted by Ronning, but had suffered because of it. His father, a tyrannical patriarch, had disowned him and compelled him to walk through the streets of Xiangfan with a wooden placard on his back saying "I am a Christian." Many people had mocked him, but he had held his head high. Later he told Halvor, "I did it for the Lord. My heart is at peace."

The salt merchant set an example by bringing his daughter to school and gradually other girls came as students. The only criterion for entrance was that they did not have bound feet or, if they did, they were required to unbind them.

Two weeks after the opening Halvor wrote to Nils: " I have 11 small boys and the ladies have five girls. We must not be discouraged. Building has begun on the dormitories and the mission work is expanding rapidly."

During this time China was at war with Japan. The whole country was in turmoil, but the ruling house, represented by the Dowager Empress Tzu Hsi, refused to accept the fact that there was a war going on. The turmoil had an unexpected effect on Ronning's mission and the school. The Manchu Bannermen, who by this time had become dissipated and lost their will to fight, periodically swept through Xiangfan to pick up conscripts to do their fighting for them. But by rights of extraterritoriality the Manchus were forbidden to enter the American mission compound. So when the watchmen at the city gates sounded gongs to signal the approach of the horsemen, the mission was suddenly filled with eligible young men who professed an urgent need to become educated Christians. Reverend Ronning accepted it as a God-given opportunity. He immediately began to exploit the situation and reveled in the chance to convert and educate these young men in spite of themselves. A church service was hurriedly arranged and continued for as long as the Manchus were combing the town for new conscripts.

'When the watchman sounded the 'all clear,' our church service was over for the day.'

When the Bannermen pounded on the mission gate, Hannah played the organ and everyone sang as loudly as possible. Hannah later noted with amusement: "When the soldiers heard the music they stopped their pounding to listen. Everyone took part in the singing but there was a lack of decision as to which tune should be sung. I played as best I could with one foot on the loud pedal but everyone sang his own song, the timing being conspicuous only by its absence. But there was one heart if not one tune. Halvor's voice rang above them all:

> *It is the secret sympathy,*
> *The silver link, the silken tie.*
> *Which Heart to Heart and mind to mind.*
> *In body and in soul can bind.*

"When the watchmen sounded the 'all clear' our church service was over for the day but we strongly urged them all to come to school before the Bannermen returned."

Halvor, for the first time, expressed some apprehension about the role of Christianity in China in a letter to Nils.

"October 1, 1894. Many people attend the church meetings now. The reasons may vary but I accept them all and try to do what I can. It is difficult for us to speak to the young men about our God. I feel an eager desire to work and teach. God will give the growth. The townspeople are beginning to send their girls to our school. This is real progress. Education enlarges the soul and broadens the mind. It opens new vistas of thought and comprehension. I don't know which will come first, education for all and then reform, or reform and then education." He ended his letter on a prophetic note, "I fear the latter will bring more violence."

Another diary entry: "October 26—Bad news for China. The Japanese are winning on land and sea. The fighting continues even though it seems hopeless. The North China Daily News says that the Japanese will be in China by November 30th with 100,000 men and capture Peking. The Japanese seem to be boiling over with hate and with lust to conquer China." The missionaries began to live in constant fear of robbers and undisciplined soldiers roaming the streets. Ronning and the other missionaries began carrying loaded revolvers and slept with knives under their pillows and hunting rifles at hand.

On December 13, 1894, in the middle of all this chaos, my father was born. Twenty-six years later he became the headmaster of Hung Wen Middle School. Chester was the first non-Chinese baby born in Xiangyang County, a distinction that he was proud of all his life.

His mother did not have enough milk for him and cow's milk was not available so, according to local custom, a Chinese "wet nurse" was employed to suckle the baby.

Almost 40 years later, when Chester was a political candidate for the Legislative Assembly of Alberta, Canada, a supporter told him that a damaging whispering campaign was spreading rapidly and if he didn't stop it he had no chance of winning the election. "They say you were born in China," he said. "They also say that your mother was unable to supply you with milk and that cow's milk was not available in China. Is that really so?"

Chester assured him that it was correct. "The worst of it is," said his supporter, "is that they say you were brought up on Chinese milk so you are partly Chinese."

Dad replied that according to that logic he might have absorbed some of the traditional wisdom of the great Chinese philosophers, which should make him the best possible member of the Legislature. Then he asked his friend to start a whispering campaign about his opponents.

"What do you know about them?' he asked.

"I have it on fairly good authority," said Chester, "that they were brought up on cow's milk, but I would not be so boorish to suggest they are part bull."

Dad told this story at every public meeting and the audiences seemed to appreciate its logic. He won the campaign.

On Christmas Day 1894, Halvor wrote to Nils:

"Merry Christmas, brother! We have a special present for you. Another son, Chester Alvin! At Christmas we had a festival for the children; 100 children present. We joined hands and danced around the tree singing and playing games.

"Good things are happening in our mission in spite of the war. Last month, an important official set a fine example by sending his daughter to our school. We had given his son refuge when the Bannermen came through looking for conscripts. As you know, few if any conscripts ever return. Other gentry followed his lead. Now, we have three schools going; the new one is for older boys. We have 50 children: 35 boys and 15 girls. First girls' school ever conducted in Hubei province. Some opposition noted. Only two girls rejected because the parents refused to unbind their feet. We are hoping they will soon have a change of heart. We are well and working with all our might."

Three years later, grandfather's little brick schoolhouse was officially sanctioned by the Chief Mandarin of Xiangfan. The school kept growing until 1899, when the Boxer Rebellion forced my grandparents with their three children to disguise themselves as Chinese peasants and escape down the Han river in a junk. Undaunted, they returned in 1900 to continue their work.

One hundred years after its founding the two-room school had grown into the largest school in the province. Now, it is the Number One Middle School of Xiangfan. There are more than 3,000 students, with the girls holding up half the sky.

Author's note: On my father's request, his six grown children returned with him to Xiangfan to celebrate his 90th birthday. Hundreds of family friends came to greet us. Many were descendants of my grandparent's students. One tearful old man grasped my father's hand and said they had played together 80 years ago. "Of course!" laughed Dad, "We used to chase paddy chickens (frogs) in the rice paddies." Another old woman asked why he spoke such good Chinese. "Because I am Chinese!" he answered. "No, that can't be," she said looking up at his blue eyes. "I was born right here," he insisted. "Well why don't you look Chinese?" "Well you see," he said in a conspiratorial tone," I have lived so long in Canada that I am beginning to look like one of them." The woman's mouth dropped open and a silver cackle rang out. "You are a character," she said slapping his arm. "He may look like a foreigner," said another, "but he sounds like a true lump of mud"—a term the natives jokingly apply to themselves. "Right," said Dad, "I'm just an old lump of mud, like the rest of you."

GAZA: THE OTHER SIDE OF POLITICS

ERIN TROWBRIDGE
February 1998

JERUSALEM—No longer a no-man's-land filled with reluctant refugees, the West Bank and the Gaza Strip are starting to feel lived in. The three million Palestinians who once felt unfairly relegated to these two stretches of rough terrain and barren coast have begun to make it their home. International and local developers are renovating the crumbling buildings, hollowed by war, paving the dirt roads disfigured by tanks and digging irrigation ditches and new water systems to bring life back to this land.

The plans are there and the work has started, but the territory now controlled by the Palestinian National Authority still has the look and feel of a third-world country, a long way from the prosperity of neighboring Israel's "land of milk and honey."

Politicians and developers are looking optimistically to the days when Gaza will be a tourist hot-spot and the West Bank will be a self-contained industrial nation. In the meantime, the word on the streets still carries a note of desperation as people say that new streets, parks and buildings don't mean a thing if they don't have jobs or homes and if their nation has an uncertain future.

"I've been out of work for over a year and a half and my life now is like a wheel that doesn't turn," said Mohammed Dola, 35, of his lifestyle in the Al-Shatte refugee camp in Gaza. "I'm living like an old man, just letting the hours pass until I can go to sleep again."

Unfortunately, Dola's plight is not uncommon in Gaza and the West Bank. A stone's throw away from their prosperous Israeli neighbors, Palestinians are trying to move forward from the day-to-day existence that has become status quo during the last 50 years and create industries and infrastructures that will improve their lives in the short term, and allow them to gain a grip on their future.

404

Towns in the West Bank, like Hebron, Jericho and Nablus, whose names call to mind images of the intifada and Israeli tanks, are now centers of intensive development programs.

The road leading to Nablus ducks in and out of the heavy fog blanketing the mountains of the northern West Bank region. Olive trees, symbolic for the Palestinian people because of their deep roots and long life, line the roadside and scent the air with an earthy mustiness. Nablus, the second largest city in the West Bank, is situated in a valley and along the slopes of two mountains. The city of 130,000 people is nicknamed "mountain of fire" both for its geographical location and for its revolutionary history. The recent protests over the possibility of American air strikes against Iraq reached their zenith here when Israeli soldiers came in to quiet the demonstrators. On the gray stone walls of a building dating back more than a thousand years, "Beware of Informants" is scrawled in Arabic, a remnant of the recent Israeli occupation of this city.

> *Officials say that Israeli security measures have caused the loss of many Palestinians' jobs, with the result that their incomes, already low, have plummeted.*

The long struggle over national boundaries and mutual recognition has left both Israel and Palestine with thousands of citizens dead, wounded or imprisoned. Palestinian officials say that since the signing of the peace agreements, Israel has stepped up security, making it virtually impossible for residents of certain areas under the Palestinian Authority to move freely or continue their work in Israel.

Frequent closures that restrict movement into and out of the Occupied Territories have had a devastating impact on the Palestinian economy. According to the United Nations Economic and Social Council Report issued in January, the closures have contributed to maintaining unemployment rates of 30 percent in the West Bank and 40 percent in Gaza. Since the signing of the Oslo Agreement in 1993, the report says, Palestinian incomes have dropped from an average of $1,800 to $950 in the West Bank and from $1,200 to $600 in Gaza.

Despite these problems, some progress is being made. In just the past two years, the United Nations Development Programme (UNDP) alone has funneled $155 million in international aid for the development of infrastructure in the West Bank and Gaza. Sewage systems, irrigation, water storage and distribution systems, schools, farming cooperatives and markets to help sustain small business owners are all works in progress.

The UNDP's Programme of Assistance to the Palestinian People (PAPP) "has always maintained that the person, an individual, is at the center of any development," said Timothy Rothermel, Special Representative to the UNDP/PAPP. "This new situation here is that there is a government and not-a-government at the same time," he added. "It is a 'Palestinian Authority.' There is no cabinet or anything. But before 1993, UNDP had to go through Israel and we would get held up in proposals and approvals. Now we can make the propositions and go straight to work."

In almost every area of the West Bank and Gaza, developers are focusing their efforts on architectural renovations, sewage and water distribution systems.

"The next war on this land will be a water war," said Ghassan W. Shakah, the Mayor of Nablus and a member of the Executive Committee of the Palestine Liberation Organization. "After 30 years of occupation, we have lost everything. We've spent the last three years working with the UNDP to develop the infrastructure of the city, but our priority now is to find more resources and improve our water system. Without proper and cheap water, there can be no civilization. Our systems suffered under the occupation and now we have to rebuild. We are working and have accomplished much, but this is just one step in a long march."

'The next war on this land will be a water war,' said the Mayor of Nablus. 'Without proper and cheap water, there can be no civilization,' he added.

The cobblestone paths that twist through the city's center are made up of stones that date back thousands of years. Small businesses line the streets, their storefronts filled incongruously with old tires, ironing boards, shoes and freshly baked bread. Part of the rebuilding project involves relocating the city's shopkeepers into co-operatively-run long, sheltered corridors that criss cross the downtown area. The goal is to enable these small-business owners to meet and anticipate demand by sharing their information and buying their goods wholesale.

The rehabilitation of the old city and the organization of the shopkeepers was one of the first development projects carried out in Nablus. More recently, the $5.6 million of international aid that UNDP has administered here over the last decade is being used for renovations to both the old city and to the water and sewage systems.

"The water projects here have been some of the most successful we've done in all of the area," said Walid Hasna, Chief of the UNDP's engineering unit. "There were seven pre-existing, completely functioning streams that were all connected through underground tunnels that were built by the Romans. We only had to renovate the pipes and we had enough water to take care of the whole city without having to pump it in from an outside source. We were able to reduce the loss of water by 50 percent in less than three years."

The challenge: improving on civic improvements left behind by the ancient Romans.

The water problem is echoed by development workers and government officials in cities and villages throughout the Palestinian territories.

But also mentioned frequently is the fact that much of this land's infrastructure was built almost two thousand years ago by the Romans. The ancient reservoirs and aqueducts have withstood the harsh climate and the centuries.

Engineers need only to install new pipes to make the existing systems functional. By renovating the existing water systems, the nearby cities can provide enough water to meet their needs, reducing their costs and ending their reliance on water purchased from their Israeli neighbors.

Outside of Hebron, a smaller city in the south of the West Bank, an ancient irrigation system in Beit Kahel was revitalized to provide the local farmers with a better supply. In the city itself, UNDP workers, aided by $2 million in funding from Japan, are working on creating sewage systems that will bring sanitation to 95 percent of the people, as compared with only 55 percent now.

"This is an ancient city, named after the father of Abraham," said Hebron's Deputy Mayor. "Since 1967 and the Six Day War, this city has been a hotbed of violence. Now we are facing incredible water shortages, receiving at times less than one quarter of the water we need."

The problem that development workers have in the rural area surrounding Hebron, they say, is not the rugged landscape but rather the Israeli formalities.

"The Israelis monitor our work very closely because this is in area that they still occupy," said Bruno Lemarquis, Head of Agricultural and Rural Development with the UNDP. "Our projects have to qualify as 'land development' and not 'construction.' We cannot build anew, but can only improve what already exists. So the UNDP has contracted with local nongovernmental organizations to help us restructure these ancient irrigation systems and we've been successful."

The farms Larmarquis points out are simple and small, with little patches of land fenced in with intricately stacked stones.

"We didn't have any major problems until a month and a half ago," he said. "After we had finished $12,000 work developing some land, the Israelis came in and claimed it was their land and bulldozed down all of our work. They had waited until we were completely finished. It is the first time in 15 years that a UNDP project has been destroyed."

Though development workers try to do their work outside of politics, incidents like that in Hebron are frequent and run-ins are occasionally unavoidable.

"In this area, everything is political," said Rothermel. "We should be speaking about development, not politics, but in a situation like this it is impossible to separate the two. Our goal is just to make life here as comfortable as possible."

Klaus Schwab, founder of the World Economic Forum in Geneva, sees the future borderless world of globalization as tough on nation-alistic leaders but a paradise for "creative entrepreneurs," the leaders he sees as forces for creative change. This is the optimistic view: Globalization is the catalyst which will enable us to synthesize political and business goals with the social goals of environmental sustainability and human development. In specific areas of population, development and environment, other Earth Times writers see the roots of the future resting very much in the recent past—a decade of unprecedented international emphasis on human and social needs, documented by the decade's numerous world conferences. Blueprints for action have been written, digested, argued over, and re-written. Paula DiPerna echoes the wide-spread sense that now the issue is implementation, not ideas. Writing about "Water and the Relevance of Technology," she says the reality is "there has been more policy discussed than plumbing installed."

Gulfs separating the industrialized "North" and the developing "South," and the other divisions between national groups, will clearly have to be bridged, at least in part, before the utterances of the international policy-makers give way to whole-hearted acceptance and realistic—and perhaps more unselfish—commitment of money and resources.

SECTION 9

LOOKING AHEAD

POPULATION: WHAT CAN WE EXPECT IN THE NEW MILLENNIUM?

JYOTI SHANKAR SINGH
March 1999

The environment, population, poverty alleviation, and empowerment of women were among the major substantive themes of global conferences organized by the United Nations in the 1990s. Taken together, these themes also formed part of a common international agenda on sustainable development. All of the themes received worldwide public and media attention because of the global conferences. The plans and programs they agreed upon have generated a considerable amount of action and follow-up by governments, nongovernmental organizations and the international community—all of which is encouraging as we head into the new millennium.

A crowded season of five-year reviews of these world conferences is already upon us. The fifth anniversary review of the 1992 Earth Summit (Rio+5) took place in 1997, with what most observers describe as mixed results; few of the additional resources that the Summit urged for sustainable development have been forthcoming. In June 1999, a special session of the UN General Assembly was scheduled to review the Program of Action of the 1994 International Conference on Population and Development. In the year 2000, two more special sessions are scheduled: one from September 5 to 9 in New York on the implementation of the Platform of Action of the 1995 World Conference on Women (Beijing+5), and a special session in Geneva in June to focus on a review of the implementation of the Copenhagen Declaration and the Program of Action of the 1995 World Summit on Social Development (Copenhagen+5).

These reviews are expected to refocus public awareness on the themes of the earlier global conferences, to underline their interconnectedness and to generate extensive media coverage. They should also help to focus attention on newly emerging issues as well as those issues that have gained urgency in the interim.

The ICPD+5 as well as Copenhagen+5 and Beijing+5 underline the increasing acceptance by governments and civil society organizations of the goals and objectives of their respective programs. But they also point out that progress has been slow in many areas because of political, sociocultural, managerial or resource constraints—and that there are major difficulties and challenges ahead.

In the area of population and development, the review has focused attention on seven major topics: adolescent health, maternal mortality, HIV/AIDS, aging, migration, integration of family planning with other reproductive health services, and the population-development interrelationship. Political, legal and social issues relating to the role and status of women form part of the main agenda of the follow-up to both Cairo and Beijing. Poverty alleviation is a common thread in all of the review processes, and it is a major theme of the Copenhagen+5 process. It is difficult to see what tangible progress can be reported on this theme. The number of those regarded as living in absolute poverty has actually gone up in the late 1990s. Pious pronouncements at the global level have been rarely followed up with meaningful action at the national level. What is needed now is a sustained commitment to employment creation and income generating activities, measures to improve health and educational services, and implementation of policies aimed at achieving economic and social equity.

Civil society organizations, including NGOs, women's groups and community groups, played an increasingly important role in the major UN conferences. The five-year reviews are likely to further strengthen their role and to enlarge the modalities of their participation in future follow-up activities. Partnerships among UN agencies, civil society organizations and the private sector will be emphasized; and South-South cooperation, at both the governmental and nongovernmental levels, will certainly receive a boost.

One hopes that the international community, including major donors, will increase financial and technical support for the follow-up activities.

Given the continuing decline in the level of official development assistance—the figure for 1999 is expected to be barely $45 billion, a decline of 10 percent from 1998—this will perhaps be one of the more difficult goals to achieve. But it is worth pursuing, if we still are committed to moral and development imperatives.

WHAT TO DO ABOUT CLIMATE CHANGE

SIR JOHN BROWNE
September 1997

The science of climate change is still provisional. Perhaps all science is provisional. But some things are clear. The concentration of carbon dioxide in the atmosphere is rising, and the temperature of the Earth's surface is increasing. It is hard to isolate cause and effect. But there is now an effective consensus that there is a discernible human influence on the climate, and a link between the concentration of carbon dioxide and the increase in temperature.

The forecast of the Intergovernmental Panel on Climate Change is that over the next century temperatures might rise by between 1 and 3.5 degrees centigrade, and that sea levels might rise by between 15 and 95 centimeters.

Those are wide margins of error and there remain large areas of uncertainty—about cause and effect, and more importantly about the consequences. But it would be unwise and potentially dangerous to ignore the mounting concern. There is no immediate crisis and we have time. But we do need to take precautionary action now.

Developing the right policies to deal with the situation will be a complex process. The problem won't be solved by denying or restricting the economic expectations of the people of Asia or Africa or Latin America. Nor will it be resolved by destroying the living standards of the developed world. The first would be immoral, the second unrealistic.

The challenge is to achieve growth, and a continuing rise in the living standards of all the people of the world in a way which isn't destructive. And what is at stake is economic activity as a whole not simply the transportation sector. Of all the carbon emissions which result from global human activity, only 20 percent comes from the transportation sector. The remaining 80 percent comes from industry, from power generation, and from the domestic and commercial sectors.

So how should we approach this complex challenge? I approach it as a businessman and as an optimist. Optimism, after all, is a prior condition for being in business. That doesn't mean that I think there are easy or cost free solutions. But on the basis of experience I do think we can find a constructive way forward.

The industry has responded successfully to many challenges in the past and I find a lot of support among our staff for an approach which accepts the problem as another challenge, instead of trying to deny that it exists.

I'm speaking as a businessman not a politician. Politicians must define policy but business has a responsibility to help work out how that policy can be delivered. Our role is to bring realism and practicality. We're now in the run up to the conference in Kyoto (in December 1997). I think it is important to see that conference in perspective. The problem of climate change will not be resolved at any single summit meeting. As an issue, climate change is on a par with the development of an open world trading system or the process of disarmament. It will take time.

Climate change is a long term problem and what matters now is that we begin to take rational precautionary steps even if there are still areas of uncertainty and disagreement. We can't wait for a finished, polished solution which has unanimous endorsement. Any agreement seems most likely to be around objectives and aspirations rather than around a detailed program.

There may be a target for an overall reduction in emissions by 2005 or 2010 but that will just be the beginning. The next step will be to develop the means through which any target can be achieved. The important thing is that the various policy instruments which governments could use, such as taxation, carbon trading and joint implementation, are well designed and establish the right incentives for action by those whose choices and decisions can make a difference.

Without the right incentives there will be very little practical action—just words. But with the right incentives in place, there is a lot that could be done.

Simply adopting current best practice and technology would be an enormous benefit and in the emerging markets would have a parallel and highly positive benefit for economic activity as a whole. It is possible to develop oil fields without flaring, to improve engine quality, to run cleaner power stations, and to develop measures of conservation.

It is possible to use combined heat and power plants to increase the efficiency of energy use. BP Energy, our energy management business, is already involved in this process and its efforts have cut carbon dioxide emissions in Britain by a quarter of a million tons. Combined heat and power capacity has risen by 50 percent since 1989 and there is huge scope to take that further. It is possible to encourage a more rapid turnover of capital stock to encourage work on reinjection and on reforestation. All those steps could make a contribution to an overall solution. Climate change is a matter for public policy and political decisions. But business can't be passive in the process. It isn't enough to ask for acts of leadership from politicians.

Tony Blair said in New York not long ago that "no country can opt out of global warming or fence-in its own climate." Nor can any company. The oil industry and its employees are part of society and we have to set a constructive example. I recently set out our objectives in this area. Some of them are external activities such as supporting scientific research and taking part in joint implementation initiatives. Let me concentrate on the internal steps we're taking. First of all on photovolatics and the development of a solar power business. There is no doubt that there is sufficient sunlight to generate all the energy the world needs. But at the moment it generates just 0.001 percent of the world total, some 1,500 GWh, which is only around 0.4 percent of the total annual electricity consumption in Britain. The trends in photovoltaics are very encouraging but there are still obstacles. The acceptability of solar energy to the consumer will determine whether we can achieve the necessary economies of scale in production and the technology also needs to improve. Again I'm optimistic. By 2020, I believe up to 5 percent of world energy could be supplied by renewable energies such as solar power. The pattern of energy use isn't static. Technology and markets move, and it is possible that in 50 years, renewable energy could supply half the world's needs.

> *Climate change is a matter for public policy and political decisions; business cannot be passive.*

It is in that context that we see solar energy as a significant long term business opportunity. We continue to develop the technology and to build the market. We are testing what is possible by using solar power on some of our retail sites and on bigger projects as well, including the site of the athletes' village for the next Olympics in Sydney, Australia. But it is a long term process.

For the foreseeable future, oil and gas will be required to meet the world's energy needs. The world's population is growing. Within the next decade or so it will grow by over a billion—in terms of people, another China.

Those people need energy for the basic necessities of heat, light and mobility. That is why we continue to explore and develop new resources and why we are so committed to ensuring that they are used with maximum efficiency, and the minimum of emissions.

I know some people say that we have already discovered enough coal, oil and gas to meet the world's needs and therefore we should stop exploring. I don't accept that logic. Our belief is that as technology moves on we can discover resources which can be developed more efficiently and with less environmental impact than many of resources already discovered but not yet developed. To believe otherwise is to deny the possibility of progress.

Efficiency can be improved and we're determined to make a constructive contribution to that effort. Accordingly, we're setting up our own process to measure and report the volumes of carbon dioxide emitted from our own operations. That system will be in place soon, and our intention is to develop a set of targets over the following two years. The results will be independently verified and published.

As a contribution to that process, we're developing our own internal emissions trading system. We'll start with a system involving 10 of our key operations. And if that works we'll expand it to cover more and eventually the entire company. Emissions trading has an excellent track record in dealing with sulphur in the US, and we want to see if we build on that experience in our own company.

No single company or country can solve the problem of climate change. It would be foolish and arrogant to pretend we can. But I hope we can make a difference not least to the tone of the debate by showing what is possible through constructive action. Climate change is a crucial issue but it is only one issue among the many we have to deal with. Doing business in the energy industry means you have to be highly competitive delivering a consistent financial performance for the benefit of those who trust you with their money. But that isn't the end of the story.

World population is still growing rapidly. How are we going to address new energy and housing needs? What about social issues?

To deliver high performance on a sustainable basis, companies have to be aware of the context in which they are working. There is clearly a growing concern in society about the actions and responsibilities of companies and, in particular, multinationals. Some part of the concern stems from the belief that large global companies have more power than many governments and that such power can and should be leveraged to particular ends.

That is certainly a view among some nongovernmental organizations—though my impression is that from any perspective, power is always elsewhere. Whatever the origin of the concern, it exists and companies have to respond. We can't put up the barricades and try to hide from the concerns of society. We're part of that society not least because our staff have views and opinions of their own which inevitably reflect the wider concerns of society.

We employ over 50,000 intelligent people and we can't expect them to forget or alter their views when they come through the door every morning. And we don't want them to because their individuality is what gives them the ability to produce ideas and to make a unique contribution.

They have hopes for the world and for their children. And they have fears. So how do we respond?

Of course, behaving ethically and with concern for people and the environment isn't something new for us. I hope, and I believe, that those things are part of the basic values of the company. But the level of concern and the scrutiny which is developing, means that we have to be more systematic.

We have to be clear what our standards are and we have to ensure those standards are being met consistently and universally. That is what we are in the process of developing.

We have a set of principles—a policy statement which covers the main areas where concerns arise: issues of health, safety and environment; financial control; ethics; employment and employment practices; and community relations.

Together they establish a "standard of care"—something which everyone who comes into contact with us should experience. And we are developing a management process which links directly to the Board through a responsible Managing Director to provide an assurance that our policies are being upheld.

We accept a responsibility for delivering that standard of care, but of course we're human. We make mistakes.

I define mistakes in two categories: Genuine mistakes undertaken with good intentions, and mistakes which are willful or careless.

The genuine mistakes we learn from so that they are never repeated. The willful mistakes we don't tolerate; they have to be penalized, because if they're not penalised the mistakes will be repeated and the standards won't be taken seriously.

We're still learning and testing the system. I think it will work and, more important, I think it has to work because I'm pretty sure that we're moving to the point where companies will have to report on what they're doing, and will have their conduct externally verified. Verification provides a factual basis to assess what has been achieved and what has still to be achieved.

It helps in these serious issues by moving us away from rhetoric and assertion. And I hope that as companies adopt verification as a standard process, so NGOs will do the same when they make claims and assertions, because that will clarify the debate and focus all our efforts, our positive energy, on dealing with the real problems.

I think there is great scope for practical constructive action across the whole agenda. I think business has a role in that and a responsibility and that includes working with others including governments and NGOs. We're committed to doing that.

THE YOUNG AND THE OLD

C. GERALD FRASER
June 1998

U NITED NATIONS–The fastest growing segments of the world's population are youth between ages of 15 and 24 and men and women over age 60. They are "the new generations" challenging society, says the 1998 State of the World Population report.

"At 1.05 billion, today's is the biggest-ever generation of young people between 15 and 24, and this age group is rapidly expanding in many countries," the report says. At the other end of the age spectrum, the report says, "There are more than 578 million people over 60, and this generation is growing at an unprecedented rate."

Over all, the momentum of population growth "has slowed, is slowing, and could slow still further in coming decades," says the report, which was published by the United Nations Population Fund and edited by Alex Marshall and William A. Ryan. Still, 80 million people are born each year. World population is about 5,929,800,000, according to the report. (And October 12, 1999, a date chosen somewhat arbitrarily, is to be observed as the "Day of 6 Billion.")

The challenge that youth present to society is the need to find jobs for them. "Lower birth rates in today's developing countries offer the possibility of a demographic bonus in the next 15-20 years," the report says, "as a 'bulge' of young people come into the workforce while fewer children are being born." This "workforce bulge," the report continues, "can be the basis for more investment, greater labor productivity and rapid development. This will generate revenues for social investments like health, education and social security, to meet the needs of both old and young and secure the basis for future development."

For demographers, children are those ages 0-18; adolescents, 10-19; youth, 15-24; young people, 10-24; dependent young, 0-15.

Some 71 countries and territories have more than 40 percent of their population under age 15. Forty-four are in Africa, 12 in Asia, eight in Arab

States and seven in Latin America.

As for aging, the over-65 populations in Europe, North America, Japan and Australasia have increased to 10-15 percent of the total and are expected to double in size within the next 30-35 years. In the most rapidly aging countries—including Japan, Germany and Italy—older people will soon account for almost 40 percent of the population, or even more.

"These changes are unprecedented in their size and speed," the report says. "The number of older persons being added to the world's population is now approaching nine million per year. Currently about 77 percent of the increase in the older population is taking place in developing regions.

"This growth will severely test the ability of families and societies to provide the financial, medical and social support older people will need," the report says. These older people will in some regions be healthier, better educated and more productive than their predecessors.

The report records Africa's total population at 778.5 million, larger than the population of Europe (729.4 million) or Latin America and the Caribbean (499.5 million combined). Asia is where the most people are: 3.588 billion—in Eastern Asia, South Eastern Asia, South Central Asia and Western Asia (sometimes called the Middle East).

"In purely economic terms," says a report tidbit, "children are an expensive investment, and their cost stimulates the desire for smaller families. It costs an average family in the United States $149,000 to raise a child from birth to age 17." Median annual income for a family of four in the US is about $50,000.

WATER AND THE RELEVANCE OF TECHNOLOGY

PAULA DiPERNA
April 1998

The rain pounded like hundreds of nails on the roof, a deafening roar of water. In Itaituba, in Brazilian Amazonia, it was the rainy season, a time of year that makes every cloud into a fist of storms and sends so much rain into the Amazon basin that river banks disappear, the rainforest floods and canoes float along as near to the treetops as birds. Rainy season brings sudden fierce downpours. But then, as suddenly as they fall, the rains can stop, leaving huge beautiful drops of water to stand on the countless leaves like crystal prisms in the reappearing sun.

The Amazon rainforest is water gone extravagant—the ultimate expression of the adage, water is the source of life.

But Amazonia and other rainforest areas are unique; most places in the world suffer a lack of water and rainfall. And it is this unpredictable and erratic distribution of water—due to natural and unnatural inequities—that has brought humanity to the threshold of a water crisis.

As nations gather in the Commission on Sustainable Development (CSD) at the United Nations in April 1998 for the sixth session of follow-up to the Earth Summit held in 1992, water problems have acquired new urgency. According to President Jacques Chirac of France, whose nation hosted a ministerial-level "International Conference on Water and Sustainable Development" in Paris recently, "The United Nations has identified 70 areas of water-related friction from the Near East to the Sahel, the drylands of Latin America and the Indian subcontinent. The risk of hostilities will grow in step with the depletion of resources. Are we going to allow the 21st Century to be the century of the water wars?"

The threat of acute conflict is compounded by the chronic human misery that flows wherever clean water does not. Roughly one billion people on Earth still have no access to drinkable water, almost four billion have no access to sanitation or sewage services. According to the World Health Organization, almost half of the people of the world suffer from water-borne or water-related diseases, which together account for roughly five million deaths a year. The World Resources Institute has estimated that by 2050, 13 to 20 percent of the world's people will be living in water-scarce countries, mostly in the Middle East and Africa—but all countries face pockets of scarcity due to drought and limited supply due to various factors.

In human terms, the statistics on lack of water access translate into roughly six hours a day spent by women and girls in Africa, for example, collecting and lugging water for family and household use from streams, rivers, ponds, puddles and public community taps, according to Unicef. In human terms, lack of water cannot be escaped.

Part of the problem derives from the nature of water itself. The fluid of nutrients and the bather of cells, water is indispensable to all living organisms. As a universal solvent, water is an essential cleaning and flushing agent for all manner of wastes, human and industrial. Yet this most vital substance is exceedingly rare. Only 2.5 percent of all water on Earth is freshwater and, of this, almost 70 percent is logistically out of reach in polar ice caps, glaciers and vast sheets of snow that never thaw. Roughly 29 percent of available freshwater is located in underground aquifers—groundwater—with the surface water of lakes, streams, swamps and soil moisture accounting for the one percent balance. It is said that usable water on Earth is in the same ratio as a teardrop on the surface of an egg.

What's more, though withdrawals of water from surface and underground sources can be replenished by rains—themselves renewed by evaporation in a constant "water cycle"—the supply of water on Earth is fixed. Absent desalination or the melting of icebergs—schemes discussed for decades already—there will never be more freshwater on Earth than there is today. Add to this situation pollution of all sorts, which further reduces the quantity of usable water, and it seems clear that to "manage water" is actually to manage scarcity. The current question is: Can scarcity be managed more fairly?

Another prong of today's water crisis is the reality that there has been more policy discussed than plumbing installed. For a finite resource, water seems to have generated a virtually infinite series of international discussions, dutifully cited as predecessors by many speakers at the recent Paris water conference as if they were mentioning venerable ancestors: the UN Water Conference in Mar del Plata in 1977; the International Drinking Water Supply and Sanitation Decade from 1981 to 1990; the Dublin International Conference on Water and Sustainable Development in 1992; the Earth

Summit in Rio de Janeiro later that year; intervening summits and conferences on women, population and urbanization; the gathering in Paris, plus a preceding meeting of experts in Zimbabwe; a further gathering in June 1998 organized by Unesco and others on "World Water Resources at the Beginning of the 21st Century"; a major water conference in the Netherlands in the year 2000; and according to a promotional brochure, "Water—the world's most important resource is coming to Melbourne," for Australia will host the 10th World Water Congress, also in 2000.

For perspective on what might be accomplished in actual water delivery hardware by that year, Gerald Ssendauala, Uganda's Minister for Natural Resources, estimated that he could get potable drinking water to the remaining half million people in the city of Kampala who have no access to it now— that is, if he could invest about $70 million in pipes, booster pumps, reservoir tracks and other needed urban infrastructure. In Paris, at a roundtable of African Ministers, he said confidently, "That amount would do it by then—I could reach the rest of the city."

Yet, it's not as if huge quantities of money haven't already been invested to achieve better water services. According to a 1997 UN report titled "Critical Trends," almost $100 billion was invested in the "water decade" to "accelerate the introduction of water services in poor regions . . . but results were mixed. Impressive gains in the number of people served were offset by population growth, especially in urban areas."

In fact, statistics on people still needing access to water have barely changed in 10 years. Dr. Mahmoud A. Abu-Zeid, Egypt's Minister of Public Works and Water Resources and President of the World Water Council—an international network of water-concerned entities—also blames population growth. In Paris, he exhorted delegates to face the fact that the "world freshwater situation has passed a critical crossroad toward a state of crisis during the last three decades." He added: "Things have been done but the population increase is overtaking the measuring stick. We are doing too little, and still more people are coming along." He described measures taken in his own country, where he is personally responsible: "In Egypt, we have a very limited amount of water, but we have improved efficiency through recycling and have raised efficiencies for irrigation from 40 to 70 percent. We use water twice at least, and of the 5,000 villages in Egypt, I would say about 85 percent of these have been provided with drinking water access, but only 45 percent with sanitation systems."

According to Ismail Serageldin, former Vice President of the World Bank for Environmentally Sustainable Development, to address basic water needs in developing countries and stay current with population trends already under way will require $60 billion to $80 billion of external investment over the next decade, of which the World Bank will be able to lend half. The rest will have to come from private investment and national budgets, but Serageldin observed that the costs, though high, were insignificant compared to the trillions of dollars moving through the global economy in capital and currency speculation each week.

Still, the prevailing question remains urgent: How to mobilize the needed funds, political will and technological expertise to meet the need? How to get the money moving toward water?

The main answer currently in the air is to make water a true product and attract private sector involvement to achieve its better distribution. This means expanding the principles of "user pays"—those who use water must pay something for it—and "polluter pays"—those who pollute water must pay the clean-up costs. At the Paris conference, Charles Josselin, France's Minister for Cooperation, went so far as to say that, "The belief that water falls freely from the sky is the main reason distribution has been so inequitable."

Water cannot be part of a pure market logic regulated only by the game of supply and demand.

Prime Minister Lionel Jospin of France both echoed and tempered this notion in his address to the closing Plenary. On the one hand, he congratulated the delegates for having "renounced the ancient belief, too long prevalent, that water is free." But, on the other hand, he added, "This economic approach to water should not be confused with a commercial vision. Water is not a product like others. It cannot be part of a pure market logic regulated only by the game of supply and demand." There is a balance to be found, continued Jospin, between the users' needs and economic costs.

In other words, the universe of free-market contradictions and complications must now be applied to water if the looming water crisis is to be solved. On some level, this could usher in a new age of water rationing by price.

But if water is now to be seen as mainly an economic good, how to retain its social value? How to price water high enough to be profitable, yet low enough to be affordable? After all, it is not as if water actually is free today. While much irrigation water may be underpriced, and there are water "poachers" and illegal hook-ups in large cities—especially among the poor who have no recourse—most municipal authorities do charge property owners for municipal water services, either directly or indirectly through property taxes.

And landlords pass these water charges on to tenants in rent. In rural areas, property owners pay for well installation and for water quality maintenance. Moreover, in poor areas in developing countries, if water has been "free," it's been because the time that women spend collecting it has gone entirely unremunerated. In reality, it is these women who are already paying dearly for water in time, exhaustion and lack of options. How then to estimate the much-acclaimed "real cost" of water in areas where it is needed most?

Can communities that have had no voice in water policy gain control over water resources?

The emphasis on water pricing is being justified on the grounds that the "user pays" principle will reduce waste and improve water use efficiency. Also, the notion of "free water" is being blamed for the failure of maintenance of water systems. Sekou Toure, President of the High Commission on Hydrology in the Côte d'Ivoire, remarked, "I've seen in my own country many times, in villages where people have been given water pumps and so forth by the government, when the pump breaks, there is no one in the village to fix it and it stays broken a long time. People have to have some stake in their own water system."

Of course one could argue that it is the state's responsibility to maintain what the state installs, but Toure's observation does capture a prevailing notion in evolving water policy—water problems can't be solved without involvement of civil society. The final declaration of the Paris Conference proclaims that "the development, management, use and protection of water should be . . . based upon a participatory decision-making process open to all users, in particular women, people living in poverty and disadvantaged groups. The role of nongovernmental organizations and other socio-economic partners remains essential."

But what does this mean in practice? Paying for water, deciding where the water should go, helping engineers locate water, owning the waterworks? Exactly how can communities that have had no voice in water policy thus far now gain real control over water resources?

For Bunker Roy, founder and Director of the Barefoot College in Tilonia, India, the answer is obvious: "Drinking water is too big an issue to be left to engineers alone . . . We need to start a serious 'unlearning' process. In fact, the biggest threat to a person in a rural village is the water engineer."

Barefoot College, started in 1972, is locally operated and offers educational and other social services in an arid area of Rajasthan State that had suffered, according to Roy, two severe droughts of six years each where "not a drop of rain fell." In the Tilonia region, Roy says, roughly 1,200 households in 12 villages have taken control of their own water supply. "The people themselves planned where the pipes were going to be dug, who's going to dig the pipes, who's going to make the tank and who is going to pay for it. It took us a long time, and some communities didn't want to pay. But in the end everyone paid and the whole system has been running for five years, and the water committee of that community is managing the whole show. They have generated about $2,000 in their account and they are rich and they are so confident and cocky and they don't really need any help from outside."

What's more, says Bunker Roy, the local system provides unprecedented reliability. "We haven't deepened traditional water sources and, through a piped system that also incorporates rainwater collection, we have been able to provide an hour of water in the morning and one in the evening to every member of the household throughout the year, whereas with the system supplied by the public engineers you are not even sure you would get water twice a week...Everyone is paying for water in a state where water is free, not so much for the water but for the person who operates the pump, repairs the pipes, changes the taps and so forth."

Roy also praised the region's system of rainwater harvesting, involving 150 villages which collect 12 million liters of rainwater each year, at a cost of 10 cents per liter. He said, "We have actually 'drought-proofed' these villages in the middle of a desert with rain harvesting structures. In Rajasthan, the rain comes like a flood. There we don't have gentle rain; we have rain where you can't see your hand put out in front of you. And, at that time, you can waste a lot of water. So we collect it and the water is used constantly and there is no question of contamination or stagnation."

Roy added, "Attendance of girls in school has gone up and first-generation learners are coming to school only because of safe, clean drinking water from the rain. The socio-economic spin-offs have been phenomenal from the rainwater structures."

On privatization and public participation, Roy's view is skeptical: "Usually, when experts talk about participation they often mean, 'We will do the major portion and for the portions we can't do, we must get communities to participate.' I think this is patronizing, unhealthy and short-sighted and not a sustainable solution today. . . . And who are we talking about in the privatization? Community-based organizations are private; they are not government. If we are talking about people who can introduce an element of privatization without the profit or commercial motive, then I am for it. But if you are going to get an organization which is completely outside the community, and a company with a profit motive and exploitive motive, then I am totally against it and we will fight it."

Roy also added, "Privatization is seen as a solution for many governments, a way of absolving their responsibilities. They are doing such a lousy job and they think privatization is one way of getting them out of this responsibility, and I think that's not the way to go about it."

Indeed, the future of fairness in water distribution may be determined by whether its status as a public good remains intact. In the hallway of the Paris conference, Brazilian Ambassador Antonio Dayrell de Lima, Director General for Special Issues in Brazil's Ministry of External Relations, shared his views of privatization of water services. He said he found Roy's narrative somewhat "idyllic and impractical compared to the problems of such big cities as Saõ Paulo," but he also noted that in Brazil, "Privatization of certain entities has actually turned out to mean assets have been sold to a privately-owned, even publicly-owned, foreign company."

Sekou Toure of Côte d'Ivoire makes a distinction he considers critical between private sector and privatization. He observes, "Whatever you say about private sector or public sector, I don't think that governments should be involved in implementing water services. We should make sure they are more efficient in formulating strategies in controlling whatever the private sector is doing. But mind you, you have to be careful, some countries have a very weak private sector, so the role of the government should be to foster private sector activities. . . . Governments are not so good at running utilities, but at the same time you have to be careful. If a public service is being run well, then there is no point in selling it off."

One of the major arguments in favor of private sector management of water services is to reduce what is indisputably profligate waste of water. For example, irrigation, which consumes 70 percent of freshwater resources in the world, loses about half of its water through evaporation, a waste that can be reduced with available new technologies. Even more disturbing, it is estimated that in cities with piped service, about half the water is lost in leaks. Yet privatization may not necessarily remedy maintenance negligence.

For example, the British publication, The Observer, reported that in England, where public water utilities were privatized in 1989, there is growing national concern that firefighting may be suffering from cost-cutting within the new private water companies. Rather than invest in fixing the leaks in the antiquated system, the companies have apparently chosen to reduce water pressure to put less wear and tear on the pipes. This has left firefighters with insufficient water pressure in some areas and caused the chief firefighter in the district of Warwick to complain that "this policy of profit is incorrect, since we are talking about the citizens' security in case of fires."

In addition to leaks, there is user waste, with great variations in consumption patterns among nations. Whereas average daily per capita use among those with water access in Africa may hover at about 30 liters per day, in Europe, average use is roughly 200 liters per day and in the US, 600 liters. But, unless water is moved from one continent to another, reduced consumption in one nation will not increase water resources in another.

Each community, in short, needs to conserve water for its own sake, including those in developed countries. In Japan, for example, a 1997 report on water consumption and management by the Organization for Economic Development and Cooperation (OECD) noted that infrastructure improvements have reduced urban water leakage from almost 20 percent in 1975 to 10 percent in 1993. Rate structures were reformed to favor small-volume users and thus encourage more fastidious use. In some cities in Australia, a very dry continent, per capita water use has dropped 20 percent in the last five years, due to conservation and other measures, and the city of Sydney is experimenting with re-use and recycling of potable drinking water.

The critical nature of water resources in developed economies is indisputable. According to the OECD, "For many countries, the availability of water may become a major determinant of economic growth, industrial structure and the national trade portfolio."

Even in New York City, blessed with a brilliant gravity-fed system of aqueducts that for decades has carried high-quality water to the city from upstate watersheds, the wake-up call has sounded. In the spring of 1998, an unusual alliance between city dwellers and rural dairy farmers was formed, precisely to exploit mutual interests and protect the city's water supply. The venerable New York City Club, a civic organization active for more than a hundred years, came out in favor of a controversial price support for dairy farmers because "well-managed dairy farms and the open space these farms represent have been identified as a preferred land use in the New York City watershed, serving an important function in preserving drinking water quality for millions of New Yorkers."

Although there appeared to be general agreement in Paris that water policy needs urgent attention, several ministers did express the worry that raising water charges could backfire, especially where very poor people are concerned.

Minister Ssendaula of Uganda said: "My concern is what can happen when you commercialize water too much. In Malawi, they increased the water tariff in the city of Blantyre, so a majority of the people got off the water system and they had a cholera outbreak."

Zimbabwe's Minister for Rural Resources and Water Development, Joice T. R. Mujuru, bucked the trend to say, "It is not possible to run away from subsidies. Water, unlike bread, has no substitute, and there has to be fair sharing. If our people are asked to pay, it will have to be very cheap, for without water there won't be any life, no towns, no development at all. In fact, we are making a deliberate move to introduce subsidies so that people who do not have water can get some." She estimated that to meet water needs and reach all unserved people in her country would require $1 billion over 10 years.

Haiti, on the other hand, doesn't even have the luxury of looking forward to expanding service. According to Yolande Paultre, a sanitary engineer who is leading water reform in Haiti as head of the Unite de Reforme du Secteur de l'Eau Potable (URSEP), "The situation has deteriorated in the last few years so much that we are just trying to get back to where we were in the 1980s. The coverage we had then has gone down, which was only about 50 percent of the urban population with access to potable water, about 70 percent of which was in public fountains, not private hook-ups, and 30 percent of the rural population. There has really been serious mismanagement of the water situation and we are in a position of trying to rebuild what we had, while we also try to completely reform and restructure the water sector."

Privatization is seen as a solution for many governments, a way of absolving their responsibilities.

At her own home, for example, Paultre says she is lucky if water comes out of the taps one or two hours a week, though she pays a monthly fee for municipal water service. She said, "I pay by the month for a few hours of water. Some neighborhoods are better off and receive some water every day. But for almost no one do the fees correspond to the water you receive."

In addition, drought and extreme deforestation have ravaged Haiti's watersheds. "Some parts of the island still have a good amount of water," Paultre said, "but there are riverbeds now so dry that children play soccer in them."

The task in Haiti, thus, is mammoth, and it is also paralyzed by politics. According to Paultre, "The water reform law is not yet approved because the Parliament is not in session and everything in the water sector depends on legal reform. We are in a transition phase and we hope that this will be unblocked soon. Our objective is to cover the urban population in 10 or 15 years, and at least 50 percent of the rural population by then. We are going to decentralize the management of water in my country. It is the only way."

A major open question intimately touches the physical environment. As pointed out in the OECD report, one of the biggest "users" of water is nature itself—wetlands, birds, butterflies, animals, plants, all living things—with no wallet to open. To better account for these natural water needs, OECD noted, "A number of countries are devoting increased attention to defining minimum flow requirements for river systems." But how to capture the value of these ecological processes in consumer water prices? Will society accept the cost of nature's water needs? And as the "user pays" principle expands, will water services necessarily flow toward those who do pay and away from such "free riders" as the environment?

Another tricky balance is that of how to orchestrate a synergy between private-sector investment and overseas development assistance (ODA). The final Paris Declaration stated: "ODA should complement and focus on programs designed for creating enabling frameworks, meeting basic needs, sustainable development, management and protection of water, protection of ecosystems and capacity building."

That's a tall order, given stagnant ODA flows and the urgency of basic needs. [Aid from donor countries to the developing nations is around $45 billion for 1999, a decline of 10 percent from 1998.]

The world community faces a nettle of water challenges likely to grow only more complex with time. In fact, water may prove to be the "see-through garment" of development policy in the 21st Century, placing success and failure in vivid view, especially as private investment is emphasized. For results will be plainly in view—is water flowing to all or not?

France's President Chirac has called for an International Academy of Water, at which nations could pool knowledge and breakthroughs in water conservation technology. Indeed, the ongoing collection of data on the status of water reserves is vital, lest water problems worsen as eager investors prospect and pump where water tables are already insufficient. However, given the study water has already received, and the extent of the problem still ahead, one must hope the ongoing discussions do not turn the next century's critical need for water action into policy mist.

HOW DONORS CAN HELP

WERNER FORNOS
May 1999

At the threshold of a new millennium, world population will surpass six billion—a staggering figure in itself but one that also represents a tripling of the planet's human numbers in little more than two generations.

Never has the correlation between rapid demographic growth, economic stagnation and social disintegration been so clearly defined. Virtually all of the world's annual population increase—98 percent—occurs in the less developed countries of Africa, Asia and Latin America, or some 100 million people each year. These are precisely the regions that experience the most direct and severe impact of poverty, hunger, unemployment and resource depletion. A few cold statistics reflect the magnitude of the connection between population and development: Approximately 1.3 billion people live in absolute poverty—surviving on the equivalent of $1 or less per day. Six hundred million people are homeless or without adequate shelter. Almost one quarter of the world's population—1.5 billion people—lack an adequate supply of drinking water. Roughly 840 million people are malnourished and 86 countries are unable to grow or purchase enough food to feed their populations. An estimated 2.3 billion people are without adequate sanitation.

In addition, environmental deterioration—much of it directly attributable to human activity—has reached chilling proportions. Twenty-six billion tons of arable topsoil vanish from the world's cropland every year. Six hundred thousand square miles of forest were cut down in the last decade. Massive deforestation leads to widespread desertification. New deserts worldwide are expected to equal the size of the continental United States by 2010. Global climate change is disrupting weather patterns, causing more severe droughts and flooding, and increased threats to human health.

Curtailing population growth alone may not dramatically reverse the planet's social and environmental ills, but unless human fertility is substantially reduced there is little hope for meaningful improvement of the human condition. Population and family planning programs are a relatively recent intervention in the world's less developed countries. Although most of these efforts were not initiated until the 1960s and 1970s, there have been a number of notable successes. Contraceptive prevalence among married women of reproductive age has increased over the past 30 years from 25 percent to 56 percent. The annual rate of world population growth has declined from 2.06 percent to 1.4 percent. Within the past decade, the annual increase in human number has slowed down from almost 90 million to less than 80 million.

While these demographic trends are both important and encouraging, they do not signal victory in the world's continuing struggle to contain its human growth. The difference between the impact of population growing by 80 million rather than by 90 million per year can be compared to the difference between the relative damage resulting from tidal waves of 80 and 90 feet.

Perhaps a more encouraging trend is the sea change in perceptions of population growth among developing world leaders that has taken place over the last quarter of this century. When the World Population Conference was held in Bucharest in 1974, the notion that enormous benefits could be derived by reducing population growth was viewed with blatant skepticism by developing world leaders. Many were of the opinion that fewer people meant fewer hands and minds to build and smaller armies to defend their countries.

There was also concern that the urging to curb population growth emanated from the industrialized world. Why should developing nations trust any admonition from their former colonial masters? These lingering doubts were readily understandable. Often, private nongovernmental organizations established family planning clinics in developing countries to demonstrate that people were comfortable with using their services before national programs were launched.

At the 1984 International Conference on Population in Mexico City, developing country delegations were virtually unanimous in their comprehension of the linkages between reducing fertility and achieving durable development progress. More than a few leaders of developing countries had learned by this time the hard lesson that a doubling of their countries' populations within 20 years, more or less, placed unbearable pressures on schools, job opportunities, hospitals and, in fact, wreaked havoc on the entire social and economic infrastructure.

When the 1994 International Conference on Population and Development was held in Cairo, population and family planning programs were in place throughout the developing world. By and large, the only remaining impediment to these programs was the objections raised by religious fundamentalists. But in countries as far apart geographically, politically and in religious beliefs as Iran and the Philippines, fundamentalist precepts and dogma are seriously challenged by the hard realities of poverty, hunger, unemployment and illiteracy.

Religious fundamentalists and their anti-family-planning political allies present an obstacle for the realization of population stabilization. Their influence has been of most concern in the United States, where Congress has cut off the US contribution to the United Nations Population Fund (UNFPA)—the largest multilateral organization providing population assistance to the world's poorest countries. But family planning opponents have been pushing this agenda for several years with sporadic victories rather than uniform success, and their influence remains primarily confined to the United States; no other industrialized country has ceased its contribution to UNFPA.

Opponents of international family planning assistance in the United States and elsewhere can be expected to accelerate charges of coercion in various developing country population programs. The cessation of the US contribution to UNFPA was attributable to allegations of force and coercion in the Chinese national family planning program, which receives assistance from the UN agency. Pronatalists have learned that while there is widespread public acceptance of voluntary abortion where it is legal, as well as sterilization, the public will not tolerate human rights violations in family planning programs. Proponents of population stabilization must be vigilant in supporting only voluntary family planning programs. At the same time, parliamentarians and policy makers must understand that some overzealous pronatalists are not above making false accusations of coercion and force.

The common denominator of the Bucharest, Mexico City and Cairo conferences was universal access to family planning information, education and services. As the 20th Century draws to a close, the most relevant change has been in the packaging of this proposition. In more recent years, the emphasis has shifted from a focus on reducing human numbers to improving reproductive health, gender equality and equity and the empowerment of women. But the bottom line—achieving a more equitable balance between population, environment and resources—remains the same.

Rapid population growth is one of the few global problems that are on the brink of a solution. There is near unanimity among world leaders that such growth is dangerously detrimental to development. The technology to solve the problem—a variety of effective and safe contraceptive methods—is available; though there is always room for improvement in the areas of safety and efficiency.

An estimated 350 million women of reproductive age lack access to family planning. Of these, studies indicate that 120 million would immediately use a contraceptive method if it were available. There is realistic hope that world population will level off at 8.5 billion, or less. Five countries—India, China, Pakistan, Indonesia and Nigeria—account for 50 percent of population increase today. By redoubling efforts in those five countries, world population can be stabilized at less than the 10 or 12 billion projected in the medium and high-projection scenarios of the United Nations Population Division.

First and foremost, stabilizing world population will require more responsible reproductive behavior by the 3 billion people—especially the men among them—who will enter their reproductive years during the next generation. This is not an insurmountable hurdle. Couples will be better educated than any previous reproductive generation and they should have access to broader contraceptive knowledge, as well as a wider choice of contraceptives that are more effective, efficient and safe than have been available to any generation heretofore.

Of equal significance is a new era of communication and information accessibility. Techniques used in modern advertising campaigns are employed to promote smaller family size and contraceptives in many developing countries. These include utilizing every conceivable medium from street theater to posters and billboards to newspapers, magazines, radio and television. Surveys and studies in all less developed regions indicate that these communication strategies have enormously bolstered public awareness of the benefits of family planning.

Last, but far from least, achieving population stabilization as soon as it is reasonably possible will require the political will to provide the necessary resources to implement universal access to family planning. The delivery of population assistance must compete with the plethora of development priorities that exist in every poor country in the world.

The cost to ensure voluntary family planning and reproductive health services by the year 2000 for every couple that needs and wants them is $17 billion—the equivalent of one week of the world's expenditure on armaments. Meeting the challenges of development in the new millennium will, in the final analysis, hinge on the budgetary priorities of world leaders: perhaps boiling down to a choice between increasing firepower or reducing fertility.

THE AFRICAN CENTURY

DJIBRIL DIALLO
June 1999

Last September at the United Nations in New York, I was honored to co-chair a town hall meeting on Africa in the 21st Century which featured the current Chairman of the Organization of African Unity, President Blaise Compaore of Burkina Faso.

President Compaore told the audience of African diplomats, UN officials, media and representatives of nongovernmental organizations that Africans are obliged to be active citizens of the world if we no longer want to be marginalized as the millennium approaches. "For so long," he said, "Africa has been torn apart—so much plagues some African countries, that we lost our landmarks. We didn't have any vision to change the course of poverty and strife which plagues African countries. We need to have aspirations."

Only a few months ago, Africa was the toast of the world as Bill Clinton embarked on the most extensive tour of Africa by any sitting US President. Enjoying a warm welcome throughout his trip, Clinton spoke of an African renaissance while commentators painted a picture of a new Africa—an Africa beyond the stories of the conflict, hunger and drought. They saw an Africa emerging as a major force in the international economic and political arena.

The sense of optimism that they espoused was not misplaced. In fact, in terms of economic performance, Africa has posted an enviable record in the past few years. From a history of negative economic growth, African nations are now achieving record levels of growth. The economies of 33 African nations are now achieving new levels of positive economic growth. In 1996, 20 countries had GDP growth of 5 percent or more. The list includes 11 countries who recorded economic growth rates of 6 percent or higher. During the same period, declines in GDP were recorded in only two of the countries for which data was available.

At the political level, the continent continues to make major strides. More and more African countries are democratizing. Multi-party elections are being held and increasing focus is being put on transparency and governance.

But even in the midst of progress, Africa remains a continent in great need. The 1998 Human Development Report reveals hard facts that show a continent that must still call on the international community for support as it seeks to reach its development goals. The Report, commissioned by the United Nations Development Programme (UNDP), focused on consumption for human development. It found that Africa continues to lag behind in many of the key human development indices. For instance, not only does Africa lag significantly behind all other regions in the consumption of goods and services, but over the last 30 years the region achieved only marginal improvements in consumption. Moreover, a serious consumption shortfall exists for most people in the region.

Some of the numbers are staggering. The report found that of the $5 trillion total consumption expenditure in the developing world in 1995, Africa accounted for only $2 billion. In 1999, the world is expected to consume $24 trillion in goods and services. Africa will account for an insignificant portion of that figure. The report also found that people around the world are consuming more in food, energy, education, transportation, communication and entertainment than ever before. They are living longer and enjoying greater personal freedom because of better access to health services, education, productive resources, credit and technologies. But do not be fooled by this global trend. Gross inequalities in consumption mean that most people in Africa are excluded from this progress since they fail to meet even the basic consumption requirements.

Gross inequalities in consumption mean that most people in Africa are excluded from progress.

Ranking countries according to their Human Development Index, the report found that out of the 174 countries it covered, the bottom 15 were from Africa. Sierra Leone brought up the rear and was followed by Niger and Burkina Faso.

Not surprisingly, the report also found that only two of the richest 225 people in the world are from Africa. The two, both white South Africans worth a combined $4 billion, account for only a meager fraction of the $1.1 billion owned by this group of the super rich.

The reason for Africa's poor showing becomes obvious when some of the data is analyzed. There is an abject lack of basic social services across the continent, creating a serious obstacle in dealing with consumption shortfalls. Of the 543 million people in the region, 184 million have no access to safe water, 436 million lack health services and 510 million are without basic sanitation.

In the area of nutrition, Africa's per capita daily calorie intake of 2,236 falls far below the developing countries' average of 2,571 calories per day and the required minimum of 2,300 calories per day. While average protein consumption is 115 grams per day in France, it is only 32 grams in Mozambique. In Sweden, Switzerland and the United States, there are more than 600 telephone lines per 1,000 people, but in Chad, there is one telephone line per 1,000. On average, sub-Saharan Africa has 12 telephone lines per 1,000 people. Also, while the industrialized countries have an average of 405 automobiles per 1,000 people, in sub-Saharan Africa, there are only 11 automobiles per 1,000.

In general, globalization has not helped Africa. Instead it has resulted in the marginalization of the people. Little direct investment has been attracted to the continent. Only 1.4 percent of the $280 billion invested around the world went to Africa in 1998. At the same time, factors such as HIV/AIDs and environmental degradation continue to wreak havoc on the continent. Almost 20 million people in Africa are living with HIV; and in many countries, the prevalence of the disease has reduced expected lifespans, reversing trends in human development. Life expectancy has been cut by as much as 16 years in parts of Uganda and, if the current trend continues, by 2010, it will be shorter by 25 years in Zimbabwe. As a consequence of the HIV/AIDS epidemic, more and more households are being headed by children following the death of parents.

But Africa's fate is one shared by millions around the world, including in the industrialized countries. In many of the inner cities of the world's richest countries, the same deprivations are present in varying degrees and forms. For instance, although the industrialized countries have achieved universal schooling and are regarded as "literate," an average of 8 percent of the adults in 12 European and North American countries were found to have such low levels of proficiency that they "cannot meet even basic reading requirements of a modern society." In the United States, functional illiteracy prevents 21 percent of the people from performing basic tasks such as reading instructions on a medicine bottle or reading a story to a child.

That many African countries were able to turn around their economies and are now enjoying growth is proof that, with the right policies and support, Africa can set itself on the path to true development. The challenge is for the international community to commit itself to giving the continent the support it needs in the new millennium, which can certainly be the African Century.

DOING GOOD: STEVEN RATTNER'S PHILANTHROPY

RICHARD F. SHEPARD
March 1998

For ordinary mortals you might call it conservation. But in the case of Steven Rattner, let's call it re-investment. Rattner is an investment banker. That's a calling that often sends shudders through people who are dedicated to achieving a salutary global environment. For them big money often seems to accompany big greed and big earthly mutilation. But it ain't necessarily so. At least not in terms of personal involvement, of bankers as well as of bootblacks.

Rattner is Deputy Chief Executive of Lazard Freres & Co. LLC, a financial wizard who founded the company's Communications Group, which has handled more than $100 billion worth of media transactions, a record in that field and certainly an eyecatcher when you're teaching basic banking to the folks in Bangladesh. He has been a key person in Microsoft's $1 billion investment in Comcast, in the sale of Continental Cablevision to US West, of Paramount Communications to Viacom, of AT&T's buy-up of McCaw Cellular Communications, of the sale of MGM studios. There, does that put him in focus?

From journalism to the highest reaches of global finance, a story of good deeds for social causes.

Not in sharp focus for those of us whose connection with any of the above goes no further than twisting a dial and sending them in a payment every month. Rattner is also that species we designate Concerned Citizen. He plays a role in environmental issues and those affecting our society in general. To put it another way, Steven Rattner is powerful.

He is probably more representative of the welcome outsider when it comes to such matters than the person who gives up everything and immolates the self on the altar of total dedication. Rattner regards himself as a spear-carrier in the ongoing drama of worthy causes rather than as a leader.

He believes that there are those more worthy of attention in such arenas. Over the years, Rattner has given millions to philanthropic causes—and his giving reflects the increasing generosity of Americans towards causes such as the environment and population. In 1998, charitable giving by Americans was projected to climb 11 percent to a record $175 billion, according to the American Association of Fund-Raising Counsel, whose not-for-profit arm, the AAFRC Trust for Philanthropy, publishes an annual report on charitable donations titled Giving USA. [According to Giving USA, individuals increased their giving by 10 percent in 1998 to $135 billion—77 percent of the overall giving total. Giving by foundations grew by 23 percent in 1998 to $17 billion—foundations are required by law to give away an amount equal to 5 percent of their assets, according to The New York Times's Karen W. Arenson. Giving USA also reported that corporate giving rose 9 percent in 1998, and amounted to 1 percent of corporate pretax income, while bequests amounted to $13.6 billion, an 8 percent increase from 1997.]

> Rattner exemplifies a new type of executive who believes that it's important to pay society back.

"I've always thought it important to put something back," he mused in a telephone interview. "There are a lot of people who do a lot. Some do more than I do. It's not a 100 percent of them. Among people in my field it's mixed. There are probably a group of people not attuned to this kind of thing. Probably a significant number do try. But there is a sense among the banking community that you put something back."

The business of "putting back" has won him seats in the board rooms of some of our most prestigious, and varied, societal enterprises as a Global Leader for Tomorrow by the World Economic Forum. Last year, he was appointed by President Clinton to the Commission to Study Capital Budgeting and he also serves on the International Competition Policy Advisory Committee. For good measure throw in boards and/or trusteeships on the Council of Foreign Relations, the Metropolitan Museum of Art, the New York Outward Bound Center, the Royal Institute of International Affairs (an associate) and the Educational Broadcasting Corporation (Channel 13), where he's chairman—and you have the picture, not all of it but most of it. He's also done work for the Nature Conservancy.

Rattner is a former correspondent for The New York Times. In the paper's Washington bureau in the late 1970s, he distinguished himself on the economics and energy beats; a couple of cover stories in The New York Times Magazine reinforced his reputation as a savvy reporter and one who enjoyed access to Washington insiders. His Washington stint earned him a posting in The Times's London bureau, where Rattner also focused on energy, including coverage of the byzantine politics of the Organization of Petroleum Exporting Countries (OPEC).

Journalism remains an abiding love for Rattner. He is also an enthusiastic alumnus, and trustee, of Brown University (class of '74, honors in economics, with a Harvey Baker Fellowship). In his time, there was less direction toward such philanthropic after-hours activity. That he finds time for philanthropy and engagement with social issues at all is testimony to a highly disciplined schedule of 18-hour days at his New York office and considerable travel (Rattner, who holds a pilot's license, often flies his own plane).

There's also his closely knit family. Maureen White, Rattner's wife, is a former investment banker who is engaged with humanitarian and refugee issues, notably at Unicef (where she has been US representative for the last several years). They have four children: Rebecca, 10; twins David and Daniel, 7; and James, 6, who's known as "Izzy."

"Through my involvement with Brown, I see the success they are having in instilling young people with a sense of community service," the 43-year old Rattner observed. "There is an emphasis on public service that is making an impression on young people."

Why this trend, perhaps not a surge, to work for the public weal on the part of those who have found success in the private sector?

"A good question, maybe we are living in a more gentle age," Rattner said. "There are a lot of ways to do it. There are those who work for profit, some who work for some profit then go to something else. There are those of us who are willing to put in time, a struggle sometimes—when you're very busy in the office there is little time left.

"These organizations are used to people who are interested in their work, but as a second priority. Some are more active, some are less. Generally, most people in business have been successful in the last few years. This has given them the desire to put things back. Very few of my friends are not involved in things that do not have a nonprofit aspect."

Rattner paused and then concluded, "I'm having fun at what I'm doing, investment banking, but can't do just that: I have to put something back."

TED TURNER, CONSERVATION, AND OUR COLLECTIVE FUTURE

MARK MURO
June 1999

The fact that Ted Turner owns a million acres of the American state of New Mexico—1 percent of the state and twice the acreage of all its national parks—speaks in a sense only to the largeness of one man's ego. Turner and his ranches, to that extent, don't stand for anything. They are aberrations—like the media mogul's 1997 pledge of $1 billion to the United Nations.

Yet from another perspective, Turner's immense real-estate kingdom does signify, and powerfully, something very important about the future. It epitomizes the growing centrality of private lands, and size, in conservation.

Begin with the sheer dimensions of Turner's three New Mexico spreads and others he owns in Montana and Wyoming. Of a size to rival numerous federal wildlife preserves, Turner's spreads reassert—admittedly in a special way—the continuing need to think big in conservation. "Big" is truly "beautiful" in ecology. Moreover, since Turner is painstakingly restoring the ranches' ecosystems, properties like his 300,000-acre Armendaris Ranch near Truth Or Consequences, New Mexico—which rivals Grand Teton National Park in size—bear special significance. They answer vibrantly to the need to preserve big wilderness, whether in Brazil or India. And they point to a future whose great story must become the reassembly of fragmented landscapes even as governments retreat and population growth tear ecosystems to pieces. Putting the pieces back together is where it's all going.

Yet more than the size of Ted Turner's eco-correct barony in America makes it significant. So, too, does its other striking attribute: its private ownership. Such ownership reorients conservation dramatically to the private lands after a long federal or governmental era of control.

In practical terms, this emphasis sharpens the realization that government conservation laws need to interface better with the private lands. Note that the Environmental Defense Fund recently observed that half or more of the species protected by America's Endangered Species Act have at least 81 percent of their habitat on private land. This suggests conservation must take more seriously the needs of land owners who insist, for example, that the Endangered Species Act unduly inconveniences people who discover endangered species on their land. This, in turn, implies that the best conservation strategies for the future, whether in Siberia or Chile, will make generous use of positive incentives for stewardship—tax breaks for conservation easements, start-up grants for green projects, bounties for inevitable development. Governments, in other words, will bring conservation about, but they won't control it, dominate it or predetermine it.

Additionally, the private status of Ted Turner's ranches touches on a deeper reason for environmentalists to look to the private lands. For a century, conservation has turned on governments' embrace of what the science writer David Quammen has called the protected-area strategy. The idea has been that governments would save nature by creating a collection of national parks, wildlife refuges and designated "wilderness" islands set apart from the surrounding disruption. And the approach has worked to an extent. All told, roughly 8,000 protected areas now exist worldwide, comprising about 4 percent of the planet's land surface.

Only now it turns out that even the largest protected areas don't work well enough. Everywhere, even within the sanctuaries, biodiversity is waning, in part thanks to the tendency of insularized or fragmented ecosystems to lose biological richness over time. The reality is that government reserves can never save enough land. And that is what makes doubly important all the private land in between those reserves, whether Ted Turner's and Jane Fonda's or yours. Here, across the 96 percent of the planet that remains unprotected, is where mankind must learn to cohabitate with nature.

This, then, is the ultimate significance of Ted Turner's great ranch—as well as of everybody's humble backyard, or the nearby logging company's holdings. Such places—all places eventually—point beyond the compartmentalized present-day world of public and private, protected and unprotected, managed and unmanaged, to a universe of shared responsibility. The planet is not a collection of reserves and pieces but one biosphere, one world. All of us must be stewards now—Ted and Jane and you and all of us.

Given that, Ted Turner is doing as great a good with his big ranches as he is doing with his big gift to the United Nations. He's showing where it's all going—and that is to the private lands, and the big places.

AND WHAT ABOUT THE SOUL?

FIELDS WICKER-MIURIN
March 1998

My perspective is one of someone who has had a privileged life. I have had a comfortable life, a protected life. I have never been tortured. I have never been persecuted or discriminated against (at least as far as I know). I have never wanted for shelter, for food or for education. Mine has been a lucky life, a life of opportunity and optimism. My perspective on the soul, therefore, reflects this life.

But I, like us all, do carry my own labels—labels which color my perspective on the 21st Century and the soul. First, there are the obvious labels. I am white, female, "young" and American. And then there are the less obvious labels: I am a Global Leader for Tomorrow, a "GLT" duly certified by the prestigious World Economic Forum—and very proud to be one. So the perspective I will give is the result of the combination of all of these labels and of the life I have lived.

What about my soul?

As we near the end of one millennium and the beginning of a new one, we often hear discussion of big trends—like globalization and its impact on peoples of different cultures and societies around the world; like technology and the rapid progress being made in bringing parts of the world together, perhaps leaving other parts—and people—behind. But how often do we stop and ask ourselves, explicitly, about our souls? What kind of question is that? you ask. I believe, especially as we approach the new millennium, it is a very pertinent question to ask. And it was one on which I was asked to comment at the World Economic Forum's Annual Meeting at Davos in February 1998. As I thought about the 21st Century and my soul, I realized I had three very simple but fundamental beliefs.

The first is, I hope, uncontroversial, and that is that the soul is important. It is more important than most political and business leaders realize, and that is our challenge. Our soul is what differentiates us (or at least what we believe differentiates us) from other forms of life; it's what makes us human.

Therefore, if we ignore it, we risk losing our humanity. South Africa's Archbishop Desmond Tutu—a Nobel Laureate—speaks of *ubuntu*, the marvelous African concept of humanity through the interconnectedness of humans. I am human because of my dependence on you and interconnectedness with you. This makes me think of the opening lines of a poem written almost 200 years ago by William Wordsworth, which go like this:

The world is too much with us, late and soon
getting and spending we lay waste our powers
little we see in Nature that is ours
We have given our hearts away, a sordid boon

Which brings me to my second belief: If we don't want to give our hearts away, if we really do believe our soul is important, then we have to nourish it, to feed it, to nurture it. When our body is hungry, we feed it. When our body and our minds are tired, we sleep. But what do we do about our soul? What do we do to feed and nourish our soul? In the 21st Century, in order to cope with the impact of technology, with the impact of globalization and with the "death of distance," I believe we must learn how to nourish our soul, to nourish it actively and consciously, as a priority in our lives. I believe this is important, not only to flourish, but also to survive. There may be many ways we can do this. The way I have found, in my "sabbatical for my soul," is through art and creativity, empathy and compassion for our fellow human beings. To create, and to give.

There is much talk about the divide between business and the arts, between our left brain and our right brain, between our head and our heart. Although the divisions may be correct technically, I believe it is artificial in a "life" sense. For me the magic of being human is that we have both a head and a heart. Perhaps we ourselves have constructed this divide as a mistaken self-defense to "protect" us from the other half, with which we are less comfortable, believing that if we classify and categorize the unfamiliar or the uncomfortable we will be better able to cope.

I participated recently in a discussion about whether art could prepare us for the 21st Century. There was much discussion, both ways, about the role of art in terms of preparing society for anything, much less the millennium. But there was almost universal consensus when we spoke of the role of art in nourishing our souls.

Art, however expressed, overcomes the superimposed barriers—the filters—of society, of language, of custom and geography. It goes straight through all these filters, straight to the heart, to your core self, to your soul. When you listen to a beautiful sonata, or stand before a work of art that inspires you, that beauty, that art is speaking directly to you, to your heart and to your soul. And you feel it, and respond to it. And your soul quivers.

In my own experience, at the London International Festival of Theater, I have seen the power of theater to transcend borders and bring people together through the experience of participating, each in his or her own way, in works of art and creativity from around the world. This is something we need to do more of. Especially as traditional frontiers and barriers come down, we need to find new ways to bring people together. If, not, we risk losing our way, our center and our *ubuntu*.

And this brings me to my third belief and proposition. We need to have

As traditional frontiers and barriers come down, we need to find new ways to bring people together.

the courage of our convictions and of our values, especially as the boundaries and "comfort zones" of our known physical and intellectual worlds vanish and disappear. Here I am speaking not only to political and business leaders, but also to leaders of communities, of education and of culture and the arts. I am speaking to the young and the older, but especially to the young—for you are our future. As a business person, I will share a story from the business world. A while ago, a FT-SE 100 company (that is, one of the top 100 companies in Britain, cited by The Financial Times), named a woman (an American) as Chief Executive Officer. She was the first woman chief executive ever of a FT-SE 100 company. This woman was either naïve or courageous enough in one of her first interviews after her appointment to say what she really believed about management and performance.

She said that her people, her employees, came first. That is, if she cared about them and nurtured them as humans, that if she invested in their development, then they would work better, the customers would benefit and profit improvement would follow.

Well, you can imagine what happened. The shares of her company slumped while the city laughed.

One year later, when the same city analysts voted on which CEO had been most effective in managing the performance of his/her company, guess who came out on top? Yes, you're right. She did. So perhaps, slowly, we are beginning to learn.

When I look around me, the people we admire most, including my colleagues on the Davos panel (Archbishop Tutu and Elie Wiesel, both Nobel

Laureates), are those who have used their hearts as well as their heads to pursue truth, to respect the dignity of individuals, to protect and nurture mankind, to do what is right, courageously, in their own worlds, however large or small their own arena. They have shown us that we can shape the world. The world reflects our values, our priorities, not the other way around. It is up to us to shape the world we will live in the 21st Century. We have a choice. We can do nothing and watch the implications, good and bad, of the changes around us. Or we can lead through example; we can actively use our hearts to reach out to others, use our creativity to build bridges and find a common language, use our humanity to care for other humans and to nurture our souls.

We are the custodians of the values we learned from our families and through our education; it is our responsibility to pass those values on to the next generation. All of which underlines the importance of the family, of educating and caring for the young around the world, of enabling people to develop and maintain dignity in their lives through their work, whatever that work is, and through their constructive participation in society.

My generation, which will be of the age and have the experience to begin to lead in the early 21st Century, has a real responsibility to lead with courage, with honesty, with clear values and with our hearts as well as our heads.

And as we prepare for this responsibility, we ask our current leaders to show us the way, to demonstrate the same courage, integrity and humanity we will need to take the baton forward.

THE AILING ALPS AND THE FUTURE OF MOUNTAINS

PAUL HOFMANN
August 1998

INNSBRUCK, Austria—On some days this summer there was hardly any space on top of the 15,771-foot-high Mont Blanc, the loftiest peak in the Alps. The icy ledge, barely 200 feet wide, was crowded with mountain buffs and their professional guides who had just achieved the demanding ascent from Chamonix, Courmayeur or other starting points in France and Italy. Some who had made it to the summit were exhausted; others took pictures of the stunning panorama, which encompasses Lake Geneva, the Alpine ranges toward east and the Apennines in the south; and a few dudes found nothing better to do than call their loved ones at home on their cell phones: "Guess where I am."

Similar scenes could be observed atop the pale limestone towers of the Italian Dolomites which just before sunset dramatically light up in purple hues, and on many other famous heights along the 750-mile arc of Europe's principal mountain system. The Alps, sweeping from the French Mediterranean coast by way of Switzerland, Italy and Austria to Vienna and to points near the Adriatic Sea in Slovenia, are mobbed summer and winter now.

What is happening in the mountainous heart of developed Europe is paralleled by similar developments on and around the globe's other mighty ranges from Nepal to Chile. If mass alpinism isn't brought under control it threatens to destroy some of the Earth's great natural wonders.

As for Europe, in addition to experienced climbers and would-be mountaineers more than 50 million people head for the Alps each year for skiing, hiking, camping or just taking it easy for awhile. The periodic invasions of guests are lucrative for the locals but cause deepening concerns because of their ecological consequences.

The impact of mass tourism on a unique environment is compounded by severe transportation problems. More than seven million trucks and heavy rigs wheeze across the Alps every year now. At the same time some 50 million cars annually pour through the mountain passes and tunnels that are the—relatively few—gateways piercing the majestic north-south divide, the Continent's spine.

Trans-Alpine commercial traffic has increased tenfold during the last 25 years, a result of ballooning economic exchanges within the 15-nation European Union. The recent uplifting of border controls between France, Italy, Germany and Austria is bound to cause a further surge in transports across the Alps.

The heavy motor traffic peaks with car jams, often several miles long, on the motorways during the main vacation periods. The once salubrious air in the picturesque valleys and quaint towns is fouled by exhaust fumes.

The atmospheric pollution and traffic noises are major complaints from the 13 million people who live in the Alps and from a rising number of seasonal visitors. Protest movements have been active for years. In June 1998 thousands of Tyroleans blocked the motorway between Innsbruck, the regional capital, and the 4,508-foot-high Brenner Pass for 24 hours to call international attention to their plight. The organizers of the sit-in pointed out that 1.2 million trailer trucks and other commercial vehicles passed the Brenner motorway—statistically, one every 30 seconds on average—during 1997, and that according to projections their number would swell to two million by 2010.

If mass alpinism isn't brought under control it threatens to destroy some of the Earth's great natural wonders.

The inhabitants of the towns and villages along the Brenner Road describe the air and noise pollution as intolerable. They demand that an old project to modernize the venerable Brenner Railroad (built 1863-1867) be at last realized and that a long rail tunnel be built under the famous pass so that a major portion of freight traffic can be handled by goods trains.

Switzerland has warned its neighbors that by 2004 all through-freight across the Alps must be carried by rail (mainly on the Simplon and St. Gotthard lines). Already trucks of over 28 metric tons are banned from crossing the Swiss Alps. So far, less than a third of all freight hauled through the Alps rolls on rail tracks.

The vogue of Alpine vacations is blamed for even heavier ecological damage than is wrought by commercial traffic. For decades many scenic valleys and slopes have seen an explosive building and development boom—new garish hotels, boarding houses, condominiums, second homes for city dwellers, mountain refuges, eating places, cableways, chair lifts, ski runs, swimming pools, skating rinks and golf courses.

All these amenities require new access roads, water mains, sewerages and power lines. Thus the habitat of Alpine wildlife—deer, foxes, many smaller animals, freshwater fish and, in remote corners, a few wolves and brown bears—is being continuously narrowed. Lepidopterists deplore the disappearance of some butterfly species. Botanists worry about the survival of many of the 11,000 kinds of Alpine flora; 350 species of plants—including varieties of the white-dawny edelweiss (Leontopodium alpinus)—grow nowhere else. Formerly crystal-clear streams are now loaded with wastes, and the "river trout" served in wood-paneled restaurants come mostly from fish farms.

If garbage left behind by thin-air climbers today soils the Himalayas, the plague is immensely worse in the Alps. Wild animals have long learned to forage in the overflowing trash cans in the early morning hours when they aren't yet frightened away by motor traffic and yodelling tourists. But plastic bags and other debris litter also the glaciers and ravines.

In 1996 all states sharing in the mountain system agreed on an Alpine Convention aimed at safeguarding the regional biosphere; some participating countries still have to enact the document. The International Commission for the Protection of the Alps, a voluntary body, is lobbying for the extension of national parks, which today cover only one-eighth of Alpine territory.

The uniqueness of the Alps lies not only in their natural beauties but also in overwhelming evidence of very old mountain cultures. Ancient farmhouses, barns, churches, bridges, canals and trails still hold their own next to new supermarkets in mock-mountaineer style.

How old human presence in the towering mountains is was shown up by the startling discovery seven years ago of a mummified body in a glacier at 11,817 feet altitude on the main crest of the Alps between Italy and Austria. The Iceman was equipped with a flint dagger, a copper axe, a bow, arrows and other artifacts. Scientists from various nations determined that the mummy, first brought to the University of Innsbruck, was that of a shepherd or hunter who had perished, probably in a snowstorm, more than 5,000 years ago. The Iceman now rests in a controlled environment at a museum in Bolzano, the capital of the Italian South Tyrol.

Many tourists who whiz across the Brenner Pass in their cars stop in Bolzano to view the remains of the mountaineer who in the Younger Stone Age succumbed to the high mountains.

CHALLENGES FOR THE 21ST CENTURY

KLAUS SCHWAB
June 1999

The motto of the World Economic Forum and the guiding philosophy in my own life has always been "Entrepreneurship in the global public interest."

Let me start with entrepreneurship, which is best defined as daring undertaking. Vision, risk taking, courage, action—these are the dimensions of entrepreneurship. Entrepreneurship certainly means leadership, but it means more: namely, creative leadership. Whom do you consider as the true leaders in today's world who can deal with the key problems associated with population and development? Who comes to your mind? Politicians? Entrepreneurs? My guess is that the names coming up are likely to be Bill Gates (Microsoft), Jack Welch (General Electric), Percy Barnevik (Investor AB), Ted Turner (CNN)—and not necessarily Bill Clinton, Tony Blair, Jacques Chirac, Boris Yeltsin or Gerhard Schröder.

Entrepreneurs are eager to challenge rather than submit themselves to the orthodoxies of our age. They are shaping the future rather than promising it. They are movers and shakers and not firefighters. But let's not blame the politicians. Politics has always been the art of the possible, entrepreneurship the art of the impossible. If an entrepreneur says impossible, he finds himself interrupted by someone who just did it!

The 21st Century will be the age of globalization. The technological revolution of the microchip and the Internet have taught us that all types of "walls" have crumbled in a world that is becoming more virtual than material. The Web puts power in the hands of people in a way that the voting ballot could never do. The "netizen" replaces the citizen.

In a borderless world it is difficult for politicians and national leaders to flourish, to lead. Since they have to be elected, their survival depends on their ability to rescue those who are left behind by the growing forces of change. Politicians are applauded by those who regret the passing of the good old world of relative stability, of well-traced borderlines between nation-states, between social classes, between hierarchical levels. By contrast, the borderless world is a paradise for entrepreneurs.

Joseph Schumpeter, a famous Harvard professor, coined the notion of creative destruction, the perpetual cycle of destroying the old and replacing it with the new, in his book "Capitalism, Socialism and Democracy." Entrepreneurs are constructive in a reconstructive world. Unlike politicians, they are not driven by voters, who resist change, but by customers and shareholders, who make sure that only those who provide superior value in a mega-competitive world will survive and prosper.

The clash in the world is not, as Professor Samuel Huntington, another well-known Harvard faculty member, says, a "clash of civilizations." The biggest challenge for our world is the reconciliation of tradition and innovation within each civilization. And we are only at the beginning! Bill Gates' new book, "Business@the Speed of Thought," starts with the sentence, "Business is going to change more in the next 10 years than it has in the last 50." Equally, we could say, "Life is going to change more in the next 10 years than it has in the last 50."

The conflict between entrepreneurs and politicians is not only the expression of an antipolarity between a world without borders and one still built on the illusion of borders, particularly borders to protect the present against the future. No, the conflict between entrepreneurs and politicians is a violent collision between the winners and the losers of change.

Globalization is an irreversible fact of life. But "time compression," the accelerating role of change, outpaces the ability of societies, their political systems and their leaders to adjust to the new challenge brought about by globalization.

The sheer pace of change in technology, finance and workplaces has outstripped people's ability to cope. The reaction is simply to opt out because things are happening too fast. There is repulsion at the widening discrepancy between the losers and winners of globalization. But the increasing inequality is often confused with poverty even though at the bottom they may feel the same. The reality of globalization is increased inequality but also decreased poverty.

But not only the poor or the losers resist globalization; people of middle age and up perceive that globalization undermines the stability of their life achievements. They feel that they have lost control and they want to have assurance that national politicians are doing something about their "securitization."

Our whole interrelated system with its economic, political and social dimensions is under tremendous pressure. We would be deceiving ourselves if we assume that we can avoid the breakdown of the system by decoupling economics from politics and social issues. Secretary General Kofi Annan of the United Nations said [at the World Economic Forum's Annual Meeting] in Davos this year, "History teaches us that such an imbalance between the economic, social and political realms can never be sustained for very long."

Thus, "Entrepreneurship in the global public interest" is the only way to move forward. In the process of constructive deconstruction, entrepreneurs have to embrace values that show a true commitment to improving the state of the world—for all people. The prototype of the entrepreneur of the 21st Century has to be the "social" entrepreneur, or there will be no entrepreneur any more, as we will all be annihilated by social destruction. Social entrepreneurship in the 20th Century meant primarily the provision of social safety nets and other material measures to limit the damage done to the victims of the industrial revolution. But today the social responsibility of the entrepreneur has to be adapted to new realities, the "soft" issues that characterize the ongoing revolution of globalization.

Responsible globality will require adherence to a set of fundamental values. First, we have to be aware that we are living in a global village where, in principle, everybody has the capacity to be our direct neighbor and to interact with us. The "death of distance," as Francis Cairncross of The Economist puts it, means that we have to be concerned about the fundamental rights of each of those neighbors. The worldwide preservation and development of human rights is one core value of responsible globality.

Second, we are the trustees of future generations' environmental sustainability of entrepreneurship, which is another indispensable value of responsible globality.

Third, the notion of work will completely change in the new world. As a result of the fast pace of change, employment will not come from without but from within each individual. Employment has to be self-generated by permanently updating one's own capabilities. Employment becomes a function of employability. This creates a new social responsibility for any entrepreneur who provides employment. In the same way as he invests permanently in the maintenance of his physical infrastructure, he has to invest permanently in the maintenance of the employability of people. Laying off someone is not unsocial *per se* in a superflexible economy, but the same cannot be said of depriving people of continued employability. To stimulate and provide lifelong education is another core value of globality.

In conclusion, business leaders have to become business politicians and embrace, support and enact a set of core values in human rights, environmental stewardship, population and education practices. Or in broader terms: "Entrepreneurship in the global public interest" means to foster social development, sustainable development and human development. In those areas, business leaders can make a real difference both individually and through partnerships with all sectors of society.

Entrepreneurship with no social, environmental and human responsibility can easily degenerate into brutality; social, environmental and human responsibility without entrepreneurship flies by as a sweet dream—like a great vision without the necessary creation and allocation of resources. But entrepreneurship in the global public interest can change the world. The response to the industrial revolution, which shaped the course of the 20th Century, was—after much bitter suffering—the welfare state. Now the sovereignty of states is put into question as well as the sustainability of traditional collective welfare programs.

Today, at the dawn of a new century, and confronted with business that can just emigrate from national regulatory frameworks, new international regulatory systems and new standards are necessary to protect societies, individuals and the environment. This is a very difficult thing to do when there is a lack of will on the part of national governments to engage in the process of global rule setting—accelerating *de facto* the dismantling of national authority—and when institutions to enforce new global rules are still in the infant phase. In such a situation, enlightened companies have to take the lead to create progress in recivilizing capitalism by driving forward the values of a new global civic responsibility.

Globalization is a one-sided economic phenomenon. Responsible globality is different: It is economy plus society plus environmental sustainability plus human dignity. The fact that all major actors—such as the United Nations, the World Bank, the International Monetary Fund, major corporations—are trying to adopt a comprehensive approach, the approach of responsible globality, shows that the effort to define a philosophy for the 21st Century has just begun.

CONTRIBUTORS

MORRIS B. ABRAM is Chairman of UN Watch in Geneva. He was the United States Permanent Representative to the United Nations in Europe. A distinguished lawyer on civil rights, he was President of Brandeis University.

BELLA S. ABZUG was founder and Co-Chair of the Women's Environment and Development Organization. She died in 1998.

MAJAL G. AGUIRRE is at Rutgers Law School in Newark, New Jersey. A graduate of McGill University in Canada, she has lived in India, Lesotho, Switzerland, Thailand and other countries. She helped proofread this book.

LEYLA ALYANAK is a Correspondent-at-Large for The Earth Times.

NANDINI ANSARI is Director of Public Affairs at The Earth Times. She received a Bachelor's Degree in economics from Delhi University and has a diploma in Montessori teaching. Born in Kanpur, India, she moved to the United States in 1987.

HELEN ABBY BECKER is a writer based in New York, and a former associate director of the Children's Museum of Manhattan.

NICOLAAS H. BIEGMAN is former Permanent Representative of the Netherlands to the United Nations.

GEORGES BOSSOUS JR. of Haiti was Distribution Manager of The Earth Times until June 1999. He was born in Haiti and moved to the United States in 1994. He will be attending Barry University in Miami in Fall 1999.

SIR JOHN BROWNE is Chief Executive Officer of BP Amoco.

INGAR BRUEGGEMANN is Director General of the International Planned Parenthood Federation in London. She is a native of Germany, and worked formerly for the World Health Organization.

ELIZABETH BRYANT was a correspondent for The Earth Times. She has worked at news organizations in Florida and Washington, D.C.

MARIE CIEPLAK is Director of Advertising for The Earth Times.

454

WILLIAM JEFFERSON CLINTON is the 47th President of the United States. His essay was written at the invitation of The Earth Times.

MICHELE COHEN is a freelance art director and production designer. She also teaches digital art software classes.

JASON TOPPING CONE is a graduate of Franklin and Marshall College. He majored in biology and government.

JOHN CORRY is a columnist for The Earth Times. He wrote for The New York Times for many years, and is a contributor to various publications, including the American Spectator. He is also the author of several books.

STELLA DANKER is Managing Editor of The Earth Times, and a widely published writer on business and the environment. She has worked in various countries, including Britain, Japan and Singapore.

DJIBRIL DIALLO of Senegal is Director of Public Affairs at the United Nations Development Programme.

PAULA DiPERNA is President of the Joyce Foundation in Chicago. She was Chief Editorial Writer for The Earth Times for many years.

MOHAMED T. EL-ASHRY is Chairman and Chief Executive Officer of the Global Environment Facility in Washington, D.C.

IRA EPSTEIN is Graphics Editor of The Earth Times. He was born in New York and lives in Brooklyn. He received a Bachelor's Degree from the School of Visual Arts in New York and a Master's Degree from Boston University.

WERNER FORNOS is President of the Population Institute in Washington, D.C., and a frequent lecturer on social issues.

C. GERALD FRASER is Senior Editor for The Earth Times. He was with The New York Times for many years as a correspondent, columnist and editor.

JACK FREEMAN, Senior Editor and Chief Correspondent of The Earth Times, has been connected with the newspaper since 1991. He has reported from scores of countries. Earlier he was a senior writer with NBC Nightly News with Tom Brokaw. He has taught journalism at various universities in the US.

JONATHAN GULLERY is Director of Abel Graphics. He prepared the index for this book.

PRANAY GUPTE is Editor-in-Chief and Publisher of The Earth Times, which he created in 1991. He was born in Bombay and lives in Brooklyn. He received a Bachelor's Degree from Brandeis University and attended Columbia University's Graduate School of Journalism. He was a staff reporter and foreign correspondent for The New York Times for many years. Author of five books on development issues and on India, he is a columnist for Newsweek International, and a contributing editor at Forbes Magazine. He has also produced nearly 50 documentaries for public television. He appears regularly as a commentator on international issues on radio and television. He is a member of the Council on Foreign Relations.

PAUL HOFMANN has been a foreign correspondent for The New York Times, reporting from all continents for 35 years. He is the author of 12 books.

KAUKAB JHUMRA is a student at Brandeis University in Massachusetts. She is majoring in English, and served as a summer intern at this paper in 1999.

THEODORE W. KHEEL is a veteran labor lawyer and mediator in New York, and Chairman of the Earth Pledge Foundation.

DUNE LAWRENCE is a copy editor for The Earth Times. She has worked for the foreign Fulbright Program and taught English in China since graduating from Princeton University in 1997. She is scheduled to return to China to work for PLAN International.

KYU-YOUNG LEE is Production Director of The Earth Times. After studying English literature at the University of Chicago, he has been with The Earth Times at most of the major UN conferences including the Earth Summit in Rio de Janeiro. He has written for the paper from various parts of the world.

FLORA LEWIS writes a column for The Earth Times from Paris. She wrote the "Foreign Affairs" column for The New York Times for many years. She is also the author of several books on international issues.

MICHAEL LITTLEJOHNS is a correspondent for The Financial Times, based at the United Nations. He is also a columnist for The Earth Times.

JIM MACNEILL is Chairman of the International Institute for Sustainable Development in Canada. He was Secretary General of the Brundtland Commission, and a prime writer of its celebrated report, "Our Common Future." He is Editorial Chairman of The Earth Times.

MAHER MAHRAN, M.D. is a former Population Minister of Egypt. He was

Chairman of the Main Committee of the 1994 International Conference on Population and Development in Cairo.

JAMES W. MICHAELS is Senior Vice President, Editorial, at Forbes. He was Editor of Forbes Magazine for many years.

MARK MURO is an editorial writer at the Arizona Star in Tucson. He contributes regularly to The Earth Times on environmental issues.

RABYA NIZAM is Senior Editor of The Earth Times. Pakistan-born, she received her Bachelor of Arts Degree from Barnard College of Columbia University with a major in economics and political science.

GERARD PIEL was Editor and Chairman of Scientific American.

RESHMA PRAKASH is Senior Writer at The Earth Times. She has a Master's Degree in political science from the State University of New York at Albany. She has reported from various countries such as Egypt, China and Vietnam.

RON PRAMSCHUFER has spent the last 25 years in the printing industry. He co-founded RJ Communications, which assisted Earth Times Books in producing "All of Us."

SIR SHRIDATH S. RAMPHAL is Co-Chair of the Commission on Global Governance, and a former Secretary General of the Commonwealth. He also served as Minister of Justice and Attorney General of Guyana.

STEPHEN ROSE, Executive Publisher of The Earth Times, was CEO of Ted Bates International for many years.

A. M. ROSENTHAL is a columnist for The New York Times. He was Executive Editor of The Times for many years, and is a winner of the Pulitzer Prize.

BHARATI SADASIVAM is Director of Gender Studies at the Women's Environment and Development Organization. She was earlier a senior editor at The Times of India in Bombay.

NAFIS SADIK, M.D. is Executive Director of the United Nations Population Fund. She was trained as a physician in Pakistan. She holds the rank of Under Secretary General of the United Nations.

ROBERT L. SCHIFFER is a former United States diplomat who also worked for the United Nations for many years. He writes columns for The Earth Times.

KLAUS SCHWAB is founder and President of the World Economic Forum in Geneva, Switzerland.

NICOLE SCHWAB is a correspondent for The Earth Times. She received a graduate degree in 1999 from the John F. Kennedy School of Government at Harvard University.

RICHARD F. SHEPARD was a columnist for The Earth Times based in New York. He was with The New York Times for many years. He died in 1998.

SACHA SHIVDASANI is a student at the University of Rochester in New York State. She served as a summer intern at The Earth Times in 1999.

MUSA BALLA SILLA is Executive Director of the Partners in Population and Development, based in Dhaka, Bangladesh.

ANNE SILVERSTEIN is Newsbreaks Editor for The Earth Times. She served as Page One Editor at The Berkshire Eagle.

LOUIS SILVERSTEIN is Executive Editor, and designer, of The Earth Times. Formerly, he was Assistant Managing Editor of The New York Times and corporate art director of The Times Company. He has also designed numerous newspapers and magazines around the world.

STEVEN W. SINDING served as Director, Population Sciences, at the Rockefeller Foundation. He earlier held various positions with the United States Agency for International Development.

JYOTI SHANKAR SINGH is a consultant on global issues, and a columnist for The Earth Times. He was Deputy Executive Director of the United Nations Population Fund, and Executive Coordinator of the 1994 International Conference on Population and Development.

RAHUL SINGH is a syndicated columnist in India. He was earlier Editor of Reader's Digest in India, and of The Indian Express (Bombay).

VIR SINGH is a correspondent for The Earth Times based in New Delhi. He is a frequent contributor to National Public Radio.

SATYA SIVARAMAN is a writer based in Southeast Asia.

HAZEL STALOFF is a freelance editor and writer, specializing in multicultural issues and current events.

SUSAN J. TOLCHIN is Professor of Public Administration at George Mason University, and author of several books on public policy and national security.

AUDREY RONNING TOPPING is a widely published author and photojournalist, and a columnist for The Earth Times. She has written for Foreign Affairs, National Geographic and The New York Times Magazine, and other publications around the world.

SEYMOUR TOPPING is Administrator of the Pulitzer Prizes. He was Managing Editor of The New York Times for many years, and has authored a novel and works of nonfiction. He also teaches international affairs at Columbia University's Graduate School of Journalism.

PERNILLE TRANBERG is a correspondent for Politiken in Copenhagen.

ERIN TROWBRIDGE is Senior Writer at The Earth Times. She graduated from Sarah Lawrence College, and received a Master's Degree from the Columbia University Graduate School of Journalism.

PERIEL TUNALIGIL is Chief Production Editor of The Earth Times. She is a freelance art director for print and Web projects. A graduate of the University of Vienna, Austria, she also received a degree in graphic design from the School of Visual Arts in New York City.

YASNA UBEROI is Senior Editor of The Earth Times. She graduated with a degree in English and psychology from Salve Regina University in Newport, Rhode Island. She worked in advertising and marketing for four years before joining The Earth Times.

ASHALI VARMA is Editor of Choices, the magazine of the United Nations Development Programme. She was Executive Publisher for The Earth Times.

FRANK VOGL is a columnist for The Earth Times based in Washington, D.C. He is Vice Chairman of Transparency International.

TOM WICKER is a columnist for The Earth Times. A best-selling author and lecturer, he wrote the "In the Nation" column for The New York Times.

FIELDS WICKER-MIURIN is a columnist for The Earth Times based in London. She is a Senior Partner at A. T. Kearney.

SOON-YOUNG YOON is a columnist for The Earth Times. She is a noted anthropologist, and a writer on gender issues.

ACKNOWLEDGMENTS

"All of Us: Births and a Better Life—Population, Development and Environment in a Globalized World," is the first title published by Earth Times Books, a new venture of the Earth Times Foundation. The not-for-profit, nonpartisan foundation was created to publish The Earth Times, a newspaper focusing on the business of the human environment. Over the years, the foundation has become a multimedia enterprise. We publish The Earth Times in print every two weeks. We also produce a daily edition of the newspaper on the Internet—among the very first newspapers to maintain a daily edition in cyberspace. We produce documentaries for public television. And now, with "All of Us," we have launched a book publishing company. Earth Times Books plans to develop works on the environment and on interrelated subjects such as economic growth, population, gender issues, human rights, health, education, media, and science and technology. We will highlight voices of authors who have yet to be discovered by mainstream publishing houses in the industrialized countries. Our books are aimed at general audiences, but also specifically at policymakers in government, diplomacy and business. And we will reach students and teachers in high schools and colleges in the United States, Europe, Japan, and throughout the developing world.

"All of Us" owes a great deal to The Earth Times Foundation's longtime supporters in the multilateral community, especially the UN Population Fund, and to various foundations in the United States and elsewhere.

Special thanks are due to UNFPA's Executive Director, Dr. Nafis Sadik, and to her colleagues Mohammed Nizamuddin and Catherine Pierce. They were warmly supportive of this book project from the start, and we certainly appreciate their generosity and thoughtful help.

Also at UNFPA, our thanks are due to Kerstin Trone, Hirofumi Ando, Stirling D. Scruggs, Sethuramiah L. N. Rao, Kourtoum Nacro, Yegeshan Work Ayehu, Delia Barcelona, and Joyce Eadie.

Thanks, too, to Jyoti Shankar Singh—former Deputy Executive Director of the Population Fund—who encouraged the project from the beginning.

We owe a special thanks to Lily Chau of the United Nations Photo Library for her gracious help, and also to her colleagues Vina Manchanda and Reyes Renaldo. Thanks, too, to Sonia Lecca.

At The Earth Times, Yasna Uberoi made heroic efforts in helping Jack

Freeman with the selections that appear in this book. She supervised production, and in this she was ably assisted by Reshma Prakash, our paper's managing editor. Although newcomers to book publishing, they displayed superb professionalism and creativity, and this book is a tribute to their dedication and relentless energy. Other members of the small production staff at Earth Times Books worked under great pressure, too. Periel Tunaligil, Kyu-Young Lee, Michele Cohen and Ira Epstein are to be specially cited for their extraordinary work during the design and layout stages. They were always full of good cheer and good will, even during those moments when computers acted up or cable lines snapped. Good cheer also came from Stephen Rose.

Dune Lawrence assisted us ably in the copy editing. She made creative suggestions that helped the project enormously. Majal G. Aguirre also helped with the proofreading, as did our 1999 summer interns Kaukab Jhumra of Brandeis University—who was especially creative in her suggestions—and Sacha Shivdasani of the University of Rochester. Jason Topping Cone, a recent graduate of Franklin and Marshall College, was similarly helpful in the final stages of production.

Rabya Nizam and Nandini Ansari made stellar contributions, too, as did Georges Bossous Jr. and Marie Cieplak, in helping market this book. Their work illustrates how people from different backgrounds and nationalities can come together for a creative media project. Nandini Ansari even persuaded her college-bound daughter, Aliya, to help with proof-reading.

Similarly, our Webmasters in California, Annie Johnson, Betty Foster and Chuck Foster, made sterling efforts to create a special Web section for Earth Times Books (www.earthtimes.org). Our thanks also to Ron Pramschufer of RJ Communications for assisting with manufacturing the book, and to Jonathan Gullery for helping with the index.

"All of Us" would not have come to life without the guidance and passion of Louis Silverstein. Lou, former Assistant Managing Editor of The New York Times and one of the world's great designers, gave it form, shape and visual structure. No amount of thanks would be sufficient to convey our debt to Lou.

Jack Freeman, too, put in long hours on selecting articles and then editing them for publication.

A very special thanks to Hazel Staloff, a freelance writer and editor, who did an absolutely splendid job reading the text and making perceptive suggestions that significantly improved our book.

This book would not have been possible without the cooperation of various writers who made formidable efforts to update their material previously published in The Earth Times. Warm thanks to all of them.   —PRANAY GUPTE

GLOSSARY

ACET: AIDS Care, Education and Training, Uganda.

ACP: African Caribbean Pacific Group of Nations.

ACWF: All China Women's Federation.

AFPPD: Asian Forum of Parliamentarians for Population and Development.

AGENDA 21: Recommendations produced by the 1992 UN Conference on Environment and Development.

AKFED: Aga Khan Fund for Economic Development, based in Geneva.

AIDS/HIV: Acquired immune deficiency syndrome. The virus that carries AIDS is called the human immunodeficiency virus (HIV).

AKCS-Egypt: Aga Khan Cultural Services.

ANC: African National Congress.

API: American Press Institute.

ASEAN: Association of South East Asian Nations.

AZT: An anti-retroviral drug used in treatment of AIDS.

BEIJING +5: Five-year review of the Fourth World Conference on Women, to be held in New York in 2000.

BEIJING CONFERENCE: Fourth World Conference on Women, Beijing, 1995.

BGMEA: Bangladesh Garment Manufacturers and Export Association.

BKKBN: Family Planning Program, Indonesia.

BRAC: Bangladesh Rural Advancement Coalition.

BRETTON WOODS INSTITUTIONS: The creation of the International Bank for Reconstruction and Development (later known as the World Bank) and the International Monetary Fund, in July 1944 in Bretton Woods, New Hampshire, to make long-term capital available to countries after the war.

BRUNDTLAND COMMISSION: The World Commission on Environment and Development chaired by Mrs. Gro Harlem Brundtland, former Prime Minister of Norway.

CDC: Centers for Disease Control and Prevention, Atlanta.

CEDAW: Convention on the Elimination of All Forms of Discrimination Against Women, 1979.

CIDA: Canadian International Development Agency, based in Ottawa.

COPENHAGEN OR SOCIAL SUMMIT: World Summit on Social Development, Copenhagen, Denmark, 1995.

COPENHAGEN+5: The five-year review of the Copenhagen Declaration and the Program of Action of the 1995 World Summit on Social Development, planned for Geneva in 2000.

CORA: A Mexico city-based nongovernmental organization.

CPAR: Canadian Physicians for Aid and Relief.

CPR: Contraceptive prevalence rate. Refers to the percent of married women of reproductive age who use some form of contraception.

CSARO: Community Sanitation and Recycling Organization.

CSD: Commission on Sustainable Development, United Nations.

DEFORESTATION: The felling of trees, usually for commercial purposes.

DESERTIFICATION: The spread of deserts, especially severe in the Sahel region of north and central Africa, from Senegal to Somalia.

DEVELOPED WORLD: Countries that have industrialized through possessing the means and the technology to do so. Also referred to as the North, the First World and the industrialized world.

DEVELOPING WORLD: Countries that are underdeveloped and not industrialized to the extent of the developed world. Most organizations, including the United Nations, estimate that 60 to 80 percent of the world fits into this category. Also referred to as the South and third world.

EARTH SUMMIT (RIO): United Nations Conference on Environment and Development, Rio de Janeiro, Brazil, 1992.

EARTH SUMMIT+5 (RIO+5): The five-year review of the UN Conference on Environment and Development, New York, 1997.

ECOSYSTEM: The dynamic complex of plant, animal and micro-organism communities and their non-living environment interacting as a functional unit.

EEC: European Economic Community.

EMISSIONS: The release of greenhouse gases and/or their precursors into the atmosphere over a specified area and period of time.

EP3: Environmental Pollution Prevention Project.

EPA: Environmental Protection Agency, based in Washington, D.C.

EREG: Economic Revitalization and Employment Generation Program.

EU: European Union.

FACS: Foundation for American Communications.

FAO: Food and Agricultural Organization, based in Rome.

FDI: Foreign direct investment.

FGM: Female genital mutilation.

FONPAZ: Guatemala Foundation for Peace.

FPAB: Family Planning Association of Bangladesh.

G-7: Group of Seven economic superpowers: Britain, Canada, France, Germany, Italy, Japan and the United States. The heads of state meet yearly to discuss mutual economic and security interests. Now G8 (including Russia).

G-77: Group of 77. The largest third world inter-governmental organization comprising of 133 developing countries including China.

GATS: General Agreement on Trade Services.

GATT: General Agreement on Tariffs and Trade.

GDP: Gross Domestic Product. Measure of the total production and consumption of goods and services produced within a country.

GEF: Global Environment Facility, a joint effort of the World Bank and the UN.

GEP: General Electric Plastics.

GLOBAL WARMING: The gradual rise in Earth's temperature due to the accumulated effect of gases that are trapped in the atmosphere.

GNP: Gross National Product. The total market value of all the goods and services produced by a nation.

GREEN PAPER: A national agenda for environmental issues.

HABITAT II: The United Nations Conference on Human Settlements; Istanbul, Turkey, 1996.

ICBL: International Campaign to Ban Landmines.

ICDDR, B: International Center for Diarrheal Disease Research: Bangladesh.

ICG: International Crisis Group.

ICP: The second intergovernmental conference on population in Mexico City, 1984.

ICPD: International Conference on Population and Development, Cairo, 1994.

ICPD+5: Five-year review of the International Conference on Population and Development, The Hague and New York,1999.

IDA: International Development Assistance.

IFAD: International Fund for Agricultural Development, based in Rome

IMF: International Monetary Fund.

IMR: Infant Mortality Rate. The number of deaths of children under one year of age per 1,000 live births in any given year.

IOM: International Organization for Migration, based in Geneva.

IPEC: International Program on the Elimination of Child Labor.

IPPF: International Planned Parenthood Federation, based in London.

IUD: Intra-uterine contraceptive device. A very small plastic or metal device inserted into the uterus to prevent pregnancy.

LDC: Least developed countries.

LIFE EXPECTANCY: The average number of years that a child can expect to live.

LMO: Literacy Movement Organization, based in Teheran, Iran.

LTCM: Long-term credit management.

MBIs: Market-based Instruments.

MMR, Maternal Mortality Rate: The number of maternal deaths per 100,000 births in any given year.

MNCs: Multinational corporations.

NACWOLA: The National Community of Women Living With AIDS, Uganda.

NAFTA: North American Free Trade Agreement.

NATO: North Atlantic Treaty Organization, based in Brussels.

NCPD: Egypt's National Commission on Population and Development.

NGO: Nongovernmental organization. An organization centered around a cause or causes that work outside the sphere of governments. Usually not-for-profit.

NORAD: Norwegian Agency for Development Cooperation, Oslo.

NORPLANT: A contraceptive capsule inserted under the skin of the forearm of the woman, to prevent ovulation.

NPC: National Population Council, Egypt.

OAU: Organization for African Unity, based in Addis Ababa, Ethiopia.

ODA: Official development assistance, or donor-country foreign aid.

OECD: Organization for Economic Co-operation and Development, Paris.

OPEC: Organization of Petroleum Exporting Countries, based in Vienna.

ORAL CONTRACEPTIVE: "The pill." Taken every day in 21-day cycles, to prevent ovulation and pregnancy.

ORS: Oral rehydration solution.

ORT: Oral rehydration therapy.

OXFAM: International group of NGOs engaged in humanitarian work.

PKK: A family welfare movement in Indonesia.

PLATFORM OF ACTION: Recommendations that came out of the 1995 Fourth World Conference on Women in Beijing.

PREPCOM: Preparatory Committee meetings associated with UN conferences.

PROGRAM OF ACTION: Recommendations that came out of the 1994 International Conference on Population and Development.

PSS: Parivar Seva Sanstha. A grassroots organization in Pittiwas, India.

RATE OF POPULATION GROWTH: The percentile increase of the total population in a given year.

RDP: Reconstruction and Development Program, South Africa's program for the creation of jobs and homes.

RHYTHM OR NATURAL METHOD: Birth control method to prevent pregnancy.

RQN: Return of Qualified Nations program.

SECOND UN POPULATION CONFERENCE: Held in Mexico City, Mexico in 1984.

SIDA: Swedish International Development Agency, based in Stockholm.

STDs: Sexually transmitted diseases.

STIs: Sexually transmitted illnesses.

TFR: Total fertility rate. The average number of children born to a woman in her reproductive years.

TRIMS: The Uruguay Round Agreement on Trade Related Measures.

UMATI: A nongovernmental organization that promotes family planning in Tanzania.

UNAIDS: Joint United Nations Program on HIV/AIDS.

UNCED: United Nations Conference on Environment and Development, Rio de Janeiro, Brazil, 1992.

UNCHS: United Nations Centre for Human Settlements, based in Nairobi.

UNCTAD: United Nations Conference on Trade and Development, based in Geneva.

UNDP: United Nations Development Programme, based in New York.

UNEP: United Nations Environment Programme, based in Nairobi.

UNESCO: United Nations Economic, Social and Cultural Organization, based in Paris.

UNFPA: United Nations Population Fund, based in New York.

UNGASS: The United Nations General Assembly Special Session.

UNHCHR: United Nations High Commissioner for Human Rights, based in Geneva.

UNHCR: United Nations High Commission for Refugees, based in Geneva.

UNICEF: United Nations Children's Fund, based in New York.

UNIFEM: United Nations Development Fund for Women, based in New York.

UNRWA: United Nations Relief and Works for Palestine Refugees in the Near East, based in Vienna.

UPS: United Parcel Service.

USAID: US Agency for International Development.

USCBL: The US Campaign to Ban Landmines; a coalition of 225 NGOs across the US, part of the International Campaign to Ban landmines (ICBL).

VASECTOMY (MALE STERILIZATION): A permanent and usually irreversible method of male contraception.

WEDO: Women's Environment and Development Organization, New York.

WHO: World Health Organization, based in Geneva.

WPC: World Population Conference, the first intergovernmental conference on population, Romania, 1974.

WTO: World Trade Organization, based in Geneva.

—COMPILED BY RABYA NIZAM AND NANDINI ANSARI OF THE EARTH TIMES

INDEX